Approaches to Teaching the Works of Ngũgĩ wa Thiong'o

Approaches to Teaching World Literature

For a complete listing of titles, see the last pages of this book.

Approaches to Teaching the Works of Ngũgĩ wa Thiong'o

Edited by

Oliver Lovesey

The Modern Language Association of America
New York 2012

Library of Congress Cataloging-in-Publication Data

Approaches to teaching the works of Ngugi wa Thiong'o /
edited by Oliver Lovesey.
p. cm.—(Approaches to teaching world literature ; 121)
Includes bibliographical references and index.
ISBN 978-1-60329-112-5 (cloth : alk. paper)—
ISBN 978-1-60329-113-2 (pbk. : alk. paper)
1. Ngugi wa Thiong'o, 1938– —Criticism and interpretation.
2. Postcolonialism in literature.
3. Multiculturalism in literature.
4. Kenya—In literature.
I. Lovesey, Oliver.
PR9381.9.N45Z534 2012
823'.914—dc23 2012037150

Approaches to Teaching World Literature 121
ISSN 1059-1133

Cover illustration of the paperback edition:
The artwork *The Harvest* is used with permission of the artist, Naomi Wanjiku.
Mixed media, 2009

Published by The Modern Language Association of America
26 Broadway, New York, New York 10004-1789
www.mla.org

CONTENTS

PREFACE

This volume in the series Approaches to Teaching World Literature is devoted to the works, in many genres, of Ngũgĩ wa Thiong'o. He is one of the most important and celebrated writers of postindependence Africa as well as a groundbreaking postcolonial theorist. His works are taught around the world in a variety of disciplinary, interdisciplinary, and multidisciplinary courses in many different institutions and departments and at many different levels.

This volume sets out contexts for the study of Ngũgĩ and offers practical approaches to teaching individual texts. It features both preeminent international Ngũgĩ scholars and new voices. It is designed to aid scholars, teachers, and students of Ngũgĩ by suggesting ways to tackle his challenging works in the classroom.

Like the other volumes in this series, *Approaches to Teaching the Works of Ngũgĩ wa Thiong'o* is divided into two parts: "Materials" and "Approaches." The first part provides resources for the study of Ngũgĩ. The second contains essays that demonstrate the diversity of perspectives on and approaches to teaching Ngũgĩ's works.

I wish to thank Sonia Kane for her assistance and expertise in bringing this volume to fruition. A project of this nature is the work of many hands, and I thank all the contributors for their efforts and patience over its long evolution. Gĩchingiri Ndĩgĩrĩgĩ, Simon Gikandi, Evan Mwangi, Brendon Nicholls, and Marie Loughlin were especially helpful in the completion of the project.

ORATURE IN EDUCATION

Ngũgĩ wa Thiong'o

Wangarĩ, the eldest of my father's four wives, was a philosopher who cited experience and proverbs, and she was always calm, as if she had seen it all. She was the minister of culture. Her power over my father was through a look, or gesture of disapproval often accompanied by a song or proverb.

She was also a great storyteller. Every evening we children gathered around the fireside in her house, and the stories would begin. Sometimes, particularly on weekends, the young men and women with their friends would join in, and it would become a storytelling session for all. One told a story; then another person, in the audience, would say something like, That story reminds me, a signal that he or she would tell a new story, even if, as it turned out in most cases, it had nothing in common with the one preceding it.

I looked forward to these evenings. It seemed wonderful to me that such beautiful and sometimes scary stories could come out of different mouths. Best for me were those stories in which the audience joined in the singing. I hated it when people interrupted the teller to dispute the accuracy of an episode. Why not wait for their turn? In the daytime, we would try to retell among ourselves or to others the stories we had heard, but they did not come out as powerfully as those told around the fireside, the entire space jammed with eager listeners. Daylight seemed to drive stories away, as our mothers always told us.

There was one exception: my half sister Wabia. She was the fifth child or second daughter of Wangarĩ's seven children, four of whom had physical challenges of one kind or other, but not as severe as that of Gĩtogo, who lost his power of speech on the same day that Wabia lost the power to see and move. They say that the two were born with normal sight and hearing but that one day, when Wabia was carrying her baby brother on her back, they were struck by lightning. Wabia complained that somebody had put out the sun for her, and for Gĩtogo all sound. In addition her body turned to jelly: she could stand or take a step only with the aid of two walking sticks.

But it looked as if the power of sight and mobility had all gone to her voice and memory. She always lay or sat in the courtyard, under the roof of her mother's hut, except when she took a few steps in the sun. Mostly she sang, and her voice could be heard miles away. Any song she ever heard was stored in her memory, and in time she knew the melodies and words of the songs sung in church on Sundays although she never ventured there. For her, stories did not flee in daytime, and we children became the grateful recipients of her power. It is strange that in the evening she never contributed to the storytelling, but in the daytime she could retell those stories with an imagination that made them even more interesting and delightful than in their first telling, almost as if she had created them anew. She certainly re-created the gesture, the drama, and the melodies of the chorus through her voice. We had to be nice to her, to one another, and to our parents so that she would release the story in daytime. If we quarreled among ourselves or disobeyed our mothers, she said that the story refused to come, that it would come only if we promised to behave. I was one of the most obedient and would bring her water or retrieve the walking sticks for her. She also liked it that I requested her performance so persistently. Even more than her mother, Wabia's imaginative power took me to worlds unknown, worlds that I was later able to glimpse only through reading fiction.

Whenever I think of that stage of my childhood, it is in terms of the stories at Wangarĩ's hut at night and their rebirth in her daughter's voice in the day. The stories became a reservoir of images from which I drew when I began writing fiction.[1]

My writing can be divided into two periods, the English and the Gĩkũyũ. *The River Between* (1965) was my first novel to be written though the second in order of publication. Even in that early work one can see the influence of orature. I drew on proverbs mostly, but there are also references to stories and to a song, its lyrics quoted. In my second novel, the first to be published, *Weep Not, Child* (1964), the Gĩkũyũ creation myth appears in the first half of the narrative. In *A Grain of Wheat* (1967) and *Petals of Blood* (1977), proverbs, stories, and songs are part of the texture. In this period, orature acts like an authenticating system. The narrative is written in English, the characters speak English, but how does one show that they are speaking an African language and that they are molded by an African culture with roots in precolonial, premodern times? One can think of these novels and plays as translations, but mental ones, because the entire exercise takes place in the mind first. Some of the proverbs and most of the songs are given in Gĩkũyũ first, for instance, with an English translation following them.

My Gĩkũyũ-language period began with the play *Ngaahika Ndeenda (I Will Marry When I Want* [1982]), which developed in a workshop situation in the village Kamĩrĩthũ, Kenya, with peasants and workers. Ngũgĩ wa Mĩriĩ and I, both from the University of Nairobi, had worked out the initial outline and dialogue. But in discussions that followed, some of the older participants pointed out bluntly that the kind of characters we had drawn did not speak their age. Old men and women did not use the simple language we had given them. We had to go back to the script and reimagine characters and linguistic situations in the light of the comments and suggestions we received. But it was not just the form of speech. The heart of the conflict in the play unfolds in two marriage ceremonies, Christian and traditional. In both, songs and dances are central. But in the Gĩkũyũ traditional part there was a rechoreographing of a classical *gĩtiro* opera, mostly sung and danced by women. Participants had to improvise words, images, and story in a challenge-and-response structure. The entourage of the bridegroom is barred from the gates of the bride's home; the gates will open only by the persuasive depth of the entourage's words and images and by the quality of its voices. In the unpublished play *Mother, Sing for Me*, classical

Gĩkũyũ orature permeates the structure and speech. The play dramatizes the use of orature in anticolonial resistance. The orature utilizes everything from lullabies to funeral dirges. This is a far cry from the English-language play *The Black Hermit*, which I wrote and directed in 1962 in Kampala, Uganda. The destiny of the two plays is interesting: *The Black Hermit* became a school text in Kenyan schools; *Mother, Sing for Me* was banned from the Kenya National Theater. The police even locked the doors of the alternative venue at the University of Nairobi in early March 1982. A few days later, three truckloads of armed policemen were sent to the original home of the theater group and razed to the ground the group's performance space.

In my Gĩkũyũ-language novels *Devil on the Cross* (1982), *Matigari* (1986), *and Wizard of the Crow* (2006), one finds a radical departure in orature. The same formal features are used but more freely and frequently. Now there is an attempt by writers to incorporate oral fictive narratives into the novel, to make oral structure and method the foundation of an entire work. In *Devil on the Cross*, the narrative evolves as a series of actual oral stories. The novel is conceived as a tale told by a gĩcaandĩ player, a kind of griot and seer. The central section, where the action takes place in a cave, is literally a performance: the cave dwellers, experts in modern theft and robbery, give oral testimonies before a jury and a public audience about their exploits.

Performance is at the center of orature (see Ngũgĩ, *Globalectics*). In *Matigari*, every aspect of performance and other elements of orature is utilized to the fullest. The narrative itself was inspired by an oral story about a search for a cure. In the novel, that search becomes the quest for truth. Repetition, particularly in the chorus, is a common element in oral performance, because the audience needs a pause or resting moment to absorb what has happened before the next stage in the narrative. Repetition is an integral part of the structure of *Matigari*. The written that is rooted in the oral we might call literary orature or *litorature*. *Matigari* belongs to litorature.

Wizard of the Crow takes litorature a step further. Performance, as some reviewers noticed, permeates the novel. The story, the riddle, and the proverb are part of its fabric. Oral stories, retold, provide key images. For instance, at a crucial moment in the first part of the novel, Nyawĩra tells Tajirika's two children a story about how the combined efforts of a man, woman, and child drive out a human-eating ogre who occupied their house by guile and force in the absence of the owner blacksmith. Species can change form—a human being may become a bird, as in Ovid's *Metamorphosis*. The novel makes references to Indian and Chinese classic oratures by referring to the Mahabharata and Taoism. A common figure in classical oratures of most cultures is the trickster. Every character in the *Wizard* is a trickster or embodies aspects of trickery. Even those who are close do not know what they think they know about each other. In short, the magical interplay of the real and the beyond-the-real is inspired by the same element in orature.

An important part of my literary inventions is their reception. I have written—in chapter 3, "The Language of African Fiction," in my book *Decolonising the Mind*—how my novel *Devil on the Cross* was received when it first came out in Gĩkũyũ in Kenya in 1980. It was read in groups, one person reading it aloud for others to hear. Such readings took place in different locations: outside factories during the lunch hour, in public transport, and in people's homes. *Matigari* was received in a slightly different way. It came out in 1986, when the Moi dictatorship had tightened its grip on Kenyan society to the extent of banning the spread of rumors in public places. Matigari's story was renarrated orally: people now spoke about Matigari, the eponymous hero of the novel, as a real person going about the country asking questions of truth and justice. The dictatorship issued a warrant for his arrest. Learning that he was not real, the regime arrested the book instead, confiscating copies of it from bookshops and the publisher's warehouse in a coordinated police action. I don't know yet the reception of the Gĩkũyũ *Wizard of the Crow*, but from past experience one might suspect that the written has been oralized, just as many works are now read into cassettes or CDs. Technology has made the oral a modern mode of transmission, and on a global scale. Orature is coming back.

The form of my writing owes a lot to my education in orature. But orature may have done more than that: it may have ignited in me the desire to write long before I picked up a written work of fiction.

NOTE

[1] This episode is based on an excerpt from *Dreams in a Time of War*.

NGŨGĨ WA THIONG'O: IN PRAISE OF A FRIEND

Gayatri Chakravorty Spivak

I met Ngũgĩ wa Thiong'o in 1966, when he was a member of the International Writing Program at the University of Iowa and I was an assistant professor there. Paul Engle, himself quintessentially American, even Midwestern, had thought of this program and implemented it. Engle came from a kind of Bretton Woods–to-Bandung internationalism (he might not have known much about Bandung) that Ama Ata Aidoo powerfully stages in *Our Sister Killjoy*.

Bandung—the small Indonesian town where with Nkrumah of Ghana and Nehru of India in starring roles, twenty-nine nations, mostly recently independent, met to decide that they were not going to be aligned to either the Eastern or the Western Bloc but rather be a "third" world—gave great hope to such people as Paul Robeson and Richard Wright. As is well known, the political experiment came to little, but an ideology remained, and *Third World* became a much translated phrase in many languages. A remote side effect of this ideology was the possibility of a world (of) literature(s) and a new impetus to translation, mostly into English.

The writers who flocked to the Iowa program generally represented what would alter this possible side effect. They most often connected with the local transformation of the Beat beat from the indigenous Writers Workshop. They came not from Bandung but from the brilliant and unruly spirit of the 1960s. Looking back, I realize that there for the first time I knew what would be a second wave of the possibility of literatures of the world, rather different from the biases of Bandung. Even in that crowd, Ngũgĩ stood out, with the characteristic that later became his signature: an unmarked modernity. Yes he was African, deeply indebted to orature—but why should *modernity* be synonymous with *Europe*? Why should Europe have history and we tradition? Despite his own assessment of the stages in his writing, it seemed to me then that these questions were already merely rhetorical in his calm and confident presence. It is my mature judgment that this is the chief definitive characteristic of what we can call contemporary world literature, which developed as a reaction to the benevolence of Bandung's failure. Paradoxically, this characteristic may seem an obsession with tradition if it is not shared by the reader. It has led to problems when it comes to reading gendering in Ngũgĩ's texts. Feminist readers know that gendering must sometimes choose "the wrong side," as it were. Even there, however, if one pays attention to word choice and conduct of language in the Gĩkũyũ, it is hard simply to sit in judgment. Let me ask the reader to imagine John Updike as "local," ignore all his linguistic contrivances, and diagnose a problematic gender politics as a result. This issue is of course discussed in this volume.

I saw Ngũgĩ again in the 1980s in Birmingham, England, when we were both speaking at a Third Focus event, "Exile and Displacement." By then my old friend had become a hero. *Decolonising the Mind* had appeared and immediately become the controversial classic it remains to this day. His political commitment and courage, his imprisonment and exile, had given him an aura. Yet what I remember from that occasion is his infinite kindness, his gentleness. The picket-line Third Focusers objected to my love for theory, which immediately spelled elitism to them. He came to my defense, and no one could, of course, question his authority.

Decolonising the Mind was so suited to its moment in Africa that we may not notice its timeliness now. Globalization requires a few hegemonic languages—mostly European, "for international communication," although Mandarin is fighting hard. In order, however, to sustain a world that the near-abstract structures of even the impossible dream of a welfare-world globalization can nurture, this requirement must be supplemented by a deep immersion in that world's richness of language. Ngũgĩ was not simply arguing for his mother tongue, as his subsequent career has shown. He was also arguing for inhabiting nonhegemonic languages with the depth of imaginative use, while retaining English (or, mutatis mutandis, the other imperial languages) as the "first language of international communication."

Notice that this is not principally a counter-globalizing or alter-globalizing argument. I do not mean to underestimate Ngũgĩ's contribution in the struggle to establish African literature as the center of literary instruction in Africa. (How can I, when, reading Hannah Arendt's *On Violence* for a coming conference, I see her describing African literature, in 1969, as "a nonexistent [subject]" [96]?) That Ngũgĩ is a countercanon also has little to do with this question. It is an acknowledgment that English has its uses, though it must not usurp the entire epistemic and affective space of the former colony. Not to acknowledge this, to oppose this full tilt, is to legitimize by reversal, simply to give us a malevolent in place of a benevolent empire rather than dream of using capital as socialism would: welfare-world globalization. Thus does one decolonize the mind into a realistic acknowledgment of the violence of history rather than monumentalize the opposition seemingly (only seemingly) inherent in national liberation.

Decolonising the Mind has had a long history in a somewhat different and specific debate among African and Indian writers. Should one write in one's native language and achieve a small yet culturally prepared audience, or should one write in English and claim an international readership—become world literature instantly, as it were? For Ngũgĩ there was the additional desire to produce for a subaltern audience in the native language. Essays in this volume discuss what is lost when his books are read in English, a gift that would have withdrawn into subtextuality if his first writing had been in English. The course of that debate is too well known to recount here. What must, however, be noted is that for Ngũgĩ himself the position has become a double bind, where contradictory instructions come at the same time and the writer must learn how to occupy the space of that contradiction. Write in Gĩkũyũ and write the same thing again in English "to continue dialogue with all." Polycentric translation in an activist definition was Ngũgĩ's special care as the director of the erstwhile International Center for Writing and Translation at the University of California, Irvine, where I had the honor to be a member of the board.

The first language of the colonized as double bind gives us a figure for the postcolonial predicament in globality in the most vivid way. This is the secret of the struggle against dictatorship after independence. It is also from this position that Ngũgĩ's care radiates toward all the nonhegemonic languages of the world and, in principle, thinks of the possibility of translation between and among them.

From *Weep Not, Child* to the massive phenomenon of *Wizard of the Crow* these are some of the threads that have bound Ngũgĩ's work together. An account of these bindings and their many unbindings has been painstakingly recorded in the present collection.

Part One

MATERIALS

Introduction

Ngũgĩ wa Thiong'o is one of the greatest writers of postindependence Africa, and he continues to be a vibrant cultural agitator and innovator. His work is still very much in progress as he continues to publish collections of essays and novels and edits the Gĩkũyũ-language journal *Mũtiiri*. In 2002 he accepted the position of director of the International Center for Writing and Translation at the University of California, Irvine, continuing his career-long devotion to language and culture. University teaching has always been part of his life, and he remains committed to the importance of education. His works have been translated into more than thirty languages. His acclaimed new novel *Mũrogi wa Kagogo*, translated by him as *Wizard of the Crow*, appeared in 2006; it may well come to be regarded as his masterpiece. *Approaches to Teaching the Works of Ngũgĩ wa Thiong'o* explores his diverse oeuvre, reexamines its place in the canon of African and postcolonial literature and theory, and addresses its accessibility in the classroom.

This is an opportune moment for a volume on teaching Ngũgĩ, considering that a Kenyan American whose father was born forty miles from Kisumu in Kogelo in western Kenya has been elected president of the United States of America, after an election campaign in which issues of race and gender were important in the political discourse. Postcolonial, world, or, in Gayatri Chakravorty Spivak's terms, "planetary" literature (*Death* 84, 96), which includes the works of Ngũgĩ, has become an established part of the literary countercanon. Ngũgĩ was instrumental in introducing the study of African literature at the University of Nairobi in the 1970s, a curricular revolution that began as a departmental memo (Ngũgĩ, *Moving* 8–11). In this collection, Simon Gikandi discusses the significance of this educational manifesto. Ngũgĩ's work in a variety of genres has paralleled and advanced the development of the new canon, and Ngũgĩ continues to be cognizant of the role of the postcolonial intellectual in exile, serving as a teacher, a critic of Frantz Fanon's "native intellectual" (*Wretched* 209), a cyberspace oral griot, and a cultural and political activist. He is the best-known theorist of the language debate in postcolonial studies.

Although Ngũgĩ has been prolific in other genres, he is mainly taught as a novelist and postcolonial theorist. As respondents to the survey conducted for this volume indicate, his fiction is often approached through the prism of his nonfictional prose, yet his theoretical work sometimes challenges his novels. Much of his early fiction concerns the moment of Kenyan independence from Britain and the violent conflict that precipitated it. One survey respondent states that Ngũgĩ is a historical novelist, though the history his novels represent is a contested terrain and open to transformation. His texts show history from below; they are not grand narratives of global exploitation. *Caitaani Mũtharaba-inĩ* (*Devil on the Cross*) tackles the postindependence or neocolonial period in Kenya and uses the postmodern African folktale (a uniquely African version of magic realism) as well as Ngũgĩ's distinctive "Mau Mau aesthetics" (following the "Mau Mau" rebel fighters in transforming biblical stories, for example, into tools of liberation [Lovesey, *Ngũgĩ* 64–65]) to dream into being a truly independent future. Significantly, Ngũgĩ's Gĩkũyũ novels, as Ngũgĩ points out in *Decolonising the Mind*, his most commonly taught theoretical work, were first read aloud to groups of listeners in rural inns, the reader being paid in beer (82–83). None of the contributors or survey respondents, however, suggest reading these novels aloud in class, with or without the libation, to replicate their original reception.

Ngũgĩ's most recent and longest novel, *Wizard of the Crow*, describes dictatorship in a fictional African state resembling Kenya. The novel is poignant, showing a world that lies in a state of heightened security after bombings in Nairobi, New York, and elsewhere.

The global village is smaller and more fragile but in some ways seems more hopeful than before. Dictators and exporters of civil war, like Liberia's Charles Taylor, are being brought to justice, and the first- and second-generation of African strong men, like Kenya's Daniel arap Moi, are being humbled at the ballot box and sometimes at the International Criminal Court in The Hague. Elections in Kenya in 2002 signaled the political demise of Moi, who as minister for Home Affairs earlier signed the order for Ngũgĩ's political detention, without charge or trial. This new political climate permitted Ngũgĩ's return to Kenya after over two decades in exile. *Wizard* appears at a time when revisionist imperial historians, particularly in Britain, are promoting portraits of benevolent empire, though other historians, like Caroline Elkins and David Anderson, are detailing the true horrors of colonialism in Kenya. While the forces of globalization, which Ngũgĩ faces directly in *Penpoints, Gunpoints, and Dreams*, are as pervasive and destabilizing as ever, an "African renaissance," as Ngũgĩ subtitles *Something Torn and New*, his recent collection of essays, may be dawning.

This volume is divided into two parts: "Materials" and "Approaches." The first introduces resources primarily based on survey responses. The second contains twenty-two essays detailing instructors' methods of approaching Ngũgĩ's texts in the classroom.

Editions

Ngũgĩ's first published novel, *Weep Not, Child*, was issued in Heinemann's groundbreaking African Writers Series, inaugurated by Chinua Achebe's *Things Fall Apart*, and all of Ngũgĩ's English-language novels have been published by Heinemann as well as by East African Educational Publishers (EAEP). A revised Heinemann edition of Ngũgĩ's third novel, *A Grain of Wheat*, the edition used for this volume, appeared in 1986, and Penguin Modern Classics published the novel, introduced by Abdulrazak Gurnah, in 2002; *The River Between*, introduced by Jack Mapanje, in 2002; and Ngũgĩ's fourth novel, *Petals of Blood*, introduced by Moses Isegawa, in 2005. *Petals*, selected by the survey respondents as Ngũgĩ's most frequently taught novel, was first published by Heinemann in Kenya in 1977 and by E. P. Dutton in the United States in 1978. The Heinemann edition is the one used for this volume.

Ngũgĩ's three most recent Gĩkũyũ novels—*Caitaani Mũtharaba-inĩ* (*Devil on the Cross*), *Matigari ma Njirũũngi* (*Matigari*), and *Mũrogi wa Kagogo* (*Wizard of the Crow*)—were published by EAEP. *Devil*, translated by Ngũgĩ, and *Matigari*, translated by Wangũi wa Goro, were published by Heinemann and EAEP. *Wizard*, translated by Ngũgĩ, was published in hardcover by Pantheon in the United States and by Harvill Secker in the United Kingdom. A paperback edition of *Wizard* was published by Anchor in the United States (the edition used for this volume) and by Vintage in the United Kingdom. Ngũgĩ's series of children's books—*Bathitoora ya Njamba Nene* (*Njamba Nene's Pistol*), *Njamba Nene na Mbaathi ĩ Mathagu* (*Njamba Nene and the Flying Bus*), and *Njamba Nene na Cibũ Kĩng'ang'i* ("Njamba Nene and the Cruel Chief")—were published by EAEP. English translations of only the first two, by Wangũi wa Goro, have been published.

Most of Ngũgĩ's collections of critical essays were published by James Currey, EAEP, and Heinemann, with the exception of *Penpoints, Gunpoints, and Dreams*, which was published by Oxford University Press. All appear in a single edition, with the exception of *Writers in Politics* (1981) This volume uses the revised and enlarged edition of *Writers in Politics: A Re-engagement with Issues of Literature and Society*, published in 1997 by James Currey, EAEP, and Heinemann. Ngũgĩ's collection of essays, *Something Torn and New: An African Renaissance*, was published by Basic Civitas Books in New York. Ngũgĩ's prison memoir, *Detained: A Writer's Prison Diary*, was published in 1981 by Heinemann in Nairobi and London. Pantheon Books published *Dreams in a Time of War: A Childhood Memoir* in 2010. Ngũgĩ's plays have been brought out by EAEP and Heinemann.

Ngũgĩ wa Thiong'o: A Brief Biography

Ngũgĩ's personal experience has informed his creative and theoritical writing, and it plays an important part in much of the criticism about his works. The traumatic events of his life in many ways paralleled what we might call Kenya's national trauma, particularly its colonial and neocolonial narratives. Ngũgĩ is, moreover, a writer whose home thoughts were often written abroad. Ngũgĩ's novels *The River Between* and *Weep Not, Child* were written in Uganda, *A Grain of Wheat* in England, and *Petals of Blood* in England, America, the Soviet Union, and Kenya. *Matigari ma Njirũũngi* (*Matigari*) was written in England and *Mũrogi wa Kagogo* (*Wizard of the Crow*) in America. *Caitaani Mũtharaba-inĩ* (*Devil on the Cross*) was produced in Ngũgĩ's homeland but within the walls of a maximum-security prison. The location of the act of writing may account in part for the fondness for home and the anguish of exile and return, so prevalent in his fiction. His memoir *Dreams in a Time of War*, which appeared in 2010, provides much insight into his early life.

Ngũgĩ was born on 5 January 1938, in Kamĩrĩĩthũ, Limuru, Kenya. His mother was the third of his father's four wives, and Ngũgĩ was one of twenty-seven siblings. He attended both independent Gĩkũyũ and mission schools at a time when the country's anticolonial Mau Mau struggle enveloped his family: a stepbrother (in Gĩkũyũ, *muru-wa-ithe* ["belonging to the same father"]) by the name of Gitogo was killed; a brother, Wallace Mwangi, fought in the forest; and Ngũgĩ's mother was tortured. His skill in English propelled his academic success, because, as he explains in *Decolonising the Mind*, colonial authorities were training an elite for their bureaucracy, and facility in the colonial language was rewarded (10–13). He entered the prestigious Alliance High School in 1955. The irony of his position as the child of a displaced peasant family enjoying the fruits of academic success in a repressive colonial regime was made clear when he returned from school to discover his home and village obliterated as part of the colonial government's villagization policy. Designed to enclose or destroy villages to prevent them from aiding the rebel fighters in the forest, this policy effectively imprisoned an entire community.

After briefly teaching in a primary school, Ngũgĩ entered Makerere University College in Uganda, where the special subject for his BA was Joseph Conrad. One of his professors at Makerere was the future president of Kenya Mwai Kibaki, "a brilliant young lecturer" who inspired Ngũgĩ's interest in economic theory and history, including the all-important notion of the fictional nature of some economic pronouncements (*Writers in Politics* [1997] 88). Ngũgĩ wrote "The Black Messiah" in 1961 and over the next four years revised the manuscript of what would be published as *The River Between*. He also wrote newspaper articles for various Nairobi newspapers (*Sunday Post*, *Sunday Nation*, *Daily Nation*) in the period before his departure for graduate study at Leeds University. Some of these articles show a surprisingly equivocal stance regarding colonial practices, given his later positions. Ngũgĩ's precocious energy fueled a formidable productivity while he was a student: in addition to editing the journals *Penpoint* (1963–64) and *Zuka* (1965–70), he wrote the accomplished *Weep Not, Child* in 1962, and his play *The Black Hermit* was performed at Uganda's independence celebrations. His Leeds University research on Caribbean literature was published in his essay collection *Homecoming* when he began writing *A Grain of Wheat*. In 1967, the year of the publication of his third novel, Ngũgĩ joined the English department of University College, Nairobi, becoming its first

African faculty member. By 1973, he was its first African department head, and under his direction the department's curriculum was transformed to focus on African languages and literatures. In 1970, *This Time Tomorrow*, a collection of his early plays, was published, his last book to appear under the name James Ngũgĩ, though he did not change his name legally till 1977.

Petals of Blood, partly written at the Yalta guesthouse of the Soviet Writers Union, was completed in 1976, and Ngũgĩ's former teacher Mwai Kibaki attended its launch in Nairobi (*Writers in Politics* [1997] 89). Ngũgĩ began work with the Kamĩrĩĩthũ Community and Cultural Centre, where his coauthored plays were performed. In December 1977, he was detained for one year without charge or trial in Kamĩtĩ Maximum Security Prison, the order signed by Daniel arap Moi, the Kenyan vice president and minister for home affairs. After his release, Ngũgĩ was denied employment at the University of Nairobi, and he was briefly imprisoned again in 1981 and in 1982, after which he went into exile in London, aware of the danger of politically motivated assassination if he stayed in his homeland. In London, he worked for the release of Kenyan political prisoners, and in 1987 he chaired Umoja, an umbrella group of radical Kenyan organizations. His next novel, *Matigari*, was published in 1986. President Moi, believing that Matigari was a living person, issued a warrant for his arrest. Learning that he was a character in a novel, he had all bookstores in the country raided and arrested the books instead, keeping the title out of circulation for a decade. In 1993, Ngũgĩ's *Moving the Centre* appeared, and in 1998 *Penpoints, Gunpoints, and Dreams*, a series of lectures delivered at Oxford University in 1996. In 1999 Ngũgĩ gave the Ashby Lecture at Cambridge University, and in 2010 he delivered the Wellek Library Lectures in Critical Theory at the University of California, Irvine.

Ngũgĩ began using film as a vehicle in the mid-1980s, and film technique figures in the structure of *Matigari*. Like Sembène Ousmane, he considered film a more accessible medium for an illiterate mass audience in Africa. Between 1985 and 1986, he took a film course at Dramatiska Institute in Stockholm, completing a short feature about antiapartheid sanctions entitled *Blood-Grapes and Black Diamonds*, which was presented at the 1986 Edinburgh Film Festival. He made another film with students from Tanzania and Mozambique entitled *Africa in Sweden*, which focused on Western media images and European stereotypes of Africa.[1] With Manthia Diawara, Ngũgĩ codirected *Sembene: The Making of African Cinema* (1994).[2] Ngũgĩ's exile continued in the United States, where he taught at Yale (1989–92), Smith, Amherst, and New York University. From 1992 to 2002 he was professor of performance studies and Erich Maria Remarque Professor of Comparative Literature at New York University. In 1994, he and his wife, Njeeri, cofounded *Mũtiiri*, a Gĩkũyũ-language journal of literature and culture in which some of Ngũgĩ's poems appear. In April 1994, he was the subject of an international conference organized by the Ngũgĩ scholar Charles Cantalupo. To date Ngũgĩ is the recipient of seven honorary doctorates as well as many awards, including the Nonino International Prize for Literature and the Medal of the Presidency of the Italian Cabinet.

Ngũgĩ began *Wizard of the Crow* well before 2002, when he took up his position as distinguished professor of English and comparative literature in the School of Humanities as well as director of the International Center for Writing and Translation at the University of California, Irvine. The Kenyan launch for the novel in August 2004 signaled Ngũgĩ's triumphant and courageous return to Kenya after decades of exile, though it was marred by a traumatic and nearly fatal attack. In Nairobi, Njeeri was raped and Ngũgĩ beaten and his face burned with cigarettes during a robbery attempt that Ngũgĩ is convinced was politically motivated. In November 2006, Ngũgĩ was harassed and ejected from a San Francisco hotel when he was promoting *Wizard of the Crow*. This incident was internationally condemned as racially motivated. Amid the violence that erupted during the 2007 Kenyan election, Ngũgĩ publicly endorsed Mwai Kibaki in his bid for the Kenyan presidency and spoke with guarded hope of the future. Ngũgĩ's Gĩkũyũ-language journal *Mũtiiri: Journal of Culture* was launched online in late 2010. Ngũgĩ's American-born son, Mũkoma wa Ngũgĩ, a poet and also political columnist for the BBC *Focus on Africa Magazine*, published a novel in 2009 entitled *Nairobi Heat*. In early 2009, Ngũgĩ published a collection of essays based primarily on his 2006 McMillan-Stewart Lectures at Harvard University: *Something Torn and New: An African Renaissance*. *Dreams in a Time of War: A Childhood Memoir* was published in 2010, and *Globalectics: Theory and the Politics of Knowing* in 2012.

Historical and Political Contexts

Much of Ngũgĩ's work concerns the colonial, postcolonial, neocolonial, and even postneocolonial history of Kenya as well as the cultural nationalism of anticolonial forces. Ngũgĩ offers no extensive descriptive treatment of precolonial Kenya, though there are many indications of the country's precolonial cultural integrity.

Kenya's beautiful and fertile central plateau is the setting for many of Ngũgĩ's works. The plateau attracted Europeans, but unlike the precolonial Nigeria of Chinua Achebe's *Things Fall Apart*, which became a resource colony, Ngũgĩ's Kenya became a settler colony, particularly after World War II. English interest in Kenya grew from the Victorian appetite for global imperial expansion, an appetite increased by the desire to forestall German expansion. Older missionary and antislavery sentiments made an unholy alliance with commercial interest in accessing the promised riches of Uganda and in satisfying the demands of adventure tourists. Kenya Colony was created in 1920, and Europeans appropriated the sacred land of the Gĩkũyũ to establish plantations for lucrative cash crops. Conflict between missionary and Kenyan forces reached a crisis over the controversy about "female circumcision," an issue of great importance in

The River Between.[3] The colonial government imposed hut taxes and created paramount chiefs to collect them. Grievances over taxes, labor, and land impelled the formation of fledgling nationalist associations, at the same time that colonial authorities exploited traditional animosities. The settlers' happy valley turned into Britain's gulag.

The anticolonial struggle in Kenya, also called the "Mau Mau" war of resistance, is the concern of much of Ngũgĩ's early writing, and his later writing examines the Mau Mau legacy in Kenya and particularly the official refusal to address the historical record.[4] As demonstrated by recent historical accounts, such as those of Elkins and of Anderson, this conflict was far more vicious and violent than Ngũgĩ's novels suggest. The anticolonial insurgency was galvanized by decades of accumulated grievances over land appropriation, enforced labor, taxation without representation, prohibitions on raising cash crops, apartheid-like laws regarding pass cards, wage discrimination based on race, racist attitudes, and increasing unemployment (unemployment is one of the misfortunes of the ex-soldier Boro in *Weep Not, Child*). The military wing of the insurgency was the Kenya Land and Freedom Army, and Dedan Kimathi (the heroic subject of *The Trial of Dedan Kimathi* [Ngũgĩ and Mugo]) was one of its main leaders. This period is still contested in Kenya, as W. O. Maloba explains in this volume. After independence, Jomo Kenyatta said Kenyans must forgive and forget the past. But conflicting interpretations of the insurgency and their strategic deployment as a weapon of war began well before the conflict ended. Ngũgĩ's own position shifted dramatically, from the ambivalence of his early journalism (Lindfors) to one of more strident radicalism. More research on this period is needed, though it is difficult to conduct, because of the movement's covert nature, the illiteracy of many of its participants, the age of survivors, colonial propaganda providing evidence obtained under torture, and the politically sensitive nature of this history in Kenya. Gathering the oral record has become increasingly important.

In 1952, Kenya's colonial governor declared a state of emergency, allowing detention without trial and increasing the number of capital offenses. The armed struggle moved to the Aberdares and Mount Kenya. Colonial authorities began a scorched-earth policy at the forest edge and a villagization system that placed Africans behind fences in moated compounds. In 1954, Operation Anvil rounded up thousands of supporters in Nairobi and detained them in camps. Colonial troops received cash for Mau Mau suspects killed, and corpses were displayed publically. The detention camps set up to interrogate detainees are examined in detail in Elkins's *Imperial Reckoning: The Untold Story of Britain's Gulag in Kenya*, frequently cited by survey respondents, and Anderson's *Histories of the Hanged: The Dirty War in Kenya and the End of Empire*. In 1956, Field Marshal Dedan Kimathi was captured, tried, and executed. The state of emergency ended in February 1960, and Kenya became independent on 12 December 1963. Kenyatta advocated reconciliation and something resembling historical amnesia. Wealthy, politically connected Kenyans benefited from some postindependence land redistribution, but Kenyatta and his successor, Daniel arap Moi, fostered the development of a new, quasi-colonial elite. Later, Moi's kleptocratic regime would feel so threatened by Ngũgĩ's work in popular, community theater in Kenyan languages that Moi detained Ngũgĩ for a year, launched a hunt for one of Ngũgĩ's fictional characters, banned Ngũgĩ's books, and forced him into exile. Kenya was opened to the political and economic forces of globalization, which has increased the poverty of large sectors of the population. In 2002, Mwai Kibaki became Kenya's third president; in 2008, Raila Odinga became prime minister.

The Instructor's Library

Criticism

Book-Length Studies

Critical writing on Ngũgĩ's works has been a growth industry since the early 1960s, in conjunction with the canonization of postcolonial studies, and it accelerated considerably since Carol Sicherman's 1989 bibliography listed over two thousand items produced in the first twenty-five years of Ngũgĩ's writing life (*Ngũgĩ wa Thiong'o: A Bibliography*). The recent expansion in studies of Ngũgĩ's work includes four book-length monographs: Simon Gikandi's *Ngũgĩ wa Thiong'o*, Oliver Lovesey's *Ngũgĩ wa Thiong'o*, James Ogude's *Ngũgĩ's Novels and African History*, and Patrick Williams's *Ngũgĩ wa Thiong'o*. Three comparative studies have appeared: Kandioura Dramé's *The Novel as Transformation Myth: A Study of the Novels of Mongo Beti and Ngũgĩ wa Thiong'o*, Anders Breidlid's *Resistance and Consciousness in Kenya and South Africa: Subalternity and Representation in the Novels of Ngũgĩ wa Thiong'o and Alex La Guma*, and M. S. C. Okolo's comparison of Ngũgĩ and Chinua Achebe in *African Literature as Political Philosophy*. This corpus of critical material is growing, and while the current volume was in process, three of its contributors completed book-length monographs largely or wholly on Ngũgĩ: Evan Mwangi's *Africa Writes Back to Self: Metafiction, Gender, Sexuality*, Brendon Nicholls's *Ngũgĩ wa Thiong'o, Gender, and the Ethics of Postcolonial Reading*, and Gĩchingiri Ndĩgĩrĩgĩ's *Ngũgĩ wa Thiong'o's Drama and the Kamĩrĩĩthũ Popular Theater Experiment*. In 2010, Apollo Obonyo Amoko's *Postcolonialism in the Wake of the Nairobi Revolution: Ngugi wa Thiong'o and the Idea of African Literature* appeared. Amoko explores the development of some of Ngũgĩ's work in the context of a critique of the role of literature, educational institutions, and the nation-state in colonial and postcolonial Africa. Only a book-length descriptive bibliography could do justice to the breadth as well as the important interpretative divisions in this material; my purpose here is to outline key elements of the material in the light of the survey responses for this volume.

Three recent critical books were frequently mentioned in the surveys as being particularly useful. Lovesey's *Ngũgĩ wa Thiong'o* introduces teachers and students to Ngũgĩ's works and their contexts. It deals with the novels, short stories, and plays, with Ngũgĩ's editiorial work as well as his children's stories, films, and plays. The discussion of *I Will Marry When I Want* in this book was reprinted in Biodun Jeyifo's *Modern African Drama*. Survey respondants also recommended Williams's *Ngũgĩ wa Thiong'o*, which provides a lucid, forthright, and reasonably priced critical overview of Ngũgĩ's novels and essays from the perspective of the operations of power, though Williams doesn't consider Ngũgĩ's plays. Its survey of Ngũgĩ criticism focuses on divergent views of a single text, *Petals of Blood*, because of its "pivotal position" in Ngũgĩ's work and in the responses to it (166). The most noted critical work was Gikandi's monograph *Ngũgĩ wa Thiong'o*. All scholars of Ngũgĩ are indebted to Gikandi, and this book offers the most rigorous and searching investigation of the biographical, historical, cultural, stylistic, narratological, and theoretical contexts of Ngũgĩ's oeuvre. One of Gikandi's chief concerns is to correct a critical overemphasis on Ngũgĩ's literary texts as didactic diagrams of his ideas (a tendency Ngũgĩ sometimes appears to encourage [247]) and a related tendency to view these texts solely through the prism of his essays.[5] Gikandi focuses instead on Ngũgĩ's dynamic struggle to locate an artistic form to represent the elusive, contradictory postcolonial condition. Ngũgĩ wrestled with this "crisis of representation," in Fredric Jameson's phrase (qtd. in Gikandi, *Ngũgĩ* 11), in his movement from the modernist novel of bourgeois individualism to the socialist epic in his "masterpiece" *Petals of Blood* (272), and in his "Marxist—and perhaps post-Marxist" Gĩkũyũ narratives' blend of postmodern satirical allegory and the oral tradition (38).[6] Ngũgĩ's plays, despite what Gikandi considers their limited aesthetic achievement, powerfully conjure collective memories and challenge the state. *Matigari*, in Gikandi's estimate, is a performative novel of exile, signaling the beginning of Ngũgĩ's extended alienation from the heartland of his inspiration. Gikandi's analysis of Ngũgĩ's essays deals perceptively with Ngũgĩ's famous "brief break with English later in his career" before the demands of an American university position may have forced a reengagement (287). Gikandi also traces Ngũgĩ's earlier renunciation of an Anglocentric Arnoldian and Leavisite literary aesthetic, of the Christian faith, and of a Eurocentric university curriculum.

A distinctive feature of critical studies from the mid-1990s is a concern with the relation between genre and history in Ngũgĩ's work—note Ogude's excellent *Ngũgĩ's Novels and African History: Narrating the Nation*, F. Odun Balogun's *Ngugi and African Postcolonial Narrative: The Novel as Oral Narrative in Multigenre Performance*, and Michael Cook and Michael Okenimpke's *Ngũgĩ wa Thiong'o: An Exploration of His Writings*. Two somewhat older comparative studies are Dramé's monograph and Clara Tsabedze's *African Independence from*

Francophone and Anglophone Voices: A Comparative Study of the Post-independence Novels by Ngũgĩ and Sembène. A growing number of doctoral dissertations focus on Ngũgĩ's dialogue with writers such as Ayi Kwei Armah, George Lamming, and Rachid Boudjedra. Early book-length studies of Ngũgĩ that are accessible to undergraduates and provide an important link in his reception history are Clifford B. Robson's *Ngũgĩ wa Thiong'o* and Douglas Killam's *An Introduction to the Writings of Ngũgĩ*. Cogent and accessible treatments of Ngũgĩ's historiography are provided in Abdul JanMohamed's *Manichean Aesthetics: The Politics of Literature in Colonial Africa* and in David Maughan-Brown's *Land, Freedom, and Fiction: History and Ideology in Kenya*.

Collections of Essays

The first collection of essays on Ngũgĩ appeared in 1984: Killam's *Critical Perspectives on Ngugi wa Thiong'o*. It surveys the first wave of critical responses to Ngũgĩ and includes interpretations of *A Grain of Wheat* and *Petals of Blood* as both Marxist and Christian novels. Charles Cantalupo's *The World of Ngũgĩ wa Thiong'o* contains a number of important, often cited essays, such as Neil Lazarus's "(Re)turn to the People," Gikandi's discussion of melancholy and emotions in Ngũgĩ's work, and Joseph McLaren's revealing examination of the critical reception of *Petals of Blood* as a reflection of the state of African literary criticism in general. Gĩtahi Gĩtĩtĩ introduces the "recuperation" of the gĩcaandĩ in *Devil on the Cross*, a figure of importance in all Ngũgĩ's Gĩkũyũ narratives. The collection has a number of examinations of *Matigari*, including those of Balogun ("Ngũgĩ's *Matigari*") and of Lewis Nkosi.

The largest collection of essays on Ngũgĩ published in the mid-1990s is Cantalupo's *Ngũgĩ wa Thiong'o: Texts and Contexts*. It contains poetry and twenty essays selected from the nearly 150 papers presented at "the largest conference on an African writer ever held in the United States or anywhere," as Cantalupo writes in the introduction (x). The collection includes Henry Chakava's account of the dangers and rewards of publishing Ngũgĩ in Kenya and Sam Mbure's moving acknowledgment of Ngũgĩ's literary mentorship. It opens up more fully than previous collections the value of African and international comparative approaches; it also enters the area of popular culture, in Edward Wiltse's "The 'Mau Mau' in Hollywood." *Critical Essays on Ngũgĩ wa Thiong'o*, edited by Peter Nazareth, offers a selection of new essays and reprints of a number of valuable essays, including those by McLaren, Gĩtĩtĩ, and Chakava. It continues the comparative perspective of Cantalupo's second collection and includes André-Paul Michaud's examination of nature and Christine Lofin's study of landscape in Ngũgĩ's novels. The most recent collection on Ngũgĩ, *The Writer as Activist: South Asian Perspectives on Ngũgĩ wa Thiong'o*, edited by Bernth Lindfors and Bala Kothandaraman, moves the center of Ngũgĩ studies to South Asia, though some of the collection's scholars now live in the United States. The essays demonstrate a concern with a shared colonial and postcolonial experience and a sensitive consideration of the question of language and translation.

Individual Essays

The following essays are a representative selection of those that deal with themes of history and gender in Ngũgĩ's work. Sicherman's important essay on Ngũgĩ's engagement with history ("Ngũgĩ wa Thiong'o and the Writing of Kenyan History") is still relevant (it appears in Nazareth's *Critical Essays*). A good starting place for a study of Ngũgĩ's treatment of gender is Florence Stratton's "Gender on the Agenda: Novels of the 1980s by Ngũgĩ and Achebe," in her *Contemporary African Literature and the Politics of Gender*; Charles Nama's "Daughters of Moombi: Ngũgĩ's Heroines and Traditional Gikuyu Aesthetics" and Tobe Levin's "Women as Scapegoats of Culture and Cult: An Activist's View of Female Circumcision in Ngũgĩ's *The River Between*," both in *Ngambika: Studies of Women in African Literature*, edited by Carole Boyce Davies and Anne Adams Graves; or Jennifer Evans's "Women and Resistance in Ngũgĩ's *Devil on the Cross*," in a special issue of *African Literature Today* on representations of women. Elleke Boehmer's "The Master's Dance to the Master's Voice: Revolutionary Nationalism and the Representation of Women in the Writing of Ngũgĩ wa Thiong'o" and Nicholls's "The Landscape of Insurgency: Mau Mau, Ngũgĩ wa Thiong'o and Gender" are also valuable.

Reference Works

Bibliographies

Sicherman compiled two excellent bibliographic resources on Ngũgĩ. *Ngũgĩ wa Thiong'o: A Bibliography of Primary and Secondary Sources, 1957–1987* indexes almost two thousand items on Ngũgĩ and related subjects. Part 4 of *Ngũgĩ wa Thiong'o: The Making of a Rebel* is a thirty-four-page listing of secondary sources, and the rest of the book contains a vast number of documents relating to his work. *The Writer as Activist: South Asian Perspectives on Ngũgĩ wa Thiong'o*, edited by Lindfors and Kothandaraman, contains a valuable "Checklist of South Asian Scholarship" from 1975 to 1997 that indicates the range and depth of Ngũgĩ scholarship in South Asia alone. The *MLA International Bibliography* provides a broad range of the most recent as well as older items on Ngũgĩ's works.

Biographical Material and Interviews

Although there is no biography of Ngũgĩ—Peter Kimani is at work on one, to be published by East African Educational Publishers—some of the author's personal essays (and he is a master of the genre) as well as his two memoirs recount key events in his life and may be taken together to form episodes in the emerging genre of postcolonial autobiography. A powerful section in Ngũgĩ's most influential critical work, *Decolonising the Mind*, details the humiliating physical and emotional punishments inflicted on African children attending a colonial school for speaking their own language. Children were driven to inform on classmates (10–13). Ngũgĩ expands on this material in "Recovering the Original" and recalls these episodes again in *Moving the Centre*, focusing on the profound psychological violence done to Kenyan children and their linguistic culture: "English was made to look as if it was the language spoken by God" (33). In "Biggles, Mau Mau and I," from *Moving the Centre*, Ngũgĩ offers the paradox of his position as a schoolboy encouraged in his education by his brother, while that very brother, a fighter in the anticolonial Mau Mau forces, was being bombed in the forests of Mount Kenya by the Royal Air Force (136–41).

A number of Ngũgĩ's autobiographical essays address his participation in events that in retrospect appear monumental. "A Novel in Politics: The Launching of *Petals of Blood*," in *Writers in Politics*, addresses his growing disillusionment with writing what he termed "Afro-Saxon literature" amid the growing political oppression and widespread poverty in Kenya, although the essay ends with a reflection on the still bleaker twenty-first-century Kenya in the shadow of globalization (93). Part of the essay "Enactments of Power: The Politics of Performance Space," in *Penpoints, Gunpoints, and Dreams*, gives the political context of the first Kenyan performance of *The Trial of Dedan Kimathi* in October 1976, slotted into the National Theater's schedule between "a French ballet and a British farce" (43). The venue is located beside the colonial Norfolk Hotel, which overlooks the site of a 1922 colonial massacre (40–51). "Women in Cultural Work: The Fate of Kamiriithu People's Theater in Kenya," in *Barrel of a Pen: Resistance to Repression in Neo-colonial Kenya*, is a moving account of his involvement in collaborative community theater and the hostile government response that culminated in the theater's obliteration and his detention (43–51). In addition, Ngũgĩ's book-length treatment of his imprisonment, *Detained: A Writer's Prison Diary*, tells the story of his arrest in December 1977 and year-long detention, without charge or trial, as prisoner K6, 77, in cell 16 of Kamĩtĩ Maximum Security Prison, where Dedan Kimathi was hanged. *Detained* is a story of extreme hardship but also the triumphant story of the creation of *Devil on the Cross*, the novel written in Gĩkũyũ on toilet paper in the neocolonial prison.

Ngũgĩ's *Moving the Centre* contains a reflection on his experiences teaching at Yale Univeristy and on the support for his writing in Gĩkũyũ. He also speaks about the open debate on literature and politics that he encountered:

> The kind of issues we are raising in the classrooms of Yale would land all of us in prison for anything between one and ten years. I tell the students this, and they look amazed since what we are saying is nothing particularly revolutionary. We are only looking at the relevance of fiction to the facts of life! (157)

Moving the Centre concludes with a personal essay on a return to East Africa—not Kenya, from which he was still barred—and the moving sense of homecoming but also continuing exile despite the "Kenya I always carry with me" (174). He writes of the surreal nature of the political dictatorship, under which a warrant was issued for the arrest of a character in his novel, and of his fond anticipation of postdictatorship, pan-African unity in "the United States of Africa" (176).

A picture of Ngũgĩ's early life and education, the initial seeds of a biography, emerges in Sicherman's "Ngũgĩ's Colonial Education: 'The Subversion . . . of the African *Mind*,'" reprinted in Nazareth's *Critical Essays on Ngũgĩ wa Thiong'o*. The introduction to that volume, entitled "Saint Ngũgĩ," also presents Nazareth's reflections on his memories of Ngũgĩ as a student at Makerere and Leeds. As a fellow English honors student at Makerere University College, Nazareth offered advice to Ngũgĩ on the coming final exams, but "I do not know whether he used it since he went mountain climbing the weekend before his finals, feeling nobody had the right to judge him" (1–2). Gikandi addresses Ngũgĩ's colonial schooling and particularly its emphasis on English and Christianity (*Ngũgĩ* 250–52). Sicherman provides additional material about Ngũgĩ's educational experience at Alliance and Makerere in "Ngũgĩ's British Education." Ngũgĩ's *Dreams in a Time of War: A Childhood Memoir* provides a moving account of his early life on the eve of the national trauma. A second volume of the memoir, "In the House of the Interpreter," is forthcoming.

Ngũgĩ has been generous and forthcoming in interviews over many decades. These dialogues are full of personal anecdotes and may be an excellent starting point for the instructor approaching the teaching of Ngũgĩ for the first time. Cantalupo's *World of Ngũgĩ wa Thiong'o* contains a revealing phone interview with a high school student studying one of Ngũgĩ's plays. Ngũgĩ is interviewed by Reinhard Sander and Ian Munro ("Tolstoy") and by Bettye J. Parker in Killam's *Critical Perspectives on Ngugi wa Thiong'o*. There is an interview with the author conducted in the late 1970s by Katebalirwe Amooti wa Irumba, included in an appendix to his doctoral dissertation, about Ngũgĩ's early childhood. *The Writer as Activist* contains two interviews with Ngũgĩ: D. Venkat Rao's interview (Ngũgĩ, "Conversation") primarily concerns the question of language, and T. Vijay Kumar, who comments on Ngũgĩ's energy, openness, and "teacherly" clarity, focuses his questions on ideology and genre. In this interview, Ngũgĩ acknowledges "three phases" in his writing, a "shift" taking place with *Petals of Blood* ("Writer" 176). These interviews and many others have been collected in *Ngũgĩ wa Thiong'o Speaks: Interviews with the Kenyan Writer*, edited by Reinhard Sander and Bernth Lindfors. For an interview with Ngũgĩ, on *Wizard of the Crow*, see "Ngugi wa Thiong'o Interviewed."

Comparative Approaches

Because the volume of international literature that must be covered in most postcolonial literature courses is so great, because the strains of intertextuality and interdisciplinarity in Ngũgĩ's work are so rich, and because that work originates in different languages, instructors often follow a comparative methodology, considering Ngũgĩ's work in relation to other African, postcolonial, international, world, and diasporic literatures. Ngũgĩ may be read in the specific context of Kenyan colonial writing by Karen Blixen or Robert Ruark or in the broader context of such classic African texts as Chinua Achebe's *Things Fall Apart* (Nigeria), Wole Soyinka's *Death and the King's Horseman* (Nigeria), Camara Laye's *The African Child* (Guinea), and Ayi Kwei Armah's *The Beautyful Ones Are Not Yet Born* (Ghana). Texts by Ngũgĩ are also read in conjunction with other African or non-African texts: *The River Between* or *Weep Not, Child* may be read with *Things Fall Apart*, Abdulrazak Gurnah's *Paradise* (Zanzibar), or Tsitsi Dangarembga's *Nervous Conditions* (Zimbabwe); *A Grain of Wheat* may be read with Joseph Conrad's *Under Western Eyes*, *Heart of Darkness*, or *Nostromo*. A number of survey respondents teach *Petals of Blood* with Sembène's *God's Bits of Wood* (Senegal), and other respondents noted that Achebe's *Arrow of God* or *Anthills of the Savannah* make good comparisons.

While cognizant of the danger of reducing Ngũgĩ's works to mere historical or political documents, respondents said they also teach them in connection with a range of nonliterary texts. For example, *The Trial of Dedan Kimathi* is sometimes read with Ian Henderson and Philip Goodhart's *The Hunt for Kimathi* to provide both an anticolonial and a procolonial position on Kimathi, an important historical figure. Some respondents begin teaching *The River Between* by reading sections from Jomo Kenyatta's anthropological study *Facing Mount Kenya*; some teach *I Will Marry When I Want* by first presenting Bertolt Brecht's theory of drama; some teach *Petals of Blood* in conjunction with Colin Leys's *Underdevelopment in Kenya*; some teach the utopian alternatives in *Petals* with Thomas More's English Renaissance classic *Utopia* and Jameson's literary critical text *Archaeologies of the Future*.

Other literary texts mentioned by respondents that illuminate aspects of the East African and Kenyan context are the Arabic writer Tayeb Salih's *Season of Migration to the North* (Sudan); the Kenyan writer Marina Rebeka Njau's *Ripples in the Pool*; the Kenyan historical novelist Marjorie Oludhe Macgoye's *The Present Moment*; and the best-selling popular Kenyan novelist Meja Mwangi's *Carcase for Hounds*, *The Cockroach Dance*, or *The Last Plague*.

Some respondents used the comparative approach to Ngũgĩ in a range of courses. In a course on African-Caribbean literatures, one respondent examined George Lamming's *In the Castle of My Skin* in the light of Ngũgĩ's essay on the novel in *Homecoming*. Another read *Devil on the Cross* or *Matigari* in the light of Ngũgĩ's theory of language in *Decolonising the Mind*. Another compared Ngũgĩ's linguistic theory with those of Édouard Glissant, Léopold Sédar Senghor, Wole Soyinka, and Derek Walcott. Another considered how the diasporic African writer M. G. Vassanji, living in Canada, is "rewriting" Ngũgĩ in works like *The Gunny Sack* and *The Book of Secrets*.

Electronic Resources and Other Teaching Aids

Most respondents said they do not draw extensively on audiovisual or Web-based resources because of the time needed to situate Ngũgĩ's texts in their historical and cultural contexts and because of the challenge of concentrating on the texts themselves. But almost all use maps to locate Ngũgĩ's world and show the Scramble for Africa in the nineteenth century that severed communities and engendered future conflict. For undergraduates, respondents noted the value of charting characters' names and diagramming plot lines, particularly for *A Grain of Wheat* and *Petals of Blood*. One respondent directs students to produce their own study guide for the texts. Lamenting that many students have "little, if any, knowledge of Africa beyond Discovery Channel specials on animal migrations," one respondent engages students with word association exercises (e.g., *Africa*). Some respondents had a Gĩkũyũ speaker read from Gĩkũyũ texts in class to convey a sense of the rhythm of the original as well as the way that postcolonial Gĩkũyũ is inflected with Englishness. Performing or watching performances of Ngũgĩ's plays was also recommended. Some instructors ask their students to surf the Web to research the historical, political, and cultural contexts of Ngũgĩ's works. This activity increases student engagement with a text and also discourages students from regarding Ngũgĩ's works as history or anthropology. One respondent used a storytelling technique in which students were encouraged to fill gaps and make connections with other texts.

The archive of Ngũgĩ-related material on the Web and in various media is growing. There are recordings of Mau Mau songs: Joseph Kamaru's *Nyimbo Cia Mau Mau* on CD and "Twthiaga Tukenete" on *YouTube*. There is a *YouTube* version of the Gĩkũyũ song "Ngarua Ndenda" ("I Will Get Circumcised When I Want"). Sam Mbure, a Gĩkũyũ poet and Ngũgĩ scholar, reads a story in Gĩkũyũ at www.poetmbure.com/videos/video.htm. There is an open-air comedy in Gĩkũyũ at *East African Tube*. A selection of reviews of *Wizard of the Crow* is located at www.complete-review.com. Instructors might also consult Ngũgĩ's home page (www.ngũgĩwathiongo.com) for updates on his career.

Some do employ film material in their teaching of Ngũgĩ. One respondent confronts students' stereotypes of Africa directly by showing clips from Tarzan movies. Another uses Sydney Pollack's *Out of Africa* for a similar purpose. For more general introductory perspectives, some respondents use "A Legacy of Lifestyles" from Ali Mazrui's documentary series *The Africans: A Triple Heritage* or "The Swahili Coast" in the series *Wonders of the African World*, by Henry Louis Gates, Jr., or even Terry George's *Hotel Rwanda*. To address the question of cross-cultural interpretation, one respondent uses Manthia Diawara's *Rouch in Reverse*. Some respondents pair films with particular texts, such as Sembène's *Moolaadé* with *The River Between*; Euzhan Palcy's *Sugar Cane Alley* with *Weep Not, Child*; Sembène's *Xala*, Andy Wachowski and Larry Wachowski's *The Matrix*, or Fernando Meirelles's *The Constant Gardener* with *Petals of Blood*. One respondent suggested pairing *Wizard of the Crow* with Werner Herzog's documentary on Jean-Bédel Bokassa, *Echoes from a Somber Empire*.

The documentary *Mau Mau*, written by David Koff and produced and directed by Anthony Howarth and Koff, includes interviews with former insurgents like Karari Njama as well as testimony from former interrogators about torture methods. The film argues that African armed resistance followed the creation by hostile settlers of a myth about an African secret society, a myth that had British government support. There are a number of useful films about female circumcision: Penny Dedman's *Rites*, Pratibha Parmar and Alice Walker's *Warrior Marks*, and Soraya Mire's *Fire Eyes*. Cantalupo's *Against All Odds: African Languages and Literatures into the Twenty-First Century* contains material from a conference held in 2000 in Eritrea and footage of a Tigrinya translation of Ngũgĩ and Ngũgĩ wa Mĩriĩ's *I Will Marry When I Want*.

Historical and Political Resources

There is a wealth of material on Kenya's historical, political, and socioeconomic contexts. For a discussion of Gĩkũyũ history, see Godfrey Muriuki's *A History of the Kikuyu, 1500–1900*. On Gĩkũyũ collective consciousness, see Tabitha M. Kanogo's *Squatters and the Roots of Mau Mau, 1905–63*. On culture and colonialism, see Nicholas B. Dirks's introduction to his *Colonialism and Culture* and also Robert L. Tignor's *The Colonial Transformation of Kenya: The Kamba, Kikuyu, and Maasai, from 1900 to 1939*. For a discussion of national consciousness in a colonial context, see Frantz Fanon's *The Wretched of the Earth*, a work of immense importance for Ngũgĩ.

For a detailed account of the Mau Mau conflict, see Bruce Berman and John Lonsdale's *Unhappy Valley: Conflict in Kenya and Africa*, W. O. Maloba's *Mau Mau and Kenya: An Analysis of a Peasant Revolt*, Zoë Marsh and G. W. Kingsnorth's *A History of East Africa*, Theodore Natsoulas's "The Politicization of the Ban on Female Circumcision and the Rise of the Independent School Movement in Kenya," and Lynn M. Thomas's *Politics of the Womb: Women, Reproduction, and the State in Kenya*. See also Carl G. Rosberg and John Nottingham's *The Myth of "Mau Mau": Nationalism in Kenya*, Maina wa Kinyatti's *Kenya's Freedom Struggle: The Dedan Kimathi Papers*, Josiah Mwangi Kariuki's *"Mau Mau" Detainee: The Account by a Kenya African of His Experiences in Detention Camps*, Donald L. Barnett and Karari Njama's *Mau Mau from Within: Autobiography and Analysis of Kenya's Peasant Revolt*, Maloba's *African Women in Revolution*, Frank Furedi's *The Mau Mau War in Perspective*, Greet Kershaw's *Mau Mau from Below*, and E. S. Atieno Odhiambo and John Lonsdale's *Mau Mau and Nationhood*. Two enormously influential recent studies of Mau Mau and particularly the colonial detention camps are Elkins's *Imperial Reckoning* and Anderson's *Histories of the Hanged*.

NOTES

[1] Patrick Williams informed me that the only remaining copies of these two films were lost when Channel 4 in England was preparing a documentary on Ngũgĩ.

[2] An account of this film and of other film projects in which Ngũgĩ was involved appears in Lovesey, *Ngũgĩ* 99–103.

[3] *Female circumcision* is an imprecise though widely used term for various forms of female genital mutilation.

[4] *Mau Mau* was a largely meaningless, derogatory, colonial coinage and never used by the rebel forces, though it survives as the term by which this conflict is known.

[5] In a discussion of the overlooked emotional quotient of Ngũgĩ's works, Gikandi expresses his personal debt to Ngũgĩ's early novels for allowing Gikandi's recovery of a repressed past; he also voices his regret at being denied the opportunity to be Ngũgĩ's student at the University of Nairobi by Ngũgĩ's detention ("Moments").

[6] Gikandi refers to the triumph of storytelling in *Wizard of the Crow* ("Postcolonial Wizard").

Part Two

APPROACHES

Introduction

Ngũgĩ wa Thiong'o's imaginative and theoretical works have been a source of inspiration and provocation for more than one generation of readers in his Kenyan homeland and around the world. Ngũgĩ is regarded as perhaps the leading international authority on cultural decolonization, and his courageous struggle against repressive governments and the destructive force of globalization in the cultural domain has established him as a new type of global postcolonial intellectual. In many genres, he has contributed to ongoing debates about the politics of language. There is great diversity in the interpretation of his work, as this volume demonstrates, but lively and open discussion is central to his credo. In this introduction to part 2 of the volume, I explore some of the main issues and controversies raised by Ngũgĩ's writing. I also examine the pedagogical difficulties of teaching it as well as strategies for addressing those difficulties suggested in the survey responses. Finally I provide an overview of the essays that follow.

Ngũgĩ raises divisive issues, particularly about history and gender. As both W. O. Maloba and Emilia Ilieva argue in their essays in this volume, he remains a highly controversial figure in his homeland of Kenya, the setting of almost all his work, though there may be growing openness to his writing and polemics, as both Peter Simatei and Evan Mwangi contend in this volume, in part because of Kenya's shifting political climate. Some of his books have been banned in Kenya. Even the periodization of his career is a subject of contention. In this volume, F. Odun Balogun asserts the importance of the division between Ngũgĩ's earlier English and later Gĩkũyũ works and the division also between his earlier modernist narratives and his later allegorical narratives. These distinctions are reconsidered by Simon Gikandi, who writes of the "palpable ambivalence" in Ngũgĩ's early writings, then of the influence of Frantz Fanon and Marxism that led finally to the "double paradox" of his new, exiled relation to art, language, and audience.

Probably the most contentious aspect of Ngũgĩ's work is its engagement with history and, by extension, politics. Maloba, a respected Kenyan historian, explains that the major preoccupation of African historians in the 1960s and early 1970s was the ethnic origin and migration patterns of various African peoples, a program of investigation with an insidious undertone. Kenya's colonial government, for example, attempted to justify confiscation and settlement of land by Europeans with the idea that Africans were not really owners or even long-term residents. Such claims were used to rationalize the appropriation of Gĩkũyũ land in particular. The Masai people of East Africa witnessed the division of their ancestral grazing lands between two nations, Kenya and Tanzania. As Gikandi argues in *Ngũgĩ wa Thiong'o*, the very notion of a cohesive, collective identity for the Gĩkũyũ people of Kenya, the focus of much of Ngũgĩ's work, is a colonial-era invention. The Gĩkũyũ supplied themselves with a detailed history and other distinct cultural markers to meet the challenges and threats of the colonial state:

> The Gikuyu . . . carefully remade and rewrote their cultural narratives and moral economy to fit into the structures privileged by colonialism, creating an identity for themselves as a "tribe," valorizing centralizing narratives of common descent, calling attention to a common mythological pantheon, and privileging histories and temporalities that would put them, morally and conceptually, on equal terms with their colonizers. (18)

The Gĩkũyũ of central Kenya, the largest of approximately thirty ethnic groups in the country, including the Masai, share a common language, beliefs, and a clan-based kinship system. The predominance of the linguistic distinction in Gĩkũyũ identity may account in part for the emphasis that Ngũgĩ's works—his fiction, plays, and theoretical essays—place on language as the principal marker of culture and as the archive of cultural memory. However, as all Ngũgĩ's writing makes clear, land was another fundamental component of Gĩkũyũ identity, and thus when the British colonizers confiscated and resettled ancestral Gĩkũyũ land and hired Gĩkũyũ laborers to work their own soil, as Ngũgĩ describes in *Weep Not, Child*, the eruption of Gĩkũyũ outrage was limited only by the desire to stay close to their sacred inheritance at any cost.

The issue of land, or what Maloba calls "land alienation," was a main cause of the ultimately violent confrontation between Kenyan Africans, particularly the Gĩkũyũ, and the colonial government, a confrontation recounted in some detail in the essay on *Matigari* by Ali Erritouni in this volume. Kenya had been designated a settler colony, not a resource colony like Nigeria that was valued for its raw materials as well as its strategic importance in England's geopolitical competition with France, Germany, and Portugal. Because of its temperate climate, particularly in the Gĩkũyũ highlands near Nairobi, and its surprisingly fertile soil, ideal for growing gentlemanly crops, like coffee, that required large, plantation-like farms, Kenya was considered an ideal location to settle British veterans of the two world wars. The pace of settlement increased after World War II, when demobilized British soldiers were granted land, in some cases land taken from Kenyan soldiers who fought alongside the British. The accumulation of grievances over land rights, as well as unemployment and the increasingly repressive atmosphere of colonial Kenya (marked by pass cards, laws, and regulations more commonly associated with apartheid South Africa), inflamed anticolonial sentiment.

The Mau Mau struggle was primarily a Gĩkũyũ conflict, though other ethnic groups in the country were also involved, as Ngũgĩ makes clear. Ngũgĩ has been accused of promoting Gĩkũyũ cultural nationalism through his preoccupation with this conflict and his use of his mother tongue in his later work. But he advocates the promotion of all Kenyan and African languages, referring to Kenya's ethnic communities as nationalities. He has also been, for most of his career, a passionate supporter of pan-African and pan-Kenyan unity. His treatment of Mau Mau in *Weep Not, Child* laments the divisions that the conflict caused between pro- and anticolonial forces within the Gĩkũyũ community and even within families. This conflict was part of the lived experience of Ngũgĩ and his family. The Mau Mau struggle pitted the well-armed and organized colonial forces against bands of Africans, some with European military training, who took up arms after their secret societies, distinguished by oathing and other ceremonial practices, were banned in 1950. These Mau Mau fighters over time became isolated in the forests at the base of Mount Kenya. Ngũgĩ, particularly after *A Grain of Wheat*, regards this conflict unambiguously as the first important armed rebellion against colonial rule and one that set the stage for resistance and decolonization in the rest of the British Empire in the 1950s and 1960s.

In Kenya, historical research on the conflict has been hindered by political sensitivity regarding fair restitution and reconciliation at the time of independence, as well as by anxiety about keeping alive the issues of the conflict. Research has been made difficult also by the illiteracy of many of the combatants. Jomo Kenyatta, Kenya's first prime minister and later president, on his election launched a policy encouraging the forgiveness of past wrongs but also the forgetting of still-unresolved grievances. The unwillingness to address this past—for example, through some version of the Truth and Reconciliation Commission established successfully later in postapartheid South Africa—has made the study of Kenyan history problematic and adversely affected social, economic, and political development. Ngũgĩ's historical subject and its controversial nature are variously addressed in this volume's essays by Maloba, James Ogude, and Patrick Williams. Maloba is critical of what he perceives as Ngũgĩ's idealizing tendency in his treatment of the conflict and especially in the handling of the historic role of the iconic figure of the Mau Mau leader Dedan Kimathi, whereas Ogude and Williams trace connections between Kenyan and broader African postcolonial historiography.

Gender issues in Ngũgĩ's works are addressed in this volume by Brendon Nicholls, Bonnie Roos, Gĩchingiri Ndĩgĩrĩgĩ, Evan Mwangi, and Simatei. Roos and Ndĩgĩrĩgĩ investigate very different "heroic" figures in Ngũgĩ's novels: a Nobel Prize–winning environmental activist, and also a prostitute. Nicholls and Mwangi both address the controversial topic of female circumcision, clitoridectomy, or female genital mutilation. This practice is central to Ngũgĩ's first written novel, *The River Between*, where it is the locus of opposition between the missionaries and Gĩkũyũ traditionalists. The confrontation between the two groups took place over women's bodies, when missionary groups refused to admit circumcised girls into their schools. Ngũgĩ's treatment of this practice was influenced by Kenyatta's *Facing Mount Kenya: The Tribal Life of the Gikuyu*, and Ngũgĩ at one point nearly became Kenyatta's biographer. Ngũgĩ's use of *Facing Mount Kenya*, like Chinua Achebe's use of the anthropologist G. T. Basden's *Niger Ibos* when writing *Things Fall Apart*, indicates the profound disruption caused by colonization: to recover a meaningful cultural past, these groundbreaking African authors turned to the discourse of Western anthropology. As Terence Ranger indicates in a broader discussion of this phenomenon in "The Invention of Tradition in Colonial Africa," the cultural cohesion that these early novels conjure may be the result of the work of a passionate but nevertheless "invented tradition." However, as Ngũgĩ's own "Orature in Education" in this volume illustrates so powerfully, his upbringing gave him a direct connection to the tradition of Gĩkũyũ orature, the origin of all his imaginative writing. He discusses the performative basis of Gĩkũyũ orature as well as the nature of "litorature."

Kenyatta's *Facing Mount Kenya*, an anthropological study of the Gĩkũyũ, was written at the London School of Economics under the supervision of the structural-functionalist anthropologist Bronislaw Malinowski. Malinowski advocated participatory examinations of culture and regarded culture as an indivisible whole. This indivisibility is emphasized in Kenyatta's treatment of female circumcision: the practice creates harmony and unity among the girls involved. After the ritual, "[t]hey act as one body in all tribal matters and have a very strong bond of . . . sisterhood among themselves" (4). Moreover, sexual relations with the uninitiated are "taboo" (127). Word choice is important here. Kenyatta uses the term *circumcision* and treats both male and female ceremonies in a chapter on initiation. But female circumcision is a more dangerous operation than male circumcision and potentially catastrophic; it is the near equivalent of male castration, because it entails the excision of the clitoris and sometimes also the inner and outer lips of the vagina. The practice traditionally accompanies initiation into adult life and preparation for marriage, but it also expresses anxiety about unbridled female sexuality and the enforcement of marital fidelity. Kenyatta endorses female circumcision, bowing to the force of tradition and believing that the practice assures the survival of Gĩkũyũ cultural identity. Although *The River Between* appears to condemn the practice—the circumcized girl dies—the novel also accepts its importance as a cultural marker and, like Kenyatta, maintains that it cannot be ended rapidly. In this volume, Mwangi prefers the phrase *genital cutting* to *genital mutilation* or *female circumcision* as less freighted with cultural and ideological baggage, which Nicholls maintains cannot be separated from the subject and from the politics of gender in Ngũgĩ's fiction.

Despite the entry of African and postcolonial literatures into the literary canon, many respondents to the survey of instructors conducted in preparation for this volume noted that opportunities to teach Ngũgĩ remain limited. Even some senior postcolonial scholars have rarely taught Ngũgĩ. In my own experience in the mid-1970s in eastern Canada, a course in what was the new and innovative area of Commonwealth literature, though taught by Douglas Killam, an eminent Ngũgĩ scholar, had no place in the honors English program. Respondents said that their teaching of Ngũgĩ was restricted because there were few postcolonial course offerings and because there was general contraction. The position of postcolonial and African studies in the academy is evolving, though an implicit hierarchy exists: students study English literature in many period or genre courses but study all other literatures in English in a single course covering many literatures, nations, and regions

Ngũgĩ is taught in a wide variety of educational settings and at different academic levels because of his importance in the classic phase of postcolonial writing, his influence as a theorist, and his reputation as an engaged intellectual. He appears in interdisciplinary and multidisciplinary courses across the curriculum and well beyond traditional English studies. His works are taught in courses with such titles as Postdevelopment and Postcolonial Theory, Africas of the Mind, Reading African Cultures, Performing Power in the Postcolony, Conversations: Writers and Readers in Dialogue, and World Bank Literature.

Ngũgĩ's writing presents special challenges for students and teachers. Most non-African students are less aware of the Kenyan situation than that of South Africa. Because of this ignorance, one respondent had to "[translate] the translation" of a text like *Matigari*, filling in the cultural and historical information that the text assumes its readers know. The general image of African armed conflict, political corruption, foreign debt, pandemic disease, and ecocide tends to dominate the often pitying or dismissive and sometimes racist perceptions of undergraduate students who approach Ngũgĩ. Observing that many Western students regard twentieth-century Africa as more alien than Victorian England, one respondent "challenge[s] their presumption of a radical African difference" and shows them the implications of this presumption. Students are aware of Africa best through the benevolent, if somewhat patronizing, work of Western celebrities like Ben Affleck, Bono, Bill Gates, Bob Geldof, Angelina Jolie, and Oprah Winfrey.

Ngũgĩ's most accessible early novels (*Weep Not, Child*, *The River Between*, *A Grain of Wheat*) do not, like *Things Fall Apart*, set out in extensive detail the cultural, political, and economic context of their stories They do not begin with a precolonial, pastoral idyll but almost immediately confront uncomfortable questions. They emerge from historical but also psychological trauma, in particular from the impact of colonialism's physical violence and attempt at cultural annihilation. The central characters in *Weep Not, Child* and *The River Between* quickly become alienated from their religious, cultural, and familial roots. One survey respondent noted, however, that students often identify with the "Christian romanticism" of *Weep Not, Child*'s protagonist, overlooking "the narrative's implicit critique of Njoroge as naive and even deluded." Students are also challenged by the political engagement of Ngũgĩ's later work, which does not fit their assumptions about literary disinterestedness and the idealized study of culture in the academy. Some find "the conventions of the later 'Gĩkũyũ' fiction difficult to deal with, although those who have read medieval literature are more likely to come to terms with Ngũgĩ's fables." "Students either too eagerly embrace or dismiss" Ngũgĩ's politics, notes another respondent, and even those who embrace his political engagement tend to read these texts as historical or sociological documents and overlook their complexity as aesthetic objects.

Ngũgĩ's image as a postcolonial colossus with a cult status and iconographic reputation intimidates some students. Some respond with veneration, some with derision. Some students appear reluctant to question Ngũgĩ's positions or any aspect of his work for fear of being accused of having "colonized minds." Respondents said that some of their Kenyan students had negative preconceptions and that in both Kenya and America Gĩkũyũ speakers sometimes didn't read the Gĩkũyũ novels until they appeared in translation. One respondent reported that Kenyan students inevitably assume "they know all about Ngũgĩ," are impatient with what they perceive as his "blindness" to the impossibility of reform, and feel "let down" by his departure from Kenya. Another respondent's students complained to their department chair that they were being taught "bad books."

Among negative student responses was hostility to the "excessive didacticism" of *Petals of Blood*. Some students were "troubled" or made "uncomfortable" by "compliant" female characters and by the issues Ngũgĩ raises, such as Christian hypocrisy and "female circumcision." Some were particularly distressed to learn in documentary films that even some women supported the practice. In a post-9/11 world, students, especially in the United States, objected to Ngũgĩ's treatment of anticolonial and anti-Western violence. When the justification of violence in an era of global terrorism was debated, one respondent described a "palpable tension in the class." Respondents who have taught *A Grain of Wheat* and *Petals of Blood* for a number of years observe that students with less and less experience reading lengthy and complex narratives find Ngũgĩ's mid-career novels difficult to follow.

Survey respondents recommended a number of strategies to address these and other challenges. Most found the best approach to teaching Ngũgĩ was one anchored in participatory or dialogic activity, including group work and oral presentations to elicit student responses and allow preconceptions and bewilderment to emerge openly. Other respondents refered to the classroom as a site of postcolonial struggle, observing that the language question elicits passionate, polarized positions. Reminding students that writing does not take place in a vacuum and pointing out the historical and cultural contexts of Ngũgĩ's writings were successful strategies. Gently and respectfully, instructors approach Ngũgĩ's intimidating stature by stressing his own iconoclasm in educational settings, pointing to inconsistencies between his theory and practice, and gesturing to parallels between the issues in his work and those in the students' lives.

Respondents frequently stressed the importance of confronting and utilizing the location of teaching—for example, drawing on students' concern for the environment in presenting the importance of land in Ngũgĩ's works. Instructors encouraged students to explore links between Ngũgĩ's treatment of Kenya's national story and that of other, perhaps more familiar global situations: the American Civil War; Latin American conflicts; Canada's treatment of indigenous peoples and the legacy of the Canadian conflict between French and English; Taiwan's experience of successive colonizations; and the shifting global power relations of Britain, America, Russia, and China. Instructors also connected

Ngũgĩ's novels with other, perhaps more familiar revolutionary novels (e.g., John Steinbeck's *The Grapes of Wrath* or radical African American novels of the 1960s and 1970s) that represent a struggle against oppression based on gender, ethnicity, race, or nationality. One respondent encouraged students to confront the ethics of the committed writer as it relates to the ethical role of the reader and critic. Instructors countered the tendency to read Ngũgĩ's fiction as simply history, political science, economics, or ethnography disguised as art by a close reading of the texts stressing their narratological and stylistic aspects—from genre and structure to shifting focalization, unreliable narrators, image patterns, Christian and other allusions, and oral elements. For students having difficulty with following a complex narrative, one instructor recommended a storytelling technique that left gaps for them to fill in or in which to make comparisons with other works studied. Another recommended teaching excerpts from different Ngũgĩ novels. Generally speaking, respondents found that Ngũgĩ's novels before *Petals of Blood* were received best by lower-level undergraduate students and that those after *Petals of Blood* were more appropriate for upper-level undergraduates and graduate students.

The essays in this volume reflect the diversity not only of ways to teach Ngũgĩ but also of his influence. There are essays from major postcolonial and African literary theorists as well as from newer voices from Africa, the African diaspora, and the wider world. Much of the world is covered by the contributors' teaching experiences in Africa, Canada, Eastern Europe, England, India, Singapore, and the United States. Most of the contributors are teachers of literature, but one Kenyan historian, W. O. Maloba, writes of teaching Ngũgĩ in the history classroom. Almost all Ngũgĩ's work, from the novels to the plays, children's stories, and nonfiction prose, is treated at least briefly, and the extent of that coverage reflects its importance. The essays balance innovative approaches (teaching *Petals of Blood* as an example of World Bank literature) with traditional thematic and issue-based approaches. As befitting a study of teaching the polemical Ngũgĩ, this volume contains voices in opposition. The volume should serve to broaden the range of reference in the "planetary" classroom and to elucidate the contexts in which Ngũgĩ's works are taught and studied.

The essays are arranged in sections: "Cultural, Political, and Historical Contexts," "Language, Translation, Style," "Classroom Settings," "Teaching Ngũgĩ's Works Written in English," and "Teaching Ngũgĩ's Gĩkũyũ Novels in Translation." The essays in the first section offer broad parameters for teaching Ngũgĩ. Simon Gikandi addresses the career-long development of Ngũgĩ's "role as a public intellectual" in his creative and theoretical work while Ngũgĩ continues to negotiate the paradoxes of the postcolonial condition. Brendon Nicholls examines the developing treatment of gender in Ngũgĩ's novels as it interacts with politics. Pius Adesanmi introduces Ngũgĩ's troubled relation to the postcolonial and his preference for more precise historical designations of the colonial and neocolonial. Adesanmi puts Ngũgĩ's position on African languages and identity politics in a broad historical context. Examining Ngũgĩ's challenge to the development of professional, academic Kenyan historiography, Maloba acknowledges the author's emphasis on the importance of studying history from below and his insistence on the historian's moral imperative to address the public directly but cautions against making unambiguous assertions. Patrick Williams, comparing historical engagement in the cultural works of Ngũgĩ and Sembène Ousmane, considers how the two artists present history, in films or plays, by focusing either on historical moments or on the relation between those moments and the present; asks whether they represent historical heroes or collective history; and examines their embodiment of the confrontation between popular and official versions of history.

In "Language, Translation, Style," Michael Andindilile demonstrates the points of connection between Ngũgĩ's English and Gĩkũyũ novels, using *The River Between* and *Devil on the Cross* as examples of transliteration and translation in Ngũgĩ's multilingual universe. Evan Mwangi underscores the importance of language in Ngũgĩ, regarding all his writing, including that written in English, as a work of translation. Considering Ngũgĩ's drama, fiction, the untranslated preface to *Devil on the Cross*, and the untranslated *Njamba Nene* children's story, Mwangi shows how untranslated Gĩkũyũ and Swahili names, words, and phrases shed light on central concerns in Ngũgĩ's oeuvre. F. Odun Balogun writes about teaching Ngũgĩ's novels according to their developing narrative strategies and the genre shifting that reflects his evolving ideology.

In "Classroom Settings," James Ogude approaches Ngũgĩ's writing in the light of the popular reception of his ideas, particularly those taken from *Decolonising the Mind*, in the charged political atmosphere of national restoration in postapartheid South Africa. Ogude reflects on exile as the defining condition of postcolonial identity and on the past as a contested terrain in the postcolony. Nicholls teaches Ngũgĩ's fiction on four continents and in four very different social and political situations. Engaging Ngũgĩ's work makes the classroom itself "a model of fraught postcolonial negotiation," provoking lively and often unresolved debates. Emilia Ilieva writes of teaching *Petals of Blood* in Kenya and confronting students' entrenched views about the ideology of the novel and its author. She interprets the novel as a successful work of art in French and Bulgarian comparative contexts. Gĩchingiri Ndĩgĩrĩgĩ stresses the importance of the location of teaching in his account of his experience in offering a collaborative reading of *The Trial of Dedan Kimathi* and *I Will Marry When I Want*, asking students to consider the plays' model audiences. Students are challenged to unpack their own privileged positions regarding Kenyan colonial history and the violence of liberation theology.

In "Teaching Ngũgĩ's Works Written in English," Michael Harris approaches *A Grain of Wheat* and *Weep Not, Child* in a course on African and Caribbean literature. He places the novels in the context of anticolonial resistance and in the process draws student attention to links among Ngũgĩ, other African, and also Irish examples of resistance literature—Ngũgĩ acknowledges the Irish link in *Something Torn and New* (x–xi). Peter Nazareth examines the intertextual links between Ngũgĩ and Joseph Conrad. His study of Conrad's direct influence on *A Grain of Wheat* indicates postcolonial writers' "complex dialogue with the West." He also provides the perspective of a scholar and novelist whose connection to Ngũgĩ goes back to their days as students together in Uganda and England. Uzoma Esonwanne raises the question of representation in teaching *A Grain of Wheat*, framing the discussion by considering students' resistance to the notion of postcolonial literature as anything other than ethnography "in literary drag." Esonwanne regards Ngũgĩ's text from a narratological point of view as an example of the genre of testimony. In a reading of *Petals of Blood*, Bonnie Roos argues that Wanja represents colonial and neocolonial Kenya. As a prostitute, Wanja embodies colonial dehumanization, and her belief that she can negotiate for freedom may well be a romantic delusion Kate McInturff examines the economic and political contexts of as well as the constraints on the development of world literature. She sees *Petals of Blood* as an example of World Bank literature, suggesting that teachers and students carefully consider their own political stance as well as that of their larger institutional and national setting as it influences their reading of the unequal power relations that are at play in the novel's handling of the politics of development. Oliver Lovesey discusses Ngũgĩ's prison memoir, *Detained*, in terms of its reflections on national history and national detention, and explores connections with Wole Soyinka's *The Man Died* and Breyten Breytenbach's *The True Confessions of an Albino Terrorist*.

In "Teaching Ngũgĩ's Gĩkũyũ Novels in Translation," Peter Simatei considers *A Grain of Wheat* a transitional novel leading to *Devil on the Cross* and *Matigari*, because of its use of biblical references to voice political dissent and its stretching of the generic boundaries of the European novel. The question of redemptive violence is always troubling for students, but *Matigari*'s critique of the state's legitimacy, in Simatei's view, is unnecessarily polarized and polemical. Ali Erritouni teaches *Matigari* as *Things Fall Apart*'s sequel, Achebe's novel establishing a precolonial and colonial African context for neocolonialism's development. Following Fredric Jameson's notion of national allegory, Erritouni sees *Matigari* as a novel-allegory that locates colonialism's legacy in globalization and not simply African dictatorship. Ndĩgĩrĩgĩ considers *Wizard of the Crow*'s gendered critique of the postcolony in the light of Ngũgĩ's earlier female characters. The novel emerges as an endorsement of ecofeminist nationalism and the work of leading political figures like Wangari Maathai. Steve Gronert Ellerhoff makes a case for *Wizard*'s accessibility by virtue of its "universal" qualities.

Ngũgĩ wa Thiong'o: Writer and Critic

Simon Gikandi

Although he is known primarily as a novelist and playwright, Ngũgĩ wa Thiong'o has spent most of his career as a university professor, teaching in universities in Africa, Europe, and the United States. In this context, he has been a key participant in debates on questions of African identity, the role of culture in politics, the crisis of postcolonial society, language, and the nature and meaning of historical memory. His thinking about these issues has been generated and energized by his role as a public intellectual asked, both in his native Kenya and elsewhere in Africa, to comment on the pressing issues of the time. Ngũgĩ's essays, published in his influential collections *Homecoming*, *Writers in Politics* *Decolonising the Mind*, and *Moving the Centre,* have been instrumental in shaping the debate on culture, language, and politics in Africa. They have structured the terms of often heated polemics on ideology, language, and the role of the imaginary in the transformation of society, providing the vocabularies of these and other issues. Arguably, his essays have been more influential in the cultural politics of postcolonial Africa than his novels and plays. But Ngũgĩ would probably not accept any separation of his theoretical work from his fiction. In his introduction to *Homecoming*, he asserts that the essays collected in the book were "an integral part of the fictional world of *The River Between*, *Weep Not, Child*, and *A Grain of Wheat*" (xv).

In the Shadow of Mau Mau

Significantly, Ngũgĩ's fictional and theoretical work has been informed by his life, one lived under the shadow of a violent colonial past and in the educational institutions of colonial modernity. Ngũgĩ was born in 1938 in the village of Kamĩrĩĩthũ in central Kenya, to a family of peasants who, like the majority of Africans in the region, had lost their land to white settlers and had become categorized as squatters. At the urging of his mother, Ngũgĩ was enrolled at Kamandura Primary School, which was sponsored by the Church of Scotland, but he also briefly attended Mang'uo School, which had been founded by Gĩkũyũ Christians who broke away from the local Presbyterian church over a dispute on female circumcision in the 1920s. He was a brilliant student and a committed Christian, and at the end of his elementary education he was admitted to Alliance High School, the most exclusive secondary school for Africans in Kenya.

In the mid-1950s, when Ngũgĩ was attending Alliance High School, Kenya was going through a turbulent time. It was the middle of the Mau Mau rebellion against colonial rule and the state of emergency declared by the British government in Kenya in an attempt to control the peasants' revolt. Like most other people of his generation growing up in central Kenya, he was caught in the Mau Mau conflict in two ways. On the one hand, as aggrieved peasants, his family was sympathetic to the nationalist movement. Indeed, his older brother, Wallace Mwangi, was an active member of Mau Mau. On the other hand, Ngũgĩ belonged, because of his education, to a small, privileged elite with access to the opportunities offered by colonialism. In the midst of the Mau Mau conflict, he would go on to graduate from Alliance and be admitted to Makerere University College, the most prestigious institution of learning in East Africa.

Writer and Critic

Ngũgĩ became interested in literature at Alliance, an institution that, headed by a distinguished English mathematician named E. Cary Francis, privileged English literature, especially Shakespeare, as the key to modern civilization. Later, as a student of English at Makerere, Ngũgĩ became involved in intramural writing competitions, and in them he produced his first works, *The Black Hermit*, a play produced at the National Theater in Kampala in 1962; several short stories; and the manuscript of *The River Between*.

Ngũgĩ's first published work, *Weep Not, Child*, was autobiographical in its conception and form, an emotive narrative of the powerful and contradictory forces defining the social geography of late colonialism. Located solidly in the politics of nationalism and the violence that accompanied Kenya's transition from colonialism to decolonization, this novel signaled the emergence of the bildungsroman as the form of accounting for historical memory, loss, and aspiration. Ngũgĩ used the melancholic figure of Njoroge, who tenuously attempts to become educated as a free subject, to represent and mediate the demands of nationalism and the claims of a sentimental education.

Although Ngũgĩ was to become a powerful advocate of African cultures and the politics of decolonization in his mature works, his early writing is marked by a palpable ambivalence. This ambivalence has prompted critics to label his early thought as essentially liberal, especially in its concern with the conflicting demands made on individuals by collective entities. Indeed, the struggle between individual rights and desires on the one hand and collective demands on the other characterizes Ngũgĩ's early fiction and essays. *The River Between*, for example, is a dramatization of the struggle, over landscape and identity, between two factions of Gĩkũyũ Christians, torn not only by conflicting claims about the meaning of the land but also by their doubts about the character of the African subject and its destiny in the culture of colonialism.

In Ngũgĩ's earliest essays—often commentaries and reviews written for the Kenyan news media when he was still a student at Makerere—the newly independent Kenya is conceived as a land torn by ethnic and cultural rifts and between communalism and individualism. His goal was to find a middle ground, to position himself in the conflicted drama of decolonization and in the process recover an "African way," in which, as Ngũgĩ put it in *Homecoming*, his first collection of essays, "the community serves the individual. And the individual finds the fullest development of his personality when he is working in and for the community as a whole" (25).

The Discourse of Decolonization

After graduating from Makerere in 1963, Ngũgĩ worked briefly for the *Sunday Nation*, the largest newspaper in East Africa, before moving to Leeds for postgraduate study. It was at Leeds that his vague ideas about individualism and community began to take concrete form, usually out of conversations with radical students and lecturers. He discovered the works of Frantz Fanon, especially *The Wretched of the Earth*, which perhaps more than any other theoretical text laid the foundation for Ngũgĩ's mature thought.

Fanon's *Wretched* influenced Ngũgĩ in three areas. First, Fanon argued that culture, which he located in the materiality of social life and the narrative of decolonization, was central to the project of national consciousness. In a crucial chapter on national culture, he argued that "the native intellectual who wishes to create an authentic work of art must realize that the truths of a nation are in the first place its realities" (225). Ngũgĩ took up this theme in "Towards a National Culture," one of the seminal essays in *Homecoming*, defining culture as the result of a community's "creative struggle and progress through history" (4).

Second, Fanon wrote elaborately on the crisis of history and historiography and the problem of accounting for the African past. He particularly called attention to the dangers of imagining an African past as a mystical presence used to mask the failures of the African political class in decolonization. In Ngũgĩ's essays published in the 1970s, when Ngũgĩ was most active in Kenyan debates on culture and social transformation, he returned constantly to the difficulties of recovering the past and to the role of the writer as a communal historian. In

"The Writer and His Past," he underscored the doubleness of the project of historical recuperation—namely, the tension between the desire to understand the past in order to will decolonization into being and the dangers of the writer's "becoming too fascinated by the yesterday of his people and forgetting the present" (*Homecoming* 44).

Third, in ways that struck Ngũgĩ as prophetic, Fanon warned of the dangers of the betrayal of the narrative of nationalism by a new elite functioning under the tutelage of the former imperial powers. Writing on what he called the "pitfalls of national consciousness," Fanon warned that "instead of being the all-embracing crystallization of the innermost hopes of the whole people," national consciousness was in danger of being turned into "an empty shell, a crude and fragile travesty of what it might have been" (148). This theme—the promise and potential betrayal of national consciousness—was taken up in Ngũgĩ's mature novels, most notably *A Grain of Wheat* and *Petals of Blood*. It was the primary subject in his reflections on the role of the writer in the postcolonial state in the essays collected in *Writers in Politics*. In *Writers*, Fanon helped Ngũgĩ locate the crisis of decolonization in a historical and cultural framework and paved the way for what is now referred to as the novelist's Marxist phase.

Literature and Society

Marxism became central to Ngũgĩ's cultural project between 1970 and 1980, when Ngũgĩ taught at the University of Nairobi. During this period, he was a leading member of the radical left in East Africa, and, like many of his associates in the region, he was preoccupied by two overriding problems: the relation between writing and social life and the place of African literature in the institutions of education. In response to the first question, Ngũgĩ adopted a standard Marxist approach, defining national literature in *Writers in Politics* as "the sum total of the products of many individuals" in a society, a reflection of "collective reality," and the embodiment of a communal vision (5).

As a writer and teacher, Ngũgĩ invested heavily in the idea, inherited from the English university, that literature was central to the production of enlightened national subjects. When he was a lecturer at the University of Nairobi, he sought to transform the literature curriculum so that it could respond to the needs of the polity. In 1968, with Taban Lo Liyong and Henry Owuor Anyumba, two colleagues at the University of Nairobi, he issued a manifesto arguing for the abolition of the English department and the displacement of English literature as the center of the curriculum in literary studies. In this manifesto, published as an appendix to *Homecoming*, Ngũgĩ and his colleagues argued that the primary duty of a literature department was "to illuminate the spirit animating a people, to show how it meets new challenges, and to investigate possible areas of development and involvement" (146). The content of a literary text and its orientation, its connection to national traditions, were much more important than its language. Literature should function as the medium of national orientation, and its value should be judged by its relevance to the national and regional situation and by its "contribution towards understanding ourselves" (146).

Power and the Politics of Language

The question of language, however, became one of Ngũgĩ's main concerns in the late 1970s and early 1980s. Ngũgĩ began to advocate for the use of African languages as the medium of African expressiveness and to question the authority of literatures produced in European languages. This turn was driven by an anxiety and a desire. The anxiety was that even the most radical claims made for literature in European languages as an agent of social transformation seemed limited, given the small number of people who actually read works in those languages. The desire was to use literature as an instrument of social transformation, of a radical politics.

In the late 1970s, amid his doubts about the role of the novel in English, Ngũgĩ was invited by peasants in his home village to set up a theater group and produce a play in Gĩkũyũ. Out of this experience he became convinced that African literature in European languages was already an alienated if not a counterfeit product. The real work of social change or struggle could take place only in African languages, which seemed to engage with political problems at the most local level. Ngũgĩ's assumptions about the power of an African-language literature were reinforced by his arrest and detention in a maximum security prison from 1977 to 1978 because of his engagement with the grass roots.

In his prison memoir, *Detained*, published after he was released, Ngũgĩ reflected on his experiences as a writer making a shift from a European language and an elite university toward a serious engagement with peasants and workers in the open space of theater. He saw this shift as paradigmatic of the postcolonial state's inability to confront its compromised legacy and its impoverishment as opposed to the dynamic cultural forms that had the capacity for social critique. After he was released from prison, Ngũgĩ turned to writing fiction in Gĩkũyũ, producing two of his most innovative works, *Devil on the Cross* and *Matigari*.

The Paradox of Exile

In 1982, as the Kenyan government escalated its persecution of writers and intellectuals, Ngũgĩ found himself in exile, first in Britain and later in the United States. In exile, his thinking became more focused on the institutional and instrumental nature of politics in Africa. His critique of the dictatorship in Kenya took the form of essays published in *Barrel of a Pen*, but a more elaborate discussion of the relation between art and the state was presented in *Penpoints, Gunpoints, and Dreams*, a series of essays that came out of the Clarendon Lectures that Ngũgĩ gave at Oxford University in 1996. In *Penpoints*, he explored the diverse formal responses that artists in Africa had developed in response to the challenge of the postcolonial state, which by its very nature was antithetical to the power of the imaginary. His magisterial *Wizard of the Crow*, written at this time, enacted a radical confrontation between the institutions of power and the magic of art. But writing in exile was forcing Ngũgĩ to face the double paradox of his thinking about art, the efficacy of African languages as a conduit of the African experience, and the author's relation to his primary audience.

The first paradox was that Ngũgĩ was producing his most sustained and coherent critical work on language and literature when he was furthest removed from his linguistic sources and assumed readers. In *Decolonising the Mind*, he had established what he considered to be the phenomenology of language in the definition of the African character. He had argued that language was the carrier of a culture and its entire body of values and was thus inseparable from "ourselves as a community of human beings with a specific form and character, a specific history, a specific relationship to the world" (16). He had also argued that a native language established the harmony between the speakers and their social and natural environment, whereas colonial languages were essentially alienating.

Ngũgĩ's exile, however, represented an inescapable alienation from the sources of his language and immediate audience. Increasingly his reflections on the writer's language and commitment were becoming an attempt to reconcile the desire for locality with the reality of globalization. The tension between local and global is evident in the essays collected in *Moving the Centre*. The author's referents are often Kenyan and African, but the audience is inevitably European and American, thus the art of criticism and thinking in general become a translation of the local into the idiom of the global.

The second paradox was that the political struggles that had animated Ngũgĩ's literary and theoretical projects—the struggle against the institutions of power, the necessity for structural change, and the expansion of democratic spaces—were being undertaken in his absence. In the late 1990s and the beginning of the twenty-first century, Ngũgĩ published seminal essays on cultural freedom and on the arts and the state. Their goal, as he noted in *Moving the Centre*, was to change the terms of cultural debate itself, to move away from Eurocentrism "towards a pluralism of cultures, literatures and languages" (10). These essays constituted his intervention in postcolonial theory, yet they have circulated mostly in American and European institutions. Increasingly aware of this separation of the writer from his primary audience and sources, Ngũgĩ's thinking has turned to questions of memory, commemoration, and nostalgia, the subject of the MacMillan Stewart Lectures that he gave at Harvard University in 2006.

Ngũgĩ's More Recent Work

In *Something Torn and New*, the revised and published version of the MacMillan Lectures, Ngũgĩ reflects on the problem of memory in the encounter between Europe and Africa. He argues that in the cultures of colonialism in Africa, memory was part of a dialectic in which European colonizers set out to dislodge or devalue African memory. In addition to generating the dismemberment of African memory, colonization led to radical acts of displacement, planting European memory on "the bodies of the colonized" (9). Reacting to acts of what Ngũgĩ calls disremembering, African writers and intellectuals set out to create narratives of re-membering. A central concern of the essays collected in this volume, then, is the situation that arises when the process of memory erasure associated with the colonial apparatus of culture—including language and educational institutions—comes up against the African imperative to remember and to produce a literature that secures memory. The major African social and cultural movements of the modern period, including the idea of the African renaissance and black consciousness, are presented as the third force in the dialectic of disremembering and remembering. The task of the African writer has been to decolonize memory.

Ngũgĩ's concern with memory has also been generated by his attempts to reconcile his position as an African writer, one whose preoccupations are with the politics of culture on the continent, with his location or dislocation in American institutions, including the university system. In the Welleck Lectures, delivered at the University of California, Irvine, in 2010 and published as *Globalectics: Theory and the Politics of Knowing*, Ngũgĩ tries to reconcile his local and global concerns by developing what he calls a weak theory of globalization. His argument is that, unlike "strong theories," which have a tendency to be self-referential and detached from lived experiences, weak theory asks "a few questions that simply demand answers" (6). The measure of this kind of theory is not its sophistry but its ability to initiate cultural revolutions. One example of a weak theory that had radical consequences was the 1968 manifesto to abolish the English department at the University of Nairobi. Indeed, *Globalectics* appears to be an extension of the cultural work of the Nairobi manifesto to the global stage.

But perhaps the most important aspects of the book are Ngũgĩ's systematic exploration of the conditions in which a modern African literature has been imagined and his own role in the process. The essays in the book constitute a rereading of the European canon of letters from the English "great tradition" that produced Ngũgĩ as a writer to critiques of existing theories of globalization and postcoloniality. *Globalectics* is his singular statement on the condition of theory and the place of orature and orality in the global electronic age. There is, however, a powerful and unique autobiographical turn in *Globalectics*, and the essays need to be read in conjunction with his memoir *Dreams in a Time of War*. The autobiographical turn is powerful because it enables a subjective reading of the author's own relation to the colonial and postcolonial library. The autobiographical enables a unique reflection on the emergence of African literature. Although the four essays in the collection are informed by the preoccupations of the present—most notably the nature of the global imagination—they are also informed by a long historical view: Ngũgĩ started writing when the African textual library was made up of a handful of writers; now, over fifty years later, African literature is an indispensable part of "the globalectic reading of texts and the world" (85).

NOTE

An earlier version of this essay appeared as "Ngugi wa Thiong'o," in volume 2 of *The Oxford Encyclopedia of African Thought*, edited by F. Abiola Irele and Biodun Jeyifo (2010), and is used by permission of Oxford University Press, Inc.

Gender and the Political in Ngũgĩ's Fiction

Brendon Nicholls

When one reads Ngũgĩ's fiction, from its beginnings in *Weep Not, Child* and *The River Between* to the most recent installment in *Wizard of the Crow*, it is possible to track a development in his representations of Kenyan women. This development in what we might loosely term feminine types accompanies the larger journey toward decolonized political awakening and engagement that Ngũgĩ's fiction has undertaken. Moreover, the female characters are crucial to Ngũgĩ's constructions of Kenyan masculinity. As mutually defining fields, masculinity and femininity in Ngũgĩ's fiction cast light on his understanding of the social and political. It is in this expanded sense that I argue for the instrumental value of female characters to Ngũgĩ's formulation of a politics in his fiction. A close consideration of these women allows readers to notice how the fiction negotiates contradictions in its larger positions, especially in its social vision.

The importance of the female characters is by no means an accident of representation or a foible of the literary penchant for imaginative embellishment. Rather, these characters have material origins in the history of anticolonial struggle and in the Kenyan clitoridectomy debate in particular. The divisive issue of clitoridectomy in the late 1920s and early 1930s, which has been well documented and commented on,[1] meant that Gĩkũyũ nationalism was in part formulated around ideas of femininity and cultural practices associated with the construction of the feminine. As such, there was at this point in Kenyan history a mobilization around ideal femininity as an expression or instance of anticolonial struggle. Gĩkũyũ women's bodies and choices became metaphors for the fighting nation. Ngũgĩ's fiction takes as one of its initial points of departure this moment in the Kenyan history of struggle. Indeed, his first novel, *The River Between*, depicts the clitoridectomy debate.

This political archaeology of the feminine plays itself out in all of Ngũgĩ's fiction. The women we find there bespeak the changing political positions that the fiction is working through. Broadly speaking, the idealized early female characters, invariably virginal or motherly, correspond to forms of colonial mystification that Ngũgĩ was later to debunk comprehensively in his literary output and in his political writing. Examples of such forms are the attachments to liberal tolerance, to nonconfrontation, and to the ideal of intellectual class-ascendancy.[2] At the most elementary level, the fleeting promise of a fulfilled sexual and romantic relationship between hero and heroine (e.g., Waiyaki and Nyambura) or the fulfillment by the protagonist of his mother's desire (e.g., Nyokabi's wish for Njoroge to be educated) substitute for larger political reconciliations, which remain withheld in the immediate aftermath of Mau Mau.

Since the female characters mediate the male protagonists' relation to the political, I would suggest that they are important ideological markers in Ngũgĩ's fiction. The early female characters—from Mwihaki, Nyokabi, and Njeri to Nyambura, Muthoni, and the younger Mumbi—become complex vehicles for ideological ambivalence. As such, they allow a young and serious-minded intellectual in a newly independent postcolonial nation to manage challenging social ructions and divisive colonial legacies by the confining of contradiction to the romance of the heterosexual family. When masculine sexual aims are fused with political aims, women become the site and stake of struggle in Ngũgĩ's fiction. Furthermore, since one of the primary sites of struggle in Kenyan anticolonial resistance was the land taken from the Kenyan peasantry—especially the most arable land of the White Highlands—and given to settler farmers, Ngũgĩ's female characters are almost always associated with the landscape and with its generative potential. This association allows Ngũgĩ's fiction a referential mode in which narrative desire for a woman equates to a sovereign masculine political authority that can claim the landscape as property. The increasing proximity at work in the romantic processes of courtship equates to the reappropriation of land. Since both the land and femininity are sites of contest between the male representatives of opposing colonial and anticolonial orders, the later novels such as *Matigari* and *Devil on the Cross*, are able to develop their increasingly progressive politics without needing to question the entrenched patriarchal assumptions on which their narratives are established.

One instructive example of the positioning of Ngũgĩ's early female characters as the site and stake of struggle may be found in the construction of Nyambura and Muthoni in *The River Between*. As readers of the novel cannot fail to notice, an ideological divide between Joshua's Christian rejection of clitoridectomy and Kabonyi's traditionalist advocacy of the practice is mapped spatially onto the Kameno and Makuyu ridges. Joshua's daughters, Nyambura and Muthoni, render fluid this polarization by virtue of their hybrid cultural affiliations. Nyambura is unclitoridectomized but rejects her father's Christian dogma by declaring her love for Waiyaki, while Muthoni is clitoridectomized but professes her Christianity. Both sisters thus represent an ideological middle ground, which we might associate with the novel's privileging of the Honia River, which flows between the two ridges. Tellingly, Waiyaki's amorous relationship with Nyambura plays itself out in the intermediary space of the eponymous "river between." During their early courtship, the couple meet there on a number of occasions (74, 104). This placement of hero and heroine evidences a desire for a mediatory and reconciliatory politics, even though this politics fails when the community submits the lovers to the Kiama for judgment at the conclusion of the novel.

We find a similar spatial patterning of the political mapped through the use of gendered narrative vehicles in Ngũgĩ's later, more politically conscious novels, such as *A Grain of Wheat*. Kihika's two lovers, Wambuku and Njeri, play out the disjunctive pressures placed on the spheres of the domestic and the political during the Mau Mau insurgency. Each woman dies: Wambuku, after a beating at the digging of the Thabai trench during the villagization program, which historically employed forced removal, forced labor, curfews, and crop destruction; Njeri, during armed combat in the forest. One intuits that Kenya is rendered here as a suffering woman, and the name of the village in *Grain* reinforces this imagery. *Thabai* indexes the nettles that a starving villagized population had to scavenge for food, and also the nettles that were inserted into women's vaginas as part of the torture regime during the euphemistically named rehabilitation program, which involved a pipeline of concentration camps designed to make internees confess to having taken an oath of Mau Mau allegiance (see Barnett and Njama 209). Moreover, Gikonyo's name denotes "navel" and was Mau Mau parlance for the Lincoln bombers that gave birth to destructive payloads when their infrared technology located heat sources in the forest. When we read such a wartime landscape metonymically, we discover images of alien penetration *Thabai* and alien begetting (*Gikonyo*) that find their narrative incarnation in Mumbi's child by Karanja.

Gikonyo and Mumbi are characters encumbered with political but also mythical functions. Their names are associated with the foundation of the Gĩkũyũ people by the legendary Gĩkũyũ and Mumbi, male and female archetypes in prehistory. But there is a secondary resonance in the immediate present of the novel: Gĩkũyũ and Mumbi was also one of the names that the Kenya Land and Freedom Army called itself. It never used the name Mau Mau. Finally, *Gikonyo and Mumbi* index an as yet unachieved postindependence utopia that is deferred beyond the chronological frame of *A Grain of Wheat*. We see this in Gikonyo and Mumbi's imminent sexual reconciliation at the end of the novel, which we are told will "see the birth of a new Kenya" (105). Given that Gikonyo and Mumbi correspond with Gĩkũyũ and Mumbi's unbroken transhistorical lineage running from the foundation myth through Mau Mau to decolonization I would argue that the family is a metaphor for the historical consistency of nationhood in *Grain*.

The emphasis on motherhood and the family as a corollary for a harmonic social order disappears in Ngũgĩ's fiction as the disappointments of political independence emerge during the 1970s. In other words, as Ngũgĩ realizes that extraterritorial oppression is at work in neocolonial capital's expropriation of Kenya's resources and its exploitation of Kenyan labor, it becomes impossible to rely on an ideal of the feminine that is linked to a disposition of landscape. The struggle is quite simply no longer territorial, and the earlier referential model must give way to new modes of abstraction. Accordingly, we find an increasing prevalence of single mothers (Warĩĩng'a in *Devil*) and prostitutes in the later fiction (Wanja in *Petals* and Gũthera in *Matigari*). The polymorphous affiliations and proclivities of these women replace the earlier generative potential of the virgin or mother. If the family in *Grain* corresponds to the nation, then the breaching of the family's boundaries by the single mother and the prostitute in *Petals of Blood*, *Devil on the Cross*, and *Matigari* corresponds to the transnational character of multinational corporations and their protean ability to exploit Africa through the abstract mechanisms of monetary exchange.

At the level of political analysis, these later female characters model a form of economic relation without borders, in which the single mother's absconding partner or the prostitute's changeable clientele betoken the substitutability of the paterfamilias.[3]

While this erosion of the paterfamilias is a structural corollary to the dynamics of neocolonialism, Ngũgĩ's later fiction attempts nonetheless to bring these women back into the fold through two recuperative mechanisms. The first is to redeem the female character through newfound motherhood, as we see with Wanja, whose child by Abdulla at the conclusion of *Petals of Blood* renders the continuing influence of Mau Mau's revolutionary force in terms of the resumption of a lapsed patrilineage. This subterfuge ultimately fails, because the psychosexual and legal necessities of nominating a single father founders on the political necessity of representing collectivist forms of struggle. That many fathers might claim Wanja's child to be theirs is consistent with her former profession as a prostitute. Gũthera's proxy motherhood in *Matigari* founders for a different reason: she has no relation to either Matigari or to their symbolic child, Mũriũki. When Matigari escapes from the mental hospital and decides to seize back his house from John Boy, Mũriũki and Gũthera express their political common purpose in familial terms:

> "Yes. We are the children of Matigari ma Njirũũngi," Mũrũiki said. "We are the children of the patriots who survived the war."
>
> "And their wives as well!" said Gũthera, smiling. "Or which other wives and children were you looking for?" (139)

The artificiality of the family structure as a vehicle for political mobilization becomes apparent here.

If the first recuperative mechanism applied to women is newfound motherhood, the second recuperative mechanism to which Ngũgĩ's later fiction resorts in order to restore male cultural privileges is to imbue his women with masculine characteristics, as feminist critics like Elleke Boehmer ([1991] 195) and Florence Stratton ("Gender" 163) have noticed. Failing to liberate completely its female characters, the later fiction also fails to restore completely masculine privilege: neither man nor woman exists in an unreconstructed form. The gender distinctions begin to break down in exactly these last-gasp efforts to preserve them.

To read for the disseminative force of the prostitutes and single mothers in Ngũgĩ's later fiction is to discover that clitoridectomized women exceed their placement in structures of curtailment,[4] that the Mau Mau legacy is not reducible to a patrilineage, and that the manifold abuses of neocolonialism must be conquered by more than love alone. And yet, in Ngũgĩ's most recent novel, *Wizard of the Crow*, we find a genuinely feminist narrative, not only because culture more generally has moved on from earlier polarizing attitudes toward gender but also because Ngũgĩ himself has internalized feminist responses to his work. The eponymous Wizard of the Crow is a composite of the male and female protagonists, Kamĩtĩ and Nyawĩra. For much of the novel, Kamĩtĩ is imprisoned, just as Ngũgĩ was imprisoned in Kamĩtĩ Maximum Security Prison. While Kamĩtĩ is indisposed, Nyawĩra fulfills his wizardly functions. More important, she refuses his sexual advances until he dons a condom. She mobilizes her fellow women against domestic abuse. What we see in the composite figure of the Wizard is not gender as a position (husband, wife, virgin, mother, fallen woman) or as a metaphor (for land or nation). Instead it is understood in terms of relation, the basis of the social. In fact, the composite Wizard might be thought of as relaying masculinity through the feminine and feminity through the masculine. The Wizard is a communicative, collective mechanism in which gender is in constant and fluctuating negotiation. It is this narrative mechanism that finally maps Ngũgĩ's gender constructions unproblematically onto the social, because it resolves a model in which both men and women have an equal and coimplicated stake in their partnership against oppression.

NOTES

[1] See for example, Arnold; Rosberg and Nottingham. Gikandi emphasizes that Gĩkũyũ nationalist positions in the clitoridectomy debate may be best understood as a strategic reinvention of tradition (*Ngũgĩ* 58).

[2] For an interesting analysis of the complexities of Ngũgĩ's early ideological affiliations, see Maughan-Brown; Glenn.

[3] The single mother and the prostitute are female subjects who have occasionally suffered reversals in postindependence Kenya. As Lynn Thomas has shown, one of the criticisms of the Affiliation Act (designed to secure child support from absconding fathers) was that it encouraged women into prostitution (137). Attempts were therefore made to exclude prostitutes from the act's provisions (139).

[4] Orthodox feminist critiques of Gĩkũyũ gender politics have much to learn from scholars such as Wairimu Ngaruiya Njambi, who asserts that clitoridectomy is "inscribed in [the] history of resistance as an empowering process" (705). Emphasizing the performativity of cultural practices and the strategic invention of tradition, perspectives like this widen our understanding of cultural and gender agency. The fact remains that clitoridecomy has been inscribed in the history of resistance despite its considerable and lasting impact on women's bodies, sexuality, health, and daily lives.

Ngũgĩ and the Postcolonial

Pius Adesanmi

Ngũgĩ, African Thought, and Postcolonial Discontent

Considering his well-known ideological and political praxis, which continuously ties the African condition to the unpastness of coloniality, it almost amounts to a contradiction in terms to describe Ngũgĩ wa Thiong'o as a postcolonial intellectual. In his critical interventions as well as in his novels, he has mapped a telos of conceptual decolonization that has undergone minimal change even as Africa transitioned from colonialism to political independence. If anything, independence merely deepened his awareness of the need to shift the struggle to other aspects of the African condition that are still overdetermined by the asymmetrical relation between Africa and its former colonial masters. These include persistent manifestations of coloniality in the areas of language, culture, and historiography. Consequently Ngũgĩ almost always locates his critical interventions in the categories of the colonial and the neocolonial rather than the postcolonial.

Any attempt to establish a link between Ngũgĩ's oeuvre and the postcolonial is rendered still more problematic by the history of theoretical distrust of that concept in the broader circuits of Africanist thought. Since the publication of Niyi Osundare's *African Literature and the Crisis of Post-structuralist Theorizing*, African intellectuals have expressed varying degrees of anxiety, ranging from problematizing to rejecting altogether the postcolonial.[1] Delegitimations of the postcolonial in African theorizing result from two anxieties. First is the unresolved paradox of the provenance of postcolonial theory. As Arif Dirlik famously puts it, the postcolonial begins only "[w]hen Third World intellectuals have arrived in First World academe" (329). The argument over location and provenance sees the postcolonial as exotic and exoticizing, ensconced in bourgeois Western institutions and partaking of the very knowledge it proposes to critique. Its flirtation with the arcane language and apolitical pretensions of postmodernism has further alienated African intellectuals.

The second anxiety relates to the temporal undecidabilities of the postcolonial in relation to colonialism and its heirs in the present. African intellectuals justifiably question the suggestion, with the use of the prefix *post-*, of the pastness of the colonial. There is a third problem, only slightly related to the first two but crucial to any discursive positioning of Ngũgĩ in the matrix of the postcolonial. Postcolonial theory's drive for institutional legitimation in North American academe involved the canonization of critical voices from Latin America, India, and other Commonwealth territories of the former British Empire at the expense of Africa.[2] Black critique, such as Paul Gilroy's project on the black

Atlantic, was acknowledged only when the postcolonial began to morph into other forms of cultural critique.

A rich archive of critical interventions by African scholars and, more important, by African writers predating the critiques of the canonized trinity of the postcolonial—Edward Said, Gayatri Chakravorty Spivak, Homi Bhabha—has thus been left out of narratives of the origins of the postcolonial. This archive contains the essayistic careers of writers such as Chinua Achebe, John Pepper Clark, Lewis Nkosi, Eskia Mpahlele, Wole Soyinka, and of course Ngũgĩ. There is a serious case to be made for including the vast body of critical interventions by African writers in the 1950s–1970s in the foundational canon of postcolonial discourse (Adesanmi). Works by creative writers, alongside key texts like Chinweizu's *The West and the Rest of Us* and Walter Rodney's *How Europe Underdeveloped Africa* or critiques like Peter Ekeh's seminal "Colonialism and the Two Publics in Africa," demonstrate that African writers and intellectuals were preoccupied with postcolonial discourse in the areas of subaltern histories, gender, identity, and culture long before Said, Spivak, and Bhabha made that discourse fashionable. Ngũgĩ's critical oeuvre constitutes the most cogent illustration of the affective links between African thought and the postcolonial.

Who Speaks for Kenyan Pasts?

Dipesh Chakrabarty offers a grim description of the prospects of subaltern histories in ex-colonial spaces:

> [I]nsofar as the academic discourse of history—that is, "history" as a discourse produced at the institutional site of the university—is concerned, "Europe" remains the sovereign, theoretical subject of all histories, including the ones we call "Indian," "Chinese," "Kenyan," and so on. There is a peculiar way in which all these other histories tend to become variations on a master narrative that could be called "the history of Europe." In this sense, "Indian" history itself is in a position of subalternity; one can only articulate subaltern subject positions in the name of this history. (1)

Chakrabarty underscores both the significance of historical retrieval to postcolonial praxis and the need to identify and privilege what his Subaltern Studies Group refers to as the little voices of history. Recording those voices is especially appropriate in the African context, where they were first occluded by the civilizational myths of colonialism. They were later erased in nationalist narratives and in decolonization agendas largely reduced to autobiographies of a handful of national and pan-African male heroes. Ngũgĩ's critical interventions since the second half of the twentieth century—and definitely after Kenya's independence—therefore represent one of the most enduring attempts at a postcolonial decentering of Europe and de-elitizing of the narratives of nationalism, decolonization, and independence in Kenya.

Like Chakrabarty, Ngũgĩ begins his project of postcolonial reinscription of the little voices of Kenya's history by acknowledging the cultural domination of Euromodernity in the postcolony. Writes Ngũgĩ in *Writers in Politics: Essays*:

> A central fact of Kenyan life today is the fierce struggle between the cultural forces representing foreign interests and those representing patriotic national interests. This cultural struggle may not always be obvious to a casual observer, for such a person will almost certainly be struck by the virtual domination of Kenyan life by foreigners and foreign imperialist cultural interests. (42)

For Ngũgĩ, historical retrieval and freedom from cultural domination are two sides of the same coin in an overall strategy of postcolonial self-fashioning and self-writing. But the histories and cultures that need to be recentered in the context of Kenya's struggle for dignity and identity remain the narratives and experiences of the Kenyan masses, continuously figured in his work as active agents in the making of Kenya. Postcolonial textual reinscriptions of the hitherto colonized and exploited native other often abhor reifying the masses as fixed victims of history. The argument holds that the colonized were never passive and unvoiced while their histories, cultures, and lives were subjected to the imperial gaze and acts of violence. Rather, theoretical practices failed to seek out those hidden voices in their spaces of enunciation and agency, hence the postcolonial's fixation on voicing and agency.

Ngũgĩ's thought epitomizes this strategy. Part of his genius lies precisely in not speaking for the workers and peasants who are omnipresent in his writings. Instead, Ngũgĩ accounts for their voices and agency in ways that make the workers and peasants come alive in the text. His portrayal of them in the play *I Will Marry When I Want* is most vivid. An excerpt from the play appears in his collection of essays *Barrel of a Pen*. In "A Worker Talks to a Peasant," the story of the composition of this play is itself an indication of Ngũgĩ's investment in the agency of the little voices of history. In several of his books, he tells of the creation of the Kamĩrĩĩthũ Community Education and Cultural Centre, a community theater project whose goal was to make the villagers at Kamĩrĩĩthũ the voices of their own history in the struggle against colonial and neocolonial cultural domination.[3] Despite harassment and intimidation by the postcolonial state, the Kamĩrĩĩthũ project forged a theater of the people, rooted in their histories, cultures, and quotidian experiences. It also returned the aesthetics of African drama to its roots in a postcolonial cultural context where European aesthetic tastes and practices in the arts were being actively promoted and subsidized by the state.

Ngũgĩ's commitment to center the history and voices of Kenya's peasants and workers is evident elsewhere in his creative corpus. Indeed, one of his major contributions to the plot structure of African fiction lies in capturing the multiple voices of subaltern characters. This kind of narration stands in sharp contrast to that of Achebe's *Things Fall Apart* (1958), where the plot revolves around the trajectory and agency—or lack thereof—of one hero. Multiple voicing is central to the structure of three of Ngũgĩ's novels: *A Grain of Wheat*, *Petals of Blood*, and *Wizard of the Crow*. Collectively, these novels present Kenya's colonial and postcolonial history from below, their ideological strategy belonging to the sort of historical revisionist praxis Howard Zinn uses in his *People's History of the United States of America*.

Caliban Redux

The language question has become one of the vexed issues of identity and cultural authenticity in the African postcolony. What does it mean to articulate a pan-African identity whose validity across the continent depends on its ability to circulate in the languages of colonial domination? The language debate first started at a conference of African writers held at Makerere College, Uganda, in 1962. Most of the new names in African literatures in European languages attended. Obi Wali, a Nigerian critic, stirred the hornet's nest with his presentation, "The Dead-End of African Literature?" He argued that creative works written by Africans in the European languages of colonial domination did not qualify to be called African literature. At best they belonged in the European literary pantheon, albeit with an African flavor. Wali's conference presentation was subsequently published by the influential journal *Transition* and thus commenced a vehement and ongoing debate on the ontology of African letters. Wali's radical position excluded canonical works of the first generation of modern African writers, including Chinua Achebe's *Things Fall Apart*.

If Wali inaugurated the language debate in the 1960s, Ngũgĩ in the course of the next four decades became its most vocal and famous exponent. Ngũgĩ recast the issue by using one of the most important tropes in postcolonial theorizing: Caliban. The figure of Caliban in *The Tempest* has made that Shakespearean text the subject of numerous postcolonial reappropriations—not least because Caliban's seizure of the master's language and Caliban's dissident act of turning around to look the master in the face and curse him in the master's own language mirror the resistance practiced by writers from the former British and French empires. Caliban's turning the master's language and the civilization it carries against the master gave postcolonial theory a formidable thematic leitmotif: the idea of the empire writing back.

Two African writers, John Pepper Clark in "The Legacy of Caliban" and Niyi Osundare in "Caliban's Gamble," explored the intersections of the Caliban trope with African literary identity, but Ngũgĩ went further—and he is unique in this respect—by articulating a praxis in which Caliban returns not just to write back and curse in the master's language but to reject it and revalidate Caliban's original language as the first step in the project of cultural decolonization and redefinition of the self. Ngũgĩ's decades-long campaign for a return to African languages not only in African writing but also in other spheres of cultural expression is indicative of what the philosopher Sanya Osha has described as "a radical reformulation of postcoloniality itself along lines dictated by an unambiguous politics of indigeneity" (23).

Although Ngũgĩ returns to the language question in almost every essay he has written since the Makerere conference in 1962, it is in *Decolonising the Mind* that he presents the most sustained elaboration of the problems of colonial languages in postcolonial Africa. He understands that language involves culture, civilization, and a total worldview. He is therefore concerned that reality in postcolonial Kenya—and Africa by extension—is shaped largely by such foreign languages as English, French, and Portuguese. These languages inaugurate new forms of sociality, new modalities of subjecthood, and new modes of civic interpellation by the postcolony, all of which exclude the vast majority of Africans who do not speak them.

Ngũgĩ's intervention in the language question dramatizes the asymmetries of power between African and European languages. The continued dominance of European languages in Africa, long after political independence, mirrors the condition of Africa in the neocolonial order into which the continent transitioned. Language becomes a key feature of Ngũgĩ's conceptualization of the unpastness of imperialism in the African world, hence the need to include language in what Ngũgĩ calls "the stuggle for cultural freedoms" (*Moving*).

Ngũgĩ, in classifying texts in Western languages as African literature, coins the term *Europhonism* to describe them ("Europhonism"). He reviews the nearly four decades of his engagement with language and decolonization:

> In most of my publications, . . . I have tried to argue that the language question is so crucial because language occupies a significant position in the entire hierarchy of the organization of wealth, power, and values in a society. . . . Language is a product of a community in its economic, political, and cultural evolution in time and space. . . . [It] is also the producer of a community, for it . . . enables humans to negotiate effectively their way into and out of nature and . . . makes possible their multifaceted evolution. It is in that very negotiation that a community comes to know itself as . . . different from others. . . . [S]uch a community develops knowledges which are passed from generation to generation and which become the . . . stuff of [its] way of life. . . . Language carries the cultural universe of the community and in that universe also resides the entire body of values held by that community. Every community . . . has notions of what is right and wrong, of the bad and the good, of the ugly and the beautiful, in short a system of ethics and aesthetics . . . [that] forms the basis of [its] identity. . . .
>
> Empire builders have always known that and . . . clearly saw the importance of delinking the elites of the dominated communities from their languages and literally transplanting their minds in the languages of the imperial center. . . . [When] the traditional elite resisted the transplant, . . .

> the empire builders simply manufactured a new elite through a massive cultural surgery carried out in the theaters of the new schools and colleges. The aim . . . was to turn the elite into beings for others even in their conception of themselves. Examples abound and we do not even have to go to the special case of plantation slavery where whole communities were delinked from the languages of their original homes. (2–3)

I have quoted Ngũgĩ extensively to underscore the importance he attaches to his view of language as the principal instrument of imperialism. In culture, therefore, Europhonism becomes a continuation of a neocolonial order. It mirrors the workings of a global postcolonial capitalistic order that continues to drain Africa of its vital resources. Hence, for Ngũgĩ, Europhonism is parasitic, draining African languages of their genius:

> Europhonism has no language or a cultural universe of its own. The literature it generates—Europhone Literature—is given identity in the market place of all writings in European tongues by all the reservoir of images in African life and languages. It has therefore a negative, almost parasitic side to it. Like a leech it sucks blood and stamina from African languages and it never gives anything back to the people who created the languages and the orature from which it draws so freely to give it that identity in the market place of world-wide writings in European tongues. (7)

Ngũgĩ moved beyond theorizing the question of language in the African postcolony to praxis, writing novels first in Gĩkũyũ as an ultimate act of postcolonial decolonization.

What's in a Name?

I conclude this survey of Ngũgĩ's links to postcolonial critique by examining the significance of his trajectory from committed Christian schoolboy to the Marxist writer who renounced Christianity and his baptismal name, James, as colonial. The transition from James Ngũgĩ to Ngũgĩ wa Thiong'o is a most apt summary of the writer's concept of decolonization as a process rooted in the return to and revalidation of indigenous modes of self-fashioning. Discussing the politics of African names in the context of European cultural imperialism, Osundare captures the impulse behind Ngũgĩ's rejection of his foreign name and explains why the act qualifies as a postcolonial affirmation of the self:

> The world is shaped—and frequently determined—by the words we use for expressing it. In naming the world we also name ourselves, evoking a recognizable, tangible construct of that panoply of realities which constitute what we call the human experience. Names serve as the door to the house of experience, a guide to hidden meanings in the shadowy

> nooks of time and place. Names tell stories, liberate or imprison; they may also serve as self-fulfilling prophecies. Names commit; which is why the Yoruba say that it is only mad people who do not mind what names they are called, or who refuse to see the difference between the names they choose to bear and the ones the world prefers to call them by. The negative "politics of representation" so famous in contemporary literary discourse is very much the product of misapprehension as it is of misnaming and mis-verbalization. (*African Literature* 11)

Ngũgĩ wa Thiong'o freed James Ngũgĩ from the grips of colonial misnaming. He thus clears the path for a politics of decolonization that is at once marked by localized engagements of culture in Africa—and by global aspirations for freedom from capitalist domination and enduring structures of oppression, so that space may be created "for a hundred flowers to bloom," as he puts it so memorably, echoing Mao Tse-tung, in *Moving the Centre* (12).

NOTES

[1] Osundare uses *poststructuralist* and *postcolonial* as interchangeable terms in his stinging critique of postcolonial discourse from an African perspective. See the essays collected in Magubane, *Postmodernism*.

[2] In "Africa, India, and the Postcolonial," I explore in detail the relative absence of African thought and thinkers in mainstream postcolonial theorizing.

[3] See chapter 2 of *Decolonising the Mind* for details on the Kamĩrĩĩthũ project.

Ngũgĩ and Kenya's History

W. O. Maloba

1

Kenya, Ngũgĩ's home country, was one of the few full-fledged settler colonies in Africa. The meaning of this distinction was that the local African owners of the land were subjected to drastic and sustained forms of economic exploitation and political repression. Social relationships and other cultural dynamics of the Africans that in the precolonial past had been an integral part of society were also disrupted. Land alienation and imposition of settler capitalism brought economic hardship to the majority of the Africans in Central Province, the province affected most by the demands of colonial rule. Even those Africans who lived outside the settler domain, the so-called White Highlands, were actively incorporated in the economics of colonialism through the supply of their labor. This incorporation applied especially to the inhabitants of present-day Western and Nyanza Provinces, the Abaluyia and the Luo.

The spread of colonial rule was often followed by missionary influence. Acting as cultural agents of colonialism, missionaries effected far-reaching and long-lasting changes in African communities.[1]

In Central Province, where Ngũgĩ was born and grew up, the overriding reality during colonial rule was land scarcity for Africans. Displaced peasants were actively enlisted as rural proletariat, working on farms owned by white settlers. Others drifted to the urban centers; others maintained a precarious existence as landless peasants in the congested rural areas. Poverty and economic desperation were widespread. Not surprisingly, land emerged as the single most important issue around which nationalism developed. It came to symbolize economic livelihood, political freedom, and cultural pride. It was a powerful summary of hopes and aspirations. The colonial government considered land the ultimate symbol of domination. Since the white settlers ruled the politics and economics of the colony, there was no way any compromise over African demands for land reform could be arrived at without seriously undermining the social fabric that had been created and was being maintained to benefit the foreigners. It is against this background of land and what land meant that we must understand the rise of the Mau Mau peasant revolt in Kenya and Ngũgĩ's interpretation of Kenya's history.

From childhood Ngũgĩ knew he was a victim of land alienation by white settlers: "I grew up in a small village. My father with his four wives had no land. They lived as tenants-at-will on somebody else's land" (*Homecoming* 48).[2] He grew up in a social environment in which the dispossessed peasants eked out a living as toiling squatters on white farms. What is crucial for our discussion is that the cause of the hardship was clear. To all those Africans who suffered, the colonial government and more specifically the white settlers were the source of their economic deprivation, misery, and political repression. Peace could not return to the land unless and until the tillers of the land reclaimed ownership of it. During the Mau Mau peasant revolt, the loyalists were despised not just for being collaborators but also because in supporting the enemy they made the attainment of land, and therefore progress and dignity, impossible for the majority of the peasants in Central Province. This should be clearly understood, for Mau Mau and its aftermath have provided Ngũgĩ's fiction with some key themes for over thirty years.

Conscious of the economic hardship suffered by his people and of the political and cultural brutality leveled against them in the colonial and postcolonial periods, Ngũgĩ has written basically to chronicle and expose this injustice. Like any sensitive writer, he also writes to understand: "My writing is really an attempt to understand myself and my situation in society and in history" (Preface xii). The importance of this statement is that self-comprehension for Ngũgĩ is linked to comprehension of society. This connection is clearly illustrated when we trace his evolution as a writer.

Like other pioneering African writers of the early 1960s, Ngũgĩ was in his initial books largely concerned with the cultural clash between Africans and Europeans during colonialism. The inability and in many cases refusal of Europeans to comprehend the cultural complexities of the Africans and their societies led to confrontation and violence. It planted the seed of a suspicion that has continued to characterize the relation between Africa and the West. Chinua Achebe's early novels, especially *Things Fall Apart*, pointed the way for subsequent African writers: they demonstrate the richness of precolonial African culture and describe the advent of imperialism and then the destruction of African culture.

Ngũgĩ felt that Africa's cultural destruction was linked to economic exploitation. Africa was not only culturally dominated during colonialism but was also economically exploited. Clearly then this past was more than a portrait of "egalitarian peasant communities, and of empires rising and falling"; it was the story of "continued exploitation at the hands of the West" (*Homecoming* 45). More important to Ngũgĩ than mere economic history was this relation of inequality, the exploitation of Africa by the West in both past and present. Indeed, the present was what spurred his interest in the past. The present for Ngũgĩ, is of course, postcolonial Africa.

The rise of African nationalism under colonial rule and the eventual attainment of political independence (*uhuru* is Swahili for "freedom") were closely watched by writers in Africa. Many were quick to notice the expressions of betrayal of the masses who became disillusioned with the hollow messages of the political elite and also by the greed, corruption, and repression that became standard for many regimes. Ngũgĩ was one of these writers. In his most artistically celebrated novel, *A Grain of Wheat*, he dealt not only with the tensions in the liberation movement but also with the theme of betrayal. He hinted strongly that the process of betrayal had already started in Kenya.[3] Those who fought for *uhuru* were not the chief beneficiaries of independence; those newly in power fast became wealthy and did not contribute to the ouster of British colonial rule from Kenya. Like Mugo, the main character in *Grain*, they enjoyed the rewards of mistaken heroism (19).

Since the 1970s, Ngũgĩ has turned his attention to the social, economic, and political circumstances of independent Africa. His chief concern remains the exposure of the crimes of the comprador class in Kenya. Identifying with the peasants and workers, whose labor is exploited and who are politically repressed, he has singled out foreign domination of the Kenyan economy as the basis of the national misery. Through his writing he seeks to describe and explain this domination, drawing on a variant of Marxist interpretation of history to analyze imperialism and its expansion, social classes and the class struggle, and then national liberation and socialist reconstruction in Kenya (and Africa in general). A literature of commitment has been the inevitable result of his militancy. In his writings since the 1970s, Ngũgĩ tries to explain to the peasants and workers of Kenya the nature and operations of imperialism in their country. The class distinctions among his characters are clearly drawn, especially in *Petals of Blood* and, written in prison during his detention, *Devil on the Cross*.[4] He has seized on essay writing in journals and books, and then plays, believing that these are probably more effective conveyors of his major beliefs and concerns.

In his search for historical explanations that would offer legitimacy and respectability to his political program, Ngũgĩ has been frustrated. He is not a historian himself and feels that professional historians in Kenya have failed in their national duty, writing bourgeoisie history that has accorded the ruling class some legitimacy. Although he expressed these misgivings long before 1978,[5] it was not until his release from detention that he set out what may be loosely called his theory of history, in *Detained*. Also in 1978 he leveled some of his harshest criticisms against the writing and practice of history in Kenya.

2

Why is history important to Ngũgĩ? As a writer, he has argued that a "novelist is haunted by a sense of the past," that the novelist's "work is often an attempt to come to terms with the 'thing that has been,' a struggle, as it were, to sensitively register his encounter with history, his people's history" (*Homecoming* 39). To this end, Ngũgĩ supports efforts by African writers to re-create the African past, the lost glorious culture of Africa. But on this point he differs with many writers. Although applauding Achebe for his efforts in "helping his society to regain its belief in itself," Ngũgĩ does not believe that this alone can lead to a socialist reconstruction of society (Cook and Okenimkpe 212; see also Ngũgĩ, *Homecoming* 39). "Can people like Obi Okonkwo, Nanga, Odili, Max—or political parties even like the Common People's Convention," he asks, "behave in a radically different way while operating within and in fact espousing the same economic and social set-up?" (*Homecoming* 53). It is the society that needs to be changed first, for "individual honesty, integrity," et cetera cannot be relied on to provide fundamental institutional and ideological changes in society.

History, which Ngũgĩ consistently asserts is the "writer's subject matter," is characterized by him as "the process of a people acting on nature, changing it, and in so doing, acting on and changing themselves." The essence of this history at any given period is often difficult to decipher, but literature has an edge in that deciphering, since it "has often given us more and sharper insights into the moving spirit of an era than all the historical and political documents treating the same moment" (*Writers in Politics: A Re-engagement* 68). Literature thus emerges in this formulation as a valid, reliable, and even a more useful record of historical moments.

Artists should criticize their society from some historical perspective:

> It is not enough for the African artist, standing aloof, to view society and highlight its weaknesses. He must try to go beyond this, to seek out the sources, the causes and the trends of a revolutionary struggle which has already destroyed the traditional power-map drawn up by the colonialist nations. (*Homecoming* 65–66)

African writers should not remain indifferent to the everyday struggle for survival by the ordinary people in their society. Any "retreat into individualism, mysticism and formalism" is a self-serving strategy adopted by some authors in order to escape "encountering socialism as an alternative social system" (*Writers* 74, 75).

Ngũgĩ's preoccupation with history in his writings is a dogged attempt to "seek out the sources, the causes," of Africa's economic and social plight. Ngũgĩ has counseled fellow African writers against "becoming too fascinated by the yesterday" of their people "and forgetting the present" (*Homecoming* 44). He sees no inherent separation between art and politics. In his Clarendon Lectures delivered at Oxford University in 1996, he provided a spirited defense of this position: "I am not in art because of politics; I am in politics because of my artistic calling" (*Penpoints* 5). This calling has led him to identify with the struggles of the common people, who have remained "his fundamental interest and their well being his primary goal" (Okolo 37).

As he sat in detention in the Kamĩtĩ prison (outside Nairobi) under harsh and unhygienic conditions, Ngũgĩ had occasion to reflect further on Kenyan history. When he was released, he wrote *Detained*, which is more than a record of his prison experiences; it is "a radical critique of Kenya's political economy from the onset of colonialism to the present" (W. Ochieng, "Autobiography" 23). But this radical critique had a definite purpose, to highlight the tradition and practice of resistance of the Kenyan masses against foreign domination and exploitation. Thinking of the "glorious history" of resistance, Ngũgĩ saw

> Kenyan people ceaselessly struggling against Arab feudalists and slave dealers; against Portuguese marauders who opened up Africa to her four-hundred years of devastating encounter with European domination, and later against British predators trying to embrace Kenya with claws and fangs of blood; yes, a history of Kenyan people . . . creating a resistance

> culture, a revolutionary culture of courage and patriotic heroism. . . . A fight-back, creative culture, unleashing tremendous energies among the Kenyan people. (*Detained* 64; see also Gugler)

But even here he was more concerned with the present. His aim was and is to go "into the history of his people to invoke for the present generation the lesson of organized violence against unacceptable regimes" (Cook and Okenimkpe 218).

In *Detained*, Ngũgĩ offers the reader a long list of patriotic Kenyans who resisted British colonialism; he shows the trials they endured and their stubborn will and patriotic zeal. He begins with Waiyaki of the Kĩkũyũ, mentions with profound admiration the heroism of Me Kitilili of the Giriama people (Coast Province), then Koitalel of the Nandi people (Rift Valley Province). He has special admiration for the Mau Mau guerrillas, who waged "a protracted guerrilla war against a British imperialist power that used to boast of its invincibility to man or God." He honors these patriots, because in Kenyan schools "the children were taught colonial history which glorified the role of traitors — Kĩnyaanjui wa Gathirimũ, Mumia, Karũri wa Gakure, Lenana . . . — and other collaborators with the enemy" (55). Clearly a correct history for Ngũgĩ is one that emphasizes resistance against external domination and either directly or indirectly prepares the youth and the masses for their own resistance against neocolonialism since "no country can consider itself politically independent for as long as its economy and culture are dominated by foreign interests" (*Detained* xv).

In an interview published in the *Weekly Review* (Nairobi) soon after his release from detention, Ngũgĩ developed further this idea of patriotic history. He argued that "writers, historians and intellectuals must be able to tell the history of heroic resistance to foreign domination by Kenyan people," concluding that "Kenyan history, either pre-colonial or colonial, has not been written" (Interview [1978]). How far is this true?

3

African history, like African literature, was completely neglected in academic circles during the colonial era. "As African countries moved towards political independence," B. A. Ogot has written, "there was a corresponding move towards historical independence" (*Kenya* xiv). At the university level, this change was marked by a protracted struggle in East Africa. If we are to accept the account by Ogot, the most prominent pioneer African historian in Kenya, in "Three Decades of Historical Studies in East Africa," we can see the rough road that African history endured on its way to recognition. University lecturers, overwhelmingly expatriate at first, were not trained in African history. Many were prejudiced against African history and held views quite consistent with those of Hugh Trevor-Roper, who proclaimed as late as 1963 that what claimed to be African history was "largely darkness. . . . And darkness is not a subject of history" (9).

When Africans finally secured positions of influence in history departments in East African universities and colleges, they had specific goals. "The object of the new historiography was to produce Afro-centric as opposed to Euro-centric East African history" (Ogot, "Three Decades" 29). On one level, they were responding to outside prejudice against African history. They had to demonstrate that "African societies had well organized states, practised democracy, socialism, family planning, and engaged in long distance trade with properly organized markets" (29). On another level, they responded to an internal need by various ethnic groups eager to know their history, long neglected under colonialism. Ironically as political independence gave rise to one country with one flag and one anthem, historians and social scientists came forth with their studies in which particular peoples (nationalities) were emphasized. Some critics later referred to these studies sarcastically as tribal history.

In Kenya, there was a boom in history writing in the 1960s and early 1970s, along ethnic lines. After Ogot's study of the Luo (*History*) came Gideon Were's study of the Abaluyia, then Godfrey Muriuki's study of the Kĩkũyũ and William Ochieng's study of the Gusii. Others followed. Their overriding purpose was to create a precolonial past in which an African community had attained a certain level of social and political organization before the advent of colonialism. Historical reconstruction tried to show the social institutions, values, and economics of these various societies. It should be pointed out, however, that because the historians tended to write for an audience with specific interests, there was an overemphasis on migration and the origin of ethnic groups—concepts of debatable value—at the expense of following the change in social and political structures of these societies over time. They also held to the mistaken view that each ethnic group was a compact unit whose values passed from one generation to another in an unaltered form. All the same, these early works were a source of pride for the masses. As Ogot acknowledges, when the pioneer African historians wrote these histories, they had "a ready and receptive audience in the East African public" ("Three Decades" 29).

The history of colonialism was also extensively studied—perhaps overstudied—not only by local African historians but also by Africanist scholars overseas, especially Western scholars. It is now evident that most Western scholars have drifted toward topics linked to the colonial period instead of the precolonial one.

In the mid-1960s even history textbooks were written by African historians, many of them teaching at the local universities. Were's *East Africa through a Thousand Years* remained the principal textbook for high schools in Kenya (and East Africa) from the late 1960s to late 1970s. The formation of the Kenya Historical Association and the launching of its journal, *Kenya Historical Review*, provided platforms for Africans (and Africanists) to produce an Afrocentric history of Kenya. *Kenya Historical Review* was edited by Ochieng, for a long time one of the most respected history journals on the continent. Any casual survey of its articles demonstrates the extent to which colonialism and its influence were covered and debated. Kenya's history highlighting collaborators and resisters has therefore not been neglected, and it continues to be an area of interest. Admittedly some of the texts produced on these interrelated themes have not referred to collaborators and resisters as traitors and patriotic resisters, but this is different from the fact these are widely covered and studied themes in Kenyan history.

Ngũgĩ's critique, however, raises an interesting question about the value of studying the exploits and fortunes of collaborators in African history. It should be pointed out that to study collaborators is not to endorse them and their worldview. Since colonial conquest triumphed over tenacious African resistance, it would be useful to learn how the collaborators became incorporated into the colonial enterprise, useful to learn how the colonial system was established and how it functioned in the face of overt and covert African resistance after conquest. A study of the motives of these collaborators might help us decipher the roles and activities of the present ruling class in African countries. Do the rulers in this period of neocolonial mess have motives similar to those of the colonial collaborators? It is therefore not accurate that a study of collaborators diminishes or even distorts our comprehension of Kenya's history or the history of any African country.

In *Detained* and *Writers in Politics*, Ngũgĩ places a lot of emphasis on colonial history. On reading *Detained*, one gets the impression that Kenya's history started with resistance against colonialism and reached its climax in the 1950s Mau Mau peasant revolt against British colonial rule. This account provides abundant examples of resistance, but it leaves out thousands of years of African history before the 1890s. Precolonial African history and culture do not feature prominently in his critique. This surely is most unfortunate. If, as he has openly stated, his aim is to create in Africa (and therefore Kenya) "a completely socialized economy, collectively owned and controlled by the people" (*Homecoming* 13), then it is vital to study the social and economic history of precolonial African societies. The values that held those societies together have something to contribute to the reconstruction of Africa.

The "heroic and patriotic resistance" of Waiyakis, et cetera, places a lot of emphasis on the big man in history. It is these prominent figures that are studied and whose exploits are celebrated. How about the small man and woman? Can it be assumed that the history of the small people is automatically covered in the exploits of the heroes? How about contradictory tendencies in their careers? Ngũgĩ criticizes the sole credit given to Kenyatta as "father of the nation and liberation": it neglects the sacrifices of thousands of Mau Mau guerrillas and activists (*Detained* 13). In pursuing only the glorious history of prominent patriots, one ignores the history of the small people and their social circumstances. Yet a contradiction exists in Ngũgĩ's writings regarding the centrality of small people in the struggle for freedom. In his nonfiction, especially *Detained*, the emphasis is without any doubt on the big man in history, the heroic figures and their exploits. In his literary works, however, Ngũgĩ highlights the courage possessed by the small people as they struggle to overcome the enormous challenges in their everyday lives.

There is also the question of methodology in Ngũgĩ's articulation of his viewpoints on history. It is clear on reading *Detained*, *Barrel of a Pen*, and *Writers in Politics* that Ngũgĩ is not interested in the technical details of history writing that involves the cumbersome and laborious search for evidence and then the marshaling of that evidence in support of specific arguments and positions. He avoids these technical details by working with popular examples of resistance and giving them the meaning he wants. He works with examples that can be readily identified by his audience (at least in Kenya), an audience he hopes will embrace or at least be "disposed to revolutionary transformation within the society" (Ogude 31).

In *Wizard of the Crow*, Ngũgĩ satirizes the neocolonial rulers of Africa obedient to the dictates of international capital and ridicules the excessive material consumption of the ruling class. In all these writings, the examples used are indeed historical, but the interpretation of and meaning invested in them, and even their inherent symbolism, are all creative. He drives home his position on class and class struggle, on imperialism and the foreign domination of African society, and on patriotic resistance.[6] Ngũgĩ differs markedly from the professional historian. This is true even if we allow for differences of interpretation of data due to ideology and related factors. The professional historian is trained to respect evidence, cite examples, develop an argument, illustrate the argument, demonstrate knowledge of related literature on the subject, and be alert to the contradictions in human nature. Most discerning historians know that there are no heroes without flaws, that the biographies of the most admirable figures are riddled with inconsistencies. By portraying heroes without contradictions Ngũgĩ in essence fictionalizes these historical figures. Because he avoids these technicalities, his readers are most likely to remain unaware of the abundant contrary interpretations and even contradictions in the lives and careers of the heroic figures cited.

It is not surprising that some Kenyan historians have been pointed in their opposition to Ngũgĩ's foray into history and historical interpretation. Among them are Ogot, Were, Muriuki, and Ochieng. Their objections are both personal and professional. Distinguished members of the "Kenya history establishment" did not appreciate being labeled neocolonial, as producing neocolonial history. Ngũgĩ, for example, dismissed the national value of Ochieng's books because he thought most of them "were based on a neocolonial interpretation of Kenyan history" (*Detained* 132). This response displays the "common inability" and reluctance by historians in general "to accept literary interpretation of their field." And there is sustained criticism "both [of] Ngũgĩ's carelessness with details and [of] his promoting myth as history" (Sicherman, "Ngũgĩ" 310).

The centerpiece in the tension between Ngũgĩ and many professional historians in the writing of Kenya's history revolves around the origin, composition, aims, and legacy of the Mau Mau peasant revolt. Ngũgĩ is the most prominent representative of the Left in the interpretation of the Mau Mau in postcolonial Kenya Since *A Grain of Wheat*, his fiction and nonfiction have grown increasingly radical and more definite in their advocacy of a socialist agenda for Kenya and all Africa. It is the Mau Mau revolt that has inspired Ngũgĩ in this phase of his career.

Why Mau Mau? What has this peasant anticolonial revolt come to symbolize to Ngũgĩ? The first sustained intersection between myth and history on the question of the Mau Mau occurred in his play (coauthored with Mĩcere Gĩthae Mũgo), *The Trial of Dedan Kimathi*. This play is not a factual re-creation of Kimathi's interrogation before being hanged by the colonial authorities. Rather, it is "an imaginative recreation and interpretation of the collective will of the Kenyan peasants and workers in their refusal to break under sixty years of colonial torture and ruthless oppression . . . and new forms of enslavement" (Ngũgĩ and Mugo, Preface vi).

This "imaginative recreation and interpretation" means a reinvention of the Mau Mau revolt. Ngũgĩ endows the revolt with "new ideological attributes" and clarity on economic and social issues. It becomes "a socialist liberation movement that united Kenyan peasants and workers against imperialism" (Maloba, *Mau Mau* 174). Ngũgĩ has deployed, with remarkable consistency, this retooled image of the Mau Mau as a powerful weapon in his scathing critiques of Kenya's neocolonial mess. Both his fiction and nonfiction draw attention to sensitive national issues: the foreign control of the country's economy, the widening gap between the rich and the poor, internal oppression and exploitation, reliance on Western cultural productions, and lack of national initiatives to develop and celebrate traditional cultures and local languages. The ruling elite are portrayed as politically and ideologically illegitimate, having betrayed "the egalitarian and patriotic spirit" of the Mau Mau revolt (175; see also Ngũgĩ, *Barrel*; and Lovesey, *Ngũgĩ*).

Throughout these persistent efforts to make the Mau Mau revolt central to Kenya's history, Ngũgĩ has sought to guard against two developments. First, the nonheroic study of the revolt by scholars who would bury the revolt "under footnotes," thus refraining from highlighting its historical and ideological significance. Second, there is the fear that the Mau Mau revolt may be erased from the national memory—"from both scholarly and popular memory" (Williams, *Ngũgĩ* 180; see also Gikandi, *Ngũgĩ*).

Such erasure is unlikely to occur soon. Even the Right in Kenya, especially among the Kĩkũyũ, has sought to both exploit and control the memory of the revolt. Many members of the conservative elite have family ties to the home guards and other groups recruited and maintained by the colonial government to fight against the Mau Mau.

> Any identification with Mau Mau by the Kikuyu political and commercial elite is for utilitarian purposes in the struggle for dominance in Kenya and not because of the revolt's past practices. . . . The Right, therefore, has reinvented Mau Mau both to maintain the Kikuyu's compliance and also to justify its dominance on the national stage. Since the Kikuyu elite is involved in its own struggle on the national level, it needs a weapon of

> prestige to justify its dominance. That weapon is Mau Mau. It need hardly be emphasized that no registry of former key loyalists has been kept nor has there been any backlash against loyalists. As a result, any Kikuyu elite can, on a general level, identify himself with Mau Mau to justify his or her claim to dominance. This general and strategic identification with the revolt does not mean that the elite has embraced former guerrillas and their movement. (Maloba, *Mau Mau* 173)

Ngũgĩ's reinvention of the Mau Mau as a socialist liberation movement out to expel imperialism (in all its facets) from Kenya has given rise to a chorus of objections from historians and others familiar with the details of post–World War II socialist liberation movements in Africa and the rest of the Third World. In organizational and ideological terms, the Mau Mau revolt was not on the same footing with the Liberation Front of Mozambique (FRELIMO) or the African Party for the Independence of Guinea and Cape Verde (PAIGC). Although both the FRELIMO and the PAIGC relied for their growth and survival on the support of the peasants, the Mau Mau revolt was led by peasants. Unlike the Mau Mau revolt, in which "there were no revolutionary intellectuals nor cadres," the FRELIMO and the PAIGC were organized and led by "dedicated revolutionary cadre or 'political entrepreneurs,'" such as Eduardo Mondlane and Amilcar Cabral. The success of these movements also hinged on the active and sustained "politicization of the peasants . . . under the general direction of a revolutionary party" that espoused a progressive ideology (5–7).[7] This ideology, embraced by the militant and politicized peasants, consistently proposed the establishment of a new world free of imperial domination. It is also worth noting that their program included tackling what they identified as internal obstacles to equality: women's oppression and exploitation, oppressive aspects of traditional cultures, regionalism, racism, and even tribalism. All available evidence shows that the Mau Mau revolt did not possess such a program; it did not aspire to establish a socialist society in Kenya. "[N]one of the Mau Mau guerrillas claimed their movement was socialist. Kimathi himself did not make this claim" (174).

4

Still, there are lessons to be learned from Ngũgĩ's challenge to professional historians. The challenge involves the practical use of history in postcolonial Africa. Currently in Africa, local populations need an explanation for their poverty, diminished economic prospects, painful social circumstances, cultural strangulation, and political oppression. They need to know how the present relates to the past and if there is anything in their past that can be retrieved to help them confront today's problems. Is African history, and especially the African historian, able to respond to this need?

Since the 1960s there has been a significant increase in the number of books and scholarly journals devoted to African history. In the 1960s and early 1970s there was much enthusiasm for such texts, in Africa and abroad. Ethnic histories, precolonial institutions and cultures, and African resistance to colonialism were the themes pursued, giving a focus, a direction, to the study of African history. It is now difficult to discern any focus or direction. The enthusiasm in both Africa and abroad has waned. At the moment, books on South African history and politics are attracting attention. The history of South Africa has of late become a growth industry, yet even here no focus is identifiable. It seems that for both African scholars and external Africanists there is some crisis of confidence as to what should be on the agenda for African history in the next ten or twenty years.

As African history has matured as a university subject both in Africa and abroad, it has drawn heavily on theoretical paradigms coined in related fields, especially anthropology, political science, economics, and cultural studies. This borrowing has had the salutary effect of making African history more technical and rigorous in its analysis of issues. E. P. Thompson and the theoretical formulations of social history have had a tremendous influence on recent African history texts. Postmodernism has been another influence. To be sure, the relation between history and postmodernism remains complex, even contradictory. Some postmodernists "criticize conventional history and relegate it to a peripheral role in the larger scope of human affairs. They attribute little importance to history for its own sake: as witness to continuity, as testimony to the idea of progress . . ." (Roseneau 63). Still, some historians of African history have come to rely on postmodernism for insight and as a conceptual framework of analysis, especially in the study of individual choices. Under postmodernism,

> the . . . individual favors dispersion over concentration, the unrehearsed rather than the carefully organized. She/he emphasizes participation, private autonomy, personal liberation, without any need of universalistic claims or ideological consistency. The post-modern individual . . . relinquishes all normative assumptions, any possibility that one value or moral norm can ever be demonstrated to be better than any other. (54)

Derek Peterson's *Creative Writing: Translation, Bookkeeping, and the Work of Imagination in Colonial Kenya* is linked to the debates about the writing of history and literary theory. The book also takes much of its inspiration from Ngũgĩ's works, especially his play *Ngaahika Ndeenda*, which was performed at Kamĩrĩĩthũ, near Ngũgĩ's home in Kenya, as a community production: ordinary peasants were actors, audience, and critics of both the script and actual performance. Peterson's intent in writing his book was to show that "texts crystallize changeable social relationships, fire people with visions of the future, and inspire them to act" (xi).

Unfortunately many of the history texts produced under the influence of postmodernism have been remote, dull, too technical, and obscure, especially to nonhistorians. Obscurity seems to be gaining ground as a mark of excellence in scholarship. African history was more lively and seen by the general public and students (especially in Africa) as relevant when its products were informative and accessible. To be sure, this problem is not limited to African history.

In United States history, Richard Morris remarks that "relatively few works of history possess a literary distinction and treatment likely to appeal to a larger public." He concluded somewhat sadly that "more and more, it would seem, historians are writing for one another." To write "up-to-date syntheses of historical research and interpretation in a way that has universal appeal" is not to forsake scholarship (299). In African history, if historians continue to "write for one another," their research will have little influence. As debates rage over Africa, both on the continent and abroad, historians will find that their knowledge is not informing on the issues on the table. There is of course no guarantee that any well-researched, accessible, and interesting text will affect social discussions or even political decisions. But good history should at least inform, educate, dispel myths, demystify concepts, and identify trends.

Ngũgĩ's challenge to African historians has now been expanded to apply to all African intellectuals. In his keynote address at the thirtieth anniversary celebration of the Council for the Development of Social Science Research in Africa, given in 2003 in Dakar, Senegal, he stated that "African intellectuals and their production" were not "really connected to the continent," since "[e]ven a cursory glance shows that there is clearly a discrepancy between the quality and quantity of this knowledge production and the quality and quantity of its consumption by the general populace" ("Europhone" 157). His critical observation inevitably leads to these questions: Who is the primary audience of African intellectuals? How does this audience influence, if not shape, the consideration of the challenges Africa faces, especially in the postcolonial period? What is the mark of relevance for African intellectuals in their relation with Africa? "We cannot afford," Ngũgĩ cautioned fellow African scholars, "to be intellectual outsiders in our own land" (164).

Broadly, Ngũgĩ believes that two issues are interrelated: exposure of the rapaciousness of imperialism and its African agents; the language question. He correctly sees little if any difference between globalization and imperialism:

> [T]he major character of the emerging globe is the division of the world into a minority of very wealthy creditor nations, mostly Western (and which, incidentally, also harbour weapons of mass destruction), and the majority debtor nations, mostly African, Asian and South American (which, incidentally, are always buying arms from the same dominant group); . . . and a poor social majority. The world is now occupied by opposing extremes of poverty and wealth, the poor ironically adding to the wealth of the wealthy through debt slavery. (155–56)

The poverty of African countries and peoples has in recent years, especially in the West, been explained culturally. The culprit is traditional African culture, the principal impediment to Africa's drive toward market capitalism and prosperity. Whenever prescribed Western economic remedies—for example, the structural adjustment programs—fail to alleviate Africa's poverty, Westerners and their financial institutions have characteristically responded

> not by questioning the adequacy of the remedies but by blaming Third World peoples for their lack of entrepreneurial spirit or market orientation. If they have failed to prosper despite all the excellent advice, it is because something is the matter with them: They missed the Protestant Reformation, or they are crippled by the disabling legacy of colonial Europe, or their IQs are too low. (De Soto 4)

African intellectuals have the duty to demystify and debunk the rationale of imperialism. To be able to do this, they must realize that

> [t]he fundamental opposition in Africa today is between Western imperialism and capitalism, on one hand, and national liberation and socialism, on the other: between a small class of native "haves," which is tied to international capital, and the masses of the people. (Ngũgĩ, *Writers* 74)

On this question there can be no neutrality. Joseph Ki-Zerbo asked:

> [C]an one afford to be neutral in an African state where de facto monopartism reigns supreme? Can one be a passive observer before unfolding unipolar thought, be it endogenous or exogenous? Can the intellectual encamp like a hardened nomad in an oasis while all around him are raging genocides, mass movements of refugees, tortures and mutilations, random destruction of the environment . . . ? (80)

To be neutral is essentially to support, directly or indirectly, an oppressive and exploitative status quo.

The way forward is through revolution. For Ngũgĩ, "it is only a revolution that can restore to Africa and its people the positive self-image and confidence necessary for the radical transformation of society." Art is a crucial component of this complex undertaking. There is no room here for the notion of art for art's sake. Rather, art must serve as a vehicle in the radical politicization of the masses in their march toward revolution. Thus "the essence of art is to serve the struggle of the people against their exploiters" (Okolo 102).

On language, Ngũgĩ has over the last twenty years emerged as perhaps Africa's most prominent proponent of the use of traditional African languages in the writing of literature and even general scholarship. His radical position on language is taken in the context of a continent and a people that have yet to achieve cultural independence.

> Africa's failure to assert its cultural autonomy manifests itself most sharply with language, since facility in language of the former metropole remains

> a key to elite status through much of Africa. Indigenous languages, while vibrant socially, continue to have low status in education, administration, and big business. (Laitin 131)

What have been the long-term consequences of this phenomenon? According to Ngũgĩ, European languages in Africa attained "the level of an ideal whose achievement was the pinnacle of pure enlightenment" ("Europhone" 158). Language therefore became an effective and enduring vehicle in the perpetuation of Western cultural imperialism in Africa.

The drive toward cultural independence and also toward the "democratization of knowledge" led Ngũgĩ to insist, with unyielding consistency, "that it is very important for African writers to use African languages for their creative expression." European languages are not only constant symbols and facilitators of cultural imperialism, they are also spoken by few in Africa—"the tip of every nationality, which means that when African writers write in these languages, in English or French or in Portuguese, they are basically addressing themselves to that very tiny minority—that is, the apex of each of these nationalities." Thus it is crucial for the African writer to be continually reminded that "the majority of the African people speak African languages" ("Language" 144).

The audience for African writers will increase considerably if they write in an African language. First, native speakers of the language will read the work; then it will be translated. Ngũgĩ states, "I know that when I am writing in Kikuyu I am reaching many more people within that nationality than if I wrote in English. Everything in English would reach only a small percent of the population." Translation will ensure that his works are "available in other African languages," in Kenya and in other African countries (145).

Ngũgĩ does not consider the enterprise of African writers writing in an African language to be contrary to the ideals or "the ideology of continental unity." Translation of literature from one African language into several will lead to a necessary redefinition of pan-Africanism:

> We have to look at pan-Africanism as a people-to-people relationship and not one between the heads of states or that of the intellectual and Western-educated elite held together by their common inheritance of European languages and their roots in a European memory of place, organization of knowledge and conceptualization of reality. ("Europhone" 162)

This innovative critique by Ngũgĩ on the question of language and production of knowledge in Africa has yet to be endorsed by most African writers and scholars. Legitimate questions were raised regarding the competency of some writers and scholars in their native language. Ngũgĩ argues, "[A]ll writers that I know could effectively use [an] African [language] and write as well [in it] as, if not better than, in the English language" ("Language" 150). But is this true? Do many African writers and scholars have Ngũgĩ's choice? "This question arises," Daniel Kunene writes, "because it is implicitly assumed that African writers know at least one African language, have acquired at least one colonial or settler language, and therefore have a choice" (12).

Some African writers and scholars speak their native language fluently but lack the ability to compose a work of literature or scholarship in it. Some are not even fluent speakers of their native language. Finally, there are some to whom it may be difficult to ascribe a native African language. Will the rich and varied contributions by such writers to African literature and scholarship be discounted? Will their authenticity as African writers and scholars be questioned?

Ngũgĩ and his supporters have argued that European languages in Africa, especially English, have become vehicles "in constituting and maintaining an indigenous elite class" and are therefore linked to imperialism (Roy 173). To what extent does acquisition of a European language mean entry into the elite class in present-day Africa? The spread of education in the postcolonial period and the subsequent increase in unemployment of the educated, especially due to structural adjustment programs, have resulted in many educated Africans who can speak a European language but do not belong to the political and economic elite.

Nor are all African intellectuals whose scholarly contributions are written in a European language supporters of imperialism. No evidence suggests that all Africans who do not speak a European language are patriotic, revolutionary, and hostile to external influences. On the contrary, acceptance of the basic tenets of imperialism and admiration for capitalist solutions and Western cultural values can and have been expressed in native languages. Language alone is not enough to create and sustain a revolutionary, anti-imperialist culture. The link between language and socialist revolution or radicalism in Africa has yet to be proved by Ngũgĩ.

One of the most regrettable outcomes of the structural adjustment programs in Africa has been the erasing of the gains of independence, especially in education. Illiteracy has spread in societies that remain poor and dependent, including illiteracy in native languages. Poverty and the struggle for survival under these programs have left peasants and workers with minimal if any disposable income to buy books in any language.

Ngũgĩ's wish to see the establishment of socialist revolutionary societies in Africa is connected to his choice to write principally in his native Gĩkũyũ after 1986; the choice "was dictated by a redefinition of his target audience for sociopolitical reasons" (Kunene 12). The writing of plays for the Kamĩrĩĩthũ Community Centre near his home in Kenya was done to inspire and politicize the masses. "This shift of focus, one may even call it a maturing of political vision from liberal humanism to . . . 'a new revolutionary practice of writing/cultural production,' required him to write in the language of his audience" (Roy 171). These plays and musicals for the uneducated are consistent with Ngũgĩ's belief that art can be marshaled as a weapon for revolution.

Ngũgĩ's writings have yet to clarify how these two radical aims, socialist revolution and literature in an African language, strategically reinforce each other in African countries. Are these two projects to be undertaken concurrently? If not, which should lead the way? Since 1986, Ngũgĩ has placed more emphasis on language:

> I believe that the language issue is the key, not the only one, but definitely a very very important key to the decolonization process. What is really happening is that African thought, literary thought, is imprisoned in foreign languages. African literature and African thought, even at their most radical, even at their most revolutionary, are alienated from the majority. ("Language" 146)

NOTES

[1] The question of the cultural impact of colonialism on Africa continues to generate heated discussion. See, for example, Ajayi; Boahen.

[2] Ngũgĩ adds that "[h]arvests were often poor" and that his family at this stage "had one meal a day—late in the evening" (48).

[3] For a critical analysis of *A Grain of Wheat* and the theme of betrayal, see Cook and Okenimkpe.

[4] Ngũgĩ was detained in Kamiti Prison, Nairobi, from 31 December 1977 to 12 December 1978. He was released a few months after Kenyatta's death.

[5] Some of these misgivings were voiced in his address to the Kenya Historical Association in 1968, later published in *Homecoming* (39–46).

[6] Consider Ngũgĩ's interpretation of the role of Dedan Kimathi in the Mau Mau revolt. In *The Trial of Dedan Kimathi* (coauthored with Micere Githae Mugo), Ngũgĩ portrays Kimathi as a socialist revolutionary leader consistently and unwaveringly out to oust imperialism and build a socialist Kenya. The evidence available does not in any way support this portrayal. See Maloba, *Mau Mau*; Davidson, *People's Cause*; and Chaliand. Atieno Odhiambo believes that the class composition of Mau Mau precluded it from having "a high level of class consciousness" (385). See also Maina wa Kinyatti; Mazrui (*Africans*). This challenge to Ngũgĩ's reinvention of Mau Mau does not by any means seek to discount the brutality of the British armed forces in Kenya during the revolt. This brutality is well-known and much studied. Elkins's *Imperial Reckoning* and Anderson's *Histories of the Hanged* provide details of this story. But neither Elkins nor Anderson claims that Mau Mau was a socialist movement. The question raised in this essay is Ngũgĩ's creative reinvention of Mau Mau as a socialist revolutionary movement.

[7] On socialist ideology and Mau Mau, Mazrui has argued, "Mau Mau movement remained uninformed about the question of class alliances" ("Ideology" 60). Maina wa Kinyatti, a leading figure in the radical interpretation of history, expresses serious doubts about the ideology underpinning this revolt: "There was no ideological struggle within the Mau Mau movement to transform nationalist consciousness into class consciousness, nor was there a serious systematic analysis of imperialism, the class struggle, and the relation of socialism to the Kenya revolutionary process" (12).

Ngũgĩ and Sembène: Teaching the Text of History

Patrick Williams

> *History* does *nothing*; it "possesses *no* immense wealth"; it "wages *no* battles." It is man, real living man, that does all that, and that possesses and fights; "history" is not a person apart, using man as a means for its own particular aims; history is nothing but the activity of man pursuing his aims.
>
> —Marx, "The Holy Family"

This essay will examine various elements of the engagement with history in the work of Ngũgĩ wa Thiong'o and of Ousmane Sembène, two of the best known, as well as the most respected, postcolonial cultural producers from Africa. Although there are important differences between them—for instance, Ngũgĩ followed the English-instituted colonial education system all the way to becoming the first black professor of English at the University of Nairobi, while Sembène was largely self-taught—it is the similarities that are more significant. These include a commitment (perhaps more long-term and more thoroughgoing in the case of Sembène) to a Marxist perspective, which in turn has helped make them two of the most unremittingly oppositional figures in the postcolonial field. Both are multitalented. Sembène is best known as a filmmaker novelist, and short story writer, but he has also produced poetry and nonfiction as well as an adaptation of his most famous novel, *God's Bits of Wood* for the stage; Ngũgĩ is a novelist, short story writer, dramatist, essayist (and one-time aspiring filmmaker). Both are champions of the use of indigenous languages in their work, and while that might appear initially off-putting to their audiences in other cultures, the texts that carry these languages are formed by their authors' democratic politics, and as such are accessible, teachable, though variously demanding of their audiences. The accessibility is such that a text like *The River Between* can readily be taught in secondary school, while the formal, cultural, linguistic, and political challenges posed by Ngũgĩ's later works make them eminently suitable for undergraduate and postgraduate courses. (I have, for example, taught them in introductory courses in postcolonial literature as well as specialist ones in contemporary African cultural production, where the greater level of cultural knowledge that students can bring results in analysis of appropriate complexity.) Most importantly perhaps, both Ngũgĩ and Sembène are committed to politically aware cultural practices, which are necessarily simultaneously historically aware, and it is that historical awareness this essay aims to address (though given the limitations of space, it cannot do much more than sketch in some of the range of productive interrelations in the work of these two friends). Historical awareness forms one of the essential conditions for the foundational narratives of postcolonial polities; it is, however, no less important for students getting to grips with these varied cultures and the texts they produce, and both written work and classroom discussion benefit visibly from it.

> Here then is an adequate revolution for me to espouse—to help my society regain belief in itself and put away the complexes of the years of denigration and self-abasement. And it is essentially a question of education, in the best sense of that word. . . . I would be quite satisfied if my novels (especially the ones I set in the past) did no more than teach my readers that their past—with all its imperfections—was not one long night of savagery from which the first Europeans acting on God's behalf delivered them. (Achebe, "Novelist" 44, 45)

At least since Chinua Achebe's famous pronouncement, the necessary engagement of postcolonial cultural producers in the business of historical recovery, remembering, and reconstruction as the starting point for a (national) pedagogical project has appeared something of a given—unquestioned, possibly unquestionable. One result of that much-repeated, seemingly unavoidable task is that, in certain quarters among writers, critics, filmmakers—and students, addressing questions of history has a yawn-inducing quality. "Been there . . . done that. . . ." At the same time, for both Sembène and Ngũgĩ, engagement with history remains centrally important, regardless of any repetitiveness that the (to their way of thinking) absolutely necessary struggle involves: "For every image of the past that is not recognized by the present as one of its own concerns threatens to disappear irretrievably." As Walter Benjamin famously goes on to say, "Only that historian will have the gift of fanning the spark of hope in the past who is firmly convinced that *even the dead* will not be safe from the enemy if he wins. And this enemy has not ceased to be victorious" (257). For Sembène and Ngũgĩ, the enemy—global capitalism in its various phases and guises (colonialism, followed by neocolonialism with its local indigenous bourgeoisies as intermediaries, and then globalization)—has so far not ceased to be victorious, and as we shall see, it is very much on behalf of the dead—as well as the living—that they conduct their engagement with history. Further, the very fact of working with history can seem politically significant:

> Historical reconstruction, then, the positing of global characteristics and hypotheses, the abstraction from the "blooming, buzzing confusion" of immediacy, was always a radical intervention in the here and now, and the promise of resistance to its blind fatalities.
> (Jameson, *Postmodernism* 400)

Such radical optimism notwithstanding, there remain questions regarding precisely what sort of history or whose history is being reconstructed; the manner of its reconstruction and representation; the cultural, ideological, or political agendas behind the process of reconstruction; and so on. Clearly, not just any history is automatically appropriate, useful, or even reasonably accurate; indeed, for some, almost any interest in the past can constitute a problematic distraction from the political needs of the present:

> I am convinced that it would be of the greatest interest to be able to have contact with a Negro literature or architecture of the third century before Christ. I should be very happy to know that a correspondence had flourished between some Negro philosopher and Plato. But I can absolutely not see how this fact would change anything in the lives of the eight-year-old children who labor in the cane fields of Martinique or Guadeloupe. (Fanon, *Black Skin* 230)

While Sembène might have some sympathy for Fanon's early position (one that underwent some later modification), Ngũgĩ has more consistently argued for the political utility of historical knowledge, in both his essays and his fiction.

If there is or has been an inaugural struggle for postcolonial writers to begin to reconstruct effaced histories, there is a different and arguably more challenging struggle to be waged over more "difficult" histories and narratives, where the degree of "difficulty" often equals the degree of deliberate occlusion of the history. In the case of Sembène, celebrating the collective victory of ordinary Senegalese working people in *God's Bits of Wood* may be relatively unproblematic; cataloging colonial atrocities (particularly in *Emitai* and *Camp de Thiaroye*) and indigenous postcolonial corruption (e. g., *Xala*), including its sometimes murderous excesses (*Guelwaar*), is most emphatically not. However, although different films (*Xala, Mandabi*) had scenes cut on the insistence of the Senegalese government (acting under French pressure), and *Ceddo* was banned for a number of years, Sembène never suffered personally in the way Ngũgĩ did. For Ngũgĩ, the trajectory of "difficulty" is similar: the interreligious and intracommunal conflicts of the 1930s in *The River Between* and the early depiction of the Mau Mau period in *Weep Not, Child* may be uncontroversial; the same cannot be said for the refusal to stop championing Mau Mau (particularly in *The Trial of Dedan Kimathi*) or attacking indigenous postcolonial corruption and tyranny (in *Petals of Blood*). The result of this for Ngũgĩ (and even more so his experiments in radical popular theater) was his arbitrary arrest, imprisonment without charge or trial, and his unlooked-for but possibly lifesaving move into exile following his release from prison, where works such as *Devil on the Cross*, *Matigari*, and *Wizard of the Crow*—the first of these famously written on toilet paper during his imprisonment—continue to excoriate the greed, stupidity, and brutality of postcolonial African regimes.

While some audiences may wonder how far contemporary postcolonial corruption may legitimately fit under a rubric of "history," according to Ngũgĩ and Sembène there is no contradiction whatsoever. For both, the postcolonial present is produced and informed by a past that is most recently, and oppressively, colonial, but is also composed of much more than that. For instance, on the relation between past and present in his work, Ngũgĩ comments, "I do not go outside history for my themes; they are derived from history and current social practice" ("*Matigari* as Myth" 246). For both, an understanding of which histories are working themselves out in the present is the only basis on which any intervention in the present can proceed.

Although their perspectives on history are quite similar, the way each has chosen to represent that history is different: Ngũgĩ's novels offer something like a relatively continuous history of Kenya in the twentieth and early twenty-first centuries; Sembène's historical sweep may be greater, especially in his films, but his coverage is also more spasmodic, with a stronger focus than Ngũgĩ's on the contemporary outworking of various histories and processes. In the remainder of this essay, these similarities and differences will be traced in a few representative examples of the use of history by Sembène and Ngũgĩ: individual and collective; punctual and processual, official and popular.

Punctual or Processual

One example of this, focusing on the punctual moment of the precise historical period or the broader processual sweep, is the way in which Ngũgĩ and Sembène tackle the question of female genital mutilation, particularly in Ngũgĩ's novel *The River Between* and Sembène's film *Moolaadé*. Ngũgĩ, in the first novel he wrote, sees it as emblematic of the history of Kenya in the late 1920s and early 1930s, the "punctual" moment of emergent resistance to the attempt by Church of Scotland missionaries to eradicate female genital mutilation, and as a stage in the development of more generalized anticolonial resistance. Sembène, on the other hand, in what was to be his final film, looks at it in a manner we could call "processual," in the context of the continuity of cultural forms and practices, their relationship to the past and the present, and their acceptability within an African framework.

For Ngũgĩ's central character, Waiyaki, in *River,* the perceived need to defend Gĩkũyũ practices is very much in line with the position taken by Jomo Kenyatta in *Facing Mount Kenya* in 1938, not only that European colonialism had stripped the Gĩkũyũ of their most meaningful traditions and given them nothing in return, but that the endangered practice of "circumcision" in fact united the whole community.

> Circumcision was an important ritual to the tribe. It kept people together, bound the tribe. It was at the core of the social structure, and something that gave meaning to a man's life. End the custom and the spiritual basis of the tribe's cohesion and integration would be no more.
>
> (Ngũgĩ, *River* 68)

European culture, especially in the shape of Christianity, acts as a divisive force for the Gĩkũyũ, and the community of the novel is split between those, such as Joshua, who are wholly or partially assimilated into Western ways and want to stamp out "pagan" practices, and those, like Kabonyi, who become militant cultural nationalists, dedicated to the defense of tradition and ritual. The split is literally embodied in characters like Muthoni, who, though she is the daughter of the leading Christian convert, Joshua, desperately wants to undergo excision in order to become—in her own eyes as well as those of the traditionalists—a proper member of the tribe. To general astonishment, Muthoni disobeys her overbearing father and is excised, dying soon afterward of complications, but seemingly believing that she has achieved some sort of reconciliation: "[T]ell Nyambura [her sister] I see Jesus. And I am a woman, beautiful in the tribe" (53). In this rebellion against patriarchy, Muthoni repeats the actions of a number of Kenyan women of the period, wives of converts to Anglicanism, who disobeyed their husbands in order to be excised. Unfortunately for the community of the novel, there is no reconciliation; instead, Waiyaki's project of cultural syncretism and an enlightened approach to history and tradition seems doomed by the growing power of the *kiama*, the council of traditionalists, and for the foreseeable future female genital mutilation is here to stay. The women's suffering is the price to be paid for the usefulness of the practice as the focus for resistance at that moment in history.

In *Moolaadé,* Sembène undertakes detailed scrutiny of, for him, another variously problematic African practice. Polygamy, which he saw as "an undeniable problem," had already featured in his work from *God's Bits of Wood* onward, most notably in *Xala*. While for Sembène African traditions, rituals, and cultural practices must be preserved—"Yes, ritual is very important. In Europe, it's practically disappeared. . . . My people recognize themselves through rituals. Europeans find this hard to understand. When you lose your own rituals, you lose a part of your soul" (Murphy 239)—that does not mean absolutely all of them, and certainly not at any cost. In his view, however, two things are evident: the need to assess African traditions carefully (historically, morally, politically) and the fact that addressing any problems they may present is a question for Africans and no one else. Although traditional practices can be regarded as processual, that does not prevent their being understood historically, and in the case of polygamy, its contemporary form is above all a question of the commodification of women:

> Polygamy, especially in the bourgeois or urban setting, means the wife is only some flesh for whom a commodity value is paid. . . . There is a problem, but the problem is clear because the woman's inferior status is visible. We do not, however, find a solution in the Western concept of the family, for that model only produces a deterioration in human beings. In reality, the problem should not be posed in terms of sexes but in terms of classes. (Sembène qtd. in Downing 46)

Female genital mutilation is another traditional practice that, although he understands it historically as well as in terms of its place within African culture, he cannot accept, not least because it too is based in the continuing social and physical subjugation of women. It is also—and this matters very much to Sembène—a problem affecting something like three-quarters of African countries. In *Moolaadé*, the central character, Collé, uses tradition against tradition as she invokes the ancient practice of *moolaadé* ("sanctuary") in order to protect four young girls, due to face excision, who have sought refuge with her. In taking this stand—initially against almost the whole of her community—she becomes the latest in a long line of female characters in Sembène's work who bravely resist forms of oppression—colonial, capitalist, patriarchal—no matter how historically or traditionally sanctioned these may be. Throughout his books and films, Sembène had always been, in his own words, "somewhat concerned with history and the heroism of everyday life" (Downing 41), so it is interesting that he should specifically use the phrase "heroism of everyday life" as the title for his final, unfinished trilogy, where the two completed films, *Faat Kine* and *Moolaadé*, celebrate the courage and resilience of women in the face of gendered violence.

While Collé's initial stand against oppression is taken in the name of tradition, it is a complex blend of the ancient and the modern that brings about a positive resolution. For example, the falsification of history by the local imam, who declares that female genital mutilation has always been an Islamic practice, is discovered by women listening to the radio and hearing a greater religious authority declare the opposite. Most importantly, the westernized son of the village chief returns from abroad, apparently to assume his place in history in the age-old line of inheritance, but he marks a crucial break with oppressive histories and practices by opposing his father, and siding with Collé in marrying her unmutilated daughter, an act unimaginable in a traditionalist context.

Individual or Collective

The habit of understanding history as the product of the deeds of the great (typically male) can be as hard to break in Africa as it is in the West. For instance, a central aspect of the historical role of the West African griot was to recall all the heroism and triumphs of his patron and his patron's ancestors. More recently, under the Conservative government in Britain in the 1990s there were heated debates about whether history teaching should in fact be oriented back to the study of kings and queens and great men, from which it was deemed to have slipped. To a large extent, however, both Ngũgĩ and Sembène manage to avoid that kind of historical model. Although the conventions of fiction and filmmaking require a central character for the purposes of emotional or ideological identification, neither typically succumbs to the pressure to create a hero figure, and Sembène in particular frequently avoids even the creation of an obvious central character. In the career of each, however, it is possible to point to an exception to this: in the case of Ngũgĩ, the historical "hero" is the Mau Mau leader Dedan Kimathi, hanged by the British in 1957, while for Sembène it is the nineteenth-century statesman and warrior Samory Touré, who for eighteen years led the fight against the French. Apart from their role in anticolonial struggle, there are other similarities between the two men: for example, both were vilified by the colonial powers as bloodthirsty barbarians, and were subject to historical erasure — even more by their own culture than by the West. Sembène spent several decades amassing material on Samory, and in his seventies was still talking about the film he would make on the subject, but died with this major historical project unrealized. Ngũgĩ, on the other hand, was more successful: he wrote probably his best play, *The Trial of Dedan Kimathi,* with Micere Mugo in 1976.

More important than their individual achievements, however, is what Samory and Kimathi stand for, their representative status in larger historical schema of national liberation struggles and anticolonial resistance. The corresponding shift in Ngũgĩ's writing practice from the creation of realistic individualized characters to something very different is indicated by his comment that "[t]he character of Matigari can be seen first in a general sense as representing the collective worker in history" ("*Matigari* as Myth" 243). The combined practice of downplaying central characters and having individuals embody collectivities allows both Ngũgĩ and Sembène to offer what they consider more historically honest representations of the efforts of groups, communities, whole nations — in what Marx, in the epigraph to this essay, calls the pursuit of their aims (Marx and Engels). Even in an early work like *God's Bits of Wood*, Sembène is determined to show how different oppressed groups — workers, women, colonized people — achieve collective awareness and agency in particular historical settings. In the case of Ngũgĩ, the move to more fabular and allegorical modes, which accompanied his growing use of aspects of oral literature in *Devil on the Cross*, *Matigari,* and *Wizard of the Crow*, means that the collective dimension is as likely to be transhistorical as precisely historicized. In this perspective, Matigari comes to represent not only workers but the entire nation in its five hundred years of resistance to foreign domination.

Official versus Popular

The representation of collective popular resistance is above all the history that both Ngũgĩ and Sembène wish to recover and have acknowledged. However, this postcolonial version of what, in a British context, was called "history from below" immediately comes into conflict with various forms of "official" history. For Ngũgĩ, "[t]here have been two types of history in Kenya: the *real living* history of the masses; and the *approved official* history" (*Moving* 98). As he comments in *Petals of Blood,* his novel most concerned with such questions, while the oppositions that these positions embody can still be matters of life and death, "there can be no neutral history" (*Petals* 200; for a more extensive discussion of this issue, see Williams, "'Like Wounded Birds'?").

The official history includes obviously the dominant Western version, especially that produced during the period of colonialism, as well as derivative versions produced by the (derivative) black elites who inherited power from the colonizers. This is the problem Ngũgĩ faced with particular intensity in relation to Kenya and Mau Mau, but the situation for Sembène in Senegal is broadly similar. Colonial historiography routinely ignored indigenous resistance until ignoring it became impossible, at which point it was transformed into something terrible, the epitome of treachery or barbarity. Mau Mau is the classic example of the latter. In many cases (though not all, it must be said) it was also in the interests of postindependence black elites to perpetuate Western versions, and again Kenya offers a strong example.

One obvious reason for the extreme demonization of indigenous resistance as barbaric was the (simple but inadmissible) fact that it was met with barbaric behavior by the colonizers. Sembène in particular has tried to unearth evidence of atrocities perpetrated by the French in Senegal, and says he knows of eighteen examples. Two of these were turned into films, *Emitai* and *Camp de Thiaroye*. The former tells of a massacre in 1942 of civilians who refused to hand over their rice stock requisitioned by the French military; the latter is the story of another massacre, in 1944 this time, of African soldiers recently returned from the war in Europe. Neither was officially acknowledged by the French. While Sembène is reluctant to see film as having a direct influence in politics, it is nevertheless the case that within six years of its release *Camp de Thiaroye* turned a previously unmentionable—and hence very largely forgotten—event into a day of national remembrance. The Mau Mau period unsurprisingly provides Ngũgĩ with his best examples of British atrocities, especially in the treatment of actual or suspected Mau Mau fighters in the prison camp system, and also of the general rural population in the regime of enforced villagization, the virtual creation of prisons for those not convicted of any crime. The brutality meted out to Mau Mau prisoners, culminating in the massacre at Hola camp (renamed Rira in the novel), makes a rare appearance in fiction in *A Grain of Wheat*.

For both Sembène and Ngũgĩ, official historians, black or white, colonial or postcolonial, are at the root of the problem. In Sembène's eyes, they are chronophages, literally eaters or swallowers of time, and he also likens them to undertakers, eager to bury historical events rather than bring them to life (Murphy 177–78). In the Kenyan context,

> [t]here are the official historians, the approved state historians, whose role is to give rational legitimacy to the tradition of loyalism and collaboration with imperialism. These have received state accolades and honours. But the . . . people's real history of struggle and resistance has thrown up its own historians. (Ngũgĩ, *Moving* 98)

The official historians accuse Ngũgĩ and Sembène of historical inaccuracy, exaggeration, distortion, the propagation of myth, and some of these accusations are (partially) accepted. For example, Sembène says of *Ceddo* and its compression of time, "I recognise that it may not be historical, but it is my version" (Murphy 178); while Ngũgĩ notes that *The Trial of Dedan Kimathi* may not be strictly realistic but says that this is in the service of a more important realism and relevance (Ngũgĩ and Mugo, Preface vi–vii), in the style of Bertolt Brecht. More combatively, in *Petals of Blood* he argues that it is the very inadequacy of the "history" on offer, which means that writers have to rely on legend and myth as source material, and provocatively (and unusually in the context of a novel) goes on to name the four most distinguished contemporary Kenyan historians as among those who continue to repeat theories propagated by the defenders of imperialism (67–68).

Other historians, such as Bruce Berman and John Lonsdale, who are not obviously "official," attack those whom they label "radicals" for being "cavalier" with evidence:

> Ideological heroism has been most determinedly demanded of the evidence by those who have least studied it, who can indeed sneer at those who bury Mau Mau "in a heap of footnotes." Kenyan liberals have protested against this contempt for authorised professional standards, calling it "intellectual terrorism." (298)

The quoted, unnamed (and inaccurately referenced) sneerer is Ngũgĩ. The jibe about evidence also falls very flat, in view of the findings of David Anderson and of Caroline Elkins. Their work reveals that Ngũgĩ's allegedly "exaggerated" portrayal of British repression in fact only begins to sketch in its awfulness; his reconstruction isn't nearly historical enough. The horrors of the camps, for example, may be partly depicted, but not even Ngũgĩ tackles the way in which the British and their Kenyan "loyalists" routinely tortured and murdered those whom they suspected of opposing them, or hanged them by the dozen, after "due process." That is a pity, because along with the simply appalling facts that need to be told, there are grotesque ironies that might appeal to Ngũgĩ, such as the group of detainees from Embakasi camp who managed to overpower their guards and escape. Unfortunately, they were later recaptured—and hanged for the capital crime of possessing the guards' guns.

Ngũgĩ entitled the final section of *Petals of Blood* "La Luta Continua," and even though in the kleptocratic world of Aburĩria in *Wizard of the Crow* this may have become "A loot-a continua," there is indeed a struggle to be continued. The regimes of Jomo Kenyatta and Daniel arap Moi made the most strenuous efforts to obliterate the memory of Mau Mau, and intimidate, imprison, or murder those who objected. In a different sphere of enforced amnesia, when Elkins attempted to undertake primary research into the Mau Mau period, she discovered that most of the relevant documentation had been destroyed by the British authorities, and her project suddenly became primarily one of oral history. However difficult of access the text of history may be, the example of writers and filmmakers like Ngũgĩ and Sembène, as well as historians like Elkins and Anderson, makes clear that there are more-honest narratives of history to be fought for, and taught.

LANGUAGE, TRANSLATION, STYLE

African Anglophonism, Translation, and the Teaching of Ngũgĩ's Works

Michael Andindilile

In Ngũgĩ wa Thiong'o's novel *Devil on the Cross* (written in Gĩkũyũ: *Caitaani Mũtharaba-inĩ*), we find a parable: "The flag of Independence can be likened unto a man travelling unto a far country, who called his own servants, and delivered unto them his goods . . ." (174). Ngũgĩ manipulates the biblical parable of the five talents here to expose the emptiness of political independence when it is not accompanied by economic liberty. This is one of many English passages that he presents untranslated in the Gĩkũyũ original as part of his rhetorical strategy. Although he is writing primarily for a Gĩkũyũ audience, he evidently has an eye on the international audience as well.

I encourage my students to avoid two pitfalls when they approach Ngũgĩ: reading his English fiction as if it were typically Anglo-American and reading his Ngũgĩ fiction as if it were originally written in English. In both there is an African anglophonism at work, which calls our attention to his rhetoric. After all, his fiction thrives on the revolutionary potential of language and literature. To help my students, I highlight the strategies Ngũgĩ employs in all his work: the language he uses, whether drawn from his oral culture or from English, to convey his anticolonial and anti-neocolonial message. My primary objective is to show students how his language is the key to understanding his vision of Kenya's and Africa's socioeconomics and cultures.

In a recent Anglophone African Literatures course I taught at Fordham University in which we read Ngũgĩ's *Devil on the Cross*, the students majored in English, French, and comparative literature, as well as in psychology, philosophy, and communications. They all had one thing in common: they knew very little about Africa or its literatures. One student explained her lack of background information on Africa thus. She recalled that in her elementary and high school years, Africa had not been covered as a subject except in relation to the transatlantic triangular trade that brought African slaves to the Americas. Science majors, in the more general and larger lower-division required classes, knew even less.

As Ngũgĩ's works deal with politics, economics, sociology, and history, a variety of approaches is needed in classes where students come from different backgrounds. I prefer discussion-based teaching, a self-conscious departure from the lecture-and-recitation method in which I was taught at the University of Dar es Salaam in Tanzania. I ask how Kenya historically wound up in the shape it's in, and why America, which did not originally colonize Africa, should become one of the "bad guys" in Ngũgĩ's worldview. Students see colonial and neocolonial links between England (a colonial power) and Kenya (a former colony), since the former colonized the latter, but they have difficulty associating America with colonialism or neocolonialism in Africa.

In *Decolonising the Mind*, Ngũgĩ implies that the political and ideological conflict in his fiction targets imperialism as represented by the United States and its international policy through the International Monetary Fund (IMF) (2–3).[1] His more radical novels, such as *Petals of Blood*, show how Western finance capital and transnational monopolies embodied by the IMF further marginalize the poor majority. A sociological approach helps expose students to the social contexts of Ngũgĩ's works. For example, why is land so important in Ngũgĩ's novels and the play *I Will Marry When I Want* (Ngũgĩ and Ngũgĩ wa Mĩriĩ), and what are the implications of its loss for most Kenyans? I explain that during the colonial era, land was appropriated by white settlers, hence the need to reclaim it. But political independence from Britain did not result in the poor majority assuming control of the land in neocolonial Kenya; the land remains in the hands of the rich few. Kihika, the protagonist in Ngũgĩ's *A Grain of Wheat*, says that "everybody should have a share in the common shamba [farm or land], our Kenya" and that "[t]his soil belongs to Kenyan people" (93).

Linked to the issue of land, as we see in Ngũgĩ's works, is the fact that the people who control the land also control the means of production. The contested power relations in Kenya play out among varying social forces and institutions. Marxist sociology alerts students to the political organization of the Kenyan (and African) nation-states as depicted in Ngũgĩ's novels and plays. For example, how is money used to manipulate people? *I Will Marry When I Want*, set in contemporary neocolonial Kenya, explores the relationship between the haves (represented by Ahab Kĩoi wa Kanoru) and the have-nots (the poor majority represented by Kĩgũũnda) and shows how the former manipulate the latter (as the loss of Kĩgũũnda's land title deed illustrates) to consolidate their hold on power. From a Marxist perspective, in *A Grain of Wheat* and *Petals of Blood* Ngũgĩ is reacting against the continuing survival of colonial culture in Africa.

When I introduce Ngũgĩ, I stress his involvement in the debate about the language of African literatures. We discuss the introductory chapter of

Decolonising the Mind,[2] and the students come to class with personal responses to Ngũgĩ's language argument and to the question, To what extent do you agree with Ngũgĩ that African literatures can be written only in African languages? Their responses, which generally oppose Ngũgĩ's position, provide an opportunity to clarify issues.

I usually lead our discussion of Ngũgĩ with his premise that language "is both a means of communication and a carrier of culture" (*Decolonising* 13). I explain that his insistence on writing in an indigenous African language should be seen in the broader context of building cross-cultural bridges, in which indigenous languages are not marginalized since "no culture is an island unto itself" as it "has been influenced by other cultures and other histories with which it has come into contact" ("Borders" 119). The purpose is to show that the language question is complex, having many interconnected issues.

Ngũgĩ is concerned with maintaining local cultures and speaking to and transforming them. Ultimately, such cultures should be enabled to speak directly to one another and eventually convey themeselves to the metropolitan West through translation. I agree with Ngũgĩ when he says that regardless of the language choice an African writer makes, "it does not mean you are going to invent your own history or a new world" ("Beyond Nativism" 163). In this statement lies the relevance of Ngũgĩ's English and Gĩkũyũ fiction to the study of Kenyan and African culture. The Gĩkũyũ culture portrayed in his earlier novels written in English is no less authentic than in those written later in Gĩkũyũ.

My introduction also covers the polyglossic nature of Kenya's linguistic environment, in which more than forty ethnic groups share national space. Kenyans are expected to know Kiswahili, the national language, in addition to their mother tongue, and they speak English when they are educated. English in Kenya is a language of instruction and an official language. Though the country declared Kiswahili the national language in 1969 and a language of parliament in 1974, English gets priority and has greater prestige sometimes even in linguistic spheres reserved for Kiswahili, confirming the unequal power relations Ngũgĩ seeks to redress.

Apart from *Devil on the Cross*, Ngũgĩ's first Gĩkũyũ novel, I like to teach *The River Between*, his first novel written in English and dealing with an earlier period of Kenyan history. As the style of this novel is closer to traditional Anglo-American literature than Ngũgĩ's later works, some associate *The River Between* and *Weep Not, Child* with English aesthetics. This classification occurs despite the fact that Ngũgĩ's "apparent embrace of 'Englishness'" is "riddled with ambivalence, ambiguity, and slippage" (Amoko, "Resemblance" 35). Moreover, an aesthetic that is distinctive of the anglophone African novel must negotiate among contending linguistic forces. *The River Between* and *Devil on the Cross* both belong to the realm of African, not English, aesthetics.

Ngũgĩ's novels allow us to see at work transliteration and translation, important devices in African literary discourse. Transliteration, which Michael Onwuemene interprets as "literal translation" (1057), was embraced as an integral part of African writing during the historic 1962 Conference of African Writers of English Expression held in Kampala, Uganda, about which Ezekiel Mphahlele reported, "It was generally agreed that it was better for an African writer to think and feel in his own language and then look for an English transliteration approximating the original" (qtd. in Wali 14). In Ngũgĩ's Gĩkũyũ fiction, English translation should "be seen in the same light as . . . other translations," since Ngũgĩ did not "transliterate" (Kasanga and Kalume 48).[3] That *The River Between* has been transliterated and *Devil on the Cross* translated, however, does not make one novel any easier for students than the other. As one of my students observed, translation provides only partial access to the original. That Ngũgĩ translated *Devil on the Cross* from Gĩkũyũ into English himself convinced the student of the translation's authenticity. But, the student sometimes couldn't tell when a character was actually using English in the text. The words and phrases Ngũgĩ chooses to translate and how he translates them hold the key to some of his most important themes.

Students learn that having English as a shared language does not guarantee easy and straightforward interpretation by a traditional anglophone reader of Ngũgĩ. I invite them to consider the linguistic features that make *The River Between* an archetypically African novel. Paramount is the question of how the author represents Kenyan culture in English. Students often point out the non-English words, such as "*Tiitheru*" (14; "of a truth") or expressions like "*Kagutui ka Mucii gatihakagwo Ageni*" (3; "the oilskin of the house is not for rubbing into the skin of strangers"). Ngũgĩ's retention of certain native words and expressions leads to a discussion of the relation between his Gĩkũyũ and English in the English text. For example, why does he reproduce only certain songs in Gĩkũyũ?

I draw students' attention to a hymn in Gĩkũyũ and English:

Maikarite thi Utuku
Ariithi a Mburi
Murekio wa Ngai niokire
Nake akimera o uu.

While shepherds watched their flocks by night
All seated on the ground
The angel of the Lord came down
And glory shone around. (132)

I ask why an earlier song appears only in English (93) and thus prompt students to consider what such language application reveals. We look at the word *Ngai* ("Lord" or "God") in the Gĩkũyũ song, the same word the protagonist, Waiyaki, uses to highlight the bigotry of the missionaries, who find his people "ignoran[t]" for worshipping "Murungu, Mwenenyaga, Ngai," the Gĩkũyũ god the "unerring white man had called . . . the prince of darkness" (29). Gĩkũyũ words here help undermine common misconceptions about Africa.

Some historical background can clarify the relation among colonialism, Christianity, and the English language. English was one of the languages through which the explorer, the soldier, and the missionary determined how to master, colonize, and transform the dark continent.[4] V. Y. Mudimbe's insights into how the missionaries' programs in Africa were "more complex than the simple transmission of the Christian faith" (45) explain why biblical language is an integral part of Ngũgĩ's anticolonial rhetorical strategy. I bring in Hegel's controversial remark that in "Negro life the characteristic point is the fact that consciousness has not yet attained the realization of any substantial objective existence" (93). Ngũgĩ's counterargument is implicit in his novels' use of language. The words the missionaries readily appropriate from African languages for the Judeo-Christian god demonstrate that African consciousness has attained that realization. I thus strive to make the students see beyond the surface meaning of words and recognize the connection between language and larger epistemological issues.

Students are generally fascinated with orality in Ngũgĩ's English and Gĩkũyũ fiction. We discuss the use of African songs, dance, mime, and proverbs as rhetorical tools that enrich Ngũgĩ's literary language. These forms borrowed from African oral culture, or orature, indicate the complementary nature of African oral literature and modern African writing. Antonia Kalu explains that African writers such as Ngũgĩ "embed . . . African oral narrative theoretical frameworks in plot structure and other literary techniques" (50). The point to make to students is that these African forms help Ngũgĩ communicate his message and that indigenous African culture is not inert when an African writes in English. Thus when Chinua Achebe writes, "proverbs are the palm-oil with which words are eaten" (*Things* 7), he is "drawing [our] attention to the central position that the form occupies in African speech" (Irele, *African Imagination* 32). I ask students to examine and interpret the oral features that appear in the text. For example, the proverb "The oilskin of the house is not for rubbing into the skin of strangers" is both a cultural expression and a conveyor of the values of the Gĩkũyũ. This way, the students go beyond simply identifying these oral features (which increase progressively in Ngũgĩ's fiction after *Petals of Blood*). We discuss how Ngũgĩ becomes more influenced by orality as he moves toward writing in Gĩkũyũ. When he breaks decisively with the Afro-European novel, he finds himself assimilating more and more of the Gĩkũyũ oral and prose traditions, including the narrative form of *Devil on the Cross*.

We touch on the many languages and levels of rhetoric that appear in *Devil*. Ngũgĩ explains in a footnote, "In the original work, written in Gĩkũyũ, certain words and phrases appear in English, French, Latin and [Ki]Swahili. In this translation all such words and phrases are printed in *italic* type" (10). But I am more interested in the difference that writing in Gĩkũyũ makes for Ngũgĩ. As this novel moves toward the politics of commitment, how does the instructor negotiate the bold and direct language in which the novel "declares its message about neocolonialism and the means to correct it, boldly if relentlessly, in places nearly choking on its own expression of outrage" (Lovesey, *Ngũgĩ* 65)?

I introduce the effects of colonialism and neocolonialism in Kenya, which lets students see the bigger picture. Gatuiria, one of the characters, says, "Cultural imperialism is mother to the slavery of the mind and the body . . . that persuades people to allow foreigners to tell them what to do in their own country" (58). Who is behind this cultural imperialism? Why does America, which never colonized Kenya, become implicated in the exploitation of ordinary Kenyans? America, whom Ngũgĩ identifies as the leader of imperialism, is (alongside Britain, Japan, and other Western countries) in works such as *Petals* and *Devil* the perpetrator of cultural imperialism.

Addressing common Gĩkũyũ readers directly in their language, Ngũgĩ can afford such boldness. I urge students to think of his primary audience—ordinary Gĩkũyũ people—and how they would react to such language. One student sympathized with Ngũgĩ, explaining that Americans should not be upset, because Ngũgĩ was only defending his native country. Another student thought that it was heartening to know that the intended readers were ordinary Kenyans. These responses show that Ngũgĩ's often strong positions need not stand in the way of cross-cultural dialogue.

I point out to students the linguistic layers in *Devil on the Cross*: Gĩkũyũ is the main discourse language, English the language of exploitation, and Kiswahili primarily the language of a questionable nationalistic discourse. As Mikhail Bakhtin notes, languages "do not *exclude* each other, but rather intersect with each other in many different ways" (*Dialogic Imagination* 291). The English translation of *Devil* retains phrases and passages in Kiswahili and Gĩkũyũ that highlight cultural and nationalistic elements pertaining to Kenya and its history. One needs to note the role of each language in the discourse and to consider the role reversal in which English becomes subservient to Gĩkũyũ.

In addition, Ngũgĩ links italicized English words in *Devil* with exploitation. English words and expressions such as "criminals," "thieves and robbers," "time is money" and "time is robbing time," "Kenya's own millionaires, billionaires, multi-millionaires, multi-billionaires" refer to exploitation. The author demonstrates how English, a language of power, is linked to capitalist exploitation and acculturation under neocolonialism. In a passage that draws laughter from the students and generates debate, one of the "Devil's Angels" addresses the capitalists in the cave:

> As for my children, [. . . a]ll of them speak English through the nose, exactly like people born and brought up in England. If you were to hear them speak Gĩkũyũ or Kiswahili, you would laugh until you pissed yourself. *It is so funny.* They speak the two languages as if they were Italian priests newly arrived from Rome—priests without priestly collars. (109–10)

Students begin to see Ngũgĩ's literary language in the context of a broader national and transnational discourse that Frantz Fanon talks about in *The Wretched of the Earth*, which alienates the elites from the common people.

The code switching in *Devil* is one of Ngũgĩ's anticolonial and anti-neocolonial rhetorical strategies. A speaker says, "*By the way, Miss Kareendi*, what are your plans *this weekend*? I would like you to accompany me on a small safari—*what do you say to that?*" (20). The English words reveal that he belongs to the elite class, the educated who are far removed from the reality facing common Kenyans.

Overall, students appreciate the depth of the writer's vision in both *River* and *Devil* when they can negotiate his complex linguistic landscape. They leave the classroom knowing that there is a Gĩkũyũ text out there and that reading an anglophone African novel is not the same as reading typical Anglo-American productions. In both his English and Gĩkũyũ fiction, Ngũgĩ has an English-speaking audience in mind. He also appears to write for students such as the one who said she had never been taught African literature or culture as anything but an experience of the other. Studying Ngũgĩ at the level of language means that students read African literature not simply in relation to the United States but as a complex expression of a multiply connected culture.

NOTES

[1] Ngũgĩ insists, "The fundamental opposition in Africa today is between imperialism and capitalism, on the one hand, and national liberation and socialism, on the other" (*Writers* 78–79), and the United States is cast as the leader of this imperialism. The point might be made to students that his hardening ideological stand in his later novels and in his statements in *Decolonising the Mind* is connected with his decision to write in Gĩkũyũ.

[2] I recommend that students read Ngũgĩ's *Homecoming* and *Moving the Centre*; Gikandi's "Round Table"; and Cheah, *Spectral Nationality* 349–80.

[3] Graduate students, particularly those interested in stylistics, may wish to consider how Ngũgĩ Africanizes his English. Kasanga and Kalume explain that Ngũgĩ was "keen to maintain a great number of Kiswahili and Gĩkũyũ items, syntactic structures, and even resorted to coinages and nativization of some speech function" (49).

[4] Mudimbe calls these players a "trinity" who worked out the modalities of exploiting Africans and other peoples during the spread of colonialism (46–47).

Contextualizing Untranslated Moments in Ngũgĩ's Prose and Drama

Evan Mwangi

Ngũgĩ wa Thiong'o's writing in both English and Gĩkũyũ contains numerous untranslated terms whose presence seems to assume the existence of a multilingual reader. The terms need to be explained to students, because it is unlikely that teachers will find themselves in a classroom, even in Ngũgĩ's native Kenya, where every learner understands Gĩkũyũ.[1] Some names in Ngũgĩ's work are symbolic, conveying a certain quality in a character, and may not be used by people in real life (e.g., Gĩcaamba, Kĩgũũnda, Gũthera, Thoni, Boy, Matigari, Karendi). Others are names in the Gĩkũyũ community (e.g., Mwaũra, Ruhiu, Wangarĩ, Remi, Gathoni, Gikonyo, Mũthoni, Kĩĩoi, Ndugĩre, Warĩĩnga, Karega, Wanja) but used ironically by Ngũgĩ to evoke special meanings. While Carol Sicherman's well-documented resource book *Ngũgĩ wa Thiong'o: A Bibliography of Primary and Secondary Sources, 1957–1987* has done excellent work in explaining the meanings of names and cultural institutions in Ngũgĩ's work, some of the fictional terms need to be contextualized for students to appreciate them. Contextualization will also help explain things that Ngũgĩ refers to in untranslated moments: the language issue, the class struggle, gender positions, and female genital cutting.[2]

On the basis of my experience teaching Ngũgĩ's fiction and drama at various levels in the United States and Kenya, I offer ways of helping students contextualize Gĩkũyũ and Swahili words that are left untranslated. I explain some of the gains and losses in the translated texts that students need to be aware of. Instead of teaching these works as African literature in English, I look at them as translations, because even the novels, plays, and short stories written in English before Ngũgĩ said his dramatic farewell to the language as a medium of creative writing were conceived in Gĩkũyũ and translated mentally into English.[3]

The Participatory Approach

In all my courses, whether they deal with literary theory, literary criticism, African literature, or postcolonial studies, I incorporate a text or two by Ngũgĩ, because his arguments stir debate in the classroom and because his work lends itself to comparison with that of other writers, from Africa and elsewhere in the world. But whenever I have taught him—at the University of Nairobi, Ohio University, and Northwestern University, at both the undergraduate and graduate levels—I have had to address translation questions. In Nairobi, the classes were big, at times numbering as many as two hundred students. They focused on Ngũgĩ's earlier novels, which the students could use when they became high school teachers. Except for a couple of exchange students from America and Turkey, the students at the University of Nairobi were Kenyan nationals, but they came from different ethnic backgrounds and did not all understand Gĩkũyũ. The Gĩkũyũ words had to be handled with care. A word like *kĩhĩĩ* ("uncircumcised boy") would be offensive to communities that did not circumcise their males. At Ohio University, the classes were smaller (averaging about forty students), but they were much less diverse than in Nairobi. At Northwestern, they were even smaller but more diverse, with students from America, Europe, Asia, and Africa. Those from Africa, including Kenyans, were not fluent in Gĩkũyũ.

In freshmen courses, Ngũgĩ's books are well received by the students because of their use of popular culture and their treatment of such emotionally changed themes as colonialism and gender oppression. Following suggestions by students in course evaluations in a third-year class in African literature at Northwestern, I try to incorporate an early and later Ngũgĩ novel so that the shifts in the author's views can be seen. The longer and more complex works, such as *Petals of Blood* and *Wizard of the Crow,* are better taught at the graduate level. I have used them, with *Devil on the Cross,* to discuss the intersection of realist and antirealist techniques in African literature. At both the University of Nairobi and Ohio University, I taught Ngũgĩ's oeuvre, including his Gĩkũyũ poetry, with an emphasis on language and gender issues.

I recommend a participatory approach, because Ngũgĩ believes that the failure of institutions in Africa results from not involving ordinary people in decision making. His fiction and drama suggest that the colonial government and the missionaries failed to transform African institutions positively because of the Europeans' reluctance to involve local communities. Students enjoy discussing the issues that Ngũgĩ raises and role-playing scenes and situations from his prose and drama. Writing short response papers builds confidence in their reading skills, especially when they come from a non-African background and feel inadequate to handle foreign literature. Undergraduates students explore Ngũgĩ's relevance, the parallels between the society presented in his work and conditions in the developed world and in their personal lives. Sixty-second papers at the end of a lesson, in which students write anonymously about what they failed to understand or what they learned, can help the teacher explain the text and the context in further detail at the beginning of the next lesson and also evaluate the effectiveness of the teaching.

Female Genital Cutting and Translation in The River Between

Ngũgĩ considers his early works products of a naive phase in his ideological development, before he started analyzing the world from a Marxist perspective. But I find them particularly appealing to students, perhaps because the works deal with the problems of young people from the perspective of a young author. They are open-ended and ambivalent on sensitive issues in a way that makes them amenable to classroom debate. *The River Between*'s presentation of female genital cutting is a good example. Describing the conflict between European and African cultures, the novel occupies the same place as Chinua Achebe's *Things Fall Apart* in giving students a glimpse of the complexity of precolonial Africa.

Although Ngũgĩ is famous in Africa, most American students have not heard about him, but some have read *Things Fall Apart* before their freshman year. They should all be encouraged to read it in order to appreciate better *The River Between*. While the percentage of students who have not heard about Ngũgĩ remains constant, the percentage familiar with Achebe rises every year, probably because Achebe is becoming part of the high school English and cultural studies curricula in the United States.

Ngũgĩ's novel, like Achebe's, points to the possibility of peaceful coexistence between Western values and African practices. Without celebrating imperialism, both authors show Africans accepting positive aspects of Western culture and abandoning their own antidevelopment practices without abandoning their culture. But *The River Between* is ambivalent about female genital cutting; it does not come out as strongly against it as students would like. The novel confirms for students the stereotype of Africa as a continent that does not respect women's rights, but the female genital cutting it presents is not as severe as that carried out in many parts of Africa.[4] Achebe's novel, which is likely the only African novel the students have read before coming to *The River Between*, is wrongly interpreted in Western institutions as an Afrocentric rejection of all things Western; students see it as supporting female circumcision in opposition to Christian modernity. Achebe's presentation of Okonkwo's typical African masculinism is mistaken for an endorsement of his behavior. Further, West African novels, such as *Things Fall Apart* or Flora Nwapa's *Efuru*, treat female genital cutting so subtly that nonindigenous people miss references to it. Described euphemistically as "taking a bath," the practice is not condemned in the novels as strongly as, for example, the killing of twins.[5]

It is not surprising, then that students believe that Ngũgĩ endorses female circumcision as a social practice that helps Africans retain their cultural purity in the face of colonial predation. Yet a few untranslated moments in *The River Between* signal that he is opposed to the practice. He finds it repugnant but does not want to condemn it in the Eurocentric grammar of missionaries and colonial administrators.[6] For a perspective critical of Ngũgĩ's presentation of female circumcision, students should read Elleke Boehmer's "The Master's Dance to the Master's Voice," which argues that Ngũgĩ sacrifices women's agency to the nationalist and socialist project in his writing, where women are used as props for ideology. Brendon Nicholls's "Clitoridectomy and Gikuyu Nationalism in Ngũgĩ wa Thiong'o's *The River Between*" makes the same argument. But is Ngũgĩ really a neonationalist who finds redeeming value in female circumcision? Other critics, such as Patrick Williams, argue against the position that he presents women as lacking agency (*Ngũgĩ* 33–35). For Williams, female genital cutting is a practice through which women seize agency in a male-dominated colonial world.

Most of the criticism against Achebe and Ngũgĩ comes from Western-based white feminists. I ask students to make their own arguments against female genital cutting and compare them with those made by the missionaries in the novel in the banning of the practice. The scientific and feminist reasons that the students provide are usually different from the patronizing dismissal by the missionaries. It becomes clear that the missionaries' project is not feminist; it is imperialistic, an example of what Gayatri Chakravorty Spivak famously called, in the Indian colonial context, "White men saving brown women from brown men" ("Can the Subaltern" 297). Though they appear benevolent in their opposition to oppressive practices, the missionaries and colonial officers in *The River Between* do not have the welfare of non-Western women at heart. In fact, women who underwent the practice were punished by the church and expelled from mission schools instead of being given refuge there.

I request a student volunteer to read a paragraph in chapter 14 of the novel, in which circumcision is seemingly defended:

> Circumcision was an important ritual to the tribe. It kept people together, bound the tribe. It was at the core of the social structure, and something that gave meaning to a man's life. End the custom and the spiritual basis of the tribe's cohesion and integration would be no more. The cry was up. Gikuyu Karinga. Keep the tribe pure. Tutikwenda Irigu. It was a soul's cry, a soul's wish. (68)[7]

In African studies, the term *tribe* is discouraged as a descriptor of an African society. But by using it here and at various key moments in the novel, especially those involving Muthoni after her circumcision, the novelist is not necessarily looking down on his culture. The word appears as the English equivalent of *rurĩrĩ* ("nation"), there being no Gĩkũyũ word for *tribe*. In the English context the expressions "Gĩkũyũ Karinga" and "Tutikwenda Irigu" present a difficulty for the reader, even an indigenous Gĩkũyũ reader. The novel italicizes all the non-English words it uses and, further, translates them, signaling to the reader its theme of cultural synthesis, yet the Gĩkũyũ in this paragraph is neither italicized nor translated.

The use of the words is reminiscent of the defamiliarization device that Victor Shklovsky advances in "Art as Technique." Locating literariness in the way a text deautomatizes language by making familiar experiences unfamiliar, he argues that the purpose of art is "to increase the difficulty and length of perception because the process of perception is an aesthetic end in itself and must be prolonged" (800). Ngũgĩ does this well in *The River Between*, using Gĩkũyũ words for estrangement. One has to pay attention to who is speaking in the story to appreciate the author's position on the issues that the Gĩkũyũ words express.

For instance, the narrator distances himself from the term applied to women who have not undergone genital cutting: "*irĩgũ*."[8]

Because the Gĩkũyũ words are not italicized, it might appear as if Ngũgĩ is domesticating into English these statements in support of female genital cutting and in pursuit of ethnic purity. But this passage describes the views of those who advocate pure Gĩkũyũ (*Gĩkũyũ karĩng'a*). The narrator disempowers the advocates by not supplying the English. They suffer from cultural insularity, inaccessible to a non-Gĩkũyũ audience. The orthography indicates problems in representing Gĩkũyũ in English—problems that were later addressed by a committee on which Ngũgĩ sat (Biersteker, "Gĩkũyũ Literature" 310). Though the tilde had been incorporated by the United Gĩkũyũ Language Committee in 1949 to distinguish vowel height, it is not used in *Gĩkũyũ karĩng'a* ("pure *Gĩkũyũ*") and *tũtikwenda irĩgũ* ("we don't want uncircumcised women"). By reproducing the purists' mantras in the present tense and in the original language but without quotation marks, the narrator mocks people like Kabonyi, who fail to understand that although rites of passage are important, they need not include the cutting of women's bodies and that the society should replace that initiation rite with one that is gender-sensitive. Further, the text suggests that the ethnic purity to which Kabonyi aspires is an illusion, because as long as the school offers modern education, it cannot be *karĩng'a*. The songs in praise of modern learning, with which Waiyaki's students move their parents to tears, are borrowed not from English but from neighboring communities, indicating that modern education has spread to other areas and the society can borrow from other African societies instead of insisting on nativist purity. *Karinga* in the novel can be read as a contested sign: Kabonyi and his followers mouth it not to pursue tribal purity but to contradict Waiyaki and seize supremacy.

As in Ngũgĩ's overtly socialist novels, which come later, the characters' names in *The River Between* are symbolic though their symbolism will not be evident to a non-Gĩkũyũ speaker, as the names are left untranslated. The underlying theme is the need to abandon claims to cultural purity made by those supporting female circumcision. Kabonyi's name could be an intended anagram of Nyokabi, a name that features in *Weep Not, Child*.[9] A woman's name, *Nyokabi* means "one who originally came from Ukabi, the land of the Maasai." Bearing a name that does not exist in Gĩkũyũ culture indicates that Kabonyi, despite his hostility to things foreign, is himself a foreigner. The name tells the reader that Kabonyi's fundamentalist position in favor of cultural purity is self-serving and self-contradictory. Nyambura's name, on the other hand, is a common Gĩkũyũ name but has a prefix (*nya-*) borrowed from the Luo culture, the supposed nemesis of the Gĩkũyũs. *Nyambura* means "the one who brings rain." Unlike her sister Muthoni (a common Gĩkũyũ name, reserved for children named after their father's mother-in-law), Nyambura does not undergo genital cutting. Given the predominance of the river and water in the novel, Nyambura symbolizes the future of the nation, while the circumcised Muthoni (the in-law) is the foreigner. Although he contrasts her with Nyambura and has her die from her wound after circumcision, Ngũgĩ does not condemn Muthoni the way the missionaries cursed circumcised girls in central Kenya in the 1930s. He pays her the respect due to an in-law. Her name suggests *thoni* (Gĩkũyũ for "shyness"), like the shy character Thoni in *The Black Hermit,* which was written around the same time as *The River Between,* while Ngũgĩ was a student at Makerere University College, and Gathoni in Ngũgĩ and Ngũgĩ wa Mĩriĩ's *Ngaahika Ndeenda* (*I Will Marry When I Want*).

In *The River Between,* Muthoni does not show the deference that her name evokes. As Williams notes, she is one of the most transgressive female characters in African literature (*Ngũgĩ* 33–34). Indeed, during the ritual dances, it is Waiyaki who comes across as *muthoni*, shy to join in the revelry as Muthoni dances with abandon. But Nyambura takes the transgression further, because after Muthoni sneaks out of the church to get circumcised, Nyambura openly protests against her draconian father in front of his congregation. Students see that protest is possible without having to harm one's body. Ultimately, the class appreciates that Ngũgĩ opposes female genital cutting as a rite of passage. His point in the novel is that the missionaries and the colonial government should not use the practice to demonize the Africans and rationalize colonialism or to dismiss wholesale African cultures as barbaric.

Children's Books and the Theme of Language

Ngũgĩ's children's books, composed in Gĩkũyũ in the 1980s, at the height of his preoccupation with the mother tongue debate, help us understand those aspects of language that Ngũgĩ advocates in his essays and novels. It is hard to teach these stories, because not all have been translated into English. They are pervaded by English words, phrases, and narratives, which we also find in his Gĩkũyũ novel *Matigari ma Njirũũngi,* where long passages in English are left untranslated into Gĩkũyũ. The children's stories show students the persistant influence of English culture on former British colonies in Africa. Although Ngũgĩ is against English as a colonial language, it haunts his writing in Gĩkũyũ—including the most anticolonial texts for child readers, who could not have experienced classical colonialism in Kenya.

The three Njamba Nene children's stories depict the adventures of a boy (*Njamba Nene* in Gĩkũyũ means "great hero") who bears the same name as Nyakinyua's heroic husband and freedom fighter in Ngũgĩ's *Petals of Blood.* The stories instruct young readers in anti-imperialism, which is seen as a taking up of arms against an oppressive political order. They advocate a cultural renaissance and make fun of those who embrace a Western value system. Njamba Nene fights a guerrilla war against the British colonizers and their African cronies. A staunch believer in the traditional culture, he urges the use of the mother tongue and local knowledge in modern cultural production. The stories are *Njamba Nene na Mbaathi ĩ Mathagu*, published in Gĩkũyũ in 1982 and in an English translation by Wangũi wa Goro as *Njamba Nene and the Flying Bus* in 1986; *Bathitoora ya Njamba Nene*, published in Gĩkũyũ in 1984 and in English as *Njamba Nene's Pistol* by Wangũi wa Goro in 1986; and *Njamba Nene na Cibũ Kĩng'ang' i* ("Njamba Nene and Chief Kĩng'ang'i"), published so far only in Gĩkũyũ, in 1986. In *Njamba Nene na Cibũ Kĩng'ang'i*, the young hero successfully avenges the death of his mother at the hands of an African colonial chief, King'ang'i (the name derives from the Gĩkũyũ word for crocodile). Aided by a girl, Njeeri, Njamba Nene raids a colonial post sarcastically called Hiti Ke ("For you to eat, Mr. Hyena"), where the colonial government killed his mother. He wounds Chief King'ang'i. Impersonating a doctor and nurse, Njamba Nene and Njeeri follow him to the emergency room and finish him off.

Ngũgĩ uses the texts to reverse the linguistic influence of neoimperialism by inspiring in children an interest in literatures in local languages—but even here he seems to assume a child readership that is already steeped in the Englishness that he is attempting to dismantle. In *Njamba Nene na Mbaathi ĩ Mathagu*, Ngũgĩ attacks the English language. John Bull, Njamba Nene's brainwashed African teacher, leads the African children in a song in English, which, when sung as a Gĩkũyũ song, yields absurdity:

Raandanĩci Mbaana	London's burner
Raandanĩci Mbaana	London's burner
Rũkũ rwa nda	Firewood in the belly
Rũkũ rwa nda	Firewood in the belly
Baaya nĩ Baaya	Fire is fire
Baaya nĩ Baaya	Fire is fire
Boro nĩ wota	Boro, warm yourself
Boro nĩ wota.	Boro, warm yourself
	(*Njamba Nene na Mbaathi* 10; *Njamba Nene and the Flying Bus* 12)[10]

The Gĩkũyũ song is meaningless, an empty imitation of the English song "London's Burning," which commemorates the 1666 Great Fire of London:

London's burning, London's burning,
Look yonder! Look yonder!
Fire, fire! Fire, fire!
Pour on water, pour on water! (Bullock 13)

The children think they are culturally superior in singing this song instead of the Gĩkũyũ children's poetry that Njamba Nene presents, but they are singing nonsense. Although London is dispossessed by the fire, the children interpret London as possessing the burner. Boro (a rare Gĩkũyũ name, found in *Weep Not, Child*) is invited to warm himself by the fireside (*ota*). Child readers will not understand the linguistic palimpsest behind Ngũgĩ's humor unless they know the English nursery rhyme that is being mimicked. The assumption in the story is that Njamba Nene's schoolmates do know it and therefore appreciate the parody and the teacher's misusage.[11]

Aware of the difficulty of teaching Ngũgĩ's works in Gĩkũyũ to students who do not speak the language, I read aloud the first few passages of *Njamba Nene na Cibũ Kĩng'ang'i* and *Mũrogi wa Kagogo* (*Wizard of the Crow*) in Gĩkũyũ, so students can hear localized versions of English words in these works. Njamba Nene's mother is killed at the "*bũũthiti-inĩ ya Hiti-Ke*" (1; "Hiti-Ke Post"), *post* being localized as *bĩĩthiti.* In *Mũrogi wa Kagogo,* the first content word in the long novel is *thiorĩ* ("theory"), expressing the speculation about the president's strange illness. Providing students with the visual appearance of the Gĩkũyũ narratives also shows them how colonial structures are deeply entrenched in local African lives. In the Gĩkũyũ edition of *Matigari ma Njirũũngi*, as Matigari searches for his home, which is now occupied by neocolonialists, we encounter Nyakerũ (a white man) and Nyakairũ (his black crony) conversing in English (38-46).[12] That their dialogue is given in italics but not translated into Gĩkũyũ indicates that the Gĩkũyũ reader has no problem understanding the highly idiomatic conversation between the two. The cover of *Njamba Nene na Cibu King'ang'i* shows the young "doctor" Njamba Nene and the "nurse" Njeeri going to what is inscribed in English as the "casualty" ward.

The Novels of Disillusionment

In Ngũgĩ's political novels of disillusionment, untranslated expressions signal the unfulfilled promise of political liberation. The narrator of *A Grain of Wheat* reiterates as a song interlude the untranslated ditty referring to the ancestral founders of the ethnic group (Gĩkũyũ and Mũmbi). The song underlines the plight of the community under colonialism and neocolonialism:

> Gĩkũyũ na Mumbi
> Gĩkũyũ na Mumbi
> Gĩkũyũ na Mumbi
> Nikihiu ngwatiro. (106)

"Nikuhiu ngwatiro" ("it is burnt at the handle," "the situation is bad," "life is intolerable") points to the dysfunctional status of the nation under colonialism. The image of a tool whose handle has been burned reminds readers of Gikonyo the carpenter, whom we encounter just before the outbreak of the Mau Mau war fixing a new handle. He must leave his shop to fight in the bush, yet after independence the nation is still out of joint. Even characters like Gikonyo (meaning "navel" or "umbilical cord") who have taken over the mantle of leadership cannot fix the problems facing the independent nation or deliver it from its neocolonial shackles.

Students are intrigued by the untranslated chant *Thai thathaiya Ngai, Thaai* ("peace and praises to God") that we hear as the call for prayer among the fighters (21). In contemporary Kenya, the ancient words evoke not reverence for God, as they used to during the period portrayed in the novel, but Gĩkũyũ ethnic chauvinism. Twenty years later, Ngũgĩ reincarnates the chant in *Matigari* (1986) in a strategy that uses a traditional practice to confront the excesses of the neocolonial government. In the 1980s and after, expressions like *Thai thathaiya Ngai, Thaai* were perverted by tribalist organizations like the dreaded Mungiki (a violent nativist underground organization that advocates, among other things, the forcible circumcision of women) into a call for Gĩkũyũ supremacy. Most Gĩkũyũs would be hesitant to utter the chant, viewing such holy words with dread. Writers living in exile may be unaware of changes like this one happening in their culture.[13]

Before his fatal shooting by Kihika's gun, the colonial district officer Thomas Robson mouths Swahili words that are left untranslated and unitalicized despite their centrality in grounding the irony of the scene and in revealing the sadism of colonialism. The words also demonstate that a local language can be used to block the interests of the community:

> Near the jeep, his teeth could be heard chattering and clicking, so that Tom was forced to laugh. "Usiogope Mzee," he called jovially as if to reassure the man. "Tom will not eat you." Suddenly the old man straightened himself, whipped something from his pocket, and two thick shots thudded into Tom's body. Before the frightened policemen could do anything, the man had jumped across the hedge, towards the Indian shops.
>
> (*Grain* 187)

Usiogope mzee means "Don't fear, old man" or "Take it easy, old man." The colonial officer thinks that Kihika, a dangerous freedom fighter, is a helpless old man like the ones he is used to harassing at the height of colonial rule in the 1950s. Although the word *mzee* ("old") indicates respect, Tom uses it to express his contempt for the ordinary African man.

Ngũgĩ also uses untranslated or mistranslated Africanisms when Gikonyo promises to carve a stool for Mumbi, a symbol of their reconciliation. The species of the wood is untranslated: "He would carve the stool from a Muiri stem, a hardwood that grew around Kirinyaga and Nyandarwa hills" (244). The statement defines *Prunus africana* in Gĩkũyũ terms, from Gikonyo's perspective. Because the tree grows in other areas, beyond that context, *muiri* suggests the narrow-mindedness with which members of the Kenyan elite, like Gikonyo, define African concepts and practices, a narrow-mindedness that will be the bane of the continent. In the novel we have already seen that the local leadership has betrayed the ideals of the war of freedom. Gikonyo betrayed the oath by developing a capitalist business. Despite his possible reconciliation with Mumbi as the novel comes to an end, his view of things will remain narrow, contaminated by the profiteering instinct.

This self-interest is underlined by an untranslated proverb uttered by Warui, one of the old men in the story: "It is the old saying come true: *Kamwene kabagio ira*" (172). The proverb, roughly equivalent to "Charity begins at home," refers to the Gĩkũyũ initiation ceremony in which a boy is given *ira* (whitish cold stuff) to numb his penis before circumcision. The proverb expresses the need to take special care of the local and individual. Ngũgĩ's use of Gĩkũyũ without translation spurs readers to seek its meaning. The kind of participatory reading he desires will result. It also metalinguistically forecasts the author's decision to start writing in his mother tongue. At the same time, the proverb is ironic: the attitude of characters using the untranslated language resembles the ethnocentricism and nepotism of the leadership in postcolonial Kenya.

Untranslated Taboo Language in Petals of Blood

Petals of Blood leaves Gĩkũyũ taboo words untranslated, yet translated taboo words are used liberally, even when they are transcribed from an oral text. Their presence in the novel, as later in *Devil on the Cross,* implies the triumph of evil in a postcolony that is now defined by dirtiness and degeneracy. In *Petals of Blood* and *Devil on the Cross*, Ngũgĩ delivers swear words in the register of the male. Women in the lawyer Chui's home, for example, sing a sexually innocuous but politically laden song: Irish potatoes are peeled at the home of Kenya's first lady, Ngina (*Petals* 145–50, 207–09).[14] In the song, Irish potatoes are equated with modernization (*ngirigaca* is "agriculture") as opposed to the more traditional tubers, and Ngina is the role model for Gĩkũyũ women who have embraced modernity. When the men take over the song, they sing of female circumcision, using expressions that the author dares not put in his mother tongue; the expressions are given in English but truncated with dashes because they are so offensive, referring to female genitalia with greater force than English equivalents, there being no neutral word in Gĩkũyũ for the vagina. The narrator seems to be happy with the song, describing the taboo parts as "juicy sections" (150).

After the Ilmorog residents partake of the traditional brew, they utter obscenities openly in the traditional songs they sing. The taboo words are either unscripted or euphemized in translation. Njuguna and Nyakinyua—the Ilmorog male elder and female elder, respectively—are particularly outrageous in the parts they sing (207–09). Their words are translated into English, which is not as strong as the language used in the circumcision song sung in Gĩkũyũ (150). The text thus cleans up the obscenities of the traditional culture while invoking them as a gesture against capitalistic modernity. The euphemisms and silences do not fully erase Gĩkũyũ patriarchy and its obsessions. When debating the relative importance of male and female categories, Njuguna says, "Is it not a man who sleeps, *hmmm! hmmm!* You know where?" (162). The "*hmmm! hmmm!*"

replaces an obscenity that refers to sexual activity. The new expression defers meaning for greater effect, to Njuguna's amusement.

The text also gives women taboo expressions. When Munira's mucus accidentally flies into Nyakinyua's face, the Gĩkũyũ words the old woman uses in reaction are taboo, designating a woman's sexual organ (7). Although the Dutton edition of the novel explains in a footnote that the words are "[a] curse expressing shock" (*Petals* [1978] 7), no translation is provided, because their foulness cannot be expressed in any other language. Their italicization on the printed page draws readers' attention to their indecency. Abdulla jokingly uses a worse version of the expression when ordering a beer for Munira: "Gatutu Gaka, bring another beer" (11). The untranslated expression is a variant term for the female genitalia; the sense is "you undersized cunt." Later, Abdulla takes pleasure in repeating an Indian's Swahili swearwords that refer to a mother's genitalia (253). The expression collocates with the Swahili word for female genitalia and the Gĩkũyũ word *nyukua*, a derogatory term for "mother." This is the kind of language that one would encounter in a Kenyan bar. With Abdulla's expression, Ngũgĩ signifies that women in the postcolony have become such a degraded category that even otherwise admirable characters use misogynistic vulgarity to express themselves.

Swearwords come from drunkards or from old people like Nyakinyua or Njuguna, who in Gĩkũyũ culture may use language that a young person, such as Wanja in the novel, may not. Nyakinyua utters words like *nduri* ("cunts") often because as an old woman she is no threat to the Gĩkũyũ patriarchy; her expletives, for all their dirtiness, are to be read as part of the novel's attempt at humor. Although Nyakinyua's insults are in Gĩkũyũ, they do not sound as offensive as Wanja's rant, in English, against her "cunt . . . this hole" (293).

Gĩcaandĩ and the Untranslated Preface in Devil on the Cross

Usually overlooked in the reading of *Devil on the Cross* is an untranslated preface in the original, *Caitaani Mũtharaba-inĩ*. A reading of the preface in a postcolonial literature class, in which this novel was one of the primary texts, revealed that Ngũgĩ prefers a participatory, reader-response approach to his work. I provided a translation of the preface in which he urges readers to construct their own meanings and not be sympathetic to the novel just because it was written in prison. The story is presented as the oral account of a self-declared traditional artist who also gives himself the grand titles Gĩcaandĩ Player and Prophet of Justice. Initially, there seems to be some correspondence between Ngũgĩ and the narrator, but they part ways as the story develops. Because the narrator's account is incomplete, the novel calls on readers to offer a counternarrative, an alternative to the way the male gĩcaandĩ artist frames the stories of women and the nation in his text. Compared with other kinds of verbal performance in the novel—for example, the thieves' verbal competition in the den—the artist's use of language is revealed to be a failure. The artist acquires the aspect of a clown as the story unfolds, despite the grand delivery expected of him.

Students see that Ngũgĩ distances himself from the gĩcaandĩ artist who tells the story. The artist is incompetent, insensitive to women, and cavalier in his treatment of weighty themes. Students note that the preface points to the unreliability of the male frame narrator. Ngũgĩ has commented on the oral and gendered imperatives that structure his novels.[15] The story may appear simplistic, obvious, and moralizing in its politics, but the preface shows students the irony that attaches to its narrator.

So that students will develop their argument further, I have them examine the narrator's failure in performance. We consider the various ways in which gĩcaandĩ is defined as a poetic and political cultural activity. A highly specialized and stylized art form, gĩcaandĩ is a genre of Gĩkũyũ poetry that encodes all aspects of Gĩkũyũ life in riddling, performed publicly by contesting poets. The inability to encode a message in metaphor or decode the metaphor of a fellow poet disqualifies a contestant. Gĩcaandĩ is also the instrument (a gourd engraved with hieroglyphs) that the oral artists rattle as they dance and riddle with other artists and the audience.[16] Members of the audience are expected to be active participants in the contest. The hieroglyphs on the gĩcaandĩ gourd indicate a poet's mastery of the techniques employed to cloak political statements in metaphor. The performance is assessed for its subversion and sophistication.[17] Students understand that the artist in the novel is quite different from the idea of an artist as presented in the preface and in various essays by Ngũgĩ. They see that although postcolonial theory insists that African literature parodies Western texts, Ngũgĩ does not spare indigenous practices and art forms from both criticism and mimicry.

Wizard of the Crow and Anglophone Gĩkũyũ

Written in exile, *Mũrogi wa Kagogo* (*Wizard of the Crow*) wins Ngũgĩ credit for capturing the dynamics of the Gĩkũyũ language, which had changed tremendously since he left the country over twenty years before. In the Gĩkũyũ original, the novel is published in three volumes: the first volume, *Mũrogi wa Kagogo: Mbuku ya Mbere na Kerĩ*, contains books 1 and 2 and came out in 2004; the second volume, *Mũrogi wa Kagogo: Mbuku ya Gatatũ*, is book 3 and came out in 2006; the third volume, *Mũrogi wa Kagogo: Mbuku ya Kana, Gatano, Gatandatũ*, containing the rest of the story, came out in 2007. That the translation appeared a year before the whole of the original appeared demonstrates to students the inequality in the publishing of European and African languages: the African languages are obviously at a disadvantage. Student also see that a translation is not necessarily inferior to its original. In *Wizard of the Crow*, the original and the translation influenced each other, as Ngũgĩ changed some parts of the original to echo the translation: his Gĩkũyũ text often borrows from the English version.

Gĩkũyũ now is anglophone and highly globalized: its use demonstrates not only its interaction with other languages of the world and its speakers' interaction with cultural texts from across the globe but also its capacity to express the new phenomena that globalization has brought to African societies. The narrator, a hybridized character, interacts with people who speak a heteroglossic Gĩkũyũ that takes words from Kiswahili and English. Words like *mithiamu* ("museum"), *randiko* ("radical"), *mbayongiraba* ("biographer"), *reboriuconi* ("revolution"), *nũtimbũkũ* ("notebook"), and *thubawanda* ("super wonder") are borrowed from English and used the way they would be spoken by a Gĩkũyũ person with some knowledge of English. Not fully integrated into the Gĩkũyũ vocabulary, they have a specialized register: not used in everyday discourse but only when one is referring to something in English and expressing it in Gĩkũyũ. The narrator could have used a Kiswahili loan word for mosque (*mũthigiti*, from *Musikiti*), for example, but he borrows the word from English, *mothiki*.[18]

In the novel, Ngũgĩ incorporates Sheng, a macaronic language of city youth that would be incomprehensible to non-Swahili speakers. In both Gĩkũyũ and English texts, the Sheng expressions are left untranslated: "'*Hũi, sasa, story zako? Ni nini makalau wanakubringia kinaa. Nĩ haarĩ wanakuitia?*' Sikiokuu asked in Sheng" (389; "Hey, wazup! What do the cops want with you? Is it some sexy hussies they want to hook you up with?"). Sheng is seen as a perverted language, used in *Wizard* only by political crooks. Positively drawn young city people like Nyawira and Kamiti do not speak it, though in reality they would be using this hybrid language in African streets.

Paradoxically, in *Decolonising the Mind* Ngũgĩ praises workers in Sierra Leone and Nigeria for developing creoles and pidgins instead of using the elite Europhone language of the exploiter class. The intermixed languages "[owe] their identities to the syntax and rhythms of African languages" and are "kept alive in the daily speech, in the ceremonies, in political struggles, above all in the rich store of orature—proverbs, stories, poems, and riddles" (23). But in *Wizard* he gives this kind of language to the ruling elites, to mock them. That the elites speak an archaic and heavily Gĩkũyũ-leaning Sheng reveals the superficiality of their use of the language of young people as well as their exploitation of women: they abuse the state machinery, such as the police force, to get hapless women for personal gratification. The Sheng expression *Story zako?* ("What's going on?," "What's your story?") is drab and not as hip as, say, "*niaje?*" (a more current version of the equivalents for Kiswahili slang *sasa* or the English *wazzup*). The elites are using a language they cannot effectively appropriate. For example, Sikiokuu ("Big Ear") speaks Sheng in a stilted and dry way and in contexts that show not only his sexual depravity but also his delusion that he is still young.

Tajirika dismisses Sikiokuu's Sheng as outdated, but when he also tries to speak the language, his Sheng is even more outdated. Ngũgĩ puns: *ũceng'e ceng'i canini* is a contemptuous neologism for "to speak Sheng a little bit"(2: 115). *Canini*, spoken by Sikiokuu, does not exist in Gĩkũyũ; it is a corruption of *hanini* and alliterates with the Sheng term *ceng'i*. Ngũgĩ not only redomesticates the runaway slang back into mainstream Gĩkũyũ but also associates it with "*ũcoga*" ("homosexuality") in an incident in which Tajirika (Swahili for "get rich quickly") and Sikiokuu are talking in sexually laden terms.[19]

Ngũgĩ does not endorse Tajirika and Sikiokuu's project of investigating *ucoga*, because Tajirika's wife, Vinjinia, whom they suspect of lesbianism, is not necessarily involved with other women. But although these depraved and chauvinistic male characters mention *ũcoga* negatively and in a scene where they are celebrating their heterosexual virility with multiple women, Ngũgĩ suggests a repressed homoerotic relationship between them. Tajirika warns Sikiokuu, "I am not here to play *Fathe* and *Mathe*" (389). "*Fathe* and *Mathe*" involve the Sheng words, derived from "father" and "mother," for a game in which children play Dad and Mom. For two adult males to play *Fathe* and *Mathe* points to a homoeroticism that echoes Luce Irigaray's equation of capitalism with homosexuality (193). The reference to *ũcoga* occurs when Tajirika mouths Sheng words to convince himself that he has become younger. Ngũgĩ associates his corruption, the linguistic death he represents, and both characters' sexual depravity with homosexual inclinations.

Wizard is extremely playful, but much of the punning and some of the satire are lost in translation. In the Gĩkũyũ edition, the Ruler, the dictatorial head of state in the novel, is given not the secular equivalent name *Mũnene* but *Mwathani*, a name reserved for Jesus in the Gĩkũyũ bible, hymns, and prayer books. Further, reading sections of the novel in Gĩkũyũ helps students appreciate the music and often brutally sarcastic alliteration. The Gĩkũyũ edition is more playful—it provides its own Web site and e-mail address for those who would like to chat with the narrator online, in the opening paragraphs of "Mbuku ya Gatatũ" (book 3). These italicized and idiosyncratic addresses are dropped in the translation. The Web joke shows that Gĩkũyũ can carry the burden of the demands of the modern world, but the point is unnecessary to make in English, which is already accepted as a language of global communication.

Drama and Language

Ngũgĩ's dramas contain numerous untranslated words, especially in the songs and expletives. In *The Trial of Dedan Kimathi* (Ngũgĩ and Mugo), it is assumed that the characters speak Gĩkũyũ although the dialogue is in English. But sometimes it is in a language other than English, and directors in places in Africa where Kiswahili or Gĩkũyũ is not spoken must replace the lines with local expressions. Waitina, a colonial officer whose name is a corruption of Whitney to connote the Gĩkũyũ obscenity for "anus," harasses locals for not carrying passbooks:

Waitina: Leta karatasi yako.
First Man: Sina.
Waitina: *[Kick!]* Sina Afande! Rudia!
First Man: Sina Afande.
Waitina: Kazi yako?
First Man: Kulima.
Waitina: Mtu ya Kimathi?
First Man: Hapana. (7)

Waitina: Let me see your identification papers.
First Man: I don't have.
Waitina: I don't have, sir! Repeat that!
First Man: I don't have, sir!
Waitina: Your work?
First Man: Farming.
Waitina: Are you a Kimathi person?
First Man: No. (my trans.)

In the scene, enacted in Kiswahili and left untranslated, Waitina is a laughable authoritarian character who demands titles of respectability such as *afande* ("sir") from peasants who regard him as an asshole. He is made more ridiculous by his vanity and gluttony.

During the stage performance of the play, the naming of Waitina in the script loses its raison d'être, because the name does not feature anywhere in the dialogue. Despite the powerful institution of British colonialism that he represents, Whitney (Waitina) is demoted in the play to the level to which the colonial government has reduced its subjects. Like them, he is not named, and when an unverbalized sobriquet is given to him, it lowers him further, because it connotes a taboo term and possibly what the community considers a signifier of perverse sexuality. In Bakhtinian grotesque realism, he is ludicrous.

The Gĩkũyũ and Kiswahili versions of Ngũgĩ wa Thiong'o and Ngũgĩ wa Mĩriĩ's *Ngaahika Ndeenda* (*I Will Marry When I Want*) are not as masculinist as the English translation of the play. Land, which is the site of ideological contestation, is equated with the penis in a translational infelicity in which Ngũgĩ renders the proverb "*mundu ainaga na gatiru gake*" (*Ngaahika* 11; "one shows off one's little possession") as "[a] man brags about his own penis, / However tiny" (*I Will Marry* 4). *Mundu* in the original is gender-neutral, and the proverb's wording has no gender weight; the translation introduces into the play *man* and *his* as well as the male sexual organ. In ordinary conversation, *gatiru* means "a small piece," and the proverb metaphorizes Kĩgũũnda's pride in his small piece of land, which he acquired honestly, unlike the ill-gotten properties of his nemesis, Ahab Kĩĩoi wa Kanoru, whom he eventually defeats in a struggle between good and evil. To translate *gatiru* as "penis" reveals the unconscious gendered dimensions of the class struggle that Ngũgĩ and Ngũgĩ stage in *I Will Marry When I Want.*

Ngũgĩ's texts, whether in English or Gĩkũyũ, demand that readers be proficient in different languages—English, Gĩkũyũ, Kiswahili, Sheng. The omission of text in an English translation can reduce the original playfulness. In *Matigari,* the female translator, Wangũi wa Goro, makes the text more gender-conscious.[20] As the novel closes, the female character Gũthera's point of view dominates, but in the original more narratorial agency is given to the male character Mũriũki. The translation is interpretative, suggesting in sentences not in the original that Matigari might be a spirit instead of a corporeal and specifically gendered hero. The often repeated questions about Matigari include three that the translator adds to include women, like Gũthera, as "matigari ma njirũũngi" ("those who survived the colonial bullets in the fight for independence, those who will stage a new revolution against neoimperialism"):

> Who is Matigari? they asked one another. How on earth are we going to recognize him? What does he look like? What nationality is he? Is Matigari a man or woman anyway? Is he young or old? Is he fat or thin? *Is he real or just a figment of people's imagination? Who or what really is Matigari ma Njirũũngi? Is he a person, or is it a spirit?*
>
> (170; emphasis added)

In Gĩkũyũ, the pronouns are not gendered. Because Matigari is not a real name in the referential world, it could designate either a man or a woman; the same ambiguity applies to the name of the heroine, Gũthera. Wangũi wa Goro neutralizes the gender bias of the translation by adding sentences that say that Matigari is not necessarily male. In the above passage, the italicized sentences show that the female translator is attempting to feminize further an already feminist text by emphasizing the androgyny of the new revolutionaries. The original foregrounds Gũthera further in its punning on her name to indicate the link between the character and ideological awareness (*gũthera*), dawning (*gũthererũka*), and forward mass flow (*gũtherera*), which are constantly repeated in the narrative. It is clearer in the original than in the translation that one cannot be *matigari* (the new, post–Mau Mau revolutionary) without all the notions that Gũthera's name suggests.

In the Gĩkũyũ version, Mũriũki, the boy revolutionary, is given prominence as the future of the struggle. When describing their different exits from Matigari's Mercedes as the novel moves toward resolution (152), the English translation lessens that prominence. The passage reads:

> *Gũthera akiumĩra gatagatĩ-inĩ ga kĩhingo gĩa kĩgaanda na njĩra ya gũthĩ ndũnyũ.*

> *Maathiianga haniini, Mũriũki akiũma mwago-inĩ wa nywee ya maciindĩci.* (136)
>
> Gũthera got out somewhere between the factory gate and the road to the market place.
>
> After driving for some time, Mũriũki got out from the pleasures and the *nywee* ["smooth movement"] of the Mercedes. (my trans.)

Nywee, an ideophone, is lost in translation. Philip Noss argues that although ideophones are common to all languages, the mastery of an African language calls for a command of them. He also notes that ideophones are more prominent in African oral performance than in Western literate cultures (46). The dropping of an ideophone in translation may be found in what he calls "the receptor culture norm" (42). In the original, *nywee* indicates free indirect discourse, expressing the comical and childish delight of the person from whose point of view the event is relayed. It expresses onomatopoeically the smooth movement and comfort in the Mercedes as perceived by Mũriũki. The sentence is therefore filtered through Mũriũki. For Gũthera, there is no expression marking her perception of the car. Much of the story in Gĩkũyũ is focalized through Matigari or Mũriũki, but the translation presents some of the sections from her perspective, making it more woman-oriented than the original.

In translation, Ngũgĩ retains his characters' Swahili and Gĩkũyũ names to suggest subtly the extratextual setting of his works despite their frequent disavowals of specificity. The use of Swahili names in *Wizard* instead of their translations, even when they derive from an event that readers have witnessed in the story and even if the names are as absurd in Kiswahili as in any other language, suggests that the novel is about President Moi's Kenya (1978–2002).[21] Although the sobriquets of Ngũgĩ's characters are symbolic and sometimes extremely ironic, they cannot be rendered in English, because they would either be a mouthful or be meaningless. Their irony and symbolism are heightened by their expression in Gĩkũyũ in a way that is not obvious; their subtlety defies translation. The character names Muthoni, Gathoni, and Thoni derive from the same word, *thoni* ("shyness," "timidity"), yet they denote differences, which are compounded by the different contexts in which Ngũgĩ uses them. Unlike Ayi Kwei Armah, who borrows names from across Africa in his later writing without indicating their source, Ngũgĩ takes his characters' names from Gĩkũyũ culture or, more recently, from Kiswahili. Thus it is easy for students to get the meanings of these names from dictionaries. But readers should be aware that the names, steeped in culture and mythology, are accessible only in a larger context.[22]

Because Ngũgĩ's translation of his own work transforms the text to acquire nuances not in the original, it would be rewarding for Gĩkũyũ readers to engage with the texts in English as well. Ngũgĩ's translation fits with that proposed by Lawrence Venuti and by Gayatri Spivak ("Translating"), among other poststructuralist translation theorists, who deemphasize both fidelity to the original and domestication of the text to the target culture. Ngũgĩ retains Gĩkũyũ and Kiswahili words not only to signal the incommensurability between languages but also to avoid subsuming the marginalized languages of the global south into the dominant languages of the West. If translation is to be taken in the wider Derridean context to cover other forms of transformation, students can explore how Ngũgĩ translates the various works he cites in his own writing.

In *The River Between,* Ngũgĩ mines Jomo Kenyatta's functionalist anthropological study *Facing Mount Kenya* for details on Gĩkũyũ culture. But while Kenyatta, the founding president of Kenya and a nationalist, openly supports female genital cutting and equates the female rite of passage with male circumcision as a gesture against colonialism, Ngũgĩ is not enamored of such notions of cultural purity. The circumcision songs in the novel are elided, and scenes of women's circumcision are disnarrated or unnarrated. This is a metalinguistic technique theorized variously by Gerald Prince and Robyn Warhol, in which a narrative excludes details about an event and forces the reader to infer through a "retrospective filling-in" what happened (Prince 30). In Prince's formulation, nonnarration or unnarration

> comprises everything that according to a given narrative cannot be narrated or is not worth narrating—either because it transgresses a law (social, authorial, generic, formal), or because it defies the powers of a particular narrator (or of any narrator), or because it falls below the so-called threshold of narratability (it is not sufficiently unusual or problematic). (25–26)[23]

We know that Muthoni has undergone female genital cutting, but the actual event is excluded from the story. It cannot be put in the category of the irrelevant in a novel whose main conflict involves the banning of this rite of passage. The event is unnarrated in that by the time the novel was written, female genital cutting had become a taboo issue in Kenya.

The narrator also refuses to include the circumcision songs. When these songs appear in Ngũgĩ's later novels, it is in narratives that indicate that female genital cutting no longer happens. The songs are used to symbolize maturity of the mind rather than marks on the body.[24] Students observe that Ngũgĩ does not advocate culturalist retention of traditional practices, especially those inimical to women's rights. He supports society's translation into modernity as long as local voices are not excluded from debate and negotiation.

NOTES

[1] Kenya's national language is Kiswahili. Gĩkũyũ is spoken by the largest ethnic group, but this group constitutes only a fraction of the national population, which speaks over fifty languages. Kenyan students are fluent in Kiswahili and English but speak vari-

ous other ethnic languages not shared with everyone in class. Kenyan college students also speak Sheng, an urban patois that mixes Kiswahili, English, and ethnic languages. Though comprehensible across ethnic boundaries, Sheng is not accepted in class, and the mention of it in Ngũgĩ's *Wizard of the Crow* is negative. Explaining Ngũgĩ's untranslated terms would therefore be necessary even in his native country.

[2]I try to be neutral in discussing the practice of female genital cutting as a rite of passage, as presented in *The River Between*. I do not take sides in the debate on whether missionaries and the colonial administration were right to ban the practice while nationalist elements supported it. For discussion on the term to use—among *female genital cutting*, *female genital modification*, *female genital mutilation*, and *female circumcision*—see Lyons; Ntarangwi; and Prazak and Coffman. Because the subject is charged, students should be allowed to use the term they prefer as long as they can justify it.

[3]Ngũgĩ uses the term "mental translation" to designate a form of literary rendition in which the narrative is conceived in one language but presented to the reader in another ("Ngũgĩ wa Thiong'o in Conversation" 403). The narrators and characters speak in Gĩkũyũ, but their words may be rendered in English.

[4]Without reducing the class to a forum on female genital cutting, the teacher could use the essays in Obioma Nnaemeka's *Female Circumcision and the Politics of Knowledge*. These essays help students see that the practice is not uniform across the world. That the practice among the Gĩkũyũ people is mild in comparison with the practice in other cultures, however, does not justify it in contemporary society. Note also that although Muthoni dies from genital cutting, it is only from a Western perspective that we can blame her death on it. In the Gĩkũyũ culture her death can be interpreted differently. Other girls undergo the procedure without dying. Muthoni may have died because she did not receive her father's blessing, as was the tradition, before her initiation. Joshua could also be to blame for not having performed the rituals expected of him as the father of an initiate and for not having forgiven his child when she was near death. As the novel suggests, a "simple sacrifice" of a ram without a blemish at the Mugumo tree might have saved Muthoni (48).

[5]For euphemism in the treatment of the ritual in Nigerian novels, see Zabus.

[6]The church ordered all its followers and those who wanted their children to receive a missionary education to oppose the custom and forbid their daughters to be circumcised: "[a]ll those who desired their children to attend the mission schools, to pledge themselves not to support this custom in any form and to refuse permission for their children to undergo the initiation rite" (Bunche 53).

[7]According to Benson's *Kikuyu-English Dictionary*, the adverb *karĩng'a* means "absolutely" (399). It is used to describe people who have rejected mainstream Christianity in colonial Kenya. Here it designates the pure, unmixed, uncontaminated, indigenous Gĩkũyũ person. Today it is a typographic error to spell it without the apostrophe and tilde. The inability of the novel to spell it properly betrays the inability to maintain the *karĩng'a* status, but Ngũgĩ's nonuse of the punctuation marks in 1965 can hardly be made to carry that much weight. The tilde, introduced as a marker of tonal vowel quality in 1949, was not adopted officially until 1980.

[8]The word *irĩgũ* (plural for *kirĩgũ*) is a derogatory and taboo reference to uncircumcised girls, and is more negative than its masculine form, *ihĩĩ* (plural for *kĩhĩĩ*), which the novel mentions several times, accompanied with English translation. *Ihĩĩ* can be used to refer to Kenyan societies that do not circumcise their men. Spelled without the tildes,

irigu in Gĩkũyũ means "banana." The taboo nature of the word is demonstrated by its deletion from the editions of the novel taught in Kenyan schools. Its masculine form *(kĩhĩĩ)* is also deleted, because of its function as an ethnic slur.

9 Some proper nouns in Ngũgĩ's works are anagrams of Gĩkũyũ names. The high school Siriana is an anagram for Ara'anisi, a Gĩkũyũ-inflected pronunciation of "Alliance," the name of Ngũgĩ's alma mater, a school that was started by an alliance of Protestant churches in colonial Kenya and that quickly became the best school in the country, a position it has retained.

10 The "translation" of the song is left out of the Gĩkũyũ edition (1982), but the English edition explains in a footnote: "The song they are singing is *London's Burning*. They sing the English words as if they are Gĩkũyũ words and reduce the song to utter nonsense" (12).

11 The teacher's name, John Bull, could be an anglicized version of John Mburu or John Ndegwa (*ndegwa* is the Gĩkũyũ word for "bull"). The name demonstrates the educated elite's mentally colonized status in neocolonial Kenya and signifies the teacher's alienation from himself and from his own community.

12 In the English translation, Nyakerũ is Robert Williams and Nyakairũ is John Boy.

13 On Mungiki and postindependence Kenyan politics, see Kagwanja, "Facing" and "'Power'"; for a sympathetic treatment of the sect, see Wamue.

14 Ngina was the official first lady during Jomo Kenyatta's reign (1963–78). She was the most famous of his four wives.

15 Ngũgĩ has commented on the gendered and oral imperatives governing *Devil on the Cross*. The writing of the novel was inspired by the resilience of Kenyan women in their struggle against oppression in present-day Kenya and throughout history (*Detained* 10). In *Decolonising the Mind*, he discusses the novel in terms of how it appropriates traditional oral literature in its production and reception by mass audiences (77–78), and in *Pen-points, Gunpoints, and Dreams* he emphasizes the emancipatory potential of the use of oral forms in African writing, saying that in *Devil* he "drew largely on orature" (124).

16 The term *gĩcaandĩ* derives from the Gĩkũyũ word *caanda* ("dance"). It is also an onomatopoeic representation of the sounds produced by the gourd with which artists accompany their riddling and dancing.

17 In defining gĩcaandĩ, Benson's *Kikuyu-English Dictionary* observes that the performance involves "riddles, conundrums in which two poets compete" (46). The literature on gĩcaandĩ by various researchers (Gĩtĩtĩ; Mutahi; Kabira and Mutahi; and Njogu, "Gĩcandi" and *Reading*) covers different aspects of the genre, but scholars almost unanimously define gĩcaandĩ in terms of the plurality of contesting voices. Gĩtĩtĩ notes "the dramatic sequence of challenge, response, conflict/tension, and reconciliation" in the poetry in Ngũgĩ's *Devil on the Cross* (122). This view is supported by Njogu's incisive dialogical analysis of gĩcaandĩ as an anticolonial poetic genre ("Gĩcandi"). Njogu salutes Ngũgĩ's efforts in *Devil*, especially in restoring a poetic genre that patronizing colonial scholars had dismissed as gibberish because they could not understand it (*Reading*). He writes that "there is a general consensus that *gĩcaandĩ* is poetry that is composed by at least two poets who enter into dialogue with each other" (155).

18 *Mũthigiti* would be a more current word than *mũthiki* for "mosque." That Ngũgĩ favors the English over Kiswahili here suggests that he has nothing against the English language per se.

[19] This incident appears in book 3 of the Gĩkũyũ edition, toward the end of section 19 (151); in the English translation, it would appear after Sikiokuu's reference to "modern African manhood" (404). The English translation has expunged Sheng from the incident in "Female Daemons," where Sikiokuu is advising Tajirika to stop beating his wife without giving up his manhood (404). The supposed Sheng words *tuknanane* ("let's be calling each other through the hotline") and *nzuribye*, which is meaningless, indicate the superficiality of the speaker. Also expunged is the sentence after the reference to wife beating and manhood: *ũgũkirĩrĩria o kĩhinda-inĩ gĩkĩ tũratuĩria na kwenjera mĩri ya ũhoro ũyũ o hamwe na ũcio wa ucoga"* (151; "You'll have to bear with not beating your wife for only this period when we are investigating Virginia's public involvement with other women and homosexuality").

[20] For a reading of the polysemantic use of Gĩkũyũ references in *Matigari*, see Biersteker's "*Matigari*." The essay reviews other work on this subject.

[21] Sikiokuu takes up his name because he undergoes surgery to lengthen his ears to serve the head of state better. The same reason applies to Machokali ("Big Tough-Looking Eyes"). Because the names are not original or found in the real world outside the text but acquired as the narrative progresses, they could have easily been translated into English. Ngũgĩ retains references to Swahili proverbs to suggest the Kenyan setting of the novel, despite its claim to be about an unnamed African country.

[22] For a discussion of some of the names, see Ndĩgĩrĩgĩ, "Character Names." Ndĩgĩrĩgĩ suggests that symbolic naming might be grounded in Ngũgĩ's later socialist realism, but name symbolism pervades his work from the beginning. It is a reflection of Gĩkũyũ folkloric tradition. Benson's *English-Kikuyu Dictionary* and *Kikuyu-English Dictionary* are excellent resources.

[23] The term *disnarration* was coined in 1980 by Prince to designate silences in a text, silences the narrator uses to tell about events other than the ones that happen in the referential world. A related term is *unnarration*, coined by Warhol; the narrator cannot tell us what happened although the narrative indicates that that event took place.

[24] In *Devil on the Cross*, Ngũgĩ says that girls are no longer circumcised in Kenya. Reference to the rite of passage in the novel appears only as a careless and innocuous metaphor for maturity. For Wambui, Warĩĩnga's daughter in the novel "is big enough to be initiated into womanhood—that is, if girls were still circumcised, as they used to be" (234). In the Gĩkũyũ original, the equivalent for "as they used to be" is absent, indicating that in indigenous discourse there appears to be no need to state that female cutting is no longer practiced.

From Imitation to Avant-Garde: Ngũgĩ's Stylistic Evolution as a Novelist

F. Odun Balogun

One of the more rewarding ways that I have found to teach Ngũgĩ as a novelist is to trace the path of his stylistic evolution from being an imitator to becoming an avant-garde experimentalist, a pacesetter. This approach enables me to examine with my students the stages in the developmental evolution of his narrative style, the contributions he made to the growth of the African novel, and the fundamental ways in which he helped change critical perception of the novel as an artistic form.

The five stages in Ngũgĩ's development are imitative realism, in *Weep Not, Child* and *The River Between*; psychological realism, in *A Grain of Wheat*; experimentations with socialist realism, in *Petals of Blood*; experimentations with the performance narrative of orature, in *Devil on the Cross*; and the generic transformation of the novel into a multiform, in *Matigari*, with the consolidation of that transformation in *Wizard of the Crow*.

An advantage of this approach is that it provides a window into several other significant aspects of Ngũgĩ's art, including the evolution of his thematic preoccupations as he moves from one artistic form to another; the historical debates in African literature (e.g., the language question) that prompted changes in his style; a comparative perspective on the novelistic influences on his writing as he moves from the nationalist ideology of Chinua Achebe in the earlier novels to the Soviet-influenced radical socialism of the later novels; and a historical perspective on the African novel as a whole, because Ngũgĩ's works are discussed in comparison with those of other African novelists and also because his role in the development of the African novel is arguably the most central.

Imitative Realism

No writer creates in a vacuum; there is always a source of influence that can be traced to explain a new writer's choice of subject matter and of the style for treating that subject. For Ngũgĩ wa Thiong'o, as for other African writers of his generation who grew up attending school during the colonial period, the first contact with written literature was the English tradition. This tradition dominated colonial education from elementary through secondary school and the university. Thus by 1961, when Ngũgĩ started writing fiction as a student at Makarere, a college of the University of London, he was familiar with English narratives from Geoffrey Chaucer, Jonathan Swift, the Brontë sisters, and Charles Dickens to Joseph Conrad and D. H. Lawrence. By that time British colonialism also had been under siege and was rapidly being dismantled under the political pressure of African nationalists like Jomo Kenyatta and Kwame

Nkrumah, whose efforts were ideologically reinforced by African anticolonial and nationalist writers like Peter Abrahams and Achebe.

Ngũgĩ was the child of parents whose family lands had been appropriated by British colonial settlers and who were compelled therefore to work for an African landowner, eking out a subsistence existence. The injustice, humiliation, exploitation, and inhumanity experienced by Ngũgĩ's family were the common lot of most Kenyans and the factors that provoked Mau Mau, the name given to the Kenyan anticolonial struggle for independence. It was inevitable that Ngũgĩ would not only completely identify with the Mau Mau independence movement but also, on becoming a writer, strive to express the same nationalist outrage against these conditions.

Ngũgĩ's first two novels, *The River Between* and *Weep Not, Child*, were motivated by the desire to expose the inhumanity of British colonialism in Kenya, notably its methods, which were brutal, and its effects, which brought social strife and political and religious division to a previously united people. It also brought economic dispossession and poverty to a people once rich in natural resources. Another effect of colonialism was the cultural humiliation visited on the people through the dismissal of the indigenous religious, educational, and social practices that Kenyans had enjoyed and been proud of. When it came to expressing these subjects in his earliest novels, Ngũgĩ naturally turned to African and not British models:

> In 1962 I was invited to that historic meeting of African writers at Makarere University College, Kampala, Uganda. The list of participants contained most of the names which have now become the subject of scholarly dissertations in universities all over the world. The title? "A Conference of *African Writers of English Expression*."
>
> I was then a student of *English* at Makarere, an overseas college of the University of London. The main attraction for me was the certain possibility of meeting Chinua Achebe. I had with me a rough typescript of a novel in progress, *Weep Not, Child*, and I wanted him to read it. In the previous year, 1961, I had completed *The River Between*, my first-ever attempt at a novel, and entered it for a writing competition organized by the East African Literature Bureau. I was keeping in step with the tradition of Peter Abrahams with his output of novels and autobiographies from *Path of Thunder* to *Tell Freedom* and followed by Chinua Achebe with his publication of *Things Fall Apart*. . . . (*Decolonising* 5)

After getting acquainted with this background, students find it easier to understand why the theme of *The River Between* and *Weep Not, Child* can be summed up with the title of Achebe's own first novel, *Things Fall Apart* (1958). In *The River Between*, colonial intrusion has led to an irreconcilable division and antagonism between Kenyans. On the one side are those who embrace, or are afraid to challenge, colonial economic, political, and cultural imposition; on the other side are nationalists who are committed to fight and dismantle colonialism. Since religious disunity is the primary symbolic idiom of Kenyan division in this novel, Joshua, the religious fanatic, represents the first group and the nationalist Waiyaki represents the second.

These opposing camps have their parallels in *Things Fall Apart*, where the action of Okoli, the colonial supporter and religious fanatic who kills the sacred python, triggers the fierce opposition of Okonkwo, the archenemy of colonialism. While Waiyaki and the other nationalists like Kabonyi and Kamau in *The River Between* seek restoration of Kenyan cultural integrity through the fight to reinstate the traditional circumcision rite, Okonkwo, a more dynamic and heroic figure in *Things Fall Apart*, fights to avenge the killing of the sacred python, symbol of the previous cultural unity in Ibo society. The python, ironically, becomes the symbol of irreconcilable division among the Ibo, much the same way as the river Honia, "which meant cure, or bring-back-to-life," becomes the ironic symbol of division now separating the two ridges Kameno and Makuyu, which are "ready to come to blows in a life and death struggle for the leadership of this isolated region" (*River* 1).

In *Weep Not, Child*, Ngũgĩ shows how the horrors of colonization further intensify during the Emergency, an intensification of oppression that provoked a corresponding escalation in the nationalist, anticolonial struggle. The people also became dramatically polarized with nationalists like Ngotho and Boro fully committed to using violence to destroy colonialism, while traitors to the nationalist cause, like Jacobo, collaborated with colonialists, like Mr. Howlands, to uphold colonialism. The horror of the violence was such that Njoroge, the teenage hero through whose consciousness events are filtered, contemplated suicide. Despite the approval of the nationalist struggle, the privileging of Njoroge's perspective on the issues suggests that education rather than armed struggle is the solution to the disunity among the people: "Whatever their differences, interest in knowledge and book-learning was the one meeting point between people such as Boro, Jacobo and Ngotho. Somehow the Gikuyu people always saw their deliverance as embodied in education" (104–05).

It is not only through their subjects that Ngũgĩ's first two novels are indebted to *Things Fall Apart* but also in their style. This is evident in at least two other ways than the use of symbolism referred to earlier. A fluid, nonintrusive narrative syntax—simple, precise diction and uncomplicated sentences—equally characterizes *Things Fall Apart*, *The River Between*, and *Weep Not, Child*. Another similarity is the adherence to the principle of verisimilitude in representation, depictions of believable and verifiable characters and situations. Although fictional, each of these works remains close to the sociological realities of the cultural milieu and colonial experiences it depicts. For instance, although both authors portray British colonialism, the settler character of Kenyan colonialism contrasts with the more benign, indirect rule characterizing British colonial administration in Nigeria.

Psychological Realism

In his first two novels, Ngũgĩ represents a period of Kenyan history through the use of setting, subject matter, characters, and an objective narrative point of view. According to Ian Watt, this is the prescriptive method by which writers achieve verisimilitude or the illusion of reality in their novels (9–34). Given his closeness to the world he depicts, Ngũgĩ could hardly be expected to display absolute impartiality in his narrative, but notable scholars of the novel concede that no writer can achieve complete objectivity (Wellek 252–53; Booth 68, 70, 78, 83; Robbe-Grillet 468). In his third novel, *A Grain of Wheat*, Ngũgĩ achieves as much impartiality as any writer could, providing not only a true representation of reality but a sympathetic one as well. He realizes that it is not enough to depict the actions of his characters; he must also recognize the complexity of life and dig beneath the surface to reveal the underlying motivations that drive human actions.

The result is an impressive, intricate narrative where idealism is compromised by reality, where betrayal is mitigated by good deeds, and where things turn out to be not what they initially appear to be. For my students to understand better Ngũgĩ's complex realism, I often ask them to read Eustace Palmer's *An Introduction to the African Novel* (24–47), which provides an illuminating, close textual analysis of Ngũgĩ's novel. Palmer observes:

> In the depth of its psychological penetration and the power of its characterization, in the subtlety of its narrative technique, in the density of its texture, and in the sophistication of its language, [*A Grain Of Wheat*] exceeds all expectations raised by the two earlier novels, promising though they were. (24)

Palmer, who sees the influence of Conrad's *Lord Jim* at work in this novel, meticulously explains the narrative strategies—the numerous flashbacks, delaying of information, multiple central characters, and frequent switching of narrative focus from character to character. Palmer admires the way Ngũgĩ makes readers suspend judgment until all the details and contradictions of a character's life, provided piecemeal through the novel, are known. After the reader has gained acquaintance with the realities that consciously and subconsciously govern—sometimes in a contradictory manner—the life of a given character, it becomes difficult to pass superficial judgment on the character. In the end, heroes become humanized by the revelation of their frailties, and villains are partially redeemed by the circumstances mitigating their crimes as well as by the occasional good deeds that they perform.

Kihika and Mugo are two such characters in *Grain*. Kihika becomes a martyr of the Mau Mau anticolonial war because he is betrayed by Mugo. But Kihika's heroic idealism is diminished as we learn of his egoism and arrogance, because these negative qualities, which promote recklessness in the face of danger, partly explain his virtue as a leader. On the other hand, Mugo does not betray Kihika in order to gain any personal advantage; he only wishes to be left alone, uninvolved in the war for independence that touches every life, so that he can pursue his personal dream of success. After the betrayal, he is filled with remorse. In his anguish, he risks his life by defending Wambuku, who although pregnant is being beaten by home guards, locals who are recruited to protect the embattled colonial government and who are much feared because of their brutality. Even more significant is the fact that Mugo can choose to hide his guilt and will never be found out, since everyone already suspects Karanja, the home guard, as the traitor. Moreover, Mugo, everywhere revered as a hero of the patriotic war, is being urged to accept political leadership in the newly independent Kenya, but Mugo makes the moral yet infinitely harder choice of publicly confessing his crime and accepting the punishment, which is death. In his transformation from villain to hero, he overshadows Kihika.

Socialist Realism

By the time Ngũgĩ wrote his fourth novel, *Petals of Blood*, his sociopolitical and literary ideology had changed from nationalism to the socialism that has since inspired both the themes and style of all his writing.

To understand this change, students need to have some familiarity with the political history of African states in the two decades that followed the attainment of independence from colonial powers in the early 1960s. First, this was the era of the Cold War, when the rival ideologies of capitalism and socialism each sought to control the soul of Africa. Second, the euphoria of independence quickly evaporated and was replaced by a great disillusionment once it became clear that independence would not bring development and prosperity to all Africans. Instead, almost every African nation soon fell under the control of a middle-class elite, which took over the reins from departing colonial administrators. The new elites behaved much as the colonial elites had, establishing an exploitative relation with the majority population, which was largely made up of peasants. African intellectuals, including writers, expressed their disillusionment in various ways. Some, like Ayi Kwei Armah, wrote devastating social critiques, as in his novel *The Beautyful Ones Are Not Yet Born* (1968). Others, like Ngũgĩ, identified the problem with capitalism and embraced socialism. Soldiers and politicians organized coups d'état and took over governance. A reading of Ngũgĩ's first book of essays, *Homecoming*, should provide students with information and the reason why Ngũgĩ chose socialism.

Among the tenets of socialist ideology are the primacy of economics in social relations; the dominance of class analysis, with emphasis on class war and the inevitability of proletarian revolution; and the belief in the philosophy of dialectical materialism as the ideological engine fueling revolutionary social change.

These tenets are prominent in *Petals of Blood*. Its characters come from two antagonistic camps, the exploited proletariat and the exploiting bourgeois elite—the former represented by Munira, Karega, Abdulla, and Wanja, the latter by Mr. Nderi wa Riera, Rev. J. Brown, and Mr. Hawkins. The narrative centers on the revolt of the proletariat against the bourgeoisie, with Karega the proletarian *positive hero* who organizes the demonstration that ends in rebellion. The revolt itself is the dialectical outcome of extreme bourgeois exploitation.

Petals is a naturalist, proletarian prose epic. Its epic quality is reflected in the national importance of its theme; the panoramic sweep of its setting, encompassing almost the whole country; its cast of four major characters, each of whom receives considerable narrative attention; and the mythic nature of the trek from Ilmorog to Nairobi. Its naturalist tendency is seen in the fact that Ngũgĩ not only links effects to their causes but goes deeper, to a scientific, documentary investigation of the causes themselves. He does not stop at connecting the plight of the Ilmorog villagers to their exploitation by neocolonial black leaders; he also explores the nature and consequences of that exploitation. Moreover, this exploitation is represented as a socially and environmentally deterministic factor in the lives of the proletariat. To deepen my students' understanding of this aspect of Ngũgĩ's novel, I may invite them to read John Steinbeck's *The Grapes of Wrath* (1939), which exhibits similar thematic and stylistic features. To facilitate the comparison, I also suggest that they read my essay "Naturalist Proletarian Prose Epics: *Petals of Blood* and *Grapes of Wrath*."

Performance Narrative

Devil on the Cross is Ngũgĩ's first novel in his native language, Gĩkũyũ, after Ngũgĩ made the historic decision not to use English as the primary language for his fiction. He has insisted that his advocacy of African-language literature should be seen in the context of his advocacy of a pluralism of world cultures, of the liberation of world cultures from the centuries-old stranglehold of Eurocentricism. His language switch has had an enormous influence on his novelistic style. By writing in Gĩkũyũ, he becomes more deeply acquainted with the performance narrative mode and stylistic devices of the oral tradition. The target audience of his Gĩkũyũ novels is his people, who thus are able to have direct access to his writing and his thoughts because these are written in their language.

By experimenting with the performance narrative style of his people's oral tradition, Ngũgĩ discovers a new way of writing that systematically and fundamentally transforms his novels by opening up multiple generic possibilities in one composition. The traditional realistic novel can deviate only so far from the realistic mode of depiction if it wants to retain its integrity, but a novel written in the performance style of oral narrative has no such anxiety. Given its tradition of accommodating multiple genres at once, an oral narrative can be performed as any number of genres, including myth, epic, hagiography, and realism.

This is the discovery that Ngũgĩ makes writing *Devil*, a novel that invites multiple reading as a fabricated myth about ogres and devils, as a performance complete with songs and dance, as a satire, as a hagiography of a Marxist heroine, and as a realistic novel of capitalist greed and exploitation. Because it is his first experiment in this narrative mode, the effort is understandably not flawless. For instance, the novel opens as a narrative by a traditional griot, with a stylistic grandeur that is too lofty to be sustained, hence the story soon switches to the voice of a modern novelist.

The Novel as a Multiform

The experiment with orature, which was partially successful in *Devil*, reached its perfection in Ngũgĩ's next novel, *Matigari*, and was further consolidated in his latest, *Wizard of the Crow*. Both novels, like *Devil*, were written in Gĩkũyũ and then translated into English. In *Matigari* and *Wizard*, Ngũgĩ transforms the novel into a multigenre. Traditionally, African writers have borrowed elements of indigenous oral narratives to enrich the composition of their novels, which essentially remain realistic, despite an occasional crossing of boundaries such as we find in the mythopoeic novels of Camara Laye and of Wole Soyinka or in the mythic histories of Armah. With Ngũgĩ, however, the novel is not merely enriched but completely transformed.

To help my students discover for themselves the multiform nature of Ngũgĩ's Gĩkũyũ novels even after the novels are translated into English, I divide the class into groups and assign each group to research the properties of a specific literary genre—myth, epic, hagiography, and the traditional realistic novel. After each group has completed this assignment and has identified the thematic and stylistic characteristics of the assigned genre, I invite them to apply these properties to the analysis of a translated Gĩkũyũ novel by Ngũgĩ. Often students require help, so I direct them to relevant secondary literature, including my book on Ngũgĩ, subtitled "The Novel as Oral Narrative in Multigenre Performance." The length of this exercise depends on student experience and the level of the class, but the outcome always fascinates: students realize that Ngũgĩ's Gĩkũyũ novels indeed are different genres in one, each genre being coherent, complete, and autonomous.

There are other valid ways, of course, to teach Ngũgĩ's novels. I find, however, that this evolution-of-style approach enables students to appreciate Ngũgĩ's tireless experimentation and his remarkable talent in finding new ways to educate and entertain the readers of his novels. It also helps students recognize the positive outcome of his radical language switch, which has led the way to his reconceptualization of the novel as a genre.

Location and History: Salient Issues in Teaching Ngũgĩ to Black South African Students

James Ogude

It is now taken for granted that whenever we teach literature, we signal the historical, social, and cultural contexts of its production. Fredric Jameson has argued that "genuine interpretation directs the attention back to history itself, and to the historical situation of the commentator as well as of the work" (*Situations* 5). He is directing our attention to the conditions of existence of a work of art—the conditions of its production and consumption. Whereas production is often embedded in the cultural artifacts themselves, consumption speaks squarely to the location of the reader, to the reader's subject position and the intellectual climate in which the reading takes place. Conditions of production speak to those things that you cannot avoid while reading Ngũgĩ—things independent of the methodological approach or theoretical protocol you adopt; the location of the reader speaks to how texts are domesticated in specific contexts and why their meanings take certain inflections. Quite often, both novice and expert readers come to texts with baggage and expectations rooted in their specific and local experiences. My teaching Ngũgĩ and writing on him for over two decades have strengthened my opinion that there is indeed a range of tropes that define his oeuvre that can be traced back to the historical situation he writes about and his own spatial and intellectual location as a writer. I have also come to accept that the location of students will invariably shape their reception of a given text.

In this essay, I draw attention to why Ngũgĩ has remained so attractive for a number of black students, especially in South Africa, where I have been teaching for close to two decades. I argue that the issues he raises spoke to the local conditions of the students and to the dominant intellectual climate in black scholarship—namely, resistance narrative against apartheid and the search for national integration that crystallized in the black consciousness movement of the late 1970s and beyond.

It became clear to me, as I taught, that one cannot understand Ngũgĩ fully without coming to terms with the conditions under which his works are produced: exile, displacement, and the consequent desire for restoration or a redemptive narrative. Students appreciate him best once they understand what underpins the lyrical narratives in his early career and the polemical elements that dominate his later texts. It is therefore not easy to grasp the full import of Ngũgĩ's works without going back to history—without evoking the past and examining how that past speaks to contemporary experience.

As early as 1972, Ngũgĩ was drawing attention to how the tyranny of the past exerts itself on his works. He writes, "The novelist is haunted by a sense of the past. His work is often an attempt to come to terms with 'the thing that has been,' a struggle as it were, to sensitively register his encounter with history, his people's history" (*Homecoming* 39). For Ngũgĩ, then, the novel is an instrument that wills history into being. As Simon Gikandi puts it, Ngũgĩ has always placed "himself at the junction where history (the context) and his writings (the text) meet" (*Ngũgĩ* 3).

Ngũgĩ's work raises issues of memory, national longing, and the intellectual elite's engagement with what Biodun Jeyifo has called "arrested decolonization." These are by no means the only issues that have come to define Ngũgĩ's work, but it is remarkable that they interface with one another and persist throughout his career regardless of the historical moment of their enunciation.

Ngũgĩ's writing is connected to his life experience, his biography. Building narrative around one's life inevitably leads to remembering as a construction of self-identity, especially when that identity has been disrupted—displaced, for example, by colonialism. Nothing illustrates this personal remembering better than the land question in Ngũgĩ's novels. Ngũgĩ returns to it precisely because it affected his entire family and therefore haunted his childhood:

> I grew up in a small village. My father with his four wives had no land. They lived as tenants-at-will on somebody else's land. Harvests were often poor. Sweetened tea with milk at any time of day was a luxury. We had one meal a day—late in the evening. Every day the women would go to their scruffy little strips of shamba. . . . Just opposite the ridge on which our village was scattered were the sprawling green fields owned by the white settlers. (*Homecoming* 48)

Alienation from the rich Gĩkũyũ land in what came to be known as the White Highlands reduced Ngũgĩ's family to squatters (*ahoi*). Memory is exercised by Ngũgĩ to show that the land, which is at the heart of the struggle in his texts, was given to his people by God, Murungu, through the Agikuyu founders: Gikuyu and Mumbi:

> If political freedom in Kenya became synonymous with repossession of the land, the spiritual and moral justification for this quest for freedom lies in the fact that this land is linked to the spiritual right of the people, the Agikuyu. The land was God-given; it was entrusted to them by their legendary ancestors as a form of covenant between God and his people. (Ogude 21)

Land alienation was more than a material loss; it was also a spiritual violation.

South African students and students from Zimbabwe who study in South Africa get quite animated whenever the land question is raised in class. They come to Ngũgĩ's text with a history of land alienation and forced removal of people from their ancestral land, a practice that has become a hallmark of the apartheid system. Yet in all settler economies land restitution remains a highly contested issue and continues to shape postindependence politics. My experience has been that black students from settler economies cannot read Ngũgĩ outside this context.

In both undergraduate and graduate classes, the popularity of Ngũgĩ rests on the fact that students empathize with the memories that he evokes in his texts. His biography is often similar to that of many students who read him. His narratives set in the emergency period between 1952 and 1960, the Mau Mau war, echo their own experiences. Like them, he was a witness and victim of a war in which family members were directly involved. Students also relate to how he uses the people's memories to provide authority and legitimacy for their struggle.

Remembering for Ngũgĩ is always connected to exile and displacement, to marginality and fragmentation, so his texts invariably convey a sense of loss and a desire for restoration. As a child, he was confronted by the daily tyranny of a colonial regime that had dispossessed his family and imposed a political hegemony over his people. As an adult, he continued to live in limbo, under the dictatorship of the postindependence regimes that sent him into prison and finally forced him into exile. It is not surprising, then, that the themes of loss and redemption, which dominate his early novels, *The River Between* and *Weep Not, Child,* become even sharper in later texts, such as *Petals of Blood* and *Matigari*. In *Matigari*, they assume an allegorical dimension. The desire for integration and wholeness in these novels is driven by the nationalist desire to find an anchor and home in a specific soil.

At the height of apartheid, Ngũgĩ was the most widely researched and the best-known African writer in South Africa. His popularity cut across the racial divide, because both the white left and the oppressed blacks could identify with the class politics that underpinned his texts and essays. In 1981, N. W. Visser, as guest editor of the prestigious journal *English in Africa*, dedicated a whole issue to Ngũgĩ. This unprecedented move signaled the important space Ngũgĩ occupied in and outside the South African academy. His works crystallized the attempt to define the self and reconstitute black identity. At the same time, they embodied the spirit of resistance whose rhetoric was class war and whose substance was the longing for a utopian state free of exploitation and repression. The response to him was therefore always emotionally and ideologically charged. It was not unusual to find collection of his essays, like *Writers in Politics*, *Barrel of a Pen*, *Decolonising the Mind*, and *Moving the Centre*, being read alongside his creative works.

In 1991, when I first taught Ngũgĩ's *A Grain of Wheat*, to a second-year African literature class, I asked the students to mention one novel by Ngũgĩ they had read. Virtually all named *Decolonising the Mind*, insisting that it was a novel. It turned out that they had read not the text but summaries of it, or accounts of it had been passed on to them by word of mouth. I was witnessing here a reading strategy that had gained ground in South Africa but is now spread across the continent. This strategy is partly a consequence of poverty: people lack the resources to buy and read books; it is also the consequence of a highly regulated public space in which radical texts are outlawed by regimes. Readers share edited and abridged versions of a banned or rare text. When a book travels by word of mouth, readers can choose what to omit and what to amplify and pass on.

Decolonising the Mind had become a traveling text among many student activists long before they saw the printed text. Why was it so popular among South African students? I soon discovered that Ngũgĩ's *Decolonising* resonated with Steve Biko's teachings, which had dominated the South African intellectual landscape over the last two decades. The text had become a summary of the core teachings of the black consciousness movement. It didn't matter whether *Decolonising* was a work of imagination or not; it spoke to a familiar context and a familiar regime of knowledge. Ngũgĩ was being read through the prism of the intellectual climate of the time. The students would soon insist that *A Grain of Wheat* decolonized their minds. The novel celebrated the heroes of struggle they could relate to that—many of their leaders, like Nelson Mandela, had been detained for years. They could also draw parallels between their homeland leaders or the local *impimpis* ("collaborators"), who had settled for a politics of compromise, and Ngũgĩ's home guards. For them, the boundary between fiction and polemical essay, between narrative and history, had collapsed. Ngũgĩ's works were relevant instruments of self-definition; Ngũgĩ himself stood at the junction between a familiar sociopolitical experience and a history that they were only beginning to grapple with. He could not be read outside this multiple context.

How else did Ngũgĩ's works resonate with South African readers? Visser's special issue of *English in Africa* provides the answer. It was ostensibly dedicated to a study of Mau Mau violence and the representation of popular struggle in Ngũgĩ's fiction, but it also dealt with the dilemmas of the intellectual elite of both white and black as they grappled with the problems that confronted their society. Was violence justified in a popular struggle? Could writers really disengage from the dominant ideologies of their time? But these were questions raised by intellectuals, mainly white liberals in the academy. For the black students, the politics of the Mau Mau war that Ngũgĩ described was more than an academic engagement; it was part of their daily experience—and it pointed to the possibility of national restoration. Ngũgĩ's redrafting of the Mau Mau war into a symbol of national cohesion, a symbol around which various segments of the nation could gather, was an expression of that longing. Ngũgĩ mobilized Mau Mau iconography in *A Grain of Wheat*, *Matigari*, *The Trial of Dedan Kimathi*, and *I Will Marry When I Want*.

Gikandi has argued that Ngũgĩ, throughout his writing career, held on to "the ideals of nationhood and the metaphysics of progress it entailed." In addition, Ngũgĩ

> needed to hold on to these ideals because cultural identity and the ideals of national community on which they were predicated were the heart and soul of his writing. The category of the nation—and its referent—would change several times in the course of Ngũgĩ's career, but so long as the national ideal remained the base of all forms of identity, he could continue to argue that his works were attempts to realize these ideals.
>
> (*Ngũgĩ* 228)

But if the ideals of nationhood underpin Ngũgĩ's writing, it is because Ngũgĩ has always written under conditions of exile and an immense dislocation of the self. He spoke directly to black South Africans who lived a life of internal exile in the land of their birth. Here was a strong parallel between the conditions of production of a writer's texts and the conditions of their consumption.

The metaphor of exile and its full effect on Ngũgĩ's life are best elaborated in his prison diary, *Detained*. In this diary, Ngũgĩ takes us into Kamĩtĩ Maximum Security Prison, cell 16, a setting that echoes Wole Soyinka's vault, Kaduna 68, in his memoir *The Man Died*. It also echoes Mandela's cell 4664 on Robben Island. In Kamĩtĩ, Ngũgĩ reflects on the space of incarceration and how it shapes his multiple identities as a writer, critic, scholar, and political activist. Kamĩtĩ reminds him of his days as a young man growing up under the shadow of colonial violence. In postindependence Kenya, prison became the space of internal exile. It was for many Kenyans what South Africa had become to many black South Africans, "the stone country," as the title of Alex La Guma's novel suggests. In both Kenya and South Africa, the regime sought to imprison its people's mind and conscience.

For Ngũgĩ, deprived of all instruments of expression and writing and separated from his community of scholars, cell 16 became an exile from the self. It was for him a close encounter with the state, daily contact with state machinery. In Kamĩtĩ, the colonial legacy repeated itself through this machinery, whose crude rituals of discipline and punishment the postindependent government had perfected. A decade later, Ngũgĩ wrote of postindependence Africa as a prison house:

> This elite, pampered with military gadgets of all kinds with which to [rein] in a restive population, has often turned an entire country into a vast prison-house. Africa is a continent alienated from itself by years of alien conquests and internal despots. Thus the state of exile in the literary landscape reflects a larger state of alienation in the society as a whole, a clear case of colonial legacy which has left scars on the body, heart, and mind of the continent. (*Moving* 107–08)

He is suggesting that the state of exile is an unavoidable condition of African literary practice: the alienation of the writer ensues from the alienation of the nation. Stuart Hall echoes Ngũgĩ's sentiments when he posits that the postcolony is a form of internal diaspora embedded in what he calls "double inscription" (247). The postcolony is diasporic to the extent that it is not able to return to the sense of community that once bound it together. The long-term effect of colonialism is the creation of a diasporic condition and a sense of homelessness. Whether we see the dismembered self as the nation or Africa, the natural path of redemption leads to the desire for integration, for a home where a redemptive narrative of liberation can begin.

Ngũgĩ's return to the Gĩkũyũ language as his medium of writing may have been motivated by a number of things, but the sense of loss and alienation that the English language and its literary tradition imposed on him played a significant role in that return. He has argued that real homecoming in African literature is not possible without an escape from the linguistic prison:

> The nineties will see more and more writers trying to break out of the linguistic prison to seek their genuine roots in the languages and rhythms of life of the dispossessed majority. Only this way will African literature find its real homecoming among the African masses who have always struggled to overcome the state of alienation. Otherwise it is doomed to die, or stagnate in the linguistic prison of its colonial legacy. (*Moving* 108)

His novels in Gĩkũyũ were also written in exile: *Devil on the Cross* was written in prison, *Matigari* in the United Kingdom, and *Wizard of the Crow* in the United States. Distanced from his subject and for over two decades locked away in the West, which his texts have incessantly criticized for its neocolonial stranglehold on his people, Ngũgĩ could reconnect with his subject only by seizing the language of his people, which has been marginalized by colonial education.

The three Gĩkũyũ novels are not steeped in the realist tradition but work through rumor and fantasy. The realistic mode is no longer adequate in representing the conditions of postcoloniality, and Ngũgĩ must marshal those idioms that are likely to capture the absurdity of the moment. Both rumor and fantasy are part of the everyday grammar that the ruled deploy to negotiate meaning in the space between fact and fiction, the public space where the rulers ritually stage their public transcripts. It is through rumor and fantasy, or what James Scott calls "hidden transcripts," that the "public transcripts" get inflected. Scott defines hidden transcripts as "discourse that takes place offstage, beyond the observation of power holders, and which tend to confirm, inflect, qualify or contradict the public transcript" (16). *Matigari* and *Wizard* are good examples of novels whose narrative is driven by hidden transcripts.

There is persistent tension in Ngũgĩ's body of work between national restoration and a colonial historiography that would suppress any radical memories of his people's history and culture: the new intellectual and political elite now fear the past more than their colonial predecessors did. Nowhere is this interrogation and revision of colonial historiography better captured than in *Petals of Blood*:

> For there are many questions about our history which remain unanswered. Our present day historians, following on similar theories yarned out by defenders of imperialism, insist we only arrived here yesterday. Where went all the Kenyan people who used to trade with China, India, Arabia long long before Vasco da Gama came to the scene and on the strength of gunpowder ushered in an era of blood and terror and instability—an era that climaxed in the reign of imperialism over Kenya? But even then these adventurers of Portuguese mercantilism were forced to build Fort Jesus, showing that Kenyan people had always been ready to resist foreign control and exploitation. The story of this heroic resistance: who will sing it? Their struggles to defend their land, their wealth, their lives: who'll tell of it? What of their earlier achievements in production that had annually attracted visitors from ancient China and India? (67)

Whether or not we agree with Ngũgĩ's total rejection of Africa's history rooted in the colonial archive and his privileging of resistance as the key plot element in African history, whether or not we agree with him that the metanarrative of the nationalist victory must be revised and reconstituted as the story of workers and peasants—history from below—is beside the point. My interest here is in the way Ngũgĩ positions himself in the making of this national project as a member of the intelligentsia, a class whose crises and contradictions he mirrors so vividly in his writing. He is unequivocal in mapping out the role for the intellectual elite as creators and brokers of culture by insisting that they provide us with a history unlike that which we have received from our colonial masters, that they interrogate the epistemological frameworks from the West that continue to shape our knowledge systems.

Even a superficial reading of Ngũgĩ's fiction and critical essays points to the conscious project of transforming our inherited notions of history, especially the position of the colonial subject as inscribed in imperial discourse. We know from the work of Michel Foucault, Hayden White (*Content* and *Tropics*), and others that the writing of history is culturally motivated and ideologically conditioned; it is a mirror of contemporary concerns and dominant institutional practices. The extent to which we are able to see history as a language, as a discourse, and as a way of seeing—a code of recognition—is also the extent to which we are able to destabilize the fixity, the givenness, of history and open it up to the transformative power of imaginative revision. If the imperial narrative attempted to read the empire's history as the history of the other, Ngũgĩ's position is that the history of Africa need not be contingent on imperial allegorizing. Allegory here is used to mean a way of representing, of speaking for the other in the enterprise of imperialism.

The issues that Ngũgĩ raises resonated with black South African students in the 1980s and early 1990s. Ngũgĩ is not simply laying claim to the terrain of culture; he also seeks to revise our notions of received history. He advocates the full restoration of historical agency, which many South Africans were groping for. His work celebrates struggle history and the triumph of the individual will. South African students, who could point to several prisoners of conscience in their midst, invariably read Ngũgĩ's works as deliberate interventions for a further mobilization for national resistance and the fight for freedom. His return to writing in an African language appealed to the rhetoric of cultural survival in a context where Afrikaans and English had both been imposed as modes of discourse and as official languages. Ngũgĩ was fueling a new intellectual project by signaling the possibility of reconnecting with local communities through language. The response to this project was particularly striking in the area of theater: the Kamĩrĩĩthũ experience pushed South African theater practitioners to experiment more boldly with local African languages. Although the idea of workshopped theater was already in vogue in South Africa in the late 1970s, plays were still confined to professional actors and largely scripted in English. The Kamĩrĩĩthũ experience created an opportunity to bridge the gap between the elite professionals and the workers and peasants. It gave South African theater artists a new grammar and conferred greater legitimacy on African languages.

The reception of Ngũgĩ's work in South Africa takes us back to Jameson's argument that the reading of any work of art will invariably be shaped by the historical situation of the writer, the conditions of production of the writer's work, and the location of the readers and what intellectual and social concerns animate their reading (*Situations* 5). In teaching Ngũgĩ in Africa, specifically in South Africa, one cannot escape issues of history, exile, memory, and the desire for restoration, because the conditions of cultural production on the continent bind both writer and reader so strongly. In Africa, people go to texts to solve moral and political problems, to look for templates they can apply to their lives.

Reading Ngũgĩ on Four Continents: Relational Aesthetics and the Global Multicultural Classroom

Brendon Nicholls

Ngũgĩ wa Thiong'o's novels and theoretical essays have become staples on university syllabi worldwide. My essay investigates some of the politically situated student responses that I have encountered while exploring the gender politics of his work in multicultural classrooms in Africa, Europe, Asia, and the United States. The most interesting pedagogical questions have arisen at moments of cultural friction, in which the ideological and aesthetic values of his work have been very much at stake. As a site of cultural contestation, Ngũgĩ's fiction and critical thought embed in the university classroom a model of fraught postcolonial negotiation from which neither professor nor student is immune. In my undergraduate teaching, I have tended to focus on the early and middle novels (from *The River Between* to *Petals of Blood*), since I view them as being foundational to an understanding of his decision to write in Gĩkũyũ. Many of the students who progress to graduate work research the politics of language in the later fiction and essays. Through a series of narratives, I demonstrate some of the postcolonial negotiations undertaken by students when they read Ngũgĩ's work. Each narrative has a pedagogical bearing and a wider relevance to Ngũgĩ scholarship.

Questions of cultural and ideological value are central to Ngũgĩ's critical thought. His critiques of colonial education, his advocacy of a radical pedagogy oriented toward the decolonization of the mind, and his call for a system of literary production geared to polycentric translation offer us innovative ways of thinking about how literature might be taught, explored, and analyzed. It is therefore unsurprising that students occasionally grapple with cognate questions in their encounters with Ngũgĩ's fiction and essays.

I began teaching Ngũgĩ's fiction to a multiethnic and multiracial cohort in a major national university in late 1994, during South Africa's transition from apartheid to democracy. This diverse group of students brought a range of educational backgrounds to their study—from those who had been historically disadvantaged by apartheid to those who had been privileged by it. The multidimensional contributions they made to our seminars meant that each brought something of value to the discussion, whether it derived from book learning or a personal experience of injustice.

Since African literature was at that time not routinely taught in the core stream of the English literature department in which I worked, offering the choice to study Ngũgĩ's fiction was designed to divert certain students from the more institutionally prestigious and highly regarded course on Shakespeare. We were keenly aware that the twinning of the syllabus into parallel Shakespearean and African tracks was an organizational subterfuge to preserve Eurocentric elitism in the mainstream of the student cohort. Black students and African literature were obviously being subjected to exclusion by design. A key reading in the course I taught was "On the Abolition of the English Department," by Ngũgĩ, Taban Lo Liyong, and Henry Owuor-Anyumba.[1] Their words were particularly instructive in our South African educational context: "Why can't African literature be at the centre so that we can view other cultures in relationship to it? . . . We reject the primacy of English literature and culture" (146). Mindful of this resonant manifesto and of the transforming society around us, the students and I lobbied for change. I remember being the only (adjunct) faculty member to vote in favor of making African literature compulsory in the second-year syllabus.[2]

In this resistant educational atmosphere, Ngũgĩ's novels must have symbolized a decolonized identity to many disadvantaged students. Their hope must have accounted for the fervor with which they attended seminars, delivered presentations, and joined in class discussion and debate. The course tracked Ngũgĩ's gender representations through his fictional accounts of the anticolonial struggle, nation formation, and neocolonialism in Kenya. I began with a class on the clitoridectomy debate and its pivotal role in the consolidation of Gĩkũyũ nationalism, then moved on to Ngũgĩ's constructions of gender as mobilizing metaphors for political struggle and the narrativization of history. Students learned that *A Grain of Wheat* represents a lineage of national struggle beginning with Gikuyu and Mumbi, the mythical male and female founders of the Gĩkũyũ community; passing through Gikuyu na Mumbi, one of the names that Mau Mau called itself (Sicherman, *Ngũgĩ wa Thiong'o: The Making* 201); and culminating with the characters in the novel, Gikonyo and Mumbi. The love relationship therefore carries a political charge. Mumbi's infidelity with Karanja and her bearing of an illegitimate child by him signify a departure from the mythical destiny implicit in the names Gikonyo and Mumbi. This destiny is restored only in Gikonyo's projected impregnation of his wife, which is predicted in the stool he carves at the end of the novel. This imaginative resolution presages the rebirth of community. I suggested to my South African students that the reclamation of motherhood in *A Grain of Wheat* is consistent with what Gayatri Chakravorty Spivak might term the "uterine social organization" (*In Other Worlds* 152) instituted by the debate about clitoridectomy, a practice in which sexual pleasure is negated for women in order that their political and cultural identities can be linked to motherhood.

This point created an immediate fault line in the learning experience of some students. "Why," one asked during a class on *The River Between*, about clitoridectomy, "should we be problematizing Ngũgĩ's fictional project with a gender critique when his fiction represents an African cultural identity that apartheid has withheld from our community for forty years?" "Identity formation," countered another, "does not end with liberation." At stake in the feminist critique of

Ngũgĩ's representations of clitoridectomy were the aspirations of hidden constituencies – the emerging cultural communities of a very recently democratic South Africa. Ngũgĩ's fiction had a pivotal importance in the students' political biographies,[3] and for this reason the act of reading critically in the classroom encountered unforeseen contextual pressures.

The fault line carried over into the students' analyses of Ngũgĩ's novels. A number of male students found nothing problematic in the use of Mumbi's reproductive potential as a metaphor for an emergent Kenya at the end of *Grain*. A decolonized nation, they argued, was the only viable basis on which to begin discussing gender equality, and in any case community was possible only if family life resumed after the fragmentations and upheavals of anticolonial struggle. A different viewpoint was offered by a group of women students. They argued that African femininity needed to be viewed not in terms of a reproductive monad but in terms of a range of possible subject positions. Ngũgĩ's early equivocation on the issue of clitoridectomy and his consistent privileging of motherhood, they continued, had the combined effect of reducing the range of possibilities open to his female characters. This inequality of opportunity, they concluded, might mean that his female characters and readers would have no stake at all in decolonized nationhood, with damaging consequences for the nation's project of reconstruction.

My next opportunity to teach one of Ngũgĩ's novels was in the United Kingdom, in a prestigious northern university. *A Grain of Wheat* featured on a postcolonial survey course alongside representative texts from Canada, Australia, the Caribbean, Aotearoa (New Zealand), South Asia, and South Africa. The course tracked the different ideas of nationhood across the constituencies of the postcolonial. The challenges of reading Ngũgĩ were different here. The classes were primarily but not exclusively composed of English students who had little experience of African literature and who were apt to treat *Grain* as if its literary merits were to be found only in comparison with other novels on the reading list. One of the critical debates the students entered into was whether or not politically engaged literature is simply polemic and for that reason unliterary. A vocal minority expressed the view that *Grain* lacked complexity and that its narrative mechanisms were too obvious to qualify as first-rate literature. To meet this objection, I offered a whistle-stop tour of the complex uses of Mugo, Mumbi, Gikonyo, General R., Koina (Koinandu), and Karanja as focalizers whose multiperspectival layerings finally produce a shared communal narrative of mutual betrayal. This excursion met with little success. Neither did a summary of Ngũgĩ's literary debt to Joseph Conrad's modernist narratorial framing devices help. Some students drew attention to Mugo's intricate association with water imagery and the likelihood that it referred to water torture in the pipeline of concentration camps through which Mau Mau suspects passed on the path to political rehabilitation. But the dissenting minority in the classroom returned to that chestnut in Ngũgĩ scholarship: literature that contains a notion of constituency or social obligation has reneged on its artistic obligations to its craft.

Finally I found an argument that worked. "If a Ugandan poet looks on starvation with outrage," I argued, "then surely that is good poetry. In other words, we cannot dismiss African literature if we are ignorant of the historical experience and cultural inheritances that shape narrative form." These inheritances for Ngũgĩ have as much to do with communal experiences of the colonial anti-insurgency tactics (for example, villagization) during the Mau Mau war as they do with his reception of Caribbean fiction. Kihika is an avatar of the boy who flees from corporal punishment during assembly in George Lamming's *In the Castle of My Skin* (35). "If we uphold a rarefied ideal of the literary that is unconnected to concrete historical experience," I suggested to my students, "then we will always exclude African literary texts. By that impoverished logic, why should anyone read African literature at all if we merely expect it to tell us of its formal underachievement?" After a few moments of thoughtful silence, the response to this argument was both admirable and sophisticated: "Perhaps what we're really looking at in *A Grain of Wheat* is an African modernism in which the quest for form is directed toward the character of national experience."

More recently, I taught classes on Ngũgĩ at a major midwestern university in North America and at a prestigious college in India. Both occasions took the format of a lecture, and my interaction with students was limited to a short question-and-answer session. The questions in these two settings could not have been more different. In North America, there was disquiet about the use of the racial markers *black* and *white* in the passage from *Weep Not, Child* in which Italian prisoners of war and "black mothers" produce children who are "not really 'white' in the usual way" (5, 6). The questioner felt that the terms *black* and *white* were ideologically suspect, even when they were used in an African novel. She said, "Ngũgĩ's first published novel is locked into a dated and debilitating politics of race, and we should now discard it in the interests of multiculturalism." I responded that Ngũgĩ's fiction certainly uses the terminology of race, but his essays are from first to last distrustful of colonial racial categories. "Race in Ngũgĩ's fiction," I continued, "is always a means to assert a communal claim on the Kenyan landscape. None of us escapes making ideological claims, even when we think we are being objective. It might be useful to think about this word *multiculturalism*. What exactly do we mean when we use that term?" "Here in America," the student replied, "it means that Americans are like the leaves in a salad, and everyone else is the dressing." As flawed as this defense of multiculturalism might appear, I have sympathy with the student's critique of Ngũgĩ. Her question shows how postcolonial critique becomes indigenized and that such indigenization is a measure of the local usefulness of postcolonial terminologies.

In my Indian guest lecture, delivered to graduate students, a similar measuring took place. I offered an extended discussion of how Ngũgĩ's referential model of language extends the nominative cultural powers of the father. His well-known claim that language is a carrier of culture is paralleled by the way a father's name asserts the father's ownership over a child resulting from the mother's labor. Relating this argument to their own postcolonial literary mappings, the students were moved to discuss the necessity for a comparable critique of the famous Bengali-language poet and novelist Bankim Chandra Chattopadhyay. Bankim's gendering of the political was a conventional and convenient vehicle for collective self-imaging, they felt, but it had received insufficient critical consideration. The two writers were similar in their championing of indigenous-language literature as well as in their gender politics. Once again, Ngũgĩ's fiction had been received not only because of its eminent contributions to the postcolonial but also because of its local application.

I have shown a series of postcolonial negotiations that an assortment of students on four continents undertook in their reception of Ngũgĩ's fiction. I now suggest that the necessity of such negotiation is already anticipated in Ngũgĩ's fiction and critical thought:

> [T]he critic, whether teacher, lecturer, interpreter or analyst, is a product of a class society. . . . Therefore their interpretation of literature and culture and history will be influenced by their philosophical standpoint, or intellectual base, and their conscious or unconscious sympathies. . . . In criticism, as in creative writing, there is an ideological struggle.
> (*Decolonising* 104–05)

The ideological struggles of students reading Ngũgĩ on four continents were not immediately coextensive with each other, nor indeed with Ngũgĩ's progressive vision set out almost two decades earlier. For such students, the transitivity of literary value is instantiated in local ideological struggles—even when those struggles constitute a critical encounter with received notions of the literary.

Once we acknowledge, along with Ngũgĩ, the materiality of all grounds of critique, we are surely also destined to acknowledge in our readings of his fiction an implicit call to relation.[4] It was this call to relation that was staged, somewhat inelegantly, in the discussions between nationalists and feminists in my South African classes on Ngũgĩ. Likewise, the question about formal complexity in my British class on *A Grain of Wheat* finally placed the idea of the literary firmly in a critique of Eurocentrism. Ngũgĩ's continuing usefulness to the North American politics of race was measured after my midwestern lecture, and his usefulness for thinking about local modes of feminist critique was considered in the discussion of Bengali literature after my lecture in India.

If Ngũgĩ's fiction does nothing else, it offers us a modeling of a call to relation. For instance, it would be impossible to think about Mau Mau in *Weep Not, Child* without considering the differences of perspective, politics, and positioning among, say, Njoroge, Ngotho, and Kamau. *The River Between*'s gendering of debate can most usefully be considered by reference to the ways in which the hybrid female subjects, Nyambura and Muthoni, become the middle ground for the oppositional identities of the Christian Joshua and the traditionalist Kabonyi. *Petals of Blood*'s accumulation of a long communal history is the result of interweaving the multiple, initially separable narratives of characters such as Munira, Wanja, Abdulla, Karega, Nyakinua, Ole Masai, and Nding'uri. Narrative in all these novels results from the discovery of relation, which also invariably culminates in the disclosure of a history.

This process reaches an apogee in the practical politics of writing in Gĩkũyũ in the later novels, *Devil on the Cross*, *Matigari*, and *Wizard of the Crow*. Written for translation, these works place Gĩkũyũ and non-Gĩkũyũ readers alike in an ethical structure in which analysis or reading must always account for the linguistically unassimilable, because a translated version of the text exists. In this fluid relational space, the mutability of translation enables unanticipated subject positions. We read a translated text always in a provisional sense, because another version of that text is doing different cultural work. Hence, as we read, we are placed in a relation with positions that are unassimilable to our own. This relation with the unassimilable is especially marked if different linguistic mediums (say, Gĩkũyũ and English) automatically exert different kinds of political claims on the world, as Ngũgĩ has argued.

Ngũgĩ's defense of language as a carrier of culture invokes forms of cultural ownership and authority, but in its invocation of relations with the unassimilable it is also a most enabling mechanism for the portability of ideas. One of the most radical possibilities opened up in Ngũgĩ's later critical work is his advocacy of a literary dialogue enabled by multilateral translation. If there are innumerable centers of culture, Ngũgĩ argues, then the global hegemony of English may be ameliorated by the act of translating canonical English works into world languages (*Decolonising* 8) or by translating the world's great vernacular oral and literary traditions into one another's languages (*Moving* 39). This polycentric idea of culture is viable only when you introduce a program of translating not just from minority languages into English or vice versa but also from Hausa into Gĩkũyũ or Zulu or Urdu or Hindi, and so on.

Ngũgĩ's critical model of linguistic activism is consistent with the trajectory of his multiperspectival narratives and with the negotiations of positionality that students invariably undertake when they read his work with the seriousness it deserves. To read Ngũgĩ for partiality of perspective almost invariably enables the progressive project of imagining one's relation to the postcolonial world. Such imagining enables the work of self-critique, since it places our readings in the context of their geopolitical circumstance.

In sum, Ngũgĩ's novels and critical writings offer our students far more than an anthropological tour of an East African society. His work demands of us—as teachers, students, readers—acts of provisional self-placement in relation to unanticipated auditors. My own response to Ngũgĩ's work continues to be shaped by its political urgency and its cultural mobility as a critique of globalization, the supposedly unifying circumstance that positions so many on unequal terms and affords them markedly lesser means. Ngũgĩ's oeuvre is about more than nation or language; it is also about our cultural disposition toward political power. To instill an awareness of this disposition in our students—wherever they are and even when that is not what we set out to teach—is perhaps the greatest gift that a progressive education can bestow.

NOTES

[1] Liyong accepted an academic appointment in exile at the University of Venda the following year.

[2] I advocated designing the syllabus in a way that accorded with wider political transformation, social inclusivity, and literary relevance. My arguments were dismissed with the spurious counterclaim that if an Africanized syllabus were allowed, the integrity of the English department would be undermined by a faculty invasion of francophone and germanophone African literature courses.

[3] This progressive generation of students, fully engaged in the struggle against apartheid, had joined various liberation movements or political parties. At the university, they committed to new struggles for the transformation of knowledge. My phrase "political biographies" attempts to convey how completely politics was lived at this time by most of them.

[4] Writing of postcolonial ethics, in particular of the relation between the postcolonial critic and the subaltern, Spivak claims, "Ethics are not a problem of knowledge but a call of relationship (where being without relationship is the limit case)" ("Echo" 190). In my view, a call to relation of this order is at stake in Ngũgĩ's fiction.

Teaching *Petals of Blood* in a Kenyan Classroom

Emilia Ilieva

Today—not unlike for the first time, over a decade ago—I find myself compelled to teach *Petals of Blood* to Kenyan undergraduate students of literature as part of a corrective endeavor: to assert that this novel is a foundational text in Kenyan literature and a masterpiece of Kenya's greatest writer, Ngũgĩ wa Thiong'o. In the mid-1990s, I was shocked to discover the barely concealed hostility with which many Kenyans spoke about Ngũgĩ, when they could not avoid speaking about him altogether. Yet few were more than remotely familiar with his works. I had until then lived in a world where he was regarded as a literary icon. But it was only at first glance that this Kenyan reversal seemed a paradox. With time, I was able to see the contextual logic behind the discomfort Ngũgĩ caused in Kenya.

Emerging young writers recently engaged in a verbal bashing of Ngũgĩ—and of his generation of writers—as part of what they probably saw as the launching of their literary careers. This attack led Evan Mwangi to observe with exasperation on the seventieth anniversary of Ngũgĩ's birth:

> Praised abroad, Ngũgĩ has, like the proverbial prophet, been vilified at home. . . . [S]ome of Kenya's wannabe novelists are defined by a malignant anti-Ngũgĩ attitude, probably inculcated by the anti-intellectual 8-4-4 school system created during the Moi era. ("Ngũgĩ")[1]

So entrenched is this negative attitude that even university students have not been able to resist it. It has had a crippling effect on their reading of Ngũgĩ, which is often, at the start, superficial and biased. I had to take this phenomenon into account in my teaching. My first task was to examine it.

Ngũgĩ's return to Kenya in 2004 after twenty-two years of exile and the ambivalent response to it provided important material for self-reflective study in class. On the one hand, there was a display of enthusiasm and celebration and the expression of hope that Ngũgĩ would "discover new ways of inspiring young Kenyans into another efflorescence of socially committed creative writing" ("Ngũgĩ: Let the Grain"). On the other hand, Ngũgĩ's books remained more or less untouchable. Ngũgĩ's publisher, Henry Chakava, chairman of East African Educational Publishers, lamented that, contrary to expectations, even after the author's highly publicized return the sales of his books had not gone up. "We don't simply want the books back in schools. . . . We want people to read Ngũgĩ's books because [they] like him for his ideas" ("Kenyans"). What he saw at work were the vestiges of a fear that had been planted in people in the late 1970s, when the Kenyan government banned Ngũgĩ's books.

Even as Chakava anticipated the return of Ngũgĩ's books to the school syllabus, insufficient as this was, an anonymous correspondent to Kenya's leading weekly newspaper, *Sunday Nation*, wondered, "Can Ngũgĩ's writing 'sow' a grain of peace in learning institutions?" The implied answer was negative, because "his best characters . . . are those who portray prowess in physical combat, bravery and moral courage in warfare" ("Can"). Having students discuss the characters in *Petals of Blood* can show how intentionally selective, literal, and constraining this reading is.

Philip Ochieng, a veteran writer, took the opportunity of Ngũgĩ's return to discuss the alleged harm "revolutionary ideas" had done to Ngũgĩ's writing. He began by dismissing an extremist critic, Omushibungo Omuholo, who in the mid-1990s had said that, after *A Grain of Wheat*, Ngũgĩ had had an "exile of thought," that he had "cast out [of] the window any pretension of creative dialogue and discourse. He instead fills the mouths of peasants with Communist outpourings" ("Some Critics" 2). For Ochieng these are the "same old juggled phrases—facile, propagandistic and unverified." But he himself concludes that "somewhere in the seventies" Ngũgĩ seems to have dropped into the pitfall of "sacrificing art on the altar of 'revolutionary' agitation" (4). He observes:

> In a work of art, such slogans as "exploitation of the masses," "toiling slaves," "imperialist intrigue" and "revolutionary heroism" must be left out altogether—not because [these realities] do not exist (they do) but only because, in a work of art, they will offend the palate of any aesthete.
> (P. Ochieng, "Revolutionary Ideas" 2)

The other aberration on Ngũgĩ's part, which has "robbed Kenya of a man who was once its greatest artist in fiction," is the writer's "fixation with a revolutionary situation which does not exist" in Kenya (3). I return to this type of ideologically overdetermined reading later but note here how rigid a position can be even as it is taken in the name of artistic freedom and the beauty of form.

In another piece, Ochieng, who was Ngũgĩ's classmate at Alliance High School, says with admiration that "of all the Alliance *alumni* since it was set up in 1926" Ngũgĩ was "the only one who internalised" the school motto, "Strong to Serve." If many proved "extremely strong, but only in self-service, only as delirious gluttons and unstoppable go-getters," Ngũgĩ "decolonised his mind in readiness for service to a community gasping for survival" ("Afro-Saxon" 3). I point out this contradiction to the students, and we ask ourselves whether the intellectual and moral stuff that go into the making of such service could really contaminate Ngũgĩ's writing, as Ochieng suggested.

Rasna Warah, a journalist and writer, raised one of those extraliterary concerns that have for long been the easy and cheap way of diminishing Ngũgĩ. Ngũgĩ had just spoken to a group of twenty young writers about a writer's responsibility to his community. Gleefully, as if she had caught him in a contradiction, Warah asked Ngũgĩ if he felt "he had betrayed Kenyans by not returning home from self-imposed exile for twenty-two years." Even though slightly uneasy that she may have sounded "insensitive," "considering that Ngũgĩ's much-awaited homecoming had been marred by a brutal attack on him and his wife," Warah claims that "it was clearly [a question] many Kenyans had been asking themselves, as was evident from the outpouring of gratitude I received when the lecture was over, and Ngũgĩ was no longer within earshot." Warah conjures up an alternative biography of Ngũgĩ, one in which he remained in Kenya and continued writing in English, "simply because the only way a poor, Third World country . . . such as Kenya can have an impact on a globalising economy is to communicate in the language of that economy, which, unfortunately, is English." I ask the students to note how the twenty writers have, by a stroke of the pen, grown into "many Kenyans" and how a hypocritically attentive audience transforms itself into a bunch of gossips. We also revisit Ngũgĩ's ideas on the use of indigenous languages in view of the contemptuous manner in which Warah dismissed them.

Three years later, Mumia Osaaji, a university lecturer, responded negatively to Ngũgĩ's keynote address at a forum of the Association of Commonwealth Literature and Language Studies in Vancouver, Canada. By his very presence at the gathering, Ngũgĩ, who had been a "consistent critic of the political, economic and cultural 'British commonwealth,'" proved that he was "mellowing." The possible reasons for this were cynically supplied: "old age and fatigue"; exile, and the consequent need for Ngũgĩ to "constantly 're-package' himself to keep the sustenance taps flowing"; and Ngũgĩ's ideological isolation following the collapse of the Communist bloc (Osaaji). It is not difficult to deconstruct this text with the students, to show the lack of any sustained argument in it, its obvious bias, its light weight.

Kiarie Kamau likened Osaaji's attack to "something that was fashionable in the 1980s when some literary scholars would rail at, and lambast Ngũgĩ, as a way of placing their names on the sands of literary times!" And as a way of pleasing the ever-watchful censor, I add. With the students I discuss the intellectual dishonesty and opportunism of which Ngũgĩ has been a victim. Gradually they realize how much of these attitudes they had unconsciously adopted and begin looking at Ngũgĩ with new eyes.

The ruling regime in Kenya, under both Presidents Kenyatta and Moi, feared any political opinion or system of thought that questioned the neocolonial nature of the society they were fashioning. Any radical critique threatened them personally, since they were the beneficiaries of the status quo. With the publication of *Petals* and the works that followed, as well as with his social, political, and cultural criticism, Ngũgĩ emerged as the most forceful critic of the system. His position was vilified as Marxist, and in Cold War Kenya Marxism had officially been branded as a subversive, unpatriotic, violence-inspiring ideology. As Ngũgĩ put it, "Today . . . [q]uestioning the exploitation and oppression of peasants and workers is Marxism and hence treason. Questioning corruption in high places is sedition" (*Barrel* 2). After the attempted coup of 1982, a decade of political repression set in, in which a writer of Ngũgĩ's mold was anathema. To condemn and ostracize him became the norm. Many intellectuals toed the line. His sympathizers among progressive Kenyans mostly chose to remain silent. Radical thinkers who admired him were subjected to similar persecution. Many were brainwashed. Njoki Wane, now a professor at the University of Toronto, says of her years of study in Kenya in the 1980s, "I thought Ngũgĩ wa Thiong'o—who spoke widely on decolonisation of the mind and promoted the virtues of African languages—was a whining and troublesome English professor. Now I know better" (Kagumba-Sibanda 12).

After the disintegration of the Soviet Union, the dismantling of socialism in Eastern Europe, the fundamental changes in post-Maoist China, and the global expansion of capitalism, the ideological and moral climate in Kenya was again not conducive to an interest in and appreciation of *Petals* (and Ngũgĩ's later works). As Gitau Warigi wrote on Ngũgĩ's homecoming, "His message of class struggle which his later books are themed on looks quaint to the Kenyan yuppies who came of age when Ngũgĩ was away. The materialism he condemned is more rampant now than it was then." I seek to make the students recognize themselves in this description. We conclude that, in Kenya, Ngũgĩ's time seems never to have come. We acknowledge how unfortunate this is and accept that we should start with ourselves to change this attitude.

My second task in teaching *Petals* is to encourage my students to read Ngũgĩ's novel on its own terms and not as a text that mirrors the author's experiences, views, and beliefs. In the class, a brilliant student made a presentation on *Petals* as the product of a highly ideological writer. His argument can be summarized as follows: In his early works, Ngũgĩ was influenced by writers who were not Marxists; in those works, he was launching a cultural campaign. But somewhere between the late 1960s and the early 1970s, he saw the light, as it were; *Petals* became his first Marxist book, with others to follow. These later books translate Marxist ideology into fiction. The student spoke at length about Marx's formation as a philosopher and gave an impressive summary of the main tenets of Marxism. According to the student, *Petals* fully lent itself to a Marxist interpretation, and he set out to demonstrate how the ideas of class, class struggle, exploitation, victory of the masses, building of a new society, and base and superstructure were reflected in the novel. The arson attack on Wanja's brothel, the student argued, is a clear example of class struggle, revolution, mass action. Similarly, Inspector Godfrey, who represents the institution of the police, exemplifies how the superstructure tries to protect the status quo.

The student concluded by saying that Ngũgĩ was perhaps justified to use the Marxist analysis until the end of the 1970s: it helped him expose injustices and betrayals in the society. But even then, his solution—a socialist revolution—was far-fetched and impractical, because there has never been a revolutionary situation in Kenya. Ngũgĩ's continued adherence to Marxism, the student averred, was naive and even preposterous, considering the discrediting of Marxism as a viable ideology and the death of communism in the world.

The class felt that the student had not done justice to the novel. I pointed out that any reading that is exclusively based on an author's perspective will always present a serious limitation and reduce the meaning of a text. In this case, it led to an ideologically overdetermined perception.

Furthermore, Marxism is still very much alive. As the editors of the journal *Rethinking Marxism* recently wrote:

> Capitalism is the only game in town—or so it seems for many of our students, colleagues, and fellow citizens. Marxists, of course, notwithstanding their many theoretical and political differences, hold a different view: that capitalism is *not* the only way of organizing a society, that another—collective or communal—world is both necessary and possible.
> ("Editors Introduction" 293)

Therefore I incorporate in our discussions some of the literary criticism on *Petals* that supports a Marxist interpretation. Chidi Amuta writes:

> In *Petals of Blood*, Ngũgĩ's consciousness is decidedly anti-imperialist while his ideological alignment is unambiguously socialist in a Marxian sense. . . . It is principally against this political and ideological background that the experiences, themes, and novelistic techniques explored and adopted in the novel can most meaningfully be understood. (144)

In his overview of the critical reception of *Petals*, Joseph McLaren remarks that practically all critics have approached the novel with "particular attention to its ideological message" (73). But although his conclusion is that "[t]he success or failure of *Petals of Blood* for a particular critic was not necessarily a function of the critic's national origin but rather based on his or her aesthetic and political criteria" (88), there is an unmistakable Kenyan dimension to some of the criticism. For example, James Ogude, contesting Ngũgĩ's understanding of Kenya's past and present, repeatedly refers to Ngũgĩ's entrapment or imprisonment or deep embeddedness in the wrong theory: "Ngũgĩ's understanding of the historical processes in Kenya is too deeply embedded in dependency theory to allow for a nuanced understanding of the complex colonial and postcolonial experience in Kenya" (32–33). A Kenyan historian with what might be a vested interest in a particular interpretation of Kenya's past feels terrorized by Ngũgĩ: "Ngũgĩ is operating beyond the limits of his role as a writer. He is terrorising us" (W. Ochieng, "Dignitaries" 48). Discussing the transformation of *theng'eta* from a "potent ritual drink" into a "debased, mass-produced substance," Patrick Williams finds it "a good illustration of the Marxist argument about the way in which capitalism turns use value . . . into exchange value" (*Ngũgĩ* 83). Instead of helping us dig deeper into the text, to see the significance of *theng'eta* in the inner world of the novel, this overdetermined reading diverts our attention from it.

Ngũgĩ's supposed Fanonism is also regularly evoked. For Kathleen Greenfield, "[t]he actions planned by both Wanja and Abdullah (sic) at the end of the novel correspond to what Fanon identifies as the prerevolutionary stage" (35).

Even for Simon Gikandi, in his excellent book-length study, Ngũgĩ is forever either echoing or learning from Fanon:

> The first part of *Petals of Blood* is actually an attempt to develop what one may call "a poetics of underdevelopment," a poetics that Ngugi had learnt from Fanon's famous critique of independence. Indeed, it is hard to miss the Fanonist project in the novel. (*Ngũgĩ* 137)

Besides suggesting a certain lack of originality on Ngũgĩ's part, the tracing of such correspondences does little to advance our understanding of the book.

If *Petals* were no more than an illustration of Marxist and Fanonist principles, it would not have enjoyed the wide appeal it has had in the world. In 1984, my translation of the novel into Bulgarian sold out in a couple of weeks. A few years before the fall of the Berlin Wall, in the predominantly dissident political climate of Eastern Europe, socialist sloganeering was the last thing that could have aroused enthusiasm among Bulgarian readers. That the book struck a chord in their hearts and minds as it did must have been for reasons other than its Marxist ideology. *Petals* was appreciated because it illuminated a great deal of the life of Kenyan people and suggested a compelling moral vision.

In class, I respond to the complaints of those uncomfortable with what they see as Ngũgĩ's ideological inclination, and we discover in the process that we are actually examining evidence not only of the validity of Ngũgĩ's messages in *Petals* but also of their continuing relevance. The critic who wants to see Ngũgĩ's work free of "revolutionary ideas" is the same one who writes:

> Despite the collapse of the Soviet Union, the world remains as faulty and as dangerous as ever. . . . I know that this unacceptable division of the world between extreme affluence and extreme indigence will continue to produce "little terrorists." This is an objective situation. It does not require a Marx, a Fanon or a Ngũgĩ to create.
> (P. Ochieng, "Revolutionary Ideas" 3)

Similarly, Warah asks, "Could it be that exile creates conditions that make your work no longer relevant to the place you come from?" But then she confirms how right Ngũgĩ has always been to distrust the ruling elite in neocolonial Kenya:

> [When Ngũgĩ left Kenya] in 1982, we knew we had a dictator as president and found ways to survive in a hostile, autocratic environment; today, our so-called liberators have proved to be no better than wolves in sheep's clothing.

For Ogude, every issue that Ngũgĩ deals with in *Petals* is more complex than the novel's treatment allows. But Williams rightly wonders, in view of the recurrence of this objection, whether

> situations and issues are necessarily always so complex. . . . [I]f individuals like Kimeria and Chui are—objectively, demonstrably—cheating, exploiting and oppressing substantial numbers of their fellow Kenyans, wherein lies the moral complexity? (*Ngũgĩ* 172)

Petals directly addresses complex Kenyan realities. The depiction of the activities of the fictional KCO (Kamwene Cultural Organization) and the tea party, for example, exposes the evil of the political manipulation of ethnic feelings with an honesty and courage never exhibited by any other writer. That Ngũgĩ is historically accurate, forward-looking, and even prophetic has been repeatedly demonstrated by events in Kenya's recent past, but never so clearly as by the politically instigated ethnic violence that followed the disputed outcome of the general election of 2007, which brought the country to the brink of civil war. Yash Pal Ghai placed the question of tribalism in a broad context:

> Our problem, fundamentally, is not tribalism, but poverty, underdevelopment, corruption, a predatory political and economic class which feeds on the resources that the state extracts from the people, the politics of patronage, seemingly based on tribalism, but more accurately based on clientalism and cronyism, disparities of wealth and opportunity, and the utter lack of accountability of the Government and other public authorities.

Isn't this what *Petals* is about?

Ngũgĩ has been persistently and angrily criticized for elevating the Mau Mau rebellion as the peak of the Kenyan people's resistance against colonial domination. The fear of recognizing Mau Mau's place in Kenyan history has in fact prevented an objective and comprehensive discussion of it in Kenyan historiography. The most important scholarly works on Mau Mau remain those written by non-Kenyans, such as Andrei Pegushev, David Anderson, and Caroline Elkins. Carol Sicherman has convincingly written about the importance of Ngũgĩ's contribution to the rewriting of Kenyan history, including that of Mau Mau ("Ngũgĩ wa Thiong'o and the Writing"). Particularly important is the need to recognize Ngũgĩ's statement in *Petals*: "Mau Mau was only a link in the chain in the long struggle of African people through different times at different places" (137). Even the central symbolic journey in the novel has a referent in Kenya's history of colonial resistance. The journey precedes and is not ethnically related to Mau Mau: the extraordinary march on Nairobi by three thousand Wakamba men, women, and children in July 1938, led by Samuel Muindi (Muindi Mbingu), was designed to meet the governor and demand the reversal of the order for the forced sale of their surplus stock for erosion control (Newman).

Ngũgĩ's heroes of resistance are not only Mau Mau fighters; they are many and come from far and wide: "Chaka . . . Toussaint . . . Samoei . . . Nat Turner . . . Arap Manyei . . . Laibon Turugat . . . Dessalines . . . Mondhlane . . . Owalo . . .

Siotune and Kiamba . . . Nkrumah . . . Cabral . . ." (137). Ogude writes, "The story of resistance and collaboration, as portrayed by Ngugi, has a certain unity of view which lacks precision when one is searching for a complex interpretation of history" (35). Ngũgĩ is not ignorant of historical complexity, but his vital and perfectly legitimate task in *Petals* is the invention of tradition. For Eric Hobsbawm, an "invented tradition" constitutes "responses to novel situations which take the form of reference to old situations, or which establish their own past by their quasi-obligatory repetition" (2). We may also say that Ngũgĩ has embraced Jean Jaurès's famous appeal: "Take from the altars of the past the fire—not the ashes" (*Jean Jaurès*).

Despite the assertion that Ngũgĩ's "presentation of religion is one-dimensional" (Ogude 41), Ngũgĩ focuses in *Petals* on that aspect of religion that worries him. As John Anonby has written, Ngũgĩ "has dramatically exemplified the futility of a professed faith that fails to address real needs, in a manner reminiscent of James 2:15–17" (112). But how can we fail to see that the two most lovable women characters in the novel, Mukami and Old Mariamu, are religious? "It was Mukami who taught me prayer," says Karega (Ngũgĩ, *Petals* [1978] 217). Of Mariamu, Munira remembers, "She was very pious in an undemonstrative way: her piety simply lay in how she carried herself; in how she talked; in her trembling, total absorption in her work" (47). Ngũgĩ is contemporary in his criticism of religion. Significantly, Kenyan church leaders reflected on their conduct since the 2005 national referendum on the proposed new constitution of the country and especially before the 2007 general election, declaring:

> We . . . own up our sins of among others taking partisan positions on national issues; elevating our ethnic identities above our Christian identity; direct involvement in party politics; and, participation in the post election violence, which are made more ominous by the deteriorating national values, sinful political strategies and failure to faithfully stand for biblical values and principles. (Kibicho and Karanja)

My next task is to place *Petals* in a proper literary context. It is certainly worth looking at the book as a political novel, according to Irving Howe's definition: "a novel in which political ideas play a dominant role or in which the political milieu is the dominant setting" (17). Many critics of *Petals* argue that art and ideology, or the aesthetic and the political, are incompatible in a work of literature (P. Ochieng, "Some Critics" and "Revolutionary Ideas"; McLaren; Williams, *Ngũgĩ* 165–80). Howe admits that in a political novel there are peculiar "internal tensions" between the purpose to engage moral sentiments, passions, and emotions as well as to "capture the quality of concrete experience" and the abstract character of ideology. But he insists that this tension lends the political novel its "interest," from which it "takes on the aura of high drama" (20). "At its best, the political novel generates such intense heat that ideas it appropriates are melted into its movement and fused with the emotions of its characters"

(21). *Petals* generates such heat. Howe further observes, "No doubt, when the armored columns of ideology troop *en masse*, they do imperil the novel's life and liveliness, but ideas, be they in free isolation or looped into formal systems, are indispensable to the serious novel" (20). Ideas were indispensable in Kenya at the time of the writing of Ngũgĩ's novel. Ngũgĩ could not have avoided his nation's turmoil and social conflict, could not have *not* written *Petals*, without becoming irrelevant.

Students should also see how *Petals* fits in the tradition of social realist writing that developed in nineteenth-century Europe. The main principles of that writing—historicism; social analysis; interaction of typical characters with typical circumstances; the endeavor through analysis to arrive at a synthesis, to convey the contradictory wholeness of human life—apply to *Petals*. Ngũgĩ's novel bears an affinity to Honoré de Balzac's works, particularly to his series of novels written in the 1830s, to which Balzac later gave the common title *Human Comedy*. I give a brief outline of these novels in class.

Balzac's French society, represented from every conceivable angle, acquires an unparalleled diversity and completeness. Balzac offers moral criticism of an entire epoch. It is a bourgeois epoch, one that has turned money into the be-all and end-all of life and has thus distorted and dehumanized human relationships. But Balzac's realism is inseparable from the humanistic quest for an ideal, and this quest results in the expression of impassioned views and opinions. That is why, even though Balzac was truly a historian, he never restricted himself to the tasks of the historian. He used his creative freedom both to express his views about human affairs and to correct history. So he portrayed a world that was both evil and capable of regeneration. The search for an alternative world a better world, is precisely what we find in *Petals*.

Ngũgĩ is even closer to Émile Zola. Zola's twenty Rougon-Macquart novels are a large-scale depiction of the huge changes in the material life and consciousness of the French people in the second half of the nineteenth century: the growth of towns, the accumulation of wealth, and the advancement of science and technology. At the same time, Zola reveals the deep antihumanity of this new civilization and seeks an alternative to bourgeois relations. In the novels *Germinal*, *Money*, and *The Downfall*, we find references to the most important political events of the 1870s–80s. *Germinal* is directly related to the intensification of the strike movement in France in the 1880s. It represents a truthful and historically insightful picture of the life of working people, particularly of the inhumane working conditions of the coal miners in northern France. This picture and the depiction of the mine workers' strike constituted a literary innovation. The idea of reawakening reflected in the title of the novel is associated with the gathering social upheavals and with Zola's optimism about the possibility of social transformation. The parallels with Ngũgĩ's novel are unmistakable.

The Bulgarian reading public linked *Petals of Blood* to their own national classic, the novel Тютюн (1951; "Tobacco"), by Dimitar Dimov. It is a novel that reveals the character of Bulgarian history, of Bulgarian capitalism, between the two world wars. Dimov depicts the sharp class conflict between the get-rich-quickly tobacco merchants and the tobacco workers. The author traces the decline and fall of the Bulgarian bourgeoisie, its moral degeneration, and highlights the determined struggle of the workers against capital. Two classes, two systems of morality, two philosophies are set against each other:

> It is as if the whole world is divided by one line into two struggling halves, into two antagonistic, opposite parts. But it is precisely this line of fire which splits the world into two, that creates at the same time the balance, the totality, the wholeness of the world. (Kujumdzhiev 14)

This observation applies to Ngũgĩ's world. The tobacco of Dimov's title, resembling the commercialized *theng'eta*, is a poisonous and deadly plant; it not only symbolizes the corrupt power of money, of the momentarily invincible magnates, but also ironically hints at the inevitable doom of the world that thrives on it.

Petals belongs to African novels of "the postcolonial stage," which Kwame Anthony Appiah calls

> novels of delegitimation: rejecting the western imperium, it is true, but also rejecting the nationalist project of the postcolonial national bourgeoisie. . . . [T]hat project [of delegitimation] . . . is grounded in an appeal to an ethical universal; indeed it is based . . . in an appeal to a certain simple respect for human suffering, a fundamental revolt against the endless misery of the last thirty years. (152)

It is this ethical universal that Ngũgĩ espouses. So the revolution that he anticipates in *Petals of Blood* and that critics dismiss, ridicule, sneer at, or celebrate may be seen as symbolic. In his novel, Kenyan society is transformable, but this transformation need not take place tomorrow, nor does it have to produce a society based on the principles of scientific socialism. Appiah's "ethical universal" brings us back to Howe and the concluding observation he makes, that "the political novelist, even as he remains fascinated by politics, urges for a moral order beyond ideology" (24). My students finally recognize Ngũgĩ's desire for such a moral order and celebrate Ngũgĩ as the exceptional Kenyan writer who has been able to envision it, securing in this way the centrality of his place in Kenyan literature.

NOTE

[1] The 8-4-4 system of education in Kenya (eight years of primary, four years of secondary, and four years of university education) was introduced in 1985, replacing the 7-4-2-3 system (seven years of primary, four years of lower secondary, two years of upper

secondary, and three years of university education), which had been in place since 1964, following independence. The change was said to be in response to the need to provide skilled labor to a country that had to fast-track its industrialization. Vocational subjects were introduced into the school curriculum to teach students technical skills. Over time, the system has been subjected to criticism, seen as not only having failed in its mandate but also having led to an overburdened curriculum, which in turn made learning exam-oriented and discouraged intellectual curiosity and sophistication, the nurturing of creativity, and the development of talents.

Teaching Ngũgĩ's Drama in the American Academy

Gĩchingiri Ndĩgĩrĩgĩ

Immediately after obtaining my PhD, I had the opportunity to teach African literature in the English department at the University of California, Los Angeles, for three quarters. Hoping to translate my dissertation research findings on Ngũgĩ's drama and theater into some immediate practical use, I taught *The Trial of Dedan Kimathi* (Ngũgĩ and Mugo) in two upper-division seminars and three formal lecture classes. One lecture course was a survey of African literature, where the text was read with other texts narrativizing anticolonial resistance—albeit with the retrospective insight from the failures of the postcolonial nation. In another lecture course, on African women's writing, we specifically attempted to read the power in the margins occupied by the character in the play known as Woman, paying attention to women's attempts at incorporating their story into history.

I will always remember a student who, in an informal review of the African women's writing class, told me that as a democratically minded person he hoped that I would consider excluding *The Trial of Dedan Kimathi* when I taught the course again. I was unable to coax him into revealing what he found so undemocratic about the play. Six months earlier, I had taught the same text to a very receptive class, a third of whom wrote their term papers on the play.

This essay reflects on the challenges I encountered in teaching Ngũgĩ's drama at various universities in the United States. It also explores aspects of Ngũgĩ's drama that could be fruitfully discussed in an American classroom. Recognizing that students are active agents in the creation of the meaning of the Ngũgĩ texts I teach, I blend reader-response theory and postcolonial criticism in exploring those areas of resistance to Ngũgĩ's drama and how students can be recruited into collaborative-corroborative reading. I have also taught *The Black Hermit*, the safest of Ngũgĩ's plays, hoping that its theme of love and suicide would enable interesting discussions about the clash of cultures, about the ethnic, gender, religious, and racial tensions in the emergent postcolonial nation.

Understandably, as committed art, Ngũgĩ's later drama is ideologically demanding, and its advocacy of the rights of the underprivileged could alienate students who occupy a position of privilege (by race, class, or nation) that they are unwilling to see challenged. The drama elaborates the inequalities between colonial centers and margins, on the one hand, and the centers and margins in the emergent neocolonial Kenyan nation, on the other. Ngũgĩ's vocalization of the marginalized is part of the resistance to the discursive practices of the Western centers and of despotic postcolonial states. Conceived as activist theater that takes "the side of the people, that . . . gives people courage and urges them to higher resolves in their struggle for total liberation . . . , [that depicts] the masses . . . in the only historically correct perspective: positively, heroically and as the true makers of history" (Ngũgĩ and Mugo, Preface vii), *Trial* puts colonialism on trial for subjecting the people to a history of oppression that culminates in the botched judicial trial of the people's hero, his wrongful sentence to hang, and the persecution of those clamoring for the liberation of their country from Western imperialism. Blaming the emerging social inequalities on the betrayal of the ideals of the anticolonial struggle, both *Trial* and *I Will Marry When I Want* sought to retrieve the people's agency in confronting the neocolonial state.

Written in English and originally performed as Kenya's entry for the second All African Festival of Arts and Culture in 1977, *Trial* was part of the official nationalism whose staging the Kenyan state elite facilitated. But when Ngũgĩ repackaged that same nationalism—that same critique of class inequalities and imperialism—in *Ngaahika Ndeenda* (1977, later translated as *I Will Marry When I Want* [1982]) in Gĩkũyũ, a language understood by the underprivileged who were the subjects and objects of its revolutionary message, and when it was performed before village audiences at Kamĩrĩĩthũ in 1977, the neocolonial state banned the performance of the play and detained Ngũgĩ without trial for a year. In 1982, the Kenyan government destroyed the communal open-air theater at Kamĩrĩĩthũ in a clampdown that eventually forced Ngũgĩ into exile. Until the mid-1990s the government refused performance licenses for *Ngaahika Ndeenda* or its translation, though *Trial* was performed fairly regularly.

Most dramatic texts are written for performance, and all dramatic performance is realized in a culture. Marvin Carlson observes that theatrical performance is a uniquely structured event for a circumscribed and often clearly identifiable audience (10). Wendell Harris writes that the meaning of a text is to be found by reconstructing the historical context in which it appears (137). He also observes that meaning in a text is connected to much more than language systems (9). I make central to my teaching the analysis of the interaction between the dramatic text (both written and performed) and its context.

I want my students to attain, as Umberto Eco would say, the specific encyclopedic competence that an author assumes a model reader will have. Eco states that the model reader is "nourished on a whole chapter of an intertextual encyclopedia" (7). Modifying Eco, Marco De Marinis posits a dramaturgy of the spectator, arguing that beyond encyclopedic competence, intertextual and ideological competence defines model spectators (103). De Marinis recognizes that even though a performance builds into its textual structure an anticipated reception (104), a spectator's understanding of the performance occurs in a situation of "controlled creative autonomy" from the dramaturgies of the director, the writer, and the performer (101). The writer structures a "dialectic between the constraints imposed by the work (the 'aesthetic text') and the possibilities left open to those who receive the work" (101). This idea accords with Eco's notion of "suggestiveness": the deliberate attempt to open the text to the free response of the addressee, enabling readers to adapt their worlds to the personal world proposed by the text (49–53). Recognizing the spectator's "creative autonomy" helps us draw connections between the individuality of spectator reception to a performance and the process of reading a work in private. For De Marinis as for Eco, spectators get the best out of a performance if they bring to it their encyclopedic, ideological, and intertextual competence.

The idea of the model reader has been discussed extensively by Eco, Carlson, and Wolfgang Iser, among others, working principally from the perspectives of reader-response theory. These critics recognize that each text, to paraphrase Iser, incorporates aspects from a variety of social, historical, cultural, and literary systems that exist as referential fields outside the text (311). Eco states that a well-organized text presupposes a model of competence that comes from outside it, but the text also works to build that competence (8). These perspectives inform the attention we pay to the extratextual referential fields in reading Ngũgĩ's drama.

My student's advice in the African women's writing class indicates that the collaborative process of creating meaning in a text poses challenges. The comment surprised me because I taught *Trial* in that particular class to foreground the interplay between nationalist causes and issues affecting women as these are portrayed in literature. The discussion had been on the margins of the larger questions of class, imperialism, power, and colonial and neocolonial politics, which come through much more forcefully when the focus is kept on Kimathi. We considered the double oppression of women by colonialism and traditional patriarchy, paying particular attention to the relationship between the Woman and Johnnie, the white colonial officer. We talked about the Woman's performance of femininity when confronted by the lascivious Johnnie, about the scene's inversion of stereotypes of African promiscuity, showing how women in the struggle used their femininity to acquire power over armed colonial officers. We also discussed the Woman's ability to outwit Johnnie by mocking his manliness: "[a] white Bwana frightened by a woman's skirt . . . and 'market' basket" (10). We compared the macho Johnnie's fright to his flight when he mistakenly assumes that the "terrorists" have come and hysterically leaves the apparently vulnerable Woman to face them by herself (12). We also probed how traditional patriarchy was being reproduced (and destabilized) in the relationship between Boy and Girl before they are conscientized by the Woman. We paid attention to the Woman's mothering role as she initiates Boy and Girl into the struggle.

Recognizing that women's contribution to Kenya's independence struggle had been overshadowed by an emphasis on the valiant efforts of the named male characters in the play—Kimathi, Stanley Mathenge, General Matenjagwo—we read the unnamed Woman as the play's moral center, paying attention to her testimony that she was a bad woman until she heard the call that is both Christian and socialist. While probing her moral and ideological reform of the next generation of revolutionaries, we discussed her approximation of the role played by the so-called civilian or passive wing of the Mau Mau. This wing supplied the fighters with food, arms and ammunition, and intelligence on government troop movements. We discussed the vision of a new Kenya devoid of class, racial, and ethnic divisions that the Woman and Kimathi seem to share. We noted the woman fighter's resolve when Kimathi is shown wavering in the guerrilla court scene in the Third Movement. Above all, we paid attention to the significance of the Woman in rehabilitating Kimathi and inverting the colonial stereotypes about him. It is through her that we learn of his softer, human side, but it is also her role to perpetuate the myth of his indomitable spirit. Even as she supports the mythologization of Kimathi, she prepares the next generation of revolutionaries to take him as their inspiration.

Students generally praised the portrait of agentive womanhood, including that of the Girl, who learns to stand up to the timid bully, Boy, and then fights beside him. The students found impressive the Woman's informed participation in liberating her country and the foregrounding of women's herstories. They were receptive to the idea that herstory helps rewrite Kenyan history by disseminating positive images of women, of Kimathi and the liberation struggle he leads. They recognized that the play was intimately connected with the politics of representation in African literature and approved of a woman who was comfortable navigating the male-female, private-public binarisms as the situation demanded.

Because we discussed each text thoroughly, I was surprised to be blindsided at the end of the quarter with the student's recommendation to drop *Trial* when I taught the class again. I suspect that, as in some other instances when I taught the play, the student had a problem with the play's critique of imperialism, of the promotion of anti-imperialism as the only historically correct perspective. Students also are generally uncomfortable with violence. My decision not to supply secondary readings on Kenya's independence struggle to this particular class may have contributed as well to the difficulty.

I had earlier taught the text to a class that found Kimathi's anticolonial resistance "so cool." The makeup of that class was more international: one student was from Kenya itself; another was from Eritrea, which had recently emerged victorious in its liberation struggle with Ethiopia; another was from Nigeria; another was from the Philippines; and another was from Chechnya. There were also two American students who devoured Fanon's chapter on colonial violence with gusto, thus making the class more inclined to accept the anticolonial violence and anticapitalist rhetoric. A student in my drama seminar openly admitted that these two aspects in *Trial* put him off. He identified with Shaw Henderson in the play. Seeking (but failing) to convince the rest of the class that the Settler and Shaw Henderson were really carrying out the white man's burden—spreading law, order, prosperity, and Christianity to a dark continent—he found the liberation theology in the play troubling. He didn't see its connection to Latin American liberation movements, didn't agree with the parallels that a student originally from Guatemala was making in her seminar presentation. He dismissed the discussion of the Christlike nature of Kimathi as blasphemy.

As for the violence, the drama student took great issue with Kimathi's order to execute the two unrepentant British soldiers in the Third Movement, seeing them as upholding British patriotism. Though reminded that the violence in the play comes primarily from the colonizers, the student saw it as maintaining law and order; for him, the Mau Mau violence was atavistic. He surfed the Internet and found some alarmist references to Kimathi and Mau Mau, which he shared with the class. He also found pictures and news stories of the ethnic cleansing that befell Kenya before the elections in December 1997, and he connected ahistorically the anticolonial violence of the 1950s with that ethnic violence in a version of Ione Leigh's argument that the Mau Mau fighters "were not fighting for independence" but simply because "it was their nature to fight and brutality was part of the native character" (17).

I bring up the drama student's response to *Trial* to highlight the ongoing politics of representation and interpretation even as canon reform appears to be on course. It is still possible to have students who have not discarded such baggage from the past. From his position of privilege, this student was unwilling to make any space for the voices from the margins. Yet the presenter did a thought-provoking job. In guiding his preparation for it, I had recommended David Maughan-Brown's *Land, Freedom, and Fiction*, the first two chapters of Ian Henderson and Philip Goodhart's *The Hunt for Dedan Kimathi*, excerpts from Leigh's *In the Shadow of the Mau Mau*, and Fanon's chapter "On Colonial Violence" in *The Wretched of the Earth.* In that drama seminar, as in the African literature survey, we were able to discuss the contexts of the Kenyan liberation struggle in some depth and also make comparisons with other liberation struggles.

Teaching an African literature survey at a different university later, I incorporated a video of the freedom struggle (David Koff's *Mau Mau*) but was unable to get the students' minds off the gory scenes of Mau Mau revenge killings. Somehow the trauma of villagization and detention without trial mostly elicited the response that the terrorists deserved what they got. But a perceptive student wrote to me after class to draw his own parallels between European colonialism in Africa and the United States military occupation of Iraq (and Korea and Vietnam before that) as only one facet of an American imperialism that increasingly took the form of the export of American consumer goods and values. I also had some students who were heavily invested in Mau Mau as a symbol of the African revolution, and they objected to my suggestion that the Mau Mau were ideologically challenged but, though they lost militarily, they raised to an intolerable level the moral and economic price of further occupying Kenya (Gordon 344; Maloba, *Mau Mau* 170). Even though I supplied two chapters from Henderson and Goodhart's *Hunt* and discussed the binarisms in the story that always appears to portray Kimathi negatively, students tended to believe the characterization of Kimathi as an intemperate brute, thief, murderer, and rapist. They were shocked to learn that the real Kimathi had a wife and children, a fact never mentioned in *Hunt* since it would make him normal.

Depending on their motivation, students may find the intertextual encyclopedia supplied either rewarding or intimidating. I have taught *Trial* in three other courses structured as African and African diaspora drama, where the play keeps good company with the drama of Amiri Baraka, James Baldwin, and August Wilson and their signifying difference with generations of white image makers. Presenting *Trial* in the context of the black arts movement in the United States, I argued that the play's politics of representation is not unusual.

Using a few experiments at cocreating the meaning of a text, I devised a series of lectures that did justice to *Trial* without overloading the students on context. Seeking to destabilize the assertion by Ngũgĩ and Micere Mugo that they had written the story of Kimathi from the only "historically correct perspective" (Preface vii), I refer students to Hayden White's argument in *Tropics of Discourse* that a historical account involves selection, ordering, and interpretation, processes that are as much intuitive as they are analytic. A historical account aspires to the coherence of a story and therefore relies on the imagination. White argues that historical facts are not so much found as constructed by the kinds of questions that investigators ask of the phenomenon before them (27–43). I point out that a literary text is even more constructed, that according to Aristotle, it attempts to present not what was but what might have been (62).

I selectively share descriptions of the Kenyan freedom struggle by Henderson, Leigh, J. C. Carothers, W. O. Maloba, David Gordon, and the more recent analysis in Atieno Odhiambo and John Lonsdale's *Mau Mau and Nationhood*. I point out that Ngũgĩ and Mugo were specifically writing to rebut some of the negative portrayals of the freedom struggle by Leigh, Henderson, Carothers, and others. As an entry point into the play proper, we normally read aloud the Settler's outburst in the courtroom and use it as an example of colonial arrogance and its monopoly on violence, which Kimathi challenges repeatedly in the play. We discuss the discursive construction of the Settler's "boys" as apolitical, docile, meek, loyal, subservient, and God-fearing, against the image of Kimathi as the brute, savage, godless instigator of terrorism. We note the charade of Kimathi's trial as an expression of British justice and discuss his interrogation of the law that judges him but that he had no role in making. I point out the irony that the Settler appoints his gun the instrument of justice, as due process is deemed too lenient when the culprit is an African.

The jailhouse trials and physical violence Kimathi experiences are connected to the exploitation of Africans from the beginning of European modernity—the part played by the mime dramatizing slavery and colonialism (4–5). We explore the biblical parallels to Kimathi's trials: scenes of torture, betrayal, scourging, and the eventual sentencing to death. We discuss the imagery of the Last Supper and Kimathi's vision for an egalitarian order on a material earth girded with humanist ideals. We probe the clash between his Marxist internationalism—his utopian vision of the workers of the world uniting—and the privileging of the struggle of the Kenyan nation. Kimathi's speeches stage the nation for readers and theater audiences by invoking a common will, shared heroes, common aspirations, a common language (Swahili), and a common history of resistance. Ngũgĩ and Mugo create characters, situations, and temporalities that look believable in the world of the play, an effect that the authors would not obtain if they were operating from the only historically correct perspective. Ultimately, I argue, *Trial* is a work of the imagination, not of ideology.

Touching on the failure of the postcolonial nation, I use Kimathi's trials as pointers to the ways that the playwrights' project of the 1970s reflects back on the mid-1950s event. Kimathi foresees that the cause will be betrayed. We discuss how the characters—for example, the Politician with his talk of "[w]e all fought for Uhuru [independence] in our different ways" (47)—anticipate the conciliatory statements that in the 1960s and 1970s would emanate from Kenyatta, Kenya's first president. The Businessman's argument that the people won the war because blacks can now sit on the boards of foreign corporations and purchase land in the former White Highlands reflects a 1960s perspective. An example of the collapsing of space and time for dramatic and political ends is the clever renaming of the historical Ian Henderson, the hunter of Kimathi, as Shaw Henderson to evoke the terror of the 1970s visited on political dissidents and criminals in equal measure by Patrick Shaw, a special police reservist.

As in the women's writing class, we discuss the power in the margins occupied by the Woman, Boy, and Girl, who are the face of a revolution that does not end with Kimathi's incarceration or imminent hanging at play's end. In conclusion I note the play's ambition to become revolutionary theater rousing audiences to overthrow dictatorial regimes; I also note that the play's language in the Kenyan setting is an obstacle to this ambition. I recommend that students read *I Will Marry*.

Carlson suggests that every text postulates its receiver as an indispensable condition of its potential for meaning (12). I have written on the dramaturgies (the director's, the writer's, the performers', and the spectators') at work in the Kamĩrĩĩthũ 1976 performances of *I Will Marry* (*Ngũgĩ wa Thiong'o's Drama* 171–76). The discomfort of the ruling government with the message of the play has been discussed extensively and eloquently by Ngũgĩ (*Detained* 80, *Barrel* 39–51, *Writers* [1981] 46–48, *Decolonising* 57–62, *Penpoints* 64–68), Simon Gikandi (*Ngũgĩ* 193–94), and Oliver Lovesey (*Ngũgĩ* 99), among others, but I have observed authorial blind spots that show how even sensitive artists can perpetuate hegemonic discourse that merits interrogation.

The model audience of the first Kamĩrĩĩthũ production, *Ngaahika Ndeenda* (Ngũgĩ and Ngũgĩ; later translated as *I Will Marry When I Want*), was structured into the play at the level of both content and form. In *Ngaahika Ndeenda,* the recourse to the Gĩkũyũ language, the incorporation of familiar popular songs, the use of the common people's speech rhythms, songs, and proverbs all helped cultivate a specifically rural audience. But that audience was not inclusive. The play was structured to appeal to workers and peasants: a male model audience. Both the main characters are male, and the dramatization focuses on male prerogatives: ownership of land, which is overtly shown to confer masculinity; ownership of property; the war in the forest; nationalism; industrial working conditions; and the imminent class struggle, whose agents are also male. Women's concerns—lack of firewood, lack of water, their exploitation as agricultural laborers—are really side issues. The work of interrogating Gĩkũyũ culture's gender insensitivities was not adequately done. The characterization of Wangeci as a grasping opportunist is problematic, and Gathoni's excision from the text, whose title misleads us to expect that her rebellion will be central to the play, points to elements of a patriarchal aesthetic.

However disengaged students might be from *I Will Marry*, I have been able to get discussion going when I remark on the silence of the women in the play. Probing Wangeci's characterization as a poor example of "women in cultural work" (Ngũgĩ, *Barrel* 39–51), we explore female agency in the play.

Carlson's argument that a text postulates its receiver as a determiner of its meaning needs to be expanded. De Marinis observes that a text must have the active cooperation of a spectator to achieve its meaning: "more than just a metaphorical co-producer of the performance, the spectator is a relatively autonomous 'maker of meanings' for the performance; its cognitive and emotive effects can only be fully actualized by the audience" (102). Thus the audience's identification with the issues raised in the play, the wariness of the state security apparatus, and the uneasiness of the men from the area with what they saw as the portrait of a domineering woman are autonomous acts of producing meaning from the text. These readings exemplify a process in which, to adapt De Marinis to the Kamĩrĩĩthũ performance, "the spectators were forced to acknowledge the irredeemably partial and subjective nature of their experience of the performance, [which] experience was now conditioned by their material position, their point of observation" (105).

Much as Ngũgĩ has been involved in what Tomaz da Silva calls in a different context "the revolt of the subjugated identities against the dominant regimes of representation," he too succumbs to the temptation to present what he sees as the universals of—progressively—Gĩkũyũ, Kenyan, African, and black culture and a utopian nation of workers and peasants. Such universals are systems of signification whose claim consists in expressing the human and the social in their totality, yet they remain systems of representation in which the particular social and discursive constructions that are partial to those groups that define the process of representation are paramount (8). In teaching *I Will Marry*, I argue that the group that controlled the process of representation was male and that therefore male systems of signification dominated the play and its reception.

Reading the model audience back into *I Will Marry* allows us to tease out the suggestiveness of the text, what Eco calls a deliberate move to open the work to the free response of the addressee. The emphasis is on the readers' utilization of their full emotional and imaginative resources, the attempt to adapt their personal world to the emotional world proposed by the text (49–53). The play's emotional world is so closely structured to the worker-peasant audience and so far removed from the average American college student's experience that students have difficulty adapting. But the gender wars resonate with them.

In reading the play's masculine codes, I emphasize Kĩgũũnda's invocation of a masculinity conferred by his piece of land. The prominent land title on one wall of his hut is accompanied by his sword, another masculine symbol. Kĩgũũnda feels emasculated when he loses the land. He becomes violent toward his wife, who constantly reminds him of his vulnerability. There is frequent stage business connected with the title deed. Kĩgũũnda's changed fortune calls for a reexamination of the traditional constructions of masculinity. His overexerted self-assertion troubled my students, but when the play was performed at Kamĩrĩĩthũ, most people sided with Kĩgũũnda. While the play seeks to reform the patriarchy, there are silences over the actual place of women in the world proposed by the text.

The play assumes a reader-spectator who knows the nuances of Gĩkũyũ culture. But the spectators at Kamĩrĩĩthũ exposed the limitations of the dramatic text as a cultural product. They found Wangeci unsympathetic as a character because she was too domineering, and they blamed Kĩgũũnda for being henpecked. The supremely confident and well-adjusted Gĩcaamba makes a case for the patriarchy to change its attitudes toward women. But in Gĩcaamba's world gender is subordinated to class, and only those aspects of the patriarchal structure that impede the advancement of the workers' cause are deemed worthy of change. Two assumptions inform Gĩcaamba's gender agenda: first, that the class war will also harmonize disparities of gender; second, that the masculine story of struggle is universal.

The play's action gravitates around male deeds. When Gĩcaamba and his wife visit the Kĩgũũndas, the two couples sit "in such a way that the men are able to talk to one another, and the two women the same" (32). But apart from the gender demarcations on stage, the women's talk is tagged as "chatter" about domestic affairs (33) as the men talk high politics—social class tensions, the betrayal of the nationalist dream, neocolonialism, the impending labor unrest—areas in which the women are minor participants if not hostile opponents.

Although Wangeci was found to be domineering and self-aggrandizing by the play's model audience, she is also paradoxically passive and unvoiced in places. She remembers the displaced Olenguruone women singing defiant songs as they passed through Limuru on their way to Yatta, but the women, like Wangeci, were otherwise passive victims. We contrast their passivity with the agency of Kĩgũũnda's fellow men:

> KĨGŨŨNDA:
> It was then
> That the state of Emergency was declared over Kenya.
> Our patriots,
> Men and women of
> Limuru and the whole country,
> Were arrested. . . .
> We were jailed,
> We were taken to detention camps,
> Some of us were crippled through beatings.
> Others were castrated.
> Our women were raped with bottles.
> Our wives and daughters raped before our eyes! (27)

As wife or daughter, the woman is already spoken for, provided for, and protected by the men. Women's trouble finding firewood and water and girls' lack of equal access to education are articulated by Gĩcaamba. We know what a hard time Kĩgũũnda has providing for his family, but we do not see that Wangeci has the same difficulties, because, when provisions are lacking, it is the failing of man the provider. Though a major character, Wangeci does little to advance women's interests. I like to invoke Anne McClintock's argument that "women's political relation to the nation is submerged in and subordinated to her social relationship to a man through marriage" (298). The men are assumed to know what is good for the women. The playwrights conflate gender and class; the needs of one are assumed to be the needs of the other. But the fictional society, like the model audience, is patriarchal, and this patriarchal structure merits more interrogation than the fleeting comments that the men are allowed.

Gathoni's marginality reinforces the disarticulation of women. Oddly, as the character whose decision resonates with the play's title, Gathoni is little involved in the dramatic action, making only two minor appearances. Her conflicts, like those of the other women, are articulated for her by Gĩcaamba. Instead of occupying the conceptual order like the males, she disrupts the play's moral and cultural universe with her uninformed reproductive function. Her changed fortunes are reported to us, not dramatized; thus her grief is appropriated as one more cause for which the agentive male seeks recompense.

This displacement of female agency attests to an authorial blind spot. The playwrights embrace the idea of giving women more progressive roles, but those roles are not made part of the fictional world. Teaching *I Will Marry When I Want*, I sensitize students to the play's interrogation of the poisoned gift of independence but also remark its imbrication in a hegemonic practice: the appropriation and constraining of the voices of oppressed women. The play has been praised for its dramatization of class conflicts, of the contradictions of imperialism and globalization, of questions about free trade, and of what Gikandi calls the recovery of resistant memories that rewrite history from below and thus challenge the postcolonial state's monopoly of the performance of meanings (*Ngũgĩ* 193–94). But the lapses enumerated above raise questions whether there is an "enduring patriarchal cast of [Ngũgĩ's] ideas [that] cannot be ignored" (Boehmer [1995] 143).

Probing Ngũgĩ's dramaturgy but also reading back model spectators into his plays, I nudge students toward the encyclopedic, ideological, and intertextual competence valorized in reader-response theory, which enables them to be receptive to postcolonial criticism and to its attention to voices from the margins. By helping them negotiate the dialectic De Marinis identifies between the constraints imposed by the "aesthetic text" and the possibilities it leaves open to those who receive it (101), we can access the vitality of the plays in ways that simultaneously affirm and contest authorial intentions. By reading back the model audience into the plays, we become model readers ourselves.

TEACHING NGŨGĨ'S WORKS WRITTEN IN ENGLISH

A Terrible Beauty Is Born: *A Grain of Wheat* and *Weep Not, Child*

Michael Harris

Ngũgĩ wa Thiong'o recalls two professional trips—one to South Korea in 2005 and one to West Germany in 1982—and how both visits made him aware of the internal conflicts that had shaped those countries' histories ("For Peace"). His novels *Weep Not, Child* and *A Grain of Wheat* dramatize a similar historic moment in Kenya: the 1950s Emergency and the so-called Mau Mau rebellion during the waning days of the British Empire in East Africa. In a 2003 conference at Macalester College in Saint Paul, Minnesota, I heard Ngũgĩ give a lecture in which he called for a new world order that would place marginalized nations, such as Kenya, in a more prominent global position ("When the Margin"). His career-long project of re-visioning African history, culture, and language and putting them at the center of international awareness is evident in both novels.

In a sophomore-level course on African and Caribbean literature that I taught for years at Central College, a private liberal arts college in Iowa, I used *Weep Not, Child* but more recently turned to *A Grain of Wheat* as a representative Ngũgĩ text in the syllabus. Although these novels are very different in their level of sophistication, I have found both to be effective in the classroom. In this essay I focus on my experience teaching *A Grain of Wheat* but also make occasional reference to the earlier novel.

In my course, I typically work with novels, trying to arrange them to reflect African history in several different regions of the continent. I include some drama (such as *Death and the King's Horseman,* by Wole Soyinka; *Dream on Monkey Mountain,* by Derek Walcott; *Woza Albert!,* by Percy Mitwa, Mbongeni Ngema, and Barney Simon; and *Sizwe Bansi Is Dead,* by Athol Fugard, John Kani, and Winston Ntshona) but depend primarily on works of fiction, because of my personal taste and training and the students' competence and interest. Thus we progress from the precolonial era (Chinua Achebe's *Things Fall Apart* and Abdulrazak Gurnah's *Paradise*) to postcolonial independence (Mariama Bâ's *So Long a Letter* and Helon Habila's *Waiting for an Angel*). Ngũgĩ's fiction is useful not only for its stylistic and technical innovation but also for the way it deals with events of historical moment affecting the continent, such as the Mau Mau conflict, which Ngũgĩ has called "the first modern anticolonial guerrilla movement in Africa" ("Interview" [Martini et al.] 139). To provide students background on this conflict, I show segments of two documentaries: "New Conflicts," from Ali Mazrui's *The Africans: A Triple Heritage*, and "The Rise of Nationalism," from Basil Davidson's *Africa*. Throughout the semester I ask my students to open each class meeting with a brief introduction to an African country. I try to time these introductions so that they match the country and region of the text we are studying. Thus students will share what they have learned through research about Kenya and other East African countries. In this way, we are able to approach Ngũgĩ's novel with some awareness of the history and cultural makeup of Kenya and, in general, East Africa.

Since much of Ngũgĩ's writing is based on his lived experience, I provide students with some background on his evolution as an artist and citizen. After *A Grain of Wheat* and *Petals of Blood,* his last novel written in English, the Gĩkũyũ novels adopt a more strident tone in their call for resistance and struggle. Carol Sicherman's "Ngũgĩ wa Thiong'o and the Writing of Kenyan History," Oliver Lovesey's "Ngũgĩ wa Thiong'o's Postnation: The Cultural Geographies of Colonial, Neocolonial, and Postnational Space," and J. Roger Kurtz's "Ngũgĩ wa Thiong'o" are helpful sources in this regard. *Grain* is obviously a more complex, sophisticated narrative than *Weep Not, Child*, but both novels raise the issue of Ngũgĩ's use of the English language early in his career and show his sustained focus on the Mau Mau conflict as a turning point in Kenya's history. A decade after *Grain* was published, Ngũgĩ would personally relive the experience of Mugo's and Gikonyo's political imprisonment, as a result of the writing and performance of his play *Ngaahika Ndeenda* (*I Will Marry When I Want*). Students are fascinated to learn of Ngũgĩ's decision later to write his plays and novels in Gĩkũyũ, and this fact creates an opportunity to discuss the postcolonial politics of language. Ngũgĩ was not alone in his decision to change his name and write in an indigenous language: the Irish poet Nuala Ní Dhomhnaill chose to write in Gaelic rather than English, the colonial language.[1]

Ngũgĩ's description of the three phases of colonial rule helps situate the narrative of Kenya's history for students:

> The first is the stage of colonial conquest. Economic and political institutions are moulded on those of the metropolitan power. . . . The second

> period is that of colonial rebellion. The masses are restive. The nationalist leaders, usually from the ranks of the educated few, organize the discontent into a weapon aimed at the throat of the master. . . . [The third period is independence.] What does this independence mean? For the peasants and the urban workers this is a period of gradual disillusionment. Independence has not given them back their land. They are still without food and clothes. (*Homecoming* 55–56)

In *Weep Not, Child,* the reader witnesses the second phase in this process; *Grain* enacts completion of the second phase and brings the reader up to the eve of phase 3. The Mazrui and Davidson documentaries illustrate how Kenya's independence was fought by Africans against Africans. As Ngũgĩ argued in his presentation at Macalester, "The colonizer did not bring an army from Europe: he made armies out of the divisions between African peoples and he helped set community against community" ("When the Margin"). There are only a handful of British colonials represented in *Grain.* I find it necessary to make sure my students realize the distinction between the "soldiers" or "home guards" (those, like Karanja, who are loyal to the British) and the "freedom fighters" (those, like Kihika, trying to end British rule). Not surprisingly, District Officer Thompson refers to the freedom fighters as "terrorists" (55, 199).

To appreciate Ngũgĩ's representation of this crucial period in Kenya's history, students need to be reminded how differently events are perceived from different points on the globe. *Grain* looks at this period from a Kenyan insider's view. Students find it interesting that *Mau Mau* was a demeaning term the British coined for the freedom fighters, not a name the fighters used for themselves. The British settlers and officials are portrayed, sometimes satirically, as strange outsiders. Ngũgĩ's shifting narrative presents challenges for the typical undergraduate. At times the reader perceives the action from inside a particular subjectivity—for instance, that of Mugo, Karanja, or Mumbi; at times an omniscient narrator relates the background of key characters, like John Thompson; and at times, a first-person communal narrator expresses the hopes, aspirations, and disappointments of the local citizens of Thabai. Chapter 13 opens with, "Most of us from Thabai first saw [Mugo] at the New Rung'ei Market the day the heavy rain fell. You remember the Wednesday, just before Independence?" (178).

The insider's perspective valorizes indigenous heroes and leaders:

> Again they recreated history, giving it life through the words and voices: land alienation, Waiyaki, Harry Thuku, taxation, conscription of labour into the whiteman's land, the break with missions, and, oh, the terrible thirst and hunger for education. They sang of Jomo. (218)

The names of these historic figures are invoked as part of an alternative insider's history involving "[t]he revolt of the peasant" (13) to achieve independence and land restitution. In *Weep Not, Child,* Njoroge's father, Ngotho, provides this history in chapter 2. Njoroge first comes to realize that the land currently owned and cultivated by the settler, Mr. Howlands, originally belonged to his family. Ngotho's lifetime ambition is to regain this ancestral land for posterity. In *Grain*, an omniscient narrator similarly tells of the progression toward Uhuru in chapter 2, which is reinforced by multiple voices in subsequent chapters as the people anticipate the approaching independence day celebrations.

Ngũgĩ's intention in *Grain* is not only to offer an insider's perspective on events involving the Emergency and the Mau Mau rebellion but also to call into question the linear concept of history itself. The narrative constantly circles back on itself. Episodes, such as Mugo's decision to betray Kihika to John Thompson, are revealed through oblique references, fragments, and hints before their full explication. In class, I use the Irish writer Eavan Boland's distinction between history and the past in her description of the 1847 famine to help students understand Ngũgĩ's treatment of Kenya's struggle for independence. Boland defines history as the "official version" of events that comprises a "narrative of concealed power." By contrast, the past is "the inert, unchangeable, sometimes brutal reality of what happened," which "in its silence and inconvenient completeness must remain in the suffering, powerless place it surely was and is" (14). Ngũgĩ draws attention to this official version of history: "Learned men will, no doubt, dig into the troubled times which we in Kenya underwent, and maybe sum up the lesson of history in a phrase. Why, let us ask them, did the incident in Rira Camp capture the imagination of the world?" (131). The incident is the beating death of thirteen "Mau Mau adherents" involved in a hunger strike. News of the scandalous event reached "the House of Commons and . . . the world press" and forced Thompson to give up his "brilliant career" as a colonial officer (46). Such an event creates a mere ripple in the narrative of history, in the story the West tells itself. The reader learns later that Mugo served time as a detainee at the Rira detention camp—often referred to as a concentration camp by the narrator—while Thompson was there. Mugo's experience represents Boland's definition of the past, for the torture of Mugo by the home guards has left him occupying a silent nightmare world, isolated from others and powerless to communicate.

The experience of Ngũgĩ and his family during the Emergency, which he weaves into his fiction, underscores his awareness of the chasm between official history and the brutal reality of the past. Kwame Anthony Appiah and Henry Louis Gates's *Africana* provides useful biographical background on the effect of the Emergency on Ngũgĩ and his family. Students are moved when they learn that Ngũgĩ's mother was arrested and tortured. Ngũgĩ drew on this experience in his depiction of Ngotho's detention and torture at the end of *Weep Not, Child*. Similarly, the episode in *Grain* in which the deaf-mute Gitogo is shot because he cannot hear the white man's warning shout to halt—"Another Mau Mau terrorist had been shot dead" (5)—is based on what happened to Ngũgĩ's stepbrother.

Ngũgĩ's portrayal of the Kenyans' chaotic, confusing experience of the Emergency corresponds to Frantz Fanon's *The Wretched of the Earth,* a text that

Ngũgĩ read carefully before he wrote *Grain.* He draws especially on Fanon's chapter "The Pitfalls of National Consciousness" in several of his critical essays as well as in his fiction. In that chapter, Fanon discusses the mistrust and factionalism that accompany independence, especially on the African continent: "To . . . [the national middle class], nationalism quite simply means the transfer into native hands of those unfair advantages which are a legacy of the colonial period" (152). Several episodes in *Grain* align with Fanon's perception of the greed spawned by decolonization and independence: Karanja's psychological "need" to wield the white man's power over his fellow Kenyans (230), Gikonyo's effort to purchase land for a cooperative business venture—aborted, because the MP to whom Gikonyo applies appropriates the land for himself.

To dramatize how the Emergency destroyed Kenyan lives, Ngũgĩ focuses on the breakup of Njoroge's family in *Weep Not, Child* and the dissolution of five interconnected lives (those of Mugo, Kihika, Karanja, Mumbi, and Gikonyo) in *Grain.* Charles Larson's chapter on *Grain* in *The Emergence of African Fiction* illuminates the central theme of community versus isolation. This theme ties directly into Ngũgĩ's perception of the Emergency as essentially a time of fragmentation and disillusionment. Instead of a joyous occasion, the *uhuru* celebrations amount to a sobering reminder of the national nightmare the country has lived through in order to become independent. Ngũgĩ stresses the importance of community in postcolonial Kenya in his essay "Kenya: The Two Rifts": "The traditional African concept of *the* community should not be forgotten in our rush for western culture and political institutions" (*Homecoming* 25). For the spirit of African community to be reconstructed, people must emerge from isolation.

Students are invariably surprised and even disappointed by the anticlimactic ending of *Grain.* I prepare them by bringing Fanon's "Pitfalls of National Consciousness" into our discussions. To portray independence as a moment in which all the loose ends of the collective trauma are tied together and the country is miraculously unified would be out of keeping with Ngũgĩ's larger purpose. Mumbi's pointed remark to Gikonyo at the end mirrors the overall sober mood of the *uhuru* ceremony: "People try to rub out things, but they cannot. Things are not so easy. . . . We need to talk, to open our hearts to one another, examine them, and then together plan the future we want. But now, I must go, for the child is ill" (247). If Gikonyo and Mumbi represent modern variations of the original man and woman in the Gĩkũyũ creation myth (Gĩkũyũ and Mumbi), Mumbi's child might stand for Kenya's future. In the aftermath of Mau Mau, the country is ill and faces the daunting realization that independence is only the beginning of a new and difficult self-examination.

I use Fanon to link Ngũgĩ's novel to other texts on our syllabus. The title of Tsitsi Dangarembga's *Nervous Conditions* is taken from *The Wretched of the Earth,* and Fanon is also cited in Habila's *Waiting for an Angel.* Like Dangarembga's Babamukuru, Tambu, and Nyasha, the characters Ngũgĩ explores in *Grain* suffer from nervous conditions, as Fanon defined the psychological state of colonization by a foreign power. *Nervous Conditions,* set in Rhodesia in the 1970s, demonstrates the effects of colonialism on education, religion, and identity. *Waiting for an Angel* describes the oppression experienced in Nigeria under General Sani Abacha's 1990s military regime, which corresponds to the third phase of ironic disillusionment in the colonization process outlined in *Wretched* and illustrated in Ngũgĩ's later work, such as *Wizard of the Crow.*

Irony is a useful term to bring up in any discussion of *Grain.* After making certain that the students have completed the novel, which I check by giving reading quizzes and eliciting their written responses to the text, I spend an entire class period asking them to list as many ironies in the narrative as they can. I find that this exercise builds on itself, and students emerge surprised by the proliferation of ironies in the story, most of which involve the miscommunication, misperception, and mistrust dividing the citizens of Thabai. Many of the ironies attach to Mugo. Whereas almost everyone in Thabai believes he is a hero who withstood torture in detention without confessing the oath, Mugo is actually the one who betrayed Kihika, and the only reason he did not confess the oath is that he never took it in the first place. It is also ironic that when Mugo betrays Kihika to John Thompson, Thompson thinks that Mugo simply wants the reward and thus spits in his face (199). Thompson has no idea of the guilt and self-doubt that drove Mugo to his door. He even believes that Mugo is secretly laughing at him (56). Also ironic are Kihika's belief that Mugo would be an excellent recruit for the freedom fighters, when that is the last thing Mugo wants, and Gikonyo's overwhelming desire to escape detention and return to his wife, only to find that in his absence she has borne another man's child. The list goes on. Through these ironies, Ngũgĩ dramatizes how history does not follow a straightforward sequence of cause and effect; instead, it often takes a circuitous path laden with misunderstanding, in which the outcome is the opposite of what one originally intended.

In his essays, such as "Towards a National Culture," in *Homecoming*, and "Matigari and the Dreams of One East Africa," in *Moving the Centre,* and in his fiction, such as *Petals of Blood,* Ngũgĩ expresses his admiration for President Julius Nyerere's socialist experiment, known as *ujamaa* (Swahili for "family" or "extended family") in Tanzania. Kenya experienced a longer, more intense colonial disruption than Tanzania did, and the resultant divisiveness among its people shows in the breakdown of Kenya's microcosmic community, represented by the five key characters in *Grain.* To illustrate this elusive ideal of the African community, I show my students *ujamaa* carvings from Tanzania depicting interconnected, mutually dependent human figures. This communal ideal is obviously absent in the various one-on-one encounters among Mugo, Gikonyo, Mumbi, Kihika, and Karanja. Githua succinctly describes the collapse of communalism brought about by colonial rule when he whispers to Mugo, "The Emergency destroyed us" (3). The novel's principal figures have to overcome their emotional paralysis and distrust if they are to achieve open communication with one another. Such communication occurs when Mumbi goes to Mugo's hut to persuade Mugo to speak at the *uhuru* ceremony and, later, when she speaks with candor to her estranged husband, Gikonyo. In those encounters, the reader sees the first signs of the birth of a new spirit of community in Kenya.

One function of history is to supply a unifying national narrative that gives shape and meaning to a people's collective life. It is the role, not only of the historian but also of the poet laureate and the nationally recognized novelist, to perform this function. *A Grain of Wheat* bears some resemblance, in this regard, to W. B. Yeats's "Easter, 1916," a poem commemorating the Easter Rising in Dublin, a historic moment that left a permanent mark on the Irish nation. Students are often unsure what to make of Mugo by the end of this novel. Is he a hero? a coward? a villain? Yeats's poem, in which the poet expresses similar uncertainty about the rebels, might help students sort out the meaning of Ngũgĩ's ending. Teaching *Grain* in conjunction with "Easter, 1916" can also lead to a class discussion about the crucial role of religion in both works—in particular, about how Ngũgĩ and Yeats (both, interestingly, nonbelievers) make use of the Christian emphasis on self-sacrifice. I explain to my students that Ngũgĩ consistently incorporated Christian themes and images into his work, in part to reach his Kenyan audience, but that his later Gĩkũyũ texts, such as *Devil on the Cross* and *Matigari,* were increasingly critical of the subtle complicity between Christianity and global capitalism in Kenya.

A Grain of Wheat is less critical of Christianity than the Gĩkũyũ novels are. Mugo, like Yeats's Easter rebels, is a sacrificial figure: he and Kihika give their lives to help bring about the birth of their nation and its independence from colonial rule. A stream of villagers—Lieutenant Koina, General R., Gikonyo, the village elders Warui and Wambui, and even Mumbi—come to his hut and implicitly outline a national narrative that will be valorized, with Mugo's help, at the *uhuru* ceremony. It is precisely for events such as the *uhuru* ceremony that history-shaping narratives are created and recited. The community's need for a hero inflates Mugo's role: "Some people said that in detention Mugo had been shot at and no bullet would touch his skin" (217). Mugo is strongly tempted to perform the scripted, self-glorifying role of the national hero called for by this memorial narrative. The reader remembers his seductive logic in betraying Kihika: "His place in society would be established. He would be half-way on the road to power. And what is greatness but power?" (197).

Mugo is rescued by Mumbi's earlier willingness to bare her soul to him, which has "cracked open his dulled inside and released imprisoned thoughts and feelings" (172). This scene offers an interesting parallel to Mwihaki's encounter with Njoroge at the end of *Weep Not, Child,* but the interaction between Mumbi and Mugo is more significant. Mumbi's openness and trust in Mugo enables him to depart from the conventional national script and make a brief but honest confession to his expectant audience, who are shocked and saddened by his revelation. Nevertheless, his willingness to sacrifice himself for the good of the community validates the prophecy in Ngũgĩ's epigraph from Corinthians: "that which thou sowest is not quickened, except it die." Like the Easter rebels in Yeats's poem, who were initially vilified by the Irish public in 1916, Mugo is condemned and taken away, also like the Easter martyrs, to be executed. The seeds of his act, however, already begin to produce grain when Gikonyo decides to emulate Mugo's "courage to face his guilt and lose everything" (245) by rebuilding his relationship with Mumbi and accepting her child as his own. From personal acts of courage like Mugo's, the reader can assume that the entire Kenyan society can and will eventually be "changed utterly," and that a "terrible beauty," in the form of a new national responsibility, will be born (Yeats 180).

NOTE

[1] Ngũgĩ makes extensive comparisons between the African and Irish colonial experiences in which both suffered loss of language, names (of natural sites, towns and cities, and people), and cultural memory. He writes, "It was astonishing to discover . . . the centrality of the Irish experience to the colonial question, especially as it relates to language, culture, and social memory. Ireland was England's first colony, and it became a prototype for all other colonies in Asia, Africa, and America" (*Something Torn* x–xi).

Teaching *A Grain of Wheat* as a Dialogue with Conrad

Peter Nazareth

In 1970, when I was working as a senior finance officer in the Ministry of Finance in Uganda, I submitted a collection of my literary essays to the East African Literature Bureau. I received a fine evaluation of the manuscript, by Angus Calder (as I discovered later), in which he stated that since I had been a fellow student of Ngũgĩ's at Makerere University College and at Leeds, I was well placed to write on Ngũgĩ. I had included in the manuscript my essay on Joseph Conrad's *Nostromo*, written as my dissertation for my postgraduate diploma in English studies at Leeds, under the direction of Arthur Ravenscroft. I had not understood or liked *Nostromo* when I first read it, but I pursued it because Ngũgĩ loved it. In fact, he wrote a brilliant essay on it, "Why *Nostromo*?" while studying Conrad as his special subject for his BA honors degree in English under David Cook at Makerere. The special subject was one of three studied in the third year, and students had to sit for almost two weeks of exams at the end of the year, the exams covering the entire three years. This meant that Ngũgĩ studied Conrad in 1963–64 and then took an exam on Conrad as part of his degree requirements.

I was already at Leeds while Ngũgĩ was studying Conrad at Makerere, but he brought his essays to Leeds, which I read there. His unpublished essay on *Nostromo* began:

> I believe that *Nostromo* is one of the greatest novels of the twentieth century; it speaks to us with a very compelling urgency, an urgency that we cannot but heed, we who have witnessed revolution after revolution in the oil-rich Middle East and in the south American states. It is a political novel; it forces us to review the relationship between our social and political institutions and the economic organization of society. In no other novel have I met the examination of the man at the top—the great political figures—but also of the man and woman at the bottom, the unknown and insignificant Teresas of the world. But more than this, *Nostromo* is a great novel of individual human relationships; it calls us to examine over and over again the relationship between political theory and practice, economic organization of society and individual morality.

The essay affected my understanding of the novel much more than did the work of the well-known scholars of Conrad I referred to in my dissertation—and if I did not mention it in my dissertation, it must have been because it was a student essay by a friend. I was particularly enlightened by Ngũgĩ's statement that the complexity of the novel lay in the fact that there was no guiding voice to lead us through the complex time structure of the novel and the equally complex moral pattern of human relationships. I am now saying, "Mea culpa," for not acknowledging Ngũgĩ's influence over forty years ago.

It was at Leeds that Ngũgĩ began writing *A Grain of Wheat*—I still remember his passing the first paragraph to me in class fourteen months after he wrote the essay on *Nostromo*. But I read the whole novel only when I was back in Uganda: I bought a copy at the Uganda Bookshop in Kampala in May 1967, a copy I still use when teaching the novel at the University of Iowa. I felt that Ngũgĩ was still strongly influenced by Conrad when he wrote the novel. So when I finally wrote the essay for my book, I mentioned how much Ngũgĩ drew from *Nostromo* in terms of theme and characters: I compared the idealist John Thompson with Charles Gould and Margery Thompson with Emilia Gould, both women starving for love as their cold husbands pursue an abstract ideal of bringing about law, order, justice, and civilization. I further said that in *A Grain of Wheat* Ngũgĩ departed from the linear structure of his first two novels, which were written before he wrote his essay on *Nostromo*. Ngũgĩ had been accused of having protagonists in his first two novels who were or saw themselves as messianic figures who ultimately failed because of large forces around them. By creating his third novel in a circular or spiral way, he created a character, like Nostromo, who was a touchstone to a whole community in motion.[1]

It was inevitable that I would notice a connection between Ngũgĩ's novel and another famous novel by Conrad, because we had a classmate, Grigor Pavlov, a Bulgarian returning home from the United Nations who decided to study at Leeds for a year and wrote a dissertation on Conrad's *Under Western Eyes*, which Ngũgĩ and I read in draft form. Pavlov thought Conrad was too pessimistic about revolutions but nevertheless said that in this novel Conrad had created "a meaningful and stirring drama of a man's conscience plagued by the ills of modern living." Pavlov concluded that Conrad faithfully captured the uncertainty, tension, and suffering of man's existence in a bourgeois world convulsed by forces beyond his control. Pavlov's last sentence was, "With Conrad, we have arrived in the twentieth century." By the time I wrote on *A Grain of Wheat*, I had lived through some convulsions in Uganda: the overthrow of the Kabaka in Buganda, the coup by Idi Amin, guerrilla fighting against the Amin regime, and botched attempts at further coups, so I felt tension as I wrote.[2]

Some of the characters in Ngũgĩ's novel are similar to those in Conrad's: Mugo resembles Razumov; Kihika, Haldin, and Mumbi, Natalia. A similar story drove the two novels: the betrayal of the revolutionary by the self-made man whom people mistake as the executed revolutionary's good friend and helper. Tova Raz read a draft of my chapter and said that the way I had written it, I could be accused of suggesting that nothing in Ngũgĩ's novel was original, that it all came from Conrad. I revised to make it clear that one writer could legitimately draw from another (see Nazareth, "Obituary"). When my book came out, an early reviewer, Jacqueline Bardolph, said that *influenced* was too weak a word to use for the relation of Ngũgĩ's texts to Conrad's (32). I agreed with her. Not only was the word weak; it was misleading, because it could be taken to mean "plagiarized."

I acquired a better understanding of Ngũgĩ's relation to Conrad when reading the scene near the end of Tayeb Salih's novel *Season of Migration to the North*. When the unnamed narrator enters the room, in a small village in the south of Sudan, of the dead or disappeared Mustafa Sa'eed (a room that has an L-shaped roof), he discovers piles of books on the shelves and on the floor, and he lists their authors. Since I teach Salih's novel in my course on Conrad and what I call Conrad's descendants, one would expect to find books by Conrad on the shelf. But there is no reference to him. Or is there? The name Brierly is mentioned. Brierly is the captain in *Lord Jim* who judges Jim and then finds himself guilty and jumps into the ocean. The name Ford Madox Ford is also listed. He cowrote two novels with Conrad, *Romance* and *The Inheritors*, and he helped edit some of Conrad's books, including (according to some scholars) the writing of four pages of *Nostromo*. The appearance of Ford Madox Ford on the bookshelf implies that Salih has been a collaborator with and an editor of Conrad in his novel (Nazareth, "Dark Heart"). The same implication applies to Ngũgĩ's relation with Conrad.

Although I have taught Ngũgĩ's novels in several courses—but chiefly in African Literature and Three African Writers—I felt there was something missing by not teaching *A Grain of Wheat* in connection with Conrad's novels. In the late 1980s, my colleague Stavros Deligiorgis suggested that I devise a course on Third World literature and yet classify it as dealing with First World, mainstream literature, as a way to get the English department to pay attention to what I was doing. I told Deligiorgis that I had been thinking of teaching selected texts by Conrad and by writers from various parts of the Third World who responded to him. He thought it was a good idea, so I planned the course. I chose six texts by Conrad, seven texts by Third World writers, and F. Scott Fitzgerald's *The Great Gatsby*:[3]

Conrad

"The Secret Sharer"
Heart of Darkness
Lord Jim
Nostromo
The Secret Agent
Under Western Eyes

Descendants of Conrad

Tayeb Salih, *Season of Migration to the North* (Sudan)
Ngũgĩ wa Thiong'o, *A Grain of Wheat* (Kenya)

Wilson Harris, *Palace of the Peacock* (Guyana)
V. S. Naipaul, *A Bend in the River* (Trinidad)
Peter Nazareth, *The General Is Up* (Uganda)
James Konrad, *Target Amin* (Uganda?)
Lloyd Fernando, *Scorpion Orchid* (Malaysia)
F. Scott Fitzgerald, *The Great Gatsby* (United States)
Ishmael Reed, *Flight to Canada* (United States)

I taught the graduate class by discussing the Conrad texts first and then the other texts. After Salih I taught *Under Western Eyes*, followed by *A Grain of Wheat*.

In the company of other Third World writers responding in their own ways to Conrad, Ngũgĩ's novel became much more flexible and open-ended. Like jazz musicians jamming, Conrad stated a theme, and others improvised on it. This process went beyond influence: it was a mirroring of Conrad, a drawing on his structure to extend it or reverse it, adding elements according to the situation or a character's cultural, social, historical perspective.

Conrad's story line was also redrawn. We know what Victor Haldin did and Razumov's betrayal of him early in *Under Western Eyes*, but we do not get to know about Mugo's betrayal of Kihika until later in Ngũgĩ's novel, and we get details of how the revolutionary came to the room of the betrayer close to the end instead of near the beginning, as in Conrad's novel. Both Haldin and Mumbi draw the confession of betrayal out of Razumov and Mugo, respectively, through the power of their eyes, but Mumbi is aware of this ability as a Gĩkũyũ woman. Her power grows out of the Gĩkũyũ legend that society was matriarchal before the men took over, so that in times of trouble women use their old power. The African lover of Kurtz becomes the revolutionary woman Njeri in Ngũgĩ's novel who loves Kihika and goes into the forest to fight with him. Haldin is closer to a Russian anarchist in not considering the consequences of his bomb throwing, while Kihika is a revolutionary Mau Mau leader who hates shedding blood and has a long-term plan to fight the imperialists. Of course each writer was addressing a different audience. Conrad's was a European (strictly English) audience. In *Heart of Darkness* he exposed the cruelties of imperialism to people who were benefiting from that imperialism and did not want to see how their well-being was established on robbery and the consequent suffering of the African people.[4]

Several years after I taught Conrad and His Descendants, the English department asked me to teach it again but this time as an undergraduate course. I worried that reading Conrad's six texts might leave undergraduate students little or no time for the other texts. Then I got the idea of intertwining the texts: two by Conrad, one by a Third World writer, then back to Conrad, and so on. I ran this idea by J. R. Kurtz, who was visiting me in Iowa at the time, and he supported it. The objective of the course was preserved in this way. Not only did we see Ngũgĩ responding to Conrad but also Conrad responding to Ngũgĩ, in the sense that the Conrad text came to the minds of the students after they read the Ngũgĩ text.

I called the new course Conrad and Descendants. It intertwined selected fiction by Conrad with works by writers who responded to Conrad, by parodying, mirroring, reversing, compressing, deconstructing, or expanding him. The influence of Conrad was examined in terms of both style and content. In content, Conrad broke up the worldview imposed by the English language, creating openings through which other writers, from worlds that had been subjected to control, were able to enter.

Students discover the story of Conrad's *Under Western Eyes* after wrestling with the complex storytelling—or story writing—of the Teacher of Languages, who derives his story from various texts, real life, and his own knowledge. Ngũgĩ's dispensing with the Teacher of Languages makes it easier for us to get to the relationship between the revolutionary and the person who betrayed him. The focus thus changes from modes of writing to the story line, which is similar to Conrad's though reversed by Ngũgĩ. Like Haldin, Kihika kills a brutal agent of an oppressive government and seeks refuge with a self-made man (Razumov, Mugo). Both self-made men (orphans in reality or by upbringing) are shaken by the presence in their room of the revolutionary whom they see as a murderer; both go out in a fever, both have hallucinations about the revolutionary, and both decide to turn the revolutionary over to the authorities, rationalizing that it is not a betrayal, since they do not believe in what the revolutionaries stand for. Both think that if they can just get the revolutionary out of their lives, they can continue pursuing their interests as before. Both acquire the reputation of having been a good friend and supporter of the executed revolutionary, and both are expected (or pressured) to stand in for the revolutionary.

Both Haldin and Kihika realize toward the end, largely thanks to the revolutionary's sister, that they have betrayed the revolutionary and thus themselves. Both confess twice, first to the sister (Natalia, Mumbi), then to the public. Razumov's first confession is witnessed by the Teacher of Languages, who tells us about it, but nobody other than Mumbi knows of Mugo's confession, and she remains silent, believing that there has been enough bloodshed. Razumov confesses to the revolutionaries, among whose company is a double agent and killer, Nikita Necator, whereas Mugo confesses to the community gathered to celebrate independence. Mugo's confession is therefore more wide-reaching. In confessing, Razumov clears the reputation of Ziemianitch, who was blamed for betraying Haldin: Ziemianitch's hanging himself was taken as proof of his remorse. Razumov's confession saves Ziemianitch's reputation, not Ziemianitch's life, although it frees Razumov from endorsing a big lie. But Mugo saved a life, because Karanja was going to be executed as the betrayer. Although both revolutionaries are eventually admired for their courage, Razumov lives while Mugo is tried and executed, not as an act of revenge but for what he did. In Mugo's case, the healing of the community begins. There is a third confession by Razumov: a complex one, in his diary, which is given to Natalia, who passes it on to the Teacher. Ngũgĩ could not have included this confession, because Mugo is not a writer.

The students discover that the chronology of Conrad's novel—what is revealed earlier, what is revealed later—is reversed by Ngũgĩ. I ask them to consider the effect of this reversal. Ngũgĩ's narrative makes us want to know more about how Kihika comes to Mugo, about why and how Mugo betrays Kihika, about how Mugo discovers that he indeed betrayed him. We become more aware in Ngũgĩ's novel of how deeply divided the Gĩkũyũ community was under British colonialism, of how some were ideologically shaped by the colonizer's system, by the educational system and the use of the Bible. In Razumov's story we know early on how and why Razumov gave Haldin up, and we wait to learn when it will be discovered and how. Only near the end is it revealed how Kihika came to Mugo's hut and what happened consequently.

African writers of the colonial, neocolonial, and postcolonial periods have had to engage in a complex dialogue with the West. Ngũgĩ takes the anarchists before the Russian Revolution and turns them into a complex portrait of the Mau Mau who fought against British imperialism. Even though the Russian anarchist and the Mau Mau fighter are both patriotic, Kihika has much more of an ideological and political agenda than Haldin, an agenda that arises out of a deep spirituality and radical interpretation of the Bible. The complexity in Ngũgĩ's novel lies in the way Kihika takes up a tool used by the British to keep the people docile, the Bible, and finds in it the inspiration to fight for the freedom of his people. Moses is read by him as a leader against oppression and slavery. Kihika further redefines the role of Christ as the Messiah by saying that the Messiah is not an individual but that people can be messiahs for one another. The oppressors can kill one messiah but not a whole movement.

The Conrad text becomes a door through which Ngũgĩ enters his own African world and thereby speaks to the world at large, the global world.

NOTES

[1] See chapters 8 and 9 of my *Literature and Society.*

[2] The botched coups and consequent killings led me to write, "As Edward Luttwak says in his book *Coup d'Etat*, '*Nostromo* is a brilliant prophetic analysis of the causes and consequences of "neocolonialism"'" (*Literature* 5).

[3] See Nazareth, "Conrad's Descendants"; C. Fox; Peters; and Shaffer.

[4] It could be argued that the unblocking of Mugo by Mumbi leads to the release of the story that Mugo has repressed, presented by the omniscient narrator. Note the similar way the horrible story told to the narrator of Salih's novel by Mustafa Sa'eed is repressed by the narrator until it is released in Mustafa's room that contains hundreds of books.

Text-Context: *A Grain of Wheat* as Testimony

Uzoma Esonwanne

A Grain of Wheat, Ngũgĩ wa Thiong'o's modernist masterpiece, is very much a staple of postcolonial and African literature courses in the North American academy today. Since it was published in 1967, this novel has claimed, and earned, its place alongside works such as Chinua Achebe's *Things Fall Apart* (1958), Ousmane Sembène's *God's Bits of Wood* (1962), and Wole Soyinka's *Death and the King's Horseman* (1975) as a classic of modern Africa's long and costly struggles against European colonialism.

But is this success of *Grain* sufficient reason to teach it? Does the dramatization of a community warily contemplating the possibility that *uhuru*, the promise of national self-determination for which a long and heroic campaign was waged against Britain's colonial state, might betray all it stands for warrant the inclusion of *Grain* in the corpus of postcolonial African texts we often teach? And if it does, how ought one to teach the novel—as a literary monument to modern African history, a narrative inquiry into the ethics of violence, or an exemplar of African literary modernism? To consider these questions today, in an environment in which the failure of many postcolonial states in Africa is often advanced as proof that decolonization was a misguided enterprise, can be quite challenging. But to address them in English literary studies, where formalist skepticism toward what Edward W. Said calls "*immediacy*, that untreated bolus of direct experience" ("*Reflections*" xvii), still runs deep, for some means to risk reducing texts to an effect rather than a cause of history (Miller 4–5). But must all attempts to teach *Grain* by engaging rigorously with the history of decolonization in Kenya cast it as a historical product? Could one not teach this novel in a manner that, far from impoverishing its textuality, makes its literariness an apprehension, on the phenomenological plane, of the immediacy of decolonization?

Few who teach postcolonial (African) literatures in North America would doubt the urgency of these questions, for at their core lies the question of contextualization in literary pedagogy. The incident that brought this problem home to me occurred a decade and a half ago, when a student, wondering out loud about the provenance of "the king's horseman" in Soyinka's *Death and the King's Horseman*, startled me into incoherence. The student wanted to know if Soyinka's title meant that Africans had horses before Europeans arrived. This was the moment when I began to worry that a pedagogy that focused narrowly or exclusively on literary form might be as likely to impoverish African postcolonial texts as one that encouraged students to read them as ethnographic and sociological documents in literary drag. I began to suspect that teaching *Death and the King's Horseman* as if its narrative events had no bearing on "real world" history might be quite different from teaching *Macbeth* that way.

Teaching *Grain*, a novel that opens with an author's note declaring that it is "set in contemporary Kenya" and "the situation and the problems" represented in the narrative "are real," as if the events in Kenya's national history to which Ngũgĩ alludes are incidental to its meaning, would be to impoverish it.

Postcolonial African literary criticism has been making this point insistently for the last four decades. In 1966, one year before the publication of *Grain*, Ben Obumselu called for criticism that is informed by knowledge of the "background" of African literature (46). A few years later, Abiola Irele, worried that interpretations lacking in knowledge of the context in which Africa's literary "half-child"—his term for the emergent African literature in European languages—was produced would threaten its growth, made a powerful plea for a sociological criticism that would be informed by deep knowledge of the ambiguous provenance of each text's literary idiom (*African Experience* 29, 34). Over the years literary scholars have defined this source in varied or modified ways—they have defined it, for example, as context, understood as "the ever-present halo around the literary work as a self-contained entity" that illuminates the text while resisting its attempt to appropriate it (Amuta 88) and as African oral discourse, "a fundamental reference of African expression" (Irele, *African Imagination* 31). But what has remained consistent is the conviction that sociological analysis that attends closely to context is the most effective method by which readers can induce African texts to yield their meanings.

Coinciding with this consolidation of sociological analyses in African literary criticism was the parallel consolidation, initially in western Europe and later in North America, of formalist criticism, which was skeptical about contextualization and referentiality.[1] But, as Said's critique suggests, the formalist view never enjoyed universal acceptance. Vocal and persuasive dissent from it was articulated by exponents of left criticism, particularly Marxist and feminist scholars, in whose projects Said finds corroboration for his insistence on the valence of immediacy in literary analyses. Such scholars often hold a complex and nuanced understanding of the historical (or social) aspect of a literary work, a work whose context has "to be *read* . . . in conjunction with, and as part of, the reading of the text" (Felman and Laub xv).[2] This notion of context breaks with its antecedents. If literary scholarship in the past aligned contextual knowledge with the provenance of writing (thus the focus on sources and backgrounds of the literary word), Shoshana Felman and Dori Laub's proposition effectively realigns that knowledge with reading (the emphasis on the reception of the literary word).

Something of this realignment can be discerned in Simon Gikandi's monograph on Ngũgĩ's texts and contexts. Gikandi presents three contexts for *Grain*: the influence on Ngũgĩ's imagination of the tragic register in which Frantz Fanon, whose *The Wretched of the Earth* Ngũgĩ may have been reading as he was writing the novel, anticipates the failure of cultural nationalism and decolonization; his subscription to the ideology of modernism, as a consequence of which he is prompted to inscribe failure as a trope of disenchantment in the novel; and his need to establish the source of his authority as a chronicler of events that were unfolding even as he was writing. All three contexts, Gikandi declares, should help us understand such "contradictory intentions" of the author as the "split between the romance of cultural nationalism and the disenchantment generated by a failed decolonization" in the "language and politics" of the novel (*Ngũgĩ* 102–06). By tightly braiding his analysis of these contexts with a close reading of the text, Gikandi offers us a rigorous exposition of the ideological, political, and authorial circumstances that inspired the formal experimentations for which *Grain* has rightly been celebrated as Ngũgĩ's most accomplished novel.

But this achievement, which recuperates the referent (the conditions of Ngũgĩ's literary production) from the oblivion into which postcolonial theory has cast it, tells us little about the interplay between text and context at the axis of reception.[3] Gikandi characterizes "Ngũgĩ's ambition" as the product of "narratives that bear witness to the historical experience" (*Ngũgĩ* 2). In reading the text and context of *Grain* simultaneously, we participate in bearing witness to experiences of "the Emergency" to which Ngũgĩ's novel gives testimony.

The first obstacle we face is how to deal with our "interests and perspectives" as readers, if these, as Ato Quayson argues, inevitably saturate any context we assign to a text (xxix). How do we engage with such interests and perspectives without sliding into guilt-laden and self-indulgent psychobabble? The answer is to approach *Grain* in much the same way that Felman approaches Albert Camus's *The Plague*. For Felman, *The Plague* inaugurates "a new form of *narrative as testimony*" that bears witness to historical contingency (the Holocaust) not by chronicling it but by "rethinking" and thus transforming it (Felman and Laub 95). The word *as* in "narrative as testimony" signals what she considers distinctive about this new form. Instead of representing the Holocaust analogically, Camus's narratives (*The Plague* and *The Fall*) testify to it by undertaking to produce their "own speech as material evidence" for its truth (5). Consequently, to read *The Plague* is to enact an utterance whose felicity (whose ability to bear witness rather than say that it is bearing witness) arises from its invocation of specific conventions in a social context.

Ngũgĩ, like Camus, belongs to the age of testimony.[4] Thus it could be said that in *Grain* he, like the Algerian French colonial writer, seeks to confront our age with "the horror" (Felman and Laub 114) of its colonial past in Kenya. Felman's analysis of *The Plague* demonstrates why distinctions are untenable between literary speech acts whose performativity is contingent on the writer and those whose performativity derives from socially bound linguistic conventions. *The Plague* is an expansive fictional world in which utterances by individual characters (the dialogues between the physician Dr. Rieux, the journalist Rambert, and Tarrou) do things; it is also an underground testimony or verbal action of resistance that actually intervenes in the anti-Nazi struggle of World War II. In other words, performativity in Camus's novel operates simultaneously on two levels: narrative diegesis (textuality) and worldly contingency (historicity).

During the pandemic that has gripped their city and severed it from the rest of the world, Dr. Rieux denies Rambert the document that would certify his health and thus allow him to flee the plague. Rieux's statement "from now on you will be from here, like everybody else" transforms Rambert, who has anchored his hope of escape in the conviction that he is "not from here," into a citizen (qtd. in Felman and Laub 107). Felman's claim that Rieux, Camus's narrator, mediates between narrative and history by doubling as "an informed and an honest" eyewitness to the plague-Holocaust (101) implies that *The Plague* is an utterance-centered performative. But her yoking of Rieux's authority as witness and his story's "truth claim," both of which she ascribes to the "carnal" (or "communal") knowledge of "victimization" he gains from seeing-witnessing and telling-narrating the plague (111), with the discharge of his obligation to history's "woes" and casualties (115), demonstrates that she never loses sight of the fact that the literary conventions of any speech act have a social origin.

So how does *The Plague* testify against the genocide perpetrated by the Nazi regime? Here Felman's argument becomes most instructive for those who, like me, may wish to read and teach *A Grain of Wheat* as a narrative of testimony. What actualizes the intervention of testimonial narrative in the real world struggles of World War II is the consciousness of writer and reader. If literature of testimony is "a *performative* engagement between consciousness and history," the writer is a subject whose art is compelled by this "ceaseless engagement" with history "to transform words into events and to make *an act* of every publication" (114). The reader's implication in the text as witness is essential to the success of the writer's project. In *The Plague*, Camus implicates the reader by aligning the reader with Rambert, who is an unwilling and belated witness. By mobilizing a narrative strategy that both replicates the conventional notion of history as event (documentary representations of the Holocaust) and uses a literary metaphor (the plague) that allegorizes the event to undercut any direct reference to history, *The Plague* aligns the reader with the character whose perspective on the city's calamity is closest to the reader's. The novel thus reenacts in narrative mode the process by which Rambert, who initially wishes to chronicle the ravages of the plague with the journalistic detachment that his profession demands, is eventually implicated in and bears witness to the plague in his own body. This process compels in the reader a cognitive transformation:

> The specific task of the literary testimony is to open up in that belated witness, which the reader now historically becomes, the imaginative capability of perceiving history—what is happening to others—*in one's own body*, with the power of sight (of insight) usually afforded only by one's own immediate physical involvement. (Felman and Laub 108)

How is *Grain* a narrative of testimony? How does Ngũgĩ's novel attempt to prompt in our students, who today are the belated witnesses of the historical event it narrates, the transformation of consciousness necessary for them to be able to perceive the Emergency in their bodies? To answer this question, let us specify how Ngũgĩ's text may allow them to perceive an event few ever heard of and to perceive it with the acuity of personal experience. First, note

Felman's suggestion that the performativity of narratives of testimony operates on multiple (linguistic and social) levels. Second, note the ascription of the text's illocutionary transformation of the reader from observer to witness to the text's narrative strategies. Finally, bear in mind that the aim of any pedagogy of postcolonial narratives of testimony is to facilitate this transformation.

But since *Grain* is hardly a postcolonial African facsimile of *The Plague*, we must proceed cautiously as we put these insights to use in explaining how *Grain* inscribes the reader as a witness in history. I make this distinction: whereas *The Plague* registers the effect of history as holocaust on Camus the onlooker or witness (Felman and Laub 96), *Grain* registers history's effects as dispossession, degradation, and alienation not just on Ngũgĩ and his compatriots, the immediate victims of the anticolonial struggle, but on their offspring as well. The narrator echoes Ngũgĩ's skepticism about colonial literature and historiography:

> Learned men will, no doubt, dig into the troubled times which we in Kenya underwent, and maybe sum up the lesson of history in a phrase. Why, let us ask them, did the incident in Rira Camp capture the imagination of the world? For there were other camps, bigger, scattered all over Kenya, from the Manda Islands in the Indian Ocean to the Magata Islands in Lake Victoria. (131)

Commenting on this passage, Gikandi observes that Ngũgĩ's narrator locates himself in the reader's "universe of discourse" by identifying himself and the reader as *us* (*Ngũgĩ* 122). In this way Ngũgĩ obtains the warrant to bear witness against testimony offered by official historiography. The testimony that *Grain* offers is counterdiscursive. Unlike *The Plague*, it bears witness not only to trauma suffered by history's victims but also against narratives that devalorize the significance of the anticolonial struggle in African history.

In bearing witness to the Emergency, *Grain* does more than chronicle the degradation into which the war for national self-determination plunges everyone, particularly the peasants who are herded into concentration camps. Over and above the historical facts recounted in the narrative are the myriad acts, both individual and collective, by which adversaries on both sides of the war bravely uphold, inadvertently compromise, or cravenly betray their ideals. If Camus metaphorizes the Holocaust as a pandemic that implicates all in the struggle against disease, Ngũgĩ represents the Emergency as recollections by which survivors individually and collectively assess the prognostic value of history. "Ngũgĩ writes from the position of one who remembers the recent African past vividly, but he does not seem to be connected to this past except through its remembrance and—ultimately—its representation in narrative" (Gikandi, *Ngũgĩ* 7).

In *Grain*, Ngũgĩ attempts to orient recollection forward rather than backward, perhaps to avoid the sense of disillusionment that, just a few years after independence, began to pervade narratives of decolonization that conflated the failure of the postcolonial nation-state in Africa with all anticolonial struggles, including those inspired by revolutionary, transnational ideals (Brown 168). *Grain* may also be read as a narrative that bears witness to Ngũgĩ's alienation from himself. "[A]utobiographical elements" (Gikandi, *Ngũgĩ* 105), such as childhood memories of assaults by British soldiers on aged relatives during the "Mau Mau Emergency," suggest that his life was not spared the ravages of war (Ngũgĩ, "'Tolstoy'" 51).[5] The orientation of memories toward the future makes it clear that in this narrative remembering is cognitive action directed to the nation's prospects: "Writing about circumstances where action is to operate is as important as the practical action itself. Action is a practice and a theory" (Ngũgĩ, "Interview" [Bardolph and Durix] 162). For Ngũgĩ, writing is proleptic.

How can the postcolonial narrative of testimony bear witness to history (the Emergency) by addressing itself to circumstances that are yet to occur? The answer lies in what the narrative constitutes as its object of address and how it addresses that object. In composing his narratives, Ngũgĩ begins with the idea that colonialism had its most damaging effect on the minds and spirits of Africans. Evidence of that damage is found in the willingness of educated Africans to distort their own histories. But his narratives focus on the consequences of this distortion for their future (*Decolonising* 9–11). Against Emman Omari's suggestion that the impossibility of producing objective accounts of historical experience renders the miseducation of the young unavoidable, Ngũgĩ insists on the need "to make Kenyans view their history correctly" as a way of ensuring that they interpret their past and perceive "their future" accurately ("Ngugi wa Thiong'o Speaks" 130). In *Decolonising the Mind*, he emphasizes the urgency of this task by characterizing English-language instruction in colonialist schools as a project of cultural alienation whose object is to sever "the mind from the body" and thus produce "a society of bodiless heads and headless bodies" (28).

Dismembered, incomplete, and disharmonious, the Kenya envisioned in this colonialist project is as far removed from an imagined community as possible. More to the point, such a Kenya could not even begin to function as the social body from whose sociolinguistic conventions Ngũgĩ's narratives could derive their illocutionary force. That body can be found only in the past, in the form of the village community that has taken an Oath of Unity, the set of pledges that include loyalty, obedience, solidarity, secrecy, and "gender discipline" (Lonsdale 429–30).[6] The value of the past in *Grain* is not so much to recall what actually happened in the Emergency as it is to anticipate a yet incomprehensible *uhuru* ("independence") in the light of undertakings made for it in the past. It is in this anticipation that Ngũgĩ's orientation of his narrator and characters' memories toward the future becomes meaningful.

To see how *Grain* addresses the future by bearing witness to history, consider New Thabai and Rira. New Thabai is a village to which residents of Old Thabai were forcibly moved after the Mau Mau assault on "the Mahee Police Post" (140). Rira is a detention camp "near the coast where no rain fell and nothing grew except sand, sand and rocks" (131–32). At Rira, a decisive confrontation takes place between the colonial state, represented by Mr. John Thompson, the commandant whose strategy for breaking inmates' resistance is to surprise them, and its recalcitrant captives, some of whom, like Mugo, were residents of Old Thabai. This confrontation leaves both Thompson and Mugo scarred. Thompson, whose decision to set his "white officers and warders on" the captives causes the death of eleven prisoners (131–34), thus precipitating the global media scandal that compels Britain to seek a negotiated settlement with Jomo Kenyatta and the nationalists, becomes a broken man. Rira—a "hunger strike, a little beating and eleven detainees"—is "the tragedy of his life," the "wound" that "had never healed," because it tarnished his reputation and banished him forever from "administration" (46). Ultimately, it is the wound that unmasks colonial ideology, the "great moral idea" of a global "British nation" (54) to which Mr. Thompson has pledged his life.

For the reclusive and self-absorbed Mugo, Rira also represents an unmasking. But what it unmasks is not, as with Thompson, a misguided commitment to a seductive national project. In contrast to other villagers, including Gikonyo, Mugo did not take the Oath. Nor did he exhibit any passion for the ideals of *ithaka na wiathi* ("self-mastery through land"), the Gĩkũyũ name for the movement in support of which the villagers joined in the national liberation struggle. He intervened when a home guard whipped Wambuku, Kihika's despondent and pregnant girlfriend, while they were digging the ditch around New Thabai. Ironically this act, which elevated him to the status of a hero in the community, was motivated by "terror" rather than by solicitude for Wambuku's welfare or by political conviction (172–73). Rira exposes in Mugo a megalomaniacal resentment of Kihika. Kihika has "a mother and a father, and a brother, and a sister" and so is willing "to play with death" (195). Mugo resents this attitude, but it also provides him with a rationale for his duplicity: "I am important. I must not die. To keep myself alive, healthy, strong—to wait for my mission in life—is a duty to myself, to men and women of tomorrow" (197).[7] He represses the memory of his betrayal of Kihika to Thompson until, two years later, Mumbi's story about her experience during the Emergency "cracked open his dulled inside and released" imprisoned emotions, setting him on the path of an unavoidable confrontation with a past that he would rather forget (172).

Rira is a synecdoche for the betrayal by Gikonyo of the communal ideals (*ithaka na wiathi*) he swore to uphold by taking the Oath of Unity. Because Thabai, the community he betrays by revealing his oath to Thompson, is also the community before whom he makes his marital vow to Mumbi, his treachery is compounded. His guilt-induced angst and disenchantment with himself and Mugo's paranoid fantasies and self-loathing may differ, but the truth to which they bear witness is similar: each tells the story of the enormous personal and communal cost of betraying his oath. Gikonyo's anxiety and Mugo's paranoia are the consequences of apathy and envy: apathy to the anticolonial struggle, envy of its local hero, Kihika. Apathy, fueled by growing despondency about the prospects of freedom, prompts Gikonyo to barter his oath in exchange for the opportunity "to see his Mumbi and take up the thread of life where he had left it" (113). But initially he shared with his compatriots a commitment to the ideals of *ithaka na wiathi*. For Karanja and Mumbi it is New Thabai, not Rira, that represents wounds suffered during the Emergency. Like their unnamed son, whose presence transforms Gikonyo and Mumbi's relationship but about whose future the novel remains silent, New Thabai, a villagization project built on the ashes of the old village to starve the forest fighters of support, testifies to Mumbi's dogged resistance and eventual capitulation to history and Karanja's violation of the Gĩkũyũ *thaahu* in exchange for the "hooded" identity of the home guard and chief (Gikandi, *Ngũgĩ* 126).

If the villagers are uncertain that *uhuru* will bring *ithaka na wiathi*, they are also uncertain of the meaning of their recollections of Rira, Thabai, and other sites of war. This uncertainty explains the ambivalence with which Ngũgĩ's characters, including such minor figures as Warui, contemplate the arrival of *uhuru*. On the one hand, they seem euphoric about its approach, their optimism stoked by nationalism. "Like Kenyatta is telling us," Warui tells Mugo, "these are days of Uhuru na Kazi" (2). On the other hand, they are leery of the future into which it will usher them. Questions abound. What will the seeds of freedom, sowed in blood during the Emergency, yield? Will *uhuru* fulfill or extinguish their hopes? They turn to memories of the war for answers—or, rather, to memories of the Emergency. The patrons of Uhuru Hotel (formerly called Mambo Leo) listen patiently to Githua's boastful retelling of his exploits during the Emergency:

> They listened to him seriously at one time nodding or shaking their heads in sympathy with the tears in Githua's voice. . . . People started talking about Kenya, the land of conflicts. "The Emergency hit us hard," some were saying. (126)

The oneiric drop of water poised over Mugo's eyes at the beginning of the narrative also expresses this turning to memories (1). In hauling himself up from his nightmare, Mugo may have resisted the threat that the past poses to his vision, but the past, in both material form (his porridge) and psychological form (his dreams), continues to haunt him. For everyone, including General R. and Lieutenant Koina, Kihika's comrades in arms, and Gikonyo and Mumbi, the past is not past; it lives on in narrative "retrospective reconstructions" of their involvement in the failed or uncompleted project of decolonization.[8] Githua's compulsive recasting of himself as a heroic victim of the Emergency is one such reconstruction.

Thabai, Rira, Yala, and Muhia are names for experiences that Ngũgĩ's characters remember (and narrate)—in accordance not with the facts but with their current self-interests: the experiences represented by these names affect their perception of and attitudes toward the future. Unfolding in the "moral and intellectual context" of a struggle whose purpose was not merely to wrest economic control of the land (*ithaka*) from the colonial state but also to create a space in which the postcolonial African subject, as citizen of an independent state, could exercise "moral agency" (*wiathi*) (Lonsdale 326–27), the experiences of the peasants at Rira and New Thabai are remembered in the form of oral memoirs. But because obligation to the collective interest is the framework for assessing their roles, and because in the Emergency none could possibly live up to the communal ideals, the idiom in which they cast their recollections is confessional. This idiom separates their narratives from those of Thompson and the historians; it possesses a counterdiscursive force. Confessional memoirs, making no claim to objectivity, do not aspire, as history does, to reconstruct Rira as a minor, peripheral episode in colonialism's otherwise triumphant tale of epic adventure. Nor do they articulate that consciousness of the individual as an agent of a divinely ordained national destiny that makes Thompson perceive Rira as tragedy. If Rira, Thabai, Yala, Muhia, and the Emergency are memoirs couched in the idiom of confession, then their function in *Grain* is to ask the reader to play the role of confidant or secret sharer that participation in confessional discourse requires.

How should students engage a historical narrative that, challenging the tragic and epic genres favored by agents of the colonial state and its historians, offers fragmentary, contradictory, and incoherent autobiographical recollections of the past instead, a narrative that solicits empathy and even identification with subjects who, far from being unwitting victims of history, are responsible for its unfolding? Students should understand that the sociolinguistic conventions of testimony are essential for grasping how *Grain* juxtaposes discourses of empire, which have shaped their views of history, against discourses of resistance that point to a dimension of human experience hitherto concealed.

A Grain of Wheat, unlike history, does not offer a definitive account or master narrative of the Emergency; neither does it espouse an agnostic attitude toward the possibility of inscribing historical experience in narrative. It bears witness to the fact that to read postcolonial narratives of testimony is, finally, to be instructed by the text on how to listen to voices whose muting in official histories of empire makes possible the amnesia if not the willed ignorance that renders impossible any genuine dialogue between heirs of empire in the metropoles and peripheries of global capitalism.

NOTES

[1] I use the terms *sociological* and *formalist* to subsume multiple modes of textual analyses. These range from Marxism and new historicism to structuralism and poststructuralism. In postcolonial literary theory and criticism, scholars who share the formalist skepticism to literary contextualization are, in general, indebted to Derrida (9).

[2] Consider the following statements: "The point I want to highlight here . . . is the degree to which the social context adduced for a literary representation is always itself a strategic selection out of a process of flux"; "I would like to note that the social in my

terms is always an object produced out of an interrogation and thus has to be *read for*" (Quayson xxix, xxxi).

[3] Gikandi is here referring to the formalist position on literary context. Also, what insider perspective means for Gikandi differs from what it means for C. L. Innes. For Gikandi, the insider's perspective is a local knowledge that generates rigorous critique; for Innes, it is "an act of *recognition* and bonding" (201).

[4] On Camus and the modes of "textual" or "literary-historical" witnessing, see Kacandes 111–15.

[5] Was Ngũgĩ shielded "from the ruptures and transformations of a dying colonialism by both Alliance High School and Makerere University College," as Gikandi alleges (*Ngũgĩ* 105–06)? Sicherman takes a contrary view (*Ngũgĩ wa Thiong'o: The Making*) 3, 4, 82

[6] For an account of the history of the oath of unity, see Sicherman, *Ngũgĩ wa Thiong'o: The Making* 49, 72–82, 147–48, 182–85, 355.

[7] For an analysis of the allegorical and ironic valence of Mugo, see Gikandi, *Ngũgĩ* 109–12.

[8] Jonathan Boyarin speaks of "the conundrum of memory as recollection versus memory as retrospective reconstruction" (3).

Degendering the Mind: On Teaching *Petals of Blood*

Bonnie Roos

> The conquest of the earth, which mostly means the taking it away from those who have a different complexion or slightly flatter noses than ourselves, is not a pretty thing when you look into it too much. What redeems it is the idea only: not a sentimental pretense, but an idea: and an unselfish belief in the idea—something you can set up, and bow down before, and offer sacrifice to. . . .
>
> —Joseph Conrad, *Heart of Darkness*

My greatest struggle in teaching postcolonial literatures here in the Texas Panhandle is not the insularity of my students, many of whom have never traveled outside the state. Instead it is a problem I have found at a variety of colleges and universities, in which well-intended students, who are confronted with the brutality that many postcolonial writers describe, go about living life as if they imagine their own world as utterly disconnected from, and unimplicated in, that brutality. This apathy is unsettling precisely because students are aware that the goods they consume are produced far away—often by poorly paid workers in dire circumstances. I find Ngũgĩ wa Thiong'o's *Petals of Blood* (1977) a strategic text to convey to my students the way their world affects others, because it reveals how our own romantic sensibilities serve to undermine our activist impulses and veil the real interrelations between ourselves and others. Issues of gender in *Petals of Blood* provide a useful demonstration of how these idealizing tendencies are interrelated and thwart our attempts at better understanding, blinding us to the real problems we must address.

The primary character in *Petals of Blood* is Wanja.[1] Wanja is indisputably heroic and self-sacrificing, even though her individual successes and defeats sometimes result in missteps. This misdirection causes many readers, including my students, to overlook her strengths—strengths derived from hardship and cynicism—and to be critical of her. They are, by extension, critical of Ngũgĩ's portrayal of her. Wanja moves, after all, among female stereotypes: she is a mother and fertility goddess, as farmer and leader with Nyakinyua of the women's growers' union and through her nurturing of Joseph and in her ongoing quest to give birth to a child; she is a symbolic virgin, wooed and fought over by three eligible bachelors (Munira, Karega, and Abdulla) until she is raped by her former lover, Kimeria; and she is a whore, as she works in bars, making money less by her waitressing than by her sexual availability.[2] Whether they are liberal feminists or religiously conservative, my students all struggle with the depiction of Wanja; they like her but find her too depraved, too cynical, or too stereotypical.

Not that I believe we are intended to fully approve of her. Wanja is, as we all are, flawed, and Ngũgĩ expects us to recognize her flaws. He uses her, somewhat problematically, as a trope, as a stand-in for all of Kenya, beautiful and strong, exploited and tarnished (see Stratton 51–53). Her roles may be conventional, but the author's efforts (reflecting the theories of Frantz Fanon) to teach a history of his people make her compatible with the roles women have played in the Gĩkũyũ and Kenyan past. This history complicates our Western stereotypes. Poor and destitute people—prostitutes like Wanja, beer sellers like Abdulla—were instrumental in the Mau Mau revolution, when men and women fought side by side (Ogot and Ochieng 35), and they have historically been seen as Kenyan working-class heroes. Traveling with the Ilmorog party to the city, rescuing Joseph, and murdering Kimeria make Wanja heir to this history and invite us, and our students, to question whether the Western term *prostitute* accurately describes this female character in the Kenyan historical context.

Kenyan history informs and is disseminated in every aspect of Ngũgĩ's work, and it is a necessaary tool in teaching *Petals*. I suggest to my students that in offering histories of the Gĩkũyũ people long before the Mau Mau revolution in *Petals*, Ngũgĩ, like many postcolonial writers, is at pains to dispel the notion of primitive African villagers, hunting and gathering, having no history or future until the advent of colonialism. He is invested in debunking the gender corollary of the myth of the prostitute—the belief in the unquestioningly subservient female subaltern who awaits the neocolonizer's eventual rescue of brown women from brown men and whose position seems confirmed by the renewed Gĩkũyũ practice of genital mutilation.[3] Some sources suggest that Gĩkũyũ women traditionally possessed exceptional sexual freedom, even in marriage, though historically such arrangements were not connected to monetary exchange.[4]

Against this cultural background, Wanja's sexuality, even her promiscuity, is not a flaw; Ngũgĩ occasionally reveals it as a strength. But of course Wanja is not merely a sexually free woman; she is a prostitute, exchanging sex for money and gifts. If, as Kenneth Little suggests, prostitution did not exist in Kenya before European colonization (94), then Wanja's profession bespeaks a condition of oppression and weakness, even if she also derives strength through its practice. By extension, Ngũgĩ suggests that in Kenya's colonial exploitation of people and land, its monetary "affairs" and international "relations," mean all its people, male and female, are made prostitutes of a kind. Because *Petals* is set after independence, Kenya's condition is seen as one of ongoing colonization, ongoing degradation. In other words, like Kenya itself, even though Wanja has the apparent choice of turning away from her profession, she willingly, consciously returns to her work as a barmaid instead of pursuing a different path.

Given that such a decision seems irrational and disempowering, I ask my students why Ngũgĩ has a woman as intelligent and strong as Wanja make it. I suggest that her predilection for romantic sentimentalism is part of the problem. What distinguishes her from the other characters is her preference for the fairy-tale ideal, even as her experiences contradict its viability. She recognizes the truth of her degradation, of her ongoing colonization, but, in the words of Joseph Conrad's Marlow, she finds that "[w]hat redeems it is the idea . . . something you can set up, and bow down before, and offer a sacrifice to" (*Heart* 141). Just as Marlow's aunt compensates for the brutality of imperialism by maintaining the illusion of missionary rescue of savage natives from cannibalism, Wanja makes the reality of her prostitution tolerable through the fantasy of chivalry, of love. She knows in her more "sober moments of reflection and self-appraisal" that she is nothing more than a prostitute; still "she liked and enjoyed the illusion of being wooed and fought over, and being bought a dress or something without her demanding it as a bargain" (56). This romantic artifice is her only consolation for being condemned to a role of subservience due to her gender and beauty. She insists, "A barmaid does not take herself to be a prostitute" (130); and she does not, at least not until the final chapters, in which she cynically becomes a madam of her own whorehouse.

Even my more conservative Texas Panhandle students find Wanja's decision to become a madam more unfortunate than damning. They are more judgmental when Wanja reveals her greatest failure to conform to the expected performance of the traditional female role of mother: through her confession to Karega at the end of the novel, we learn that in a moment of youthful desperation, she killed her first child by abandoning it in a latrine. Ngũgĩ suggests that, like Kenya itself, Wanja has destroyed all prospects for her future, even as she hopes to build a new one. Once again, Wanja is heir to Kenya's historical tragedies and failures. Infanticide, in the form of abandonment of babies in toilets and elsewhere, was not uncommon in colonial Nairobi, especially during the first half of the twentieth century (L. White, "Domestic Labor" 157).[5] This tragic experience should have made Wanja particularly attuned to the dangers of submitting her power to others, of willingly playing the role of subservience in acting as barmaid or prostitute, but it does not seem to inform her decision to become a madam. She clings to the romantic belief that she acts independently of others. Her perpetuation of the gender performance in which she engages confirms her belief that her choices are made by her alone, that others are not implicated in or by her decisions. She takes complete, private responsibility for the death of her first child and understands her subsequent difficulties as therefore deserved. In her blindness and inaction, she is curiously like my students: guilt-ridden but impotent, alternating between taking complete responsibility for their actions and taking refuge in an ignorance embodied in United States–style individualism or the opinion (largely correct here in the working-class heartland) that one has worked hard for what one has earned.

The problem with such romanticism, whether based in gender or class, is not only the perpetuation of injustice but also the silencing of story, of history, because the oppressed are too ashamed to tell their version. I point out that Wanja's truth telling about who she is and what she has done is an indispensable step on Kenya's road to self-awareness as understood by Ngũgĩ. Her truth telling gives her the strength to rise up against her male oppressors. Though she does so without deliberately intending their harm, Wanja locks the three most egregious villains in their rooms when Munira sets the whorehouse on fire. She pits men against one another. She stabs Kimeria. Her truth telling allows for a new beginning, the possibility for her to bear a second child at the end of the story.

Both subtle and brilliant in the depiction of gender in *Petals* is the way Ngũgĩ has Wanja reflect on the men around her. Just as we read stories of white protagonists as if the stories were not about race (a point Ngũgĩ makes in *Decolonising the Mind*), we typically read men as if they were genderless. This idea is debunked throughout *Petals* but particularly when Wanja is raped by Kimeria. In search of relief from the famine and of help for Joseph, a sick child, the villagers travel from Ilmorog to the city and happen on the home of Kimeria, the man who took advantage of Wanja years before. They are held hostage until Wanja is separated from the group to speak with Kimeria. When she refuses Kimeria's request to reestablish sexual relations, going so far as to threaten him with a knife, Kimeria blackmails her, threatening her and all the villagers. She returns to the villagers to consider his demands, believing she has a choice:

> The door opened and Njuguna was called outside by one of the many hands about the house. Outside Njuguna listened to the message from the chief: Wanja was a former wife of the gentleman. She had run away to Ilmorog and now she was refusing the man's bed. Njuguna came back looking reproachfully at Wanja.
>
> Njuguna explained the situation as tactfully as he could, presenting them with the harsh prospects before them.
>
> "No!" Karega shouted as soon as he got the gist of the man's demands.
>
> "Will a child die . . . will Joseph die just because . . . because . . . Besides she is . . . in a way the man's wife," insisted Njuguna. . . .
>
> "Is it true? Wanja, is it true?" Karega asked, and waited for her to answer. . . .
>
> What pained her was not so much the man's lies, not so much Njuguna's attitude, not even Karega's question, but what Njuguna had said about Joseph dying. She would be responsible for a death of another who did not even belong to her. She looked back to the origin of the journey. Maybe she was to blame. . . . [S]he raised her head and looked Karega full in the eyes.
>
> "Yes! yes!" she whispered and stood up, reaching for the door.
>
> For a second, Karega sat completely still, immobile, and gazed at the same spot: what did one believe? What really could one believe now? He stirred himself. He stood up and saw himself walk toward her and hold her by the hand just as she was about to open the door. She felt one thrilling shivering in the flesh, and raised her eyes to him in weakness and

> appeal, and then turned her eyes away, aside, waiting for judgment from him. Anything, anything but this dilemma which was also her shame.
>
> "I do not know anything," he said, a little put out by the pregnant silence in the room, "but . . . but . . . must you go?" [H]e ended rather pathetically.
>
> She looked at him again, briefly, saw the dancing intensity in his eyes, and almost hated him for his youth and his innocence. She was in that second conscious of the moral gulf of knowledge and experience between them and she steeled herself against crying. A bit impatiently, irritably in fact, she disengaged her hand, opened the door and walked out, banging the door so hard behind her that it left a tremor in the room and inside her. (155–57)

It is striking that Ngũgĩ has Kimeria demand Njuguna's acquiescence in the matter. Wanja is already in Kimeria's house, and he might do with her as he pleases. Though she has rejected him with violence, he will clearly force her to have sex with him. But he wants her complicity, not merely her physical submission.[6] So he turns to Njuguna, the male elder of the group, to plead for his marriage rights. When Njuguna returns, he is angry not with Kimeria but with Wanja.[7]

I ask my students to consider the reasons behind his anger, even though he knows Wanja's history with Kimeria. Njuguna sides with Kimeria, explaining to Karega, "she is . . . in a way the man's wife." Kimeria refused to marry Wanja; his leaving her without resources led to her killing of their child. Yet his claim that his "marriage" to her should be honored is affirmed by Njuguna; indeed, Njuguna finds her refusal to be subjugated shameful. The gender hierarchy blinds him to the terrible truth that Kimeria has not merely raped Wanja but emasculated Njuguna by exposing Njuguna's inability to protect the women in his party. To hide his humiliation, Njuguna maintains the appearance of his masculinity by taking seriously Kimeria's request for permission, a pretense of respect. Thus Kimeria uses gender to make Njuguna and the other villagers complicit in their domination. Unable to admit their shame to one another—Wanja's in failing to be a good mother, Njuguna's in failing to be a good protector—they are instead divided from one another. The gender hierarchy creates a silence in which they cannot share their feelings or help one another grieve. Njuguna takes the consolation Kimeria offers him, asserting his manhood by judging Wanja. Internalizing Njuguna's censure, Wanja reasons that because she killed her child, she deserves rape, that she brought this devastation on the villagers and on Joseph: "Maybe she was to blame." Her acceptance of her plight can be mischaracterized as acceptance of Kimeria only because she has not given it voice. She does not share her guilt with others who feel guilt, who might be able to find strength in a communal awareness of disempowerment.

Showing my students how to read these silences, to read what is unspoken and undocumented, is key to the way I teach *Petals of Blood.* It is key to understanding Karega in this scene. Karega has risen in status because of his eager, idealistic defense of the villagers; he is the voice that Wanja does not yet possess. His lackluster defense of Wanja against Kimeria and the other villagers therefore seems pathetic, both to Wanja and my students. He fails because she withheld the truth about her past: had she confessed everything, he might have been able to help. But he is immobilized by the contradictions among her, Njuguna's, and Kimeria's accounts of the story. My students admire Karega's thoughtfulness, but his search for an absolute truth is as problematic as Wanja's reliance on sentimental ideals. In his wish to defend her, he envisions himself performing manhood: "He stood up and saw himself walk toward her and hold her by the hand just as she was about to open the door." She in turn wishes to be protected by him, even if it means her continued female subservience: she "felt one thrilling shivering in the flesh, and raised her eyes to him in weakness and appeal, and then turned her eyes away, aside, waiting for judgment from him." Because he does not know the history, he is impotent to act.

Karega's quest for an ideal truth that separates villain from victim blinds Karega to the truth that nothing justifies Kimeria's forcing an unwilling woman to have sex with him. Uncomfortable that his inaction has been exposed, he, like Njuguna, blames Wanja for her unfair expectations of him. Like Njuguna, he characterizes her rape as if it were a choice: "must you go?" No sense of shared responsibility is possible in such conditions. And her expectations are in fact unfair. She assumes that because he is a man, he has more choice. Just as men judge her, she judges them when they fail to perform their acts of masculine heroism and protection. In this way, gender hierarchies set in motion a silence between Wanja and Karega and the rest of the group that alienates instead of unifies.

This scene is repeated when, in full possession of the facts, Karega more confidently judges and rejects Wanja in the end, finding her too commercially tainted to join him. My students are divided in their views of this rejection. His revolutionary politics, seen as heroic by the people in the story, requires the complete denial of capitalism. Wanja's final turn to prostitution is cynical and proclaims her readiness to accept capitalism. But his criticism of her, perhaps justified but also callous, bespeaks yet another illusion of purity: as Wanja draws a line between barmaid and prostitute, Karega draws a line between the enslaved worker and Wanja, even though both are dependent on capitalism for their livelihood. Note that Karega, though he does not work for money, is supported by those who do. For who exists in the Kenya that Ngũgĩ describes who does not sell, and become sold, for profit?

Karega judges Wanja more harshly than others because she is aware of and accepts her commercialism. Yet if Wanja's cynicism is so terrible, I ask my students, how is it that Wanja is rewarded with the possibility of a new beginning at the end of the story? Her refusal to lie about herself or her work, her refusal to accept illusions, makes her more aware than any other character in the story—including Karega, who once again divides instead of unifies. Any revolution undertaken without her—without those masses who have knowingly assumed the taint of commercialism—is destined to failure. She may not defeat the evils of capitalism, but she recognizes something in Karega's final criticism of her—something that Karega, who might otherwise be seen as Ngũgĩ's voice in the story, never understands:

> [F]ac[ing] him, hatred in her eyes, anger in her voice, proud in her bearing, . . . [she tells him] "I've tried to fight them, the only way I can. What about you? What I am, you made me. . . . I pleaded with you, shed tears, but you went away and now you dare blame me." (327)

For the first time she sees that she had only the illusion of choice, that as responsible as she is for her actions, men—even relatively kind ones, like Karega—have made her what she is.

In response to his rejection, Wanja finds truth in her earlier assessment that Karega is naive, pathetic, too wedded to his ideals. Her acceptance of the truth about herself allows her to disregard men's estimation of her worth. If Karega wins a victory with the worker uprising, Wanja has won a victory over patriarchy, which is equally important if the people are to come together in a unified whole. Ngũgĩ suggests that hierarchies, including that of gender, fragment the people and perpetuate inaction. Teaching, as Paolo Freire reminds us, can offer a similar pitfall (71–86).[8]

I find it unproductive to use postcolonial courses to demonstrate how students as consumers are complicit in making other people's lives difficult: their complicity is something they already know but feel powerless to address. Instead of reminding them of their privileges compared with the poverty of others, I use Ngũgĩ's *Petals* to show them that they have much in common with characters like Wanja, to urge them to create unities instead of divisions, to acknowledge interconnections, and to respect differences. If we see our knowledge as power for change rather than as evidence of shame and failure, we can begin to work on means of improving our world.

NOTES

[1] Certainly Ngũgĩ's story has many heroes, many peoples, yet I find Wanja, the predominant female character, to be of special importance.

[2] Though Munira is married, he keeps his wife and his life in Ilmorog almost entirely separate and considers himself available for Wanja. For various takes on Wanja's character and gender, see Cochrane; LaPin; Palmer, "Ngũgĩ's *Petals*" 273, 278–79; Evans, "Mother Africa" 58–61; Sharma, "Ngũgĩ's Apocalypse" 302; Shaw 251; Cook and Okenimkpe 105–06; and Stratton 51.

[3] Spivak, "Can the Subaltern" 297. Clitoridectomies became less common before colonization and were frowned on as barbaric during colonization but they were revived in the postcolonial era as an assertion of Kenyan nationalist independence and commitment to Gĩkũyũ heritage. But note that female subservience offered a potential common ground for colonizer and colonized. Some critics do not see female circumcision as an inherently dominating practice (Njambi).

[4] Shaw 72–73. On women's traditional roles in Gĩkũyũ society, especially in relation to land use laws, see Presley 28.

[5] Luise White's discussion of women and prostitution in Kenya in "Domestic Labor" and in *Comforts* sees these women as heroic.

[6] Students recognize in this portion of the story the trope of both the romance novel and the detective novel. Kimeria forces the unwilling bride to sleep with him; she (typically) finds that her body disobeys her mind, and she falls in love with her captor. The novels that women read condition their minds to accept male domination, aggression, and violence and even to believe they should enjoy it. Obviously such simple readings are not uncontested. See Janice Radway's *Reading the Romance*, for example. Nonetheless, Wanja suffers from this illusion even though she hates Kimeria.

[7] Nyakinyua, the elder female, is silent and all but invisible during this scene.

[8] In my courses, students usually acquiesce to my expertise and expect me to lead our classroom discussions. Our academic institutions in the United States are based on that teacher-student hierarchy. Freire suggests that this hierarchy limits the critical thinking that students bring to the classroom.

Ngũgĩ, *Petals of Blood*, and World Bank Literature

Kate McInturff

"It's the economy, stupid."

—James Carville

Where in the World?

The rubric of World Bank literature, presented by Amitava Kumar in a collection of the same name, addresses the interrelations between global socioeconomic forces and the production and reception of culture. The phrase deliberately resists easy definition, being designed partly as a "pedagogical tool" to provoke dialogue and debate (Kumar, Introd.). Cultural workers, both writers and readers, World Bank literature maintains, must recognize their engagement in the process of decolonizing the inequalities of power that play out in development strategies. The rubric offers a number of new ways to read and teach Ngũgĩ wa Thiong'o's work. First, it makes central economic and social relations in the global sphere, a question of concern to Ngũgĩ in both his fiction and criticism. Although his work is famously local in that he writes of the Gĩkũyũ and in the Gĩkũyũ language, it is deeply involved with the problems of postcolonial development. His fiction and criticism deal with relations of power. They emphasize the roles that economics and culture together play in maintaining or disrupting relations of power. So too does World Bank literature, which is predicated on the same assumption that can be found in Ngũgĩ's work: the narratives that we give and receive are profoundly affected by the material conditions in which they are produced and circulated. Moreover, narratives are themselves instruments that can change the material conditions of their readers' lives. The framework offered by World Bank literature underlines Ngũgĩ's conclusion that writers and readers of literature cannot opt out of political and economic realities.

For those who find themselves, in Timothy Mitchell's terms, "the object[s] of development," there is no choice but to engage with the economic and cultural forces that already exist in the local scene. Countries and communities that depend on foreign aid are compelled to follow the policies and economic interests of the donors of that aid. Reading Ngũgĩ's work as World Bank literature requires all students to engage equally with these issues, regardless of their location in systems of aid and trade.

The framework of World Bank literature returns teachers and students to the question of their own relation to the struggle depicted in Ngũgĩ's work and in particular to the role they play in the forms of exchange it depicts. This framework asks students to consider how they have influenced their government's activity in the local and international sphere. As students of literature, they are asked to consider how they participate in the narrative system of exchange offered by the novel and to consider with whom they empathize and in whom they invest.

Petals of Blood

Petals of Blood is, in part, a consideration of the effect of competing forms of aid and influence on Kenyan development. The title phrase is indicative of ambivalence toward all systems of exchange. The novel describes the effects of multiple systems of exchange—operating in harmony and in conflict with one another: the exchange of things of blood, the exchange of currency and property, and the exchange of narratives.

As Munira describes it in *Petals*, there is a traditional system of exchange made up of "things of blood," which are the animals that provide sustenance and family status. Animals are also exchanged on the occasion of marriage as a form of bride price. Marriageable women are equally part of the category of things of blood (18). As the narrator points out, they bring their own labor and their potential to produce children. Things of blood can be the source of conflict when opposed parties seek ownership or access to the same things (women, animals, labor, *theng'eta*). Wanja's conclusion that either "you eat or you are eaten" is consistent with the logic of this system of exchange (294). Thus, although the exchange of things of blood seems to represent a traditional system—in opposition to the Western capitalist system—it is nonetheless alienating.

The competing system of development and exchange represented by the advent of the Kenya Country Office (KCO) and the African Economic Bank is unambiguously condemned in the novel. It is worth noting that the KCO seems to be modeled on Harambee projects—a form of development that was popular in Kenya at the time of the writing of the novel (Ngau 524). Harambee projects were funded in part through donations from the community in which the project was to be executed. The premise that local ownership is essential to a development project remains central to international development today.

The history of the brewing and use of *theng'eta* parallels the history of Harambee projects in general. Peter Ngau argues that the projects initially involved "a social exchange of labor and forms of mutual assistance [and] served educational purposes, defined one's own group identity, and fostered moral values through group ethics" (524). Over the course of the 1970s, Harambee projects became increasingly restricted to cash contributions and run by local or national elites for their own benefit (533).

The cycle of the *theng'eta* project described provides the basis for the analysis of another central plank of international development: aid effectiveness. The current trend in international development, led by the Paris Declaration on Aid Effectiveness, is to measure outcomes of development processes.

The underlying notion is that social and economic development ought to be a matter of steady, measurable progress. There are evident echoes here of colonial models of upward progress toward a civilizational apogee. *Petals* provides a profound critique of linear progress and the quantification of social change.

Petals of Blood offers thanks to

> Many others
> One in the struggle
> With our people
> For total liberation
> Knowing that
> However long and arduous the struggle
> Victory is certain. (vi)

Against the confidence of this acknowledgment, the novel presents what is at best a cyclical version of progress, at worst a world repeatedly beset by natural disaster and human greed.

The road to Ilmorog plays a central role both as a symbol of change (for better and for worse) and as a material support for development. The road carries the characters of the novel back and forth among Ilmorog, Limuru, and Nairobi. It provides them with a path to return to Ilmorog to heal the wounds of their experiences of violence and exploitation; but the path also permits the entry of those destructive forces. Modern road construction provides a source of water and a reprieve from drought; it also brings to Ilmorog the KCO and the African Economic Bank.

Finally, the road is symbolic of a third system of exchange, that of narratives. The trans-Africa road records both triumph and failure and offers a positive vision of future progress. The fourth section of the novel begins:

> The Trans-Africa road linking Nairobi and Ilmorog to the many cities of our continent is justly one of the most famous highways in all the African lands, past and present. It is symbolic tribute, although an unintended one, to those who, witnessing the dread ravages of crime and treachery and greed which passed for civilisation, witnessing too the resistance waged and carried out with cracked hands and broken nails and bleeding hearts, voiced visionary dreams amidst sneers and suspicions and accusations of madness or of seeking pathways to immortality and the eternal self-glory of tyrants. (262)

There is a plurality of stories and visions embedded in Munira's narrative, and perhaps a model of progress that is achieved through the collectivity of visions:

"Many others / One in the struggle." But this collectivity is composed of individuals who suffer repeated defeats as a result of forces beyond their control. Their struggles are defined by natural disaster and by external political and economic actors: "Thus history and legend showed that Ilmorog had always been threatened by the twin cruelties of unprepared-for vagaries of nature and the uncontrolled actions of men" (111). The implication here is that the struggle for independence—the struggle over things of blood—does not and should not conclude with postcolonial statehood. As several characters remind us, quoting Oginga Odinga, they are "*Not Yet Uhuru*" (239).

This failure is not intended to suggest that the struggle should be abandoned. *Petals* places positive value on the attempts by characters to treat one another and the community with dignity and respect. In its final pages the novel reminds the reader of Wanja's earlier acts of kindness toward Joseph. It describes the positive effect her kindness had on Joseph and subsequently on those now influenced by Joseph (340). Lying in the hospital, Wanja considers, "[M]aybe life was a series of false starts, which, once discovered, called for more renewed efforts and yet another beginning" (337–38).

"Not Yet Uhuru"

Teaching Ngũgĩ's work in classrooms in Egypt and Canada has heightened rather than allayed my concern that the teaching of world literature risks functioning as a form of native intelligence—either in the sense of espionage or in the sense of aptitude. For example, world literature has been viewed as integral to the national security of the United States since its institutionalization as a field of study. This attitude was particularly apparent during the Cold War, when the United States government viewed cultural knowledge as an essential tool in the battle against communism. In 1958 the government established the National Defense Education Act (NDEA). The first, explicitly stated aim of the act was "to ensure trained manpower of sufficient quality and quantity to meet the national defense needs of the United States" (*National Defense Education Act* 11). To this end the NDEA funded foreign language education. However, the knowledge of foreign languages was not the sole aim of the funding provided for higher education. The study of foreign literature was thought to give important insights into other cultures, insights that would give the United States a strategic advantage. Thus comparative literature departments received additional funding as well.

The United States continues to fund the study of cultures and languages through the National Security Education Program (NSEP). A 2003 report to Congress indicates the perceived importance of making "a strategic investment in the competent language and cultural expertise base needed by our country to address the broad range of international and multinational issues that affect U.S. national security" (*National Security Education Program* 11). The report frames the study of foreign cultures as a necessary component of national security:

> The creation of NSEP demonstrated great foresight on the part of the U.S. Congress. Born out of after-action analyses from Desert Storm, NSEP was designed to represent a post–cold war investment in vital expertise in languages and cultures critical to U S. national security. The national emergency precipitated by the tragic events of September 11 has served to further underscore the importance of NSEP but this need had been well documented before those events. (8)

Testimony before Congress on the subject of NSEP funding not only supports the importance of this form of cultural intelligence to national security but also urges that punitive action be taken against those programs and universities that boycott NSEP funding. It identifies postcolonial studies as a particular threat to United States security (S. Kurtz).

This development provides a useful if ironic counterpoint to Ngũgĩ's argument that literature is indispensable to political change. Moreover, it asks students to consider both the advantages and disadvantages of including in a course a work on the basis of its political utility. If Kenya is of little or no security interest to Canada, for example, should the government of Canada fund the study of Kenyan literature in Canada? In a classroom that was quite literally built by the United States Agency for International Development (USAID), at the American University in Cairo, should the syllabus include works that are not in line with United States foreign policy?

Raising such questions encourages students to consider the relation of literature to political change not only as a question for someone else's culture and someone else's politics but also as a question for their own classroom, university, and community.

"Change versus More of the Same"

The drive toward empathy and understanding that underwrites the study of world literature, in its more idealistic form, is predicated on the notion that they will lead to more ethical action with respect to others—the minimal level of tolerance, according to Goethe. In my classroom, this idea has meant considering the effect of unequal relations of power on those with little or no power, as represented in novels and other literary genres. But as Susan Sontag has compellingly argued in *Regarding the Pain of Others*, there is no ethical corollary to empathy. Indeed, it is equally likely that exposure to the suffering of others will lead to fear and denial, to a retreat from action. There is also the danger of slipping into a comfortable voyeurism—armchair travel combined with a satisfying

Aristotelian experience of catharsis. The elements of a novel that relate to cultural practices are sometimes treated as interesting and distant anthropological episodes—a kind of literary Discovery Channel program. This perspective is problematic for a number of reasons, not least in that it neutralizes the political challenges of Ngũgĩ's work by confining them to a unique and distant episode in the cultural history of a foreign community. Such responses may arise not only out of a lack of information but also out of a sense of helplessness and alienation from the processes of political change. Challenging students to consider how they are implicated in the political and economic processes criticized in the novel can therefore be both frightening and empowering for them. As actors in the international economic and political system, they bear responsibility and also have the power to effect positive change.

What particularly recommends the combination of the World Bank literature framework and *Petals of Blood* is how the content and structure of the novel resist the comfort of closure. Teaching *Petals* in the framework of World Bank literature presents an opportunity for students and teachers alike to observe what role they play in the cycle of change depicted in the novel. It suggests the need to examine our consonance with the characters who exercise power cruelly over others, as much as with the characters who resist that oppression. It suggests, finally, that we ought not to pity but to consider those whom we make poor.

Detained and African Prison Diaries

Oliver Lovesey

Mindful of the danger of homogenizing the national literatures of a continent, my approach to teaching Ngũgĩ's *Detained: A Writer's Prison Diary* examines it in connection with other African prison writing. It tackles one subgenre of autobiography in African writing while paying close attention to the great diversity of historical, cultural, and linguistic contexts that frame three texts. It addresses a connection between African life writing and the lives of nations and by extension considers the role of African cultural intellectuals in the public lives of their countries.

I taught three very different prison diaries as part of the African segment of a full-year, upper-level international literature course at a four-year comprehensive institution in western Canada. The students were mostly English majors, and most had never been outside Canada. They were challenged by the very different historical and political contexts of the three works and also by the authors' very different styles. They found Breyten Breytenbach's unique style the most challenging. They typically engaged with the genre as a metaphor for existential angst but had difficulty unpacking the historical background of the texts. Reading the work of famous authors whose diaries were published after their release, students were sometimes unable to appreciate the terror of political prison for writers of conscience whose countries were engaged in civil war or in anticolonial or neocolonial struggle.

The colonial prison was the school for national leaders from Kwame Nkrumah and Kenneth Kaunda to Jomo Kenyatta. Robben Island is referred to as Mandela University. The prison diary confronts the realities of colonialism's definition of the African nation, created by colonial cartographers as a result of global imperialism and industrial capitalism, from its very center. The connection between this literature and nationhood appears in an examination of the linguistic, cultural, and ideological constraints faced by African writers imprisoned or "institutionalized" in their own countries.

Wole Soyinka was detained in Nigeria for twenty-seven months between August 1967 and October 1969 for his political activities, in the tense atmosphere leading up to the Nigerian civil war. Ngũgĩ wa Thiong'o was detained in Kenya between December 1977 and December 1978 after the enormous success of his Gĩkũyũ dramas. Breytenbach was imprisoned in South Africa for seven and a half years, under the terms of the Terrorism Act, from 25 November 1975 to 29 December 1983. These writers were imprisoned by African leaders—in *Detained*, Ngũgĩ calls them "Africa's tin gods" (142)—whose suspicion of artistic expression resulted from their own mental colonization: "[L]ike their colonial counterparts, they had become mortally afraid of the slightest manifestation of a people's culture" (71). Many African writers have been imprisoned by neocolonial governments and left their "smudges on / the blank page of this nation," in the words of Jack Mapanje in "Where Dissent Is Meat for Crocodiles" (80).[1] It is a tragic irony that Ngũgĩ read Dennis Brutus's "*Letters to Martha*" and requested Soyinka's *The Man Died* while he was himself in political prison. He even joked to his jailer about writing to the man responsible for his detention, "Jomo Kenyatta in his capacity as an ex-detainee" (4).

The imprisonment of African writers, particularly those who are politically engaged, is the incarceration of the creative national spirit seeking to define and celebrate national freedom.[2] The writer's detention is, in Ngũgĩ's words, "an admission by the detaining authorities" that their acts and words are "an immoral sale and mortgage of a whole country and its people" (*Detained* 12–13). The imprisoned writer confronts the linguistic debasement of the prison environment, the unwillingness to define the conditions of imprisonment, and the offer of release in exchange for silence. The prison diary writes the story of the nation's contradictions from the nation's very center, the state institution par excellence. Examining Ngũgĩ's *Detained*, Soyinka's *The Man Died*, and Breytenbach's *True Confessions of an Albino Terrorist*, this course of study considers the prison diary as one of the defining genres of postcolonial African literature.

The tag "self-writing" or "fictionalized version of oneself" (Davies 120) seems inadequate to define the genre of the African prison diary. J. U. Jacobs has suggested "confessional narrative" ("Confession" 125), and Govind N. Sharma has offered "consolation" ("Ngũgĩ's *Detained*") for some examples of the form. Distinguishing autobiography and diary writing by their retrospective or simultaneous handling of the temporal, we may call *The Man Died* and *Detained* diaries. *True Confessions*, however, is a retrospective autobiography, written "from hindsight, beginning from the certainty of a known end" (Egan 90).[3] These works are rooted in the assertion of individual identity in the face of brutal dehumanization, although in *True Confessions* the self functions discursively as well as referentially. These works violate the convention of private, introspective self-writing in their insistence on the typicality of experience and on its social and political context. Moreover, they are clearly mixed genres, with broken chronology, signs of extensive revision, and numerous additions.

"Life in prison," Ngũgĩ writes, "is basically a cliché: dull, mundane, monotonous, repetitious, torturous in its intended animal rhythm of eating, defecating, sleeping . . ." (*Detained* 116), not "a story of sentimental heroism" (97). "A narration of prison life is, in fact, nothing more than an account of oppressive measures in varying degrees of intensity and one's individual or collective responses to them" (100). In general, Ngũgĩ's method seems to be to "let impressions form in [his] mind until they accumulate into a composite picture" (127) In terms of genre, *Detained* is a hybrid; it collates an account of his routine at Kamĩtĩ Maximum Security Prison, essays on Kenyan colonial history and aesthetics, letters written in prison, and a metacritical account of the production of his work in progress.

In *Detained*, Ngũgĩ theorizes his narrative practice in his allegorical works, which arises from what we may call his "Mau Mau aesthetics" (Lovesey, *Ngũgĩ*

64–65). Like the seventeenth-century Puritan revolutionary John Bunyan, whose work Ngũgĩ refers to in *Decolonising the Mind*, a writer who developed the allegorical poetics of *The Pilgrim's Progress* in his spiritual autobiography, *Grace Abounding to the Chief of Sinners*, Ngũgĩ discovered the potential of transformative narrative allegory in the crucible of prison experience. His political detention forced him to confront the postcolonial "crisis of representation" (Jameson, "Third-World Literature" 81). Like the Mau Mau freedom fighters, he uses Christian narrative, transforming it into a cultural weapon. The liberation movement, he explains in the first edition of *Writers in Politics*,

> rejected the culture of the oppressor and created a popular oral literature embodying anti-exploitation values. They took Christian songs; they took even the Bible and gave these meanings and values in harmony with the aspirations of their struggle. Christians had often sung about heaven and angels, and a spiritual journey into a spiritual intangible universe where metaphysical disembodied evil and good were locked in perpetual spiritual warfare. . . . The Mau Mau revolutionaries took up the same song and tune and turned it into a song of actual political, visible material freedom and struggle for land. The battle was no longer in heaven but here on earth, in Kenya. (27)

This movement took "[t]he Christian universe and spiritual idealism . . . [and] made them stand firmly on the ground, our earth, instead of standing on their head" (29). The themes of Ngũgĩ's new narrative project, engendered in political prison, are a celebration of national culture and resistance to foreign exploitation. Ngũgĩ sees a connection between his diary of neocolonial detention and the accounts written by "Mau Mau and pre–Mau Mau detainees" [xii], because Kenya's laws have a "colonial basis" and "[d]etention [is] an instrument for colonial domination" (44).

The Man Died was written between the lines of volumes such as Soyinka's own *Idanre* and on toilet paper and cigarette packages. Soyinka's editing decisions were "all influenced by . . . my continuing capacity to affect events in my country, of effecting the very revolutionary changes to which I have become more than ever dedicated" (12). Obi Maduakor argues that "Soyinka had hoped to forge a new literary technique in *The Man Died*, a technique of 'brutal realism.'" Soyinka felt that "a book if necessary should be a hammer, a handgrenade which you detonate under a stagnant way of looking at the world" (168). The prison notes document his struggle in a combination of forms, ranging from reportage, testimony, and stream of consciousness to creation myth. He interrupts the relentless, deterministic narrative logic of the prison diary genre—the "indestructible continuum of ordeal-survival-affirmation" (11)—with an extended meditation on Nigerian national identity (154–83) in the light of its degrading colonial legacy. This somber essay, ending with the affirmation that a nation is a people, "a unit of humanity bound together by a common ideology" (183), informs the rest of his account of day-to-day drudgery and anguish. He survives through his faith in the "ethical base" of the nation (182), despite his wariness about the consequences of civil war. He never forgets the colonial stamp on the nation's identity:

> the artificiality, the cavalier arrogance, the exploitive motivations which went into the disposal of African peoples into nationalities. One overcomes the sense of humiliation which accompanies the recollection of such a genesis by establishing his essential identity as that which goes into creating the entity of a people. (175)

His meditation on the nation disrupts the plot of the prison diary narrative and allows him to recover from his captors' control over his story, to connect this history to the nation's story, and to consider the future.

Breytenbach suggests the prison diary is a distinct genre (339), the story of "four walls, a floor and a light bulb on high" (253). His confessions are an edited transcription of tapes completed in Paris in August 1983, a process that "defined the inner structure and tone of the book" (338). The account is driven by the "necessity to confess" and addressed to a shadowy implied reader, referred to as "Mr. Investigator" (14), a comrade and traitor who resembles Baudelaire's ambiguous narratee in *Les fleurs du mal*. Mr. Investigator is so well-informed that he resembles "Mr. Interrogator" (101) and another imaginary figure who "took shape in" Breytenbach shortly before his arrest for whom he gains "affection" (118, 244). Breytenbach refers to this figure variously as "my dear dead I," "my dark mirror-brother," and "[y]ou old voyeur" (255, 260, 329). The nature of this figure's construction indicates the reader's complicity produced by the act of reading Breytenbach's revelations.

This formal metafictional frame and the text's self-conscious reference to diegetic levels follow from Breytenbach's beginning his confessions by reliving the experience of endlessly rewriting accounts of himself and his activities on his initial arrest and interrogation. Breytenbach feels that he has become the interrogator's creation. Telling the fictionalized account of the actant named Galant, he begins to write himself. Because, in his imprisonment, "[w]ords have replaced my life," as he says (28), he now wishes to write himself back to life. Nevertheless, he is ever aware of the sweet treachery of words and of how his writing is a "labyrinth" and "truth is a convention" (36). He perpetually reevaluates his motivations, even suspecting, during one police interrogation, that the underground political activity leading to his arrest might have been merely "an elaborate form of self-delusion" (88). The image of the chaotic labyrinth—Brutus refers to "the labyrinth of self" in *Letters to Martha* (6)—provides Breytenbach with one of his work's central organizing metaphors. Another is the mirror. These metaphors allow the representation of the prison warders' "world of make-believe where fact and fancy mix," where "your personality is broken down, to be reassembled" (48, 129). Breytenbach tells "everything, hodge-podge . . . whichever way it comes" in a "book of et ceteras" (151, 279) like a record of incidents kept by a sergeant or warrant officer. *True Confessions* is a Taoist or Buddhist spiritual autobiography, the revelation of a bungled attempt at underground work, a sociological and political document about the apartheid prison system, and a poet's account of psychological deterioration.

Confronting prison's debasement of language is one of the common features of survival literature, such as Primo Levi's *Survival in Auschwitz*. The prison diary allegorizes linguistic colonialism, in which language becomes a prison house. The idiom of expression in these works is English, the discursive medium of the colonizer. The linguistic debasement of colonialism—the abbreviation and perversion of words into the utterance of the servant and slave as well as the colonial association of indigenous linguistic expression with the demonic—is mimicked in the prison environment. Soyinka's warders babble meaningless phrases, and Ngũgĩ is irritated by the "voices of warders," which "would grate on [his] nerves" (22), and oppressed by the language of incarceration: "Abusive language, innuendos, gibes, outright denunciation" (126). He realizes that any place acquires "its own . . . special vocabulary" (131). However, the real prison language is silence. On admission, Ngũgĩ loses his name. He is never charged or told for how long he is to be detained. He believes his detention results from his revolt against the "colonial . . . aesthetic of submissive silence" (93). In prison he struggles to find a new language of resistance, although he refuses the "entirely different language," "sprinkled of course, with occasional nationalistic slogans borrowed from past memories" (87), spoken on release by those former revolutionaries (like Kenyatta) broken by detention. Ngũgĩ is schooled by his detention: "the walls . . . have become my dictionary" (166). He begins his novel in Gĩkũyũ, translated as *Devil on the Cross*, after a jailer's lecture that Ngũgĩ is one of the educated elite who despises his own language. Through writing in Gĩkũyũ, Ngũgĩ is able to escape the isolation of detention and to connect with national issues, as he later refers to African languages as "the collective memory bank of a people's experience in history" (*Decolonising* 15). Writing *Devil on the Cross*, he affirms his "faith in the possibilities of the languages of all the different Kenyan nationalities" (*Detained* 8). Cultural expression has become his weapon of resistance and means of survival.

Soyinka's inability to talk, read, and write freely is "torture"; it condemns him to a "flotsam existence," creating doubts about "his human identity" (278). Writing the prison notes "rescues words from a debasement to which they were constantly subjected by my gaolers, a debasement which . . . constituted one of the gravest challenges to my egoist survival" (14). Most demoralizing to Soyinka are the fabricated public reports of his "chronic syphilis" (291), the publication of a mock confession, and the report of an attempted escape. He imagines his own obituary: "[T]he dramatist over-dramatizes himself once too often" (77).

For Breytenbach, imprisoned in what he refers to as "No Man's Land"—the ironic counterpoint to "paradise," his other term for South Africa / Azania—confinement is death, and as a result his account is the self-consciously fictionalized process of creating "the fragmentary scenario of my identities" (331). He becomes "a weaver of shrouds" (308). Prison is a distinct world in which language, institutionalized and dehumanized, emphasizes abusive categories. Breytenbach traces "the evolution of prison language" (177) but primarily demonstrates how this penchant for categories (from "Big Fives," or informers; and "grocery rabbits," or prisoners who sell their bodies for food to "misters," prisoners with "illusions about being human" [191]), mimics the structure of apartheid. He traces the way apartheid has debased Afrikaans, rendering it "the language of oppression and of humiliation" (354). Although as a famous Afrikaans poet he is permitted to write in prison because of pressure from intellectuals who consider his facility with the language a national treasure, Breytenbach denounces the language's ideological encoding: "In its present sociological context and political impact Afrikaans bears the stigma of being identified with the policeman, the warder, the judge and the White politician" (353–54). The chronicle of this linguistic universe attempts to overcome "the filth—the degradation of human relationships imposed on one within the interrogator-detainee or warder-prisoner context" (337). In order to purge himself of the experience, he must "vomit" up and "exteriorize" the debasement of the prison experience and its language (337, 155).

The prison diary is a detailed psychological account of a mind in sensory and emotional deprivation, an intense moral self-examination, and a forum on national issues. The individual's isolation from the community is linked to the nation's traumatized self-alienation. Ngũgĩ realizes that detention is designed to make him

> feel that he has been completely cut off from the people and hence from that group solidarity—the sense of being one with the people—which alone keeps men and women going even when menaced by truncheons, nailed boots, tear-gas and deathly whistling bullets. (20)

But he comes to define his detention in terms of national struggle and to regard acts of noncooperation with the absurd humiliation of imprisonment as taking "a principled stand on national issues" (140).

Soyinka discovers in the complex power relations of the prison community a microcosm of the national dilemma. He recognizes the residue of deep-seated colonial psychological inferiority, a condition that allows the jailers to rationalize their participation in injustice as "acts of self-preservation" (70). He refuses to sacrifice any of his commitment to national issues and social justice in exchange for freedom from injury or for an increased chance to survive. As a result, he confronts warders and refuses to cooperate. He resists the notion that prison is off bounds, outside history, a moral wild zone in which only personal survival should be considered. He agrees with

> those who acknowledge that prison is only a new stage from which the struggle must be waged, that prison, especially political prison is an artificial erection in more senses than one whose bluff must be called and whose impotence must be demonstrated. (69–70)

He must "fight for an equitable society" from within the jaws of oppressive power (70). Therefore his protest against the inhumane treatment of other prisoners becomes an act of courage that has wider political consequences. In resisting the robbery of citizenship that the neocolonial prison, like the colonial state, performs on its subject, Soyinka connects individual and collective detention.

Similarly, Breytenbach acknowledges "the need to be able to contribute something to life outside" prison during his incarceration (157). His confessions, a mythopoeic account of a journey into hell, a meditation on this experience in Buddhist terms, and a major work of sociological documentation, are also an anatomy of the apartheid prison and in a sense a dialogue with it, written to enable "national liberation" through a class-based, anticolonial, anti-imperialist struggle (384). His confessions explain in detail how an individual may dwell in the prison without ending in "psycho city," the special wing for psychiatric cases (188). He makes clear from the outset that part of him died in prison and that dehumanization results from degradation. Bare survival is "made up of a million little compromises and humiliations" (258). He learns that "if you want to remain whole, [you must] recognize the humanity of your enemy" (360). The confessions acknowledge that "violator and victim . . . are linked forever perhaps, by the obscenity of what has been revealed to you, by the sad knowledge of what people are capable of. We are all guilty" (343). Such knowledge is essential for the revolutionary militant, who must never ignore the dedication and humanity of the opponent and must not violate fundamental principles, such as the sacredness of life. The prison account reveals Breytenbach as a Buddhist revolutionary for whom right thinking and right action compel recognition of South African realities.

The African prison diary goes against the grain of official accounts of a prisoner's activities; it rewrites the official version of national history. Soyinka's meditation on his imprisonment and its writing and his reflection about the fate of the nation become a metanarrative. The writer reflects on the process by which official and unofficial, colonial, postcolonial, and neocolonial histories are encoded. The progress of his personal humiliation recalls that of the "humiliated nation," to use George Mangakis's phrase (*The Man Died* 19), under colonialism. Certain aspects of imprisonment encapsulate national history. For example, Soyinka is chained in heavy manacles "the like of which I had seen only in museums of the slave-trade" (38).

Ngũgĩ's *Detained* is an extended rewriting of Kenyan colonial and neocolonial history and aesthetics, characterized as a struggle against both foreign and domestic oppression. He reinserts those nationalist fighters and "the millions of dead and detained [who] had been wiped off the face of known and written [neocolonial] history" (89). Central to his project is the belief that in the struggle for national independence "the various nationalities" in Kenya acted together (64). He rejects the tribal determinism of colonial historians. He comes to regard his involvement in the Kamĩrĩĩthũ Community Education and Culture Centre's theater production as a continuation of the cultural program of Dedan Kimathi, whose remains lie in Ngũgĩ's prison. The center's communal "creation" of plays was a distinctively African mode of production (*Barrel* 43–45). His period of working with this collective, "the most exciting in my life and the true beginning of my education" (*Detained* 76)—allowing him to assert his peasant origins and his family's involvement in Mau Mau and to repudiate his alienating colonial education—enables the intellectual to declare, "I felt one with the people" (78). He regards the government's terror in response to the group's success as the desire to "[d]etain a whole community" (80). In default, he is detained and left "in cell 16 wrestling with multifarious demons in the dry wilderness of Kamĩtĩ Prison, contemplating the two dialectically opposed traditions of Kenyan history, culture and aesthetics" (80). Ngũgĩ will either be one of those who resist or one of those who are broken by detention and become a "colonial zombie" (83). Meditating on these options, Ngũgĩ learns that the other detainees "fall into groups that span the whole history of post-independence upheavals in Kenya" (123). His imprisonment and his writing in Gĩkũyũ, therefore, are phases in a revolutionary struggle. Ngũgĩ exults: "I am part of a living history of struggle" (124). Writing about detention represents the culmination of his narrative of postcolonial history. Through his defiance in detention and his revolutionary aesthetics and practice, he has written himself into history.

In *True Confessions*, Breytenbach must position himself historically before he can write himself back to life. He is trapped in the official "warped history of the Afrikaner," part of a system that is itself "anti-historical" (54, 116). South Africa for him is "No Man's Land. Another world. A world of genteel manners and old-fashioned picnics. And a vicious world. A land of harsh, dream-like beauty Where you can feel your skin crawling. Ever on that last lip of annihilation" (93) His confessions begin "with an appreciation of the political situation which . . . I still subscribe to" and of his recruitment in "the early 1970s for the specific purpose of creating forms of aid to militant White opposition to the Apartheid regime in the country . . ." (73, 77). The story of his imprisonment is part of the history of apartheid and the global struggle for national liberation. Underground political work, like his entry into South Africa to recruit for Okhela, "inserts itself in a long and glorious line of historical struggle" (83). Similarly, specific parts of the confessions allegorize South African history, as for example when after his release, Breytenbach apocalyptically emerges from a swim in the ocean into an integrated South Africa.

Accepting conditions for release in these prison diaries is directly related to the country's future: the closure of the prison diary, if the integrity of the writer has not been destroyed in the prison house, must point to a possible future for the nation. Created between iron brackets, the prison diary genre and prison itself enforce their own closure on writing, the closure of "either death or freedom" (Ngũgĩ, *Detained* 146). Ngũgĩ's *Detained* begins, after his release from prison, with an account of charges and accusations in the media, culminating in a "call for self-censorship" (xix). Like the beginning of *Matigari*, the beginning of *Detained* is a disillusioning homecoming after release. The narrative order of Ngũgĩ's diary resists the logic of the genre, problematizing the relation of beginning and ending, detention and freedom. His diary rejects the inevitability of release or of the definite ending of torment on release, although he admits that "dreams of freedom start at the very minute of arrest" (146). Just as he envisions his detention as part of repressive national imprisonment—and so he is caged in a "double prison" (Davies 220)—he connects genuine release with the nation's liberation, so that "prison [should not be] our destiny as a Kenyan people" (63). The prison diary's narrative closure is directly related to the destiny of the national narrative and especially to Ngũgĩ's desire for "a truly democratic Kenya in which the different . . . nationalities would freely debate the past, present and future of our country . . . ," as when the political detainees talk of rights and justice and "the walls of nationality break asunder" (113, 130). Ngũgĩ postulates what he terms "progressive nationalism" for the future (159).[4]

In his views about release, Soyinka furiously denies the eschatology of the Victorian classic realist novels he is briefly permitted to read in prison: the belief that genuine social justice exists only in heaven. Instead, he too speculates that in some mythical future the cartographer's pen may redraw Africa's nations and override the injunction:

> What God (white man) has put together, let no black man put asunder. The complications of neo-colonial politics of interference compel one to accept such a damnable catechism for now, as a pragmatic necessity. Later perhaps, the black nations will themselves sit down together, and, by agreement, set compass and square rule to paper and reformulate the life-expending, stultifying, constrictive imposition of this divine authority. (181)

As in Ngũgĩ's allegorical rewriting of biblical myth in *Matigari*, for Soyinka the sound of the horn of justice must echo on earth. In *Detained*, Ngũgĩ also rejects the quasi-religious colonial-neocolonial injunction:

> [A]ny awakening of a people to their historic mission of liberating themselves from external and internal exploitation and repression is always seen in terms of "sin" and it is often denounced with the religious rhetoric of a wronged, self-righteous god. (13)

Breytenbach, writing in 1983 and drawing on biblical parallels, narrowly avoids the dangers of making predictions. He notes, "The temptation, when writing about No Man's Land / Azania, is to pour forth visions of apocalypse. Or to give way to the temptation of trying to be a prophet. Or both" (358).

All three writers began nondocumentary writing projects while imprisoned. Ngũgĩ's *Devil on the Cross*, Soyinka's *Season of Anomy* and *A Shuttle in the Crypt*, and Breytenbach's *Mouroir: Mirrornotes of a Novel* bear the marks of their prison genesis. Paradoxically, national imprisonment, at least in Ngũgĩ's subsequent view of the Kenyan situation, has led to "a rebirth of a kind of national literature in the country" (*Moving* 94). For Soyinka, release from prison is release from death to life and a renewed affirmation of "his human identity" in community with others (278). In his diary, he assumes the role of prophet, visionary, and dreamer with "the implication . . . that the dreamer is a dreamer for society" (Jones 225). Insistent on the universal nature of experience and suspicious of "literary ideology," Soyinka celebrates the African artist's "social vision" (*Myth* 61),[5] and *The Man Died* ends with both a "spiritual indictment and affirmation" (R. Fox 209). Soyinka, while affirmative, relies on a somewhat romantic view of the intellectual and a spiritual conception of the nation. As Ngũgĩ has noted, Soyinka does not suggest clear solutions to present problems (Lazarus, *Resistance* 205). Breytenbach proposes both a radical political restructuring and the quietistic consolations of Buddhism or Taoism, which seem to mesh easily with a refined existentialist despair. In the context of South Africa's subsequent renewed sense of nationhood, he has said he feels redundant or at best ambivalent. He is suspicious of the debased language of patriotism: "Everybody who wants to be somebody in the country now lays claim to having been in the resistance movement; we are all of the ANC. Rumours of heroic feats abound" ("Afrikaner"). In *Moving the Centre*, Ngũgĩ equates an affirmative future with escape from linguistic imprisonment. Warned of an ominous "red-carpet welcome" awaiting him in Kenya in 1982, he unwillingly went into exile in England and now in the United States, sadly discovering that "[e]xile can even be worse than prison" (105, 106).

NOTES

This essay is a revised version of "Chained Letters: African Prison Diaries and National Allegory," which appeared in *Research in African Literatures* 26.4 (1995): 31–45, and it is used here with the permission of Indiana University Press.

[1] Jacobs's taxonomy of African prison writing, comprising five categories ranging from "biographical works with accounts of detention or imprisonment" to "poetry and drama dealing with detention, imprisonment, and interrogation" ("Breyten Breytenbach" 96–97) is useful, although its attempt to delineate a schematic range from history to fiction is problematic, as historical works like Breytenbach's *True Confessions* self-consciously use fictional techniques, and collections of poetry such as Dennis Brutus's *Letters to Martha* and Jack Mapanje's *The Chattering Wagtails of Mikuyu Prison* are

autobiographical. Here and in "Confession, Interrogation and Self-Interrogation in the New South African Prison Writing," Jacobs usefully lists various prison writings. The attempts at definition in Jane Wilkinson's "African Diaries" and Mineke Schipper's *Beyond the Boundaries* (see esp. 114–18) are also valuable. Ngũgĩ discusses African and especially Kenyan prison writing in a number of places (*Barrel* 65–66; *Moving* 45, 72, 93–94), and Carol Sicherman documents specific cases in *Ngugi wa Thiong'o: The Making of a Rebel* (424–28).

[2] The African prison diary has a number of the elements of Fredric Jameson's problematic but highly evocative formulation of Third World literature as national allegory ("Third-World Literature"). It allegorizes the author's imprisonment and the denial of history and truth contained in that imprisonment, and it equates personal detention and national detention. As Aijaz Ahmad has pointed out, in an essay that is often read as a companion piece to Jameson's article, the national allegory formulation is essentialist in its claims of universality, simplistic in its First and Third World binary construction, and almost romantic in theorizing a synthesis of public and private in non-Western cultures ("Jameson's Rhetoric" 3–17).

[3] Shirley Neuman's call for a "poetics of differences" (225) in the drive to define the genre of autobiography is useful in this context.

[4] On Ngũgĩ's nationalism, see my "Initiation" and "Ngũgĩ wa Thiong'o's Postnation."

[5] On Soyinka's representation of Africa, see Appiah's *In My Father's House* 78–81.

Texts and Contexts: Teaching *A Grain of Wheat* and *Matigari* in Kenya

Peter Simatei

Ngũgĩ wa Thiong'o's texts constitute a staple in literature courses at universities in Kenya. One obvious reason is his pioneering status and intense engagement with Kenya's colonial and postcolonial histories. In two undergraduate courses that I teach—one on the African novel, the other on Kenyan fiction and history—his work is central to any understanding of how the African novel evolves into a complex literary genre through appropriation of the oral narrative traditions of Africa and the domestication of European novelistic traditions and culture. His work also offers a rich site for the study of the ever-changing political project of African literature. In our local contexts, it offers critical interventions in the persistent discourses of history, nationhood, citizenship, and cultural identity. Ngũgĩ is an overtly political writer, and for a background lecture I give my students an overview of his thematic concerns, explore the nationalist and socialist ideologies that frame the politics of his engagement with the histories of colonization and decolonization in Kenya, and discuss his radical ideas about the political functions of art. I then settle on *A Grain of Wheat* and *Matigari* for in-depth analysis.

My choice of these two novels is guided by their very differences and by the fact that each represents a turning point in Ngũgĩ's writing career. It is generally agreed that *A Grain of Wheat*, with its sophisticated narrative techniques associated with European literary models, confirmed his stature as a major writer but it is also a transitional novel in the sense that Ngũgĩ would abandon its kind of complexity for the simple, folkloric form crystallized in *Matigari*. *Matigari*, although coming after *Devil on the Cross*, is Ngũgĩ's Gĩkũyũ-language novel that best blends African oral narrative techniques with elements of Western written traditions. My students, who in most cases have already encountered *The River Between* and *Weep Not, Child* in introductory courses, are able to see the complexity in theme and style of *Grain* and then the subtle simplicity of *Matigari*. I introduce *Grain* as the novel that best captures the ironies of decolonization in Kenya in the sense that while it indicts colonialism, it both celebrates and questions the triumph of the nationalist project. With a knowledge of Ngũgĩ's earlier novels, students can see the link *Grain* makes between the writer's past themes and his future concerns. Set four days before *uhuru*, its time structure is fluid, traveling to the colonial past and beyond to understand the anxieties haunting the present and their implications for the future. It is this intermediary status that makes *Grain* unique in Ngũgĩ's oeuvre.

Whenever I ask students to list striking stylistic or thematic features of this novel, they always point to Ngũgĩ's appropriation of Judeo-Christian texts, the theme of betrayal, and the multiple narrative voices. Therefore I begin analysis of the novel by first addressing the significance of the use of biblical texts in the novel. I consider, in general, African writers' appropriation of European texts and culture, where intertextual references become acts of transgression rather than an affirmation of whatever truths are expressed by such texts and cultures. Students begin to realize that *Grain* mimics the Judeo-Christian concept of salvation, but they initially have different explanations for this mimicry. One student thought that the use of the Bible showed Ngũgĩ's Christian faith, but she was perplexed when I called her attention to his disavowal of Christianity. Even assuming that he was deeply Christian when he wrote the novel, his use of Judeo-Christian texts has more to do with the possibilities for dissent offered by notions of biblical justice than with the author's faith. The class comes to understand that *Grain* mimics Christian acts of salvation in order to inaugurate its own narrative of national liberation as well as subvert the way colonial discourse reinscribes biblical texts in order to legitimate the colonial system.

The epigraph derived from the Gospel of Saint John, which yields the title of the novel, exploits the Christian concept of death and resurrection to show the inevitable sacrifices involved in any war of liberation and that selective deployment of the Old Testament enables Kihika to imagine the liberation of his people as a divine mission akin to Moses's liberation of the Jewish people from Egyptian bondage. The juxtaposition of these verses with other narratives of anticolonial struggle also translates episodes from the Judeo-Christian history of salvation into a discourse of liberation. The recasting of these verses in secular and political terms makes them assume the role of a metalanguage that envisions a new Kenya with nonviolent, Indian characteristics. In Kihika's oppositional theology, Mahatma Gandhi answered the call of Christ to "deny himself, and take up his cross" (89). Gandhi's personal sacrifice leads not to the abstract kingdom of God where Christ wants to take his adherents but to the liberation of India. For Kihika, the kingdom of heaven can be attained only through messianic sacrifice:

> "Take up my cross, is what Christ told his people," Kihika resumed in a more lighthearted tone. "If any man will come after me, let him deny himself, and take up his cross, and follow me. For whosever will save his life shall lose it: and whosoever will lose his life for my sake shall find it. Do you know why Gandhi succeeded? Because he made his people give up their fathers and mothers and serve their one Mother-India. With us, Kenya is our mother." (88–89)

Kihika's radical rereading of Christ's death connects with Kihika's belief in violence as a legitimate means to end colonialism and establish a new society: "Had Christ's death a meaning for the Children of Israel? In Kenya we want deaths which will change things, that is to say, we want true sacrifice" (95). Colonial violence and its effects on the colonized is one of the subjects in *A Grain of Wheat* that we discuss. Students explore instances of colonial violence in the text as narrated by the victims and give their views on the legitimacy of violent response to oppression. I introduce Frantz Fanon's thesis that violence is a legitimate tool of liberation and suggest that Ngũgĩ's representation of decolonization as a violent process may be influenced by it. In *The Wretched of the Earth*, decolonization was violent because it involved "quite simply the replacing of a certain 'species' of men by another 'species' of men. . . . [T]here is a total, complete, and absolute substitution" (35). To what extent, I ask students, is Kihika guided by Fanon's assertion that colonialism "is violence in its natural state, and it will only yield when confronted with greater violence" (61)? *Grain* interconnects with Fanon's thesis in many respects. Fanon's contention that anticolonial violence is a consequence of settler violence is affirmed by Kihika:

> We only hit back. You are struck on the left cheek. You turn the right cheek. One, two, three—sixty years. Then suddenly, it is always sudden, you say: I am not turning the other cheek any more. . . . [Y]ou strike back. . . . We must kill. (191)

The question of redemptive violence turns out to be quite controversial in class. Most students feel that while Ngũgĩ has an obvious affinity to Fanon and seems convinced of the necessity of revolutionary violence, *Grain* does not celebrate or exalt it. The novel resists any simplistic correlation of violence and liberation by ironizing the process of decolonization so that the postcolonial moment becomes an inversion and denial of the violence that ushered it in. I discuss irony in the novel in general and how it enables Ngũgĩ to gesture toward his future concerns such as the betrayal of the ideals of independence. The class agrees that one of the greatest ironies in the novel is Mugo's false heroism, the role Mugo plays in the unfolding drama of reversed expectations that characterizes independence celebrations. This examination of irony and the paradox of independence leads to the discussion of *Matigari*.

Being privileged to have Gĩkũyũ speakers in my class, I often asked them to read the Gĩkũyũ version of the novel first so that we could then discuss the possible reasons for the changes made in the translated text. To my surprise, these students found it easier to read the English version, because they were less fluent in written Gĩkũyũ. The other surprise was that students enjoyed studying *Grain* more than *Matigari*. The reason most gave was that the simpler plot and the plain characters in *Matigari* were not engaging.

I teach *Matigari* in the context of Ngũgĩ's project of decolonized political awakening. I consider the delegitimation of the nation-state to be the main objective of his narrative. Ngũgĩ, I suggest to the class, first maps postindependence Kenya as a neocolony dominated by foreign-owned multinationals, a domination that results in the deprivation and degradation of the masses. The task of Matigari, the allegorical hero, is to liberate the nation. Ngũgĩ frames Matigari's struggle, like that of Dedan Kimathi, the Mau Mau hero of *The Trial of Dedan Kimathi*, both in socialist terms and in a Gĩkũyũ communalist grammar. Through this allegorical character Ngũgĩ can represent as a collective entity the otherwise disparate forces opposed to neocolonialism in Kenya. Matigari is resurrected as the anticipated Mau Mau hero whose return from the forest will mark the start of a second struggle, this time to bring to completion the frustrated project of national liberation.

I ask the class to recall other depictions of the Mau Mau hero in Kenyan fiction and tell what they think makes Ngũgĩ's representation different from them. Some students recognize that because Ngũgĩ reconstructs Kenya's history according to his ideology, he often idealizes the liberation movement and its leaders. Others note that transplanting a figure who has become a subject of orature into written form leads to such a flawless hero. Matigari's messianic mission, we are told, was once decreed by the Iregi revolutionaries. It is thus located in indigenous systems of justice. But this locally inspired vision is reconfigured in a domesticated socialist discourse, so that the modest ideology of land and freedom that inspired the Mau Mau revolt is imbued with the socialist politics of class struggle. This recasting is reflected in the way Matigari's idiom of communalism and folkloric metaphors gradually develops into socialist rhetoric. Matigari himself, though initially portrayed as a folkloric hero, represents himself as a savior in a mix of Gĩkũyũ and Judeo-Christian messianic language.

Matigari changes from a man innocently looking for truth and justice to a radical revolutionary calling for the violent overthrow of the capitalist order and the postcolonial state that has engendered it. His socialist consciousness is awakened by Ngarũro wa Kĩrĩro, the workers' leader, whose rhetoric best captures the dialectic of oppressor and oppressed. For Ngũgĩ, this dialect is the paradigm that frames relationships in postcolonial Kenya:

> Ngarũro had told him that there were two camps in the country. There was that of the imperialists and their retinue of messengers, overseers,

> police and military. . . . The ideas and the culture and the history they cultivated in the land were those singing glory to the role of carrying messages. . . . On the other hand, there was the camp of the working people, with their values, their culture and their history. The ruling party of messengers was trying to imprison the real history of the working people behind bars and in detention camps. (161)

I pause here to contextualize Ngarũro's statement, refering students to *Moving the Centre: The Struggle for Cultural Freedoms*, in which Ngũgĩ distinguishes between the official history produced by the state and a popular, counterhistory of resistance against both foreign and local domination authored by "workers and peasants of all the nationalities in Kenya who in their actions and songs are saying 'No' to imperialism and its comprador alliances in Kenya" (100). How does the state produce history, and do we have only two versions of history, as Ngũgĩ implies? These are questions often posed by students. In answer to the first, I use the example of the 1970s and 1980s in Kenya, the political setting of Ngũgĩ's Marxist novels, which include *Matigari*, when the state censored what it deemed subversive forms of knowledge and culture in order to suppress alternative histories of the nation. Students are able to see that by silencing other voices the state is able to project an official account of the past that serves the purposes of the hegemonic class in Kenya.

Students can point both to real life experience and places in *Matigari* where the state refashions national history to legitimate itself and suppress other perspectives. The Voice of Truth, the ubiquitous radio station and the only one in the land, is used by the state to generate and propagate the official stance. The text obviously parodies the 1980s Kenyan one-party dictatorship, but I remind my class that *Matigari* is a work of fiction. However close to reality the novel is and no matter how plain its language appears, one should always look for strategies of defamiliarization the author uses to distance the work of art from its politics. Indeed, my students' close familiarity with the contexts of Ngũgĩ's political novels presents problems of reading. The students tend to read *Matigari* as propaganda, its hero mouthing the well-known Marxist ideology of his creator. Unless guided to understand the operations of the folkloric oral style that the novel assumes—its parabolic and allegorical nature and hence the legendary and mythical character of Matigari ma Njirũũngi—they see this novel as less sophisticated than *Wheat*. I remind the class that Ngũgĩ found alienating the formal sophistication of *Grain* and *Petals of Blood*, that his decision to write in Gĩkũyũ was made in order to reconnect with the masses or what he called the "worker/peasant readership" (*Decolonising* 77).

When we discuss the second question raised by the class concerning Ngũgĩ's construction of Kenya's national history, the same issue of propaganda arises but in a different way: it touches on his polarization of people into two camps and his division of history into only two versions. *Matigari*, more than any other novel by Ngũgĩ, foregrounds Manichaean categorizations of Kenyan society into two groups—exploiters and exploited, traitors and patriots, colonizers and colonized—and culture and history are constructed in the same way. My class is often divided on this issue. There are students who side with Ngũgĩ's view of Kenyan society, and, given the very obvious unequal socioeconomic structure of the country, one understands its persuasiveness. But further discussion on this topic shows the situation to be more complex, and the class agrees that the multifaceted and contradictory nature of relations of power in postcolonial Kenya, better represented in *Grain* and *Petals of Blood*, is reduced to a bare minimum in *Matigari*. The neat boundary that this either-or binary draws between historical actors and forces excludes ambivalent histories that cut across the dichotomy described in the novel.

I suggest to students that *Matigari* is a kind of monologue: it allows no other voices to be heard and presents its truths as absolute. Does the refusal to consider other visions result in the difficulty in joining Matigari's idealistic nationalism with the proletarian aspirations of Ngarũro wa Kĩrĩro, the striking worker? The alliance between the two signals the worker-peasant collaboration that Ngũgĩ sees as one day constituting the front that will eventually bring about a proletarian revolution. But the objectives of the two characters and the methods of attaining them do not coalesce. Ngarũro wants better pay and better conditions for the workers, and not necessarily the destruction of the capitalist system. He thus defeats the socialist agenda he tries to implement. Do not the workers find capitalism already indispensable to their lives? These are ambiguities that mark the proletarian politics in *Matigari*. As Ngarũro puts it, the dispute involving workers and factory owners is one between labor and capital. It becomes an issue of political power because the regime represents and protects the interests of capital. Presumably, a proletariat revolution would put the control of capital in the hands of workers. Yet the vision of the novel wavers between this revolution and the desire for a national community based on common interests.

I conclude by mentioning the suppressed feminist politics in the text. The existence of different "forces committed to building a new tomorrow" through resistance to neocolonial oppression is acknowledged (126), but the text treats these forces as having the same ideological objective. The monologizing character of the novel denies the expression of other acts of resistance, such as those of Gũthera. Gũthera's feminist resistance is put to the service of Matigari's nationalist, patriarchal quest.

Teaching Ngũgĩ's novels in Kenya requires that I use an intertextual approach in which the novels are brought into a dialogue with the many contexts, sources, and discourses that have influenced the writer. In this way, students come to appreciate how the writer draws on and engages with diverse traditions and histories that shape African postcolonial realities.

The Historical Context of *Matigari*

Ali Erritouni

Ngũgĩ wa Thiong'o's *Matigari* features on my syllabus alongside six texts from Africa, India, and the West Indies. I teach it as part of a 3000-level course on postcolonial literature at Kent State University. Although my students are English majors in their junior year, my course represents, for most of them, their first encounter with non-Western literatures. Moreover, hailing predominantly from white communities in Ohio, they have little contact with other ethnic groups and limited knowledge of non-European cultures. In light of their academic and cultural background, I find myself having to contextualize historically and aesthetically the texts we study, as well as having to reinforce continually the knowledge they acquire during the semester.

Rather unorthodoxly, I teach *Matigari* at the beginning of the semester immediately after Chinua Achebe's *Things Fall Apart*, even though other texts on my syllabus, notably Salman Rushdie's *Midnight's Children* and Jamaica Kincaid's *Annie John*, had been published earlier and may thus claim precedence over it. I consider *Matigari* to be, to a large extent, a sequel to *Things Fall Apart.* Simply put, while *Things Fall Apart* captures the social and cultural dislocations Africans suffered under colonial subjugation, *Matigari* examines the lingering effects of colonialism on independent Africa. Given their complementarity, I believe it is more productive to teach them in succession.

There are other reasons that prompt my choice. When reading *Matigari*, students will be better served if they are able to build on the insights into colonialism they recently gained from *Things Fall Apart*. Together, these novels will immerse students in two related periods in modern African literature. Indeed, while *Things Fall Apart* represents the endeavors of African novelists in the 1950s and early 1960s to expose colonial violence and to counter imperial misrepresentations of African cultures, *Matigari*, like many novels produced from the late 1960s to the present, examines the dismal conditions in postcolonial Africa, especially economic dependency and political repression. Following common critical practice, I call the first period the "nationalist stage" and the second the "postnationalist stage," for the nationalist sentiments and anticolonial activism that inspired the first stage have given way in the second to disillusionment with the outcome of independence.

The concerns that preoccupy *Matigari* are evident in all Ngũgĩ's postnationalist novels. However, I invariably assign it in the belief that, given the comparative simplicity of its plot, it is the least daunting for my students. Moreover, although novels such as Achebe's *Anthills of the Savannah*, Moses Isegawa's *Abyssinian Chronicles*, and Helon Habila's *Waiting for an Angel* may serve, instead of *Matigari*, as examples of the postnationalist stage, I give pride of place to *Matigari* because, unlike its rivals, it allows me to reinforce some of the issues raised in my presentation on *Things Fall Apart*, notably the effects of colonialism on Africans, and because I consider its assessment of the political and economic problems afflicting postcolonial Africa to be particularly insightful. Whereas *Anthills of the Savannah*, *Abyssinian Chronicles*, and *Waiting for an Angel* ascribe political oppression in Africa to the venality of national leaders, *Matigari* locates its origins both in the self-aggrandizing ambition of despots and in the inequitable economic structures established by global capitalism.

Matigari may be the least daunting of Ngũgĩ's postnationalist novels, but it nonetheless poses serious challenges for my students, as it engages with a host of events that have marked modern Kenya, notably British colonialism, Mau Mau's armed resistance to occupation, and neocolonialism. That it couches these events in an allegorical idiom further complicates their task. Despite having had a fair amount of training in English and American literatures, and despite the work we do on colonialism when studying *Things Fall Apart*, *Matigari* seems to defy their best efforts. Their difficulties may be summarized in two points: their training does not prepare them adequately for the particular aesthetics of *Matigari*, and they have little, if any, knowledge of the political history of modern Kenya, which is indispensable for understanding the novel.

In light of their limitations, my task, as I perceive it, is partly one of providing them with pertinent critical terminology and the historical information that would enable them to unlock the unfamiliar world of *Matigari*. Thus, I begin my two-and-a-half-hour presentation by introducing them to Fredric Jameson's "national allegory." Despite its shortcomings—which are enumerated by Aijaz Ahmad, among others—*national allegory* defines a key aesthetic principle informing many African novels and, as a result, indicates a useful pedagogical approach to *Matigari*. Jameson observes that the "radical split . . . between the poetic and the political" in Western literature is absent in postcolonial literature. Instead, postcolonial texts "project a political dimension in the form of national allegory: *the story of the private individual destiny is always an allegory of the embattled situation of the public third-world culture and society*" ("Third-World Literature" 69). Jameson's argument that postcolonial literature is fundamentally allegorical teaches the students that the characters and plot of *Matigari* acquire significance from their embeddedness in a specific moment in the political history of Kenya. It also helps them recognize that an adequate understanding of *Matigari* calls for identifying its historical context.

However, the unqualified application of "national allegory" may not only reduce the teaching of *Matigari* to a tedious task aimed at relating the text to its context; it may also lead the students to misconstrue this novel as being virtually a historical document. To help them avoid this pitfall, I point out at the outset that *Matigari* does not passively reflect the history of Kenya, explaining that it is a site of ideological conflict, where two discordant narratives pitting Mau Mau against the ruling elite vie for legitimacy, and where Ngũgĩ accords Mau Mau's narrative pride of place. It is paramount that the students recognize the historical backdrop that gives meaning to the plot and the characters; but it is equally important for them to understand that *Matigari* does not depict a cohesive history. Thus, I divide my lesson into two sessions. In the first, I relate the protagonist to the historical forces that he embodies as well as identify the historical forces that oppress him. Since his struggles and his interactions with the other characters drive the plot, I find it effective to focus on the correlation between his experiences and the historical record. In the second session, I examine *Matigari*'s intervention in the political history of modern Kenya.

The hardships and disappointments that the protagonist of *Matigari* endures cannot be understood by reference to his subjectivity, for they reflect the collective experience of Kenyans and Africans in the twentieth century. His full name, Matigari ma Njirũũngi, which means "the patriots who survived the bullets," identifies him as representing former Mau Mau fighters. However, I have found it more practical to introduce him to the students as fulfilling three distinct, albeit related, allegorical functions, which derive their significance from three corresponding historical periods. He is a colonial subject during the British occupation of Kenya, a Mau Mau fighter in the war of liberation, and a disillusioned former Mau Mau fighter contending with the failures of postcolonial Kenya.

As a colonial subject, Matigari had many obligations and few rights. His employer, Settler Williams, embodying the excesses of British colonialism, regarded him as a mere instrument of his drive to maximize his wealth. Matigari laments:

> I built the house with my own hands. But Settler Williams slept in it and I would sleep outside on the veranda. I tended the estates that spread around the house for miles. But it was Settler Williams who took home the harvest. I was left to pick anything he might have left behind. I worked all the machines and in all the industries, but it was Settler Williams who would take the profits to the bank and I would end up with the cent that he flung my way. (21)

Underlying Settler Williams's treatment of Matigari is the colonial ethos. The novel does not dwell on the fact that his claim to the farm and to Matigari's cheap labor is the outcome of colonial expropriation and coercion respectively. It assumes that its Kenyan audience would readily recognize that their unequal relationship is maintained through colonial hegemony. Students may, however, need to be reminded that, in the words of Frantz Fanon, the

> first encounter [between the colonizer and the colonized] was marked by violence and their existence together—that is to say the exploitation of the native by the settler—was carried on by dint of a great array of bayonets and cannons. (*Wretched* 36)

(At this point, students often recall our analysis of colonial violence in *Things Fall Apart*. They are especially reminded of the cruel treatment Okonkwo suffers at the hands of the District Commissioner and his minions.) In order to put an end to oppression, the natives often find themselves impelled to counter the violence of the colonizers with a violence of their own. It is this imperative that drives Matigari to the mountains and forests, where he joins Mau Mau in its fight against the British empire. This decision frees him from colonial bondage and defines him as a freedom fighter, whose ultimate goal, as he allegorically expresses it, is to regain his home on top of the hill, which Settler Williams has stolen from him and his family. Here Matigari voices a central objective behind the Mau Mau rebellion, namely, to reclaim the occupied land from the settlers and to restore it to its rightful owners. In the eyes of the colonizers, however, Mau Mau's heroic resistance was no more than the bloodlust of terrorists. The British asserted that Mau Mau was an atavistic group of malcontents bent on terrorizing diligent and peaceful European settlers. As Frank Furedi points out, "[t]he colonial government went to great lengths to portray Mau Mau as an irrational force of evil, dominated by bestial impulses" (4).

Students need to understand that the demonization of the victim, cynical as it is, is an integral part of the colonial project. (In fact, my students and I address colonial representations of the self and the other when studying *Things Fall Apart*. *Matigari* allows me to reinforce what they have already learned.) Alongside its material pursuits, colonialism disseminates a set of binary oppositions that valorize the European and demonize the native. It does not rest content with expropriating land, exploiting native labor, opening markets, and depleting the mineral resources of the subjugated countries; it also resorts to expedient representations of the self and the other in order to legitimate its enterprise and to conceal its rapacious designs. Colonialism depicts itself as the selfless agent of a moral mission; as the indispensable guarantor of political order in a backward world of puerile natives; as the bearer of progress; as the reluctant arbiter of conflicts between truculent natives; and often, in the words of Fanon, "as a mother who unceasingly restrains her fundamentally perverse offspring from managing to commit suicide and from giving free rein to its evil instincts" (*Wretched* 211).

The meticulous research done by Furedi, Caroline Elkins, and David Anderson, among others, gives the lie to the colonial assertions about Mau Mau. It shows that Mau Mau was a liberation movement whose core constituency belonged to the largest ethnic group in Kenya, the Gĩkũyũ. The alienation of their land by European settlers, as a result of the Scramble for Africa, reduced many Gĩkũyũ from independent and proud farmers to impoverished squatters. Anderson observes that "[a]mong the many grievances of the Kikuyu, the loss of lands to Europeans was the deepest felt" (21). Their attempts to regain their land through legal means invariably faced colonial indifference and arrogance. To make matters worse, as the settlers mechanized their agricultural production in the wake of World War II, they evicted most of the squatters, who now faced homelessness and starvation:

> Between 1946 and 1952 . . . more than 100,000 were forcibly "repatriated." . . . Those leaving were compelled to sell their cattle and sheep, often at knock-down prices in a flooded market, sometimes even to the same

> European farmers whose decision was the cause of their impoverishment and misery. (26)

The only recourse left for the dispossessed Gĩkũyũ was to take up arms against their oppressors.

Matigari repeatedly announces that, after protracted struggle and untold sacrifices, he defeated Settler Williams and, by extension, the colonial army. This declaration contradicts the historical record: Mau Mau proved no match for the superior military equipment of the British. The war of liberation and the emergency declared in response to it, which lasted from October 1952 to January 1960, were devastating for Mau Mau fighters and their sympathizers. As Anderson points out, "[t]he official figures set the total number of Mau Mau rebels killed at 12,000, but the real figure is likely to have been more than 20,000" (4). Moreover,

> at the peak of the emergency the British held more than 70,000 Kikuyu supporters of Mau Mau in detention camps. The vast majority of these detainees were held without trial, simply on the order of the administration, on the basis of accusation or mere suspicion. . . . In the midst of the war, draconian anti-terrorist laws were introduced suspending the human rights of suspects, imposing collective punishments, facilitating detention without trial, permitting the seizure of property of convicts, and vastly extending the death penalty to a wide range of offences. Between 1952 and 1956, when the fighting was at its worst, the Kikuyu districts of Kenya became a police state in the very fullest sense of that term. (5)

Despite its military defeat and the repressive measures its followers suffered, Mau Mau nevertheless succeeded in convincing the British that their continued occupation of Kenya was unsustainable. In December 1963, less than four years after the end of the emergency, Kenya gained its independence. It is in this context that we should place Matigari's declaration of victory over Settler Williams. Irrespective of its outcome on the battlefield, the war, he seems to say, has in the final analysis achieved its objective of liberating Kenya.

This sense of accomplishment proves short-lived. When Matigari returns from the forest in the wake of *uhuru*, or independence, he is confident that his sacrifice has helped restore Kenya's resources and land to the real "owners of the country" (74). He buries his weapons in the belief that armed resistance has fulfilled its purpose. However, he gradually comes to the disheartening realization that the correlation he has made between the end of colonialism and the inception of liberty is ill-founded. After a harrowing journey across newly independent Kenya, he witnesses, inter alia, Western domination of the economy, police brutality, government corruption, and privatization of public land. The hard-won independence from Great Britain has merely substituted one set of oppressors for another. The only difference is that, while colonialism could not conceal its white European face, independence has created a convenient facade behind which Western exploitation of Africa has nevertheless continued unabated: "Yesterday it was the whites. Today they have been joined by some blacks" (75). In other words, colonialism has metamorphosed into neocolonialism. The novel drives home this point by showing that the land and position of power that Settler Williams enjoyed during occupation have been transferred in the wake of decolonization to his son, Robert Williams, and to the son of his loyal African servant, John Boy Junior. Matigari's disillusionment is compounded by the fact that independence has largely benefited the loyalists and their children. As the Minister for Truth and Justice boasts, "we loyalists are the ones in power today" (102). Gĩkũyũ landowners and the Christian Gĩkũyũ elite made common cause and fought with the British during the war of liberation against what they perceived as Mau Mau's threat to their social standing and values. In the aftermath of the war, Great Britain remunerated them for their loyalty by grooming them for positions of power in a postcolonial Kenya. As the novel poignantly shows, although John Boy aided Settler Williams against Matigari, his son has nonetheless reaped the benefits of the independence he sought to forestall. Moreover, true to his father's legacy, Boy Junior forges a neocolonial partnership with multinational capitalism, represented by Robert Williams, in disregard of the adverse effects it has on ordinary Kenyans.

Matigari reveals that the neocolonial order has engendered the same Manichaean world that defined colonialism. On the one hand, multinational capitalists and the Kenyan political and financial elite own large tracts of fertile land, drive expensive cars, and live in lavish houses. On the other hand, ordinary women sell their bodies to eke out a living, workers endure exploitation, and orphans live in junkyards and feed on food collected from the refuse of the affluent. Given the inequalities it creates, neocolonialism must, like colonialism, resort to violence in order to maintain its hold on society. *Matigari* shows that the role of silencing popular discontent and shoring up the neocolonial order has fallen to the postcolonial nation-state, which deploys the repressive state apparatuses to achieve its objectives. The worker whom Matigari meets in a prison cell explains that "[e]very worker knows that Robert Williams and John Boy [Junior] are like twins born out of the womb of the same ogre. And you know something else? The whole police force is in the hands of these two. So are all the law courts" (65).

Kenyans—like Africans in general—fought their oppressors to establish a postcolonial dispensation that would reverse the abuses of colonialism. They believed that substituting black rulers for the white administration would usher in a more egalitarian economic and political order. They would, however, discover that the national elites could be as brutal and as impervious to their welfare as the colonial administrators they dethroned. His Excellency Ole Excellence in *Matigari* is representative of these elites, particularly Jomo Kenyatta, the first president of Kenya, and Daniel arap Moi, his vice president and successor. The edicts of Ole Excellence capture the authoritarianism of Kenyatta and arap Moi. Moreover, the bribes, or the "*personal shares*," as they are euphemistically called by the Minister for Truth and Justice (107), that Ole Excellence receives from Robert Williams indicate not only the venality at the heart of the neocolonial arrangement but also the collusion of the postcolonial leaders with multinational capitalism.

Matigari's experiences with colonialism, armed resistance, and neocolonialism coalesce at the end of the novel. The revolution Matigari initiates against Boy Junior is inspired by his recognition of the similarities between colonialism and neocolonialism and by Matigari's belief in the necessity of armed struggle in order to rid society of exploitation. Anticipating a more promising future, a new independence, he blows up the house on the hill, the very house for which he fought the colonizer, in the belief that "[i]t is better to build another house altogether—a new house" than to live with the knowledge that it is occupied by Boy Junior (139). Kenya, he determines, needs radical restructuring.

The task of identifying *Matigari*'s historical context usually takes me an hour and a half. After a brief break that serves as a temporal divider between one approach to the novel and another, I argue in the second session that *Matigari* does not merely reflect Kenya's political history but also intervenes in it in order to give voice to the silenced narrative of Mau Mau. Such a task necessitates that I begin by addressing Ngũgĩ's Marxist convictions.

Ngũgĩ believes, with Karl Marx, that the movers of history are not the world historical figures of Hegel but mostly the dominant economic forces of a given period and the political institutions that buttress them. Thus, Ngũgĩ considers the failures of independence to derive from the neocolonial order, which seeks to exploit the many for the benefit of the few. Ngũgĩ is, however, far from being a vulgar determinist. He upholds the fundamental role of economic and political institutions in shaping history but equally recognizes that, in the words of Marx, "[m]en [and women] make their own history, but they do not make it just as they please; they do not make it under circumstances chosen by themselves" (*Eighteenth Brumaire* 15).

The Marxist view of history as dialectical, in which the clash of two antagonistic forces generates an alternative order, pervades *Matigari*. This novel contends that, formidable as it is, the neocolonial order is not impregnable. The oppressed masses can overturn it and transform history in accordance with their ideals and aspirations. Their grievances against colonialism in Kenya, leading to the Mau Mau rebellion and decolonization, may be equally harnessed to effect a new independence or, in the allegorical language of the novel, a Second Coming. This is precisely the conviction that drives Matigari to destroy Boy Junior's house: "The failure of one crop does not deter one from sowing seeds again" (150). It rather allows one to build "a bigger house, a house with proper foundations, a firm foundation!" (157).

To achieve their objectives, *Matigari* suggests that the masses avail themselves of revolutionary violence. Ngũgĩ does not believe that neocolonialism will collapse under the weight of its own contradictions. He holds that only radical collective action can liberate the wretched of the earth and set the stage for a more promising future. Recalling Fanon, he does not shy away from revolutionary violence. If Fanon argues that decolonization must, given the Manichaean divisions colonialism enforces, involve "searing bullets and bloodstained knives" (*Wretched* 37), Ngũgĩ transposes this trenchant call to arms to the postcolonial era. He upholds the necessity of revolutionary violence because the masses, in his eyes, cannot achieve their objectives by negotiating with their oppressors, who will never willingly give up their economic and political interests. Matigari vainly seeks "somebody who can tell me where a person who has girded himself with a belt of peace can find truth and justice!" (92). After an agonizingly futile search for a peaceful solution to neocolonial oppression, he concludes that "[*j*]*ustice for the oppressed comes from a sharpened spear*" (131).

Matigari does not only advocate revolution but also proposes its most apposite agents. It is significant that the assault on neocolonialism is initiated by a former Mau Mau fighter (Matigari) and conceivably will be resumed by the descendant of a Mau Mau martyr (Mũriũki). *Matigari* holds that the energies that led Mau Mau to mount a staunch resistance to British imperialism can be reactivated to instigate a new phase of revolutionary activism against multinational capitalism and its Kenyan conduits. In keeping with this view, it both counters the attempts of official historiography to minimize the significance of Mau Mau in Kenyan history and redefines the politics of this movement in accordance with Ngũgĩ's Marxist convictions. Kenyatta captures the gist of the arguments made by official historiography in postcolonial Kenya when he dismisses Mau Mau as "a disease which had been eradicated, and must never be remembered again" (qtd. in Furedi 212). Echoing Kenyatta, the Minister for Truth and Justice seeks in *Matigari* to suppress the contributions of Mau Mau, casting national independence, instead, as the heroic achievement of the loyalists. He asserts, "[T]hose who joined hands with colonialists in protecting the law—*loyalists*—are really the ones who made the colonialists give us independence on a platter" (103). According Mau Mau a pivotal role in national history, *Matigari* accuses the ruling elite of doubly betraying Kenya: they collaborated with colonialism against Mau Mau, and they have acted in postcolonial Kenya as compradors for multinational capitalism.

As represented by the actions and statements of Matigari, Mau Mau emerges in the novel as hostile not only to colonial expropriation of Gĩkũyũ land but also to capitalist exploitation in general. Rejecting private property, it endorses two cornerstones of socialist economics: the primacy of labor over capital and collectivism. Matigari repeatedly declares, in what amounts to a socialist manifesto, that "[t]he house is mine because I built it. The land is mine too because I tilled it with these hands. The industries are mine because my labor built and worked them" (124). If Boy Junior excludes Matigari from the house he occupies on the grounds that "what is mine is mine" (49), Matigari invites all Kenyans to it: "Come, my people, one and all, let us enter the house together. . . . Yes, come all, and let us light a fire in the house together! Let us share the food together" (51).

The view of Mau Mau as a custodian of socialist ideals, nevertheless, owes more to Ngũgĩ's Marxism than to the historical record. Furedi points out that Mau Mau's rebellion "was not translated into a coherent political perspective.

As a result the organizational independence of Mau Mau coexisted with an ideological convergence with the more moderate elements" (138), including the loyalists. Critics have faulted Ngũgĩ for what they consider to be historically inaccurate depictions of Mau Mau. I believe their criticism stems from a failure to account for the utopian dimension of *Matigari*, a novel that does not merely reflect a specific historical moment but also seeks to redirect its course. For Ngũgĩ, a revolution spearheaded by a socialist Mau Mau would rid Kenya of the agents of neocolonialism, whether foreign or national, and would bring forth a more egalitarian society. *Matigari*'s creative approach to history accords with Ngũgĩ's view of the artist. In *Penpoints, Gunpoints, and Dreams*, he maintains that the artist must not merely duplicate the world but also improve on it:

> [The artist] looks at things not only as they are, but more essentially as they could be. Hence Aristotle's ancient observation in his *Poetics* that poetry is more universal than history, for the latter deals with things as they are, the former with things as they could be. . . . (12)

I conclude my presentation by soliciting students' comments. In their responses, they occasionally criticize *Matigari* for having a strong political agenda. I argue that their unease with politically engaged literature is the outcome of their training in a specific aesthetics—namely, the notion that art is valuable only insofar as it expresses universal truths that transcend partisan politics. Whatever its merit, this position should not, I urge, prevent them from evaluating *Matigari* on its own terms. Echoing Jameson, I add that African literature generally rejects the idea of a disengaged art or art that is severed from the daily struggles of the people. Ngũgĩ and other African writers consciously seek, often with grave consequences to themselves, to make literature relevant to society. That many African nation-states ban their work and silence them through incarceration and assassination is testimony to the relevance of their efforts. Indeed, the Kenyan government found *Matigari* to be too dangerous to be ignored. Ngũgĩ writes:

> [I]ntelligence reports had it that peasants in Central Kenya were whispering and talking about a man called Matigari who was roaming the whole country making demands about truth and justice. There were orders for his immediate arrest, but the police discovered that Matigari was only a fictional character in a book of the same name. In February 1987, the police raided all the bookshops and seized every copy of the novel. ("Note" viii)

Because the concerns that preoccupy *Matigari* cannot be exhausted in the space of one class, I ask students to read two essays that address issues I do not cover in my presentation. One essay is Oliver Lovesey's "Mau Mau Aesthetics: Later Fiction," in his *Ngũgĩ wa Thiong'o* (46–79); the other is John A. Ambanby's "*Matigari*: 'The Gospel according to Ngũgĩ,'" in his *The Kenyan Epic Novelist*

Ngũgĩ (159–99). These essays also complement my analysis of *Matigari*'s intervention in the history of Kenya. I avoid giving students extra historical material for fear of undoing my efforts to teach the novel as first and foremost an active intervention in history rather than a passive reflection of it.

The students and I keep returning to *Matigari* over the course of the semester. When we study *Midnight's Children*, for instance, we compare Ngũgĩ's understanding of political oppression in the postcolony with Rushdie's. We discuss the significance of the minimal role played by Ole Excellence as opposed to the larger-than-life role played by the Widow. Given the breadth of its preoccupations and the insights it offers, *Matigari* is simply an indispensable text in a course on postcolonial literature.

Feminist Nationalism in *Wizard of the Crow*

Gĩchingiri Ndĩgĩrĩgĩ

"When will you learn to listen to the voices of women?"
—Ngũgĩ, *Wizard of the Crow*

Nyawĩra, the heroine of Ngũgĩ wa Thiong'o's *Wizard of the Crow*, in a wide-ranging discussion with her lover, Kamĩtĩ, on Third World literature, tells him to listen to the voices of women (83). Her comment is a fitting entry point into a discussion of the teachable aspects of *Wizard*, because the novel articulates the voices of the subaltern women of the postcolonial world in a remarkable fashion. This essay follows Nyawĩra's seeing "I" and probes the ways that she speaks for herself and other women, refusing to be already spoken for by patriarchal discourses. It engages in a postcolonial feminist critique that would appear to be authorized by what the heroine calls her "political catechism":

> I believe that black has been oppressed by white; female by male; peasant by landlord; and worker by lord of capital. . . . [T]he black female worker and peasant is most oppressed. She is oppressed on account of her color like all black people in the world; she is oppressed on account of her gender like all women in the world; and she is exploited and oppressed on account of her class. . . . Three burdens she has to carry. Those who want to fight for the people in the nation and in the world must struggle for the unity and rights of the working class in their own country; fight against all discriminations based on race, ethnicity, color, and belief systems; they must struggle against all gender-based inequalities and therefore fight for the rights of women in the home, the family, the nation and the world. . . .
>
> (428)

Ngũgĩ has been lauded for creating strong women characters in his earlier fiction and drama, but those women are singularly challenged in their inability to confront and surmount the obstacles facing them at the level of class, race, and gender.[1] As nationalists or agents of social change, they invariably need a man to transform their consciousness into revolutionary action, the grand narrative that Ngũgĩ upheld in his earlier works.

The limited agency of the women characters in the earlier works contrasts starkly with the feminist nationalism in *Wizard of the Crow*. The novel makes a strong connection between the men's complicity in the betrayal and degradation of their nation and the performance of masculinity that is enacted over pliable female bodies. Unlike the essentially voiceless but strong women in Ngũgĩ's earlier writing, Nyawĩra refuses to be objectified as a good daughter and wife. She demands equal rights for women, she leads the resistance against the exploitation and degradation of the nation by transnational capital, and she mobilizes both women and men in rehabilitating nature and the environment as a corrective to the rapacious greed of the national elite working in cahoots with transnational capital. As the head of the Movement for the Voice of the People (726), Nyawĩra rewrites the image of the strong woman in Ngũgĩ's earlier writing, who was all passion but little perception, consistently the understudy in a male world, whether in resistance politics, in nationalist projects, or as a victim of male domination. Nyawĩra's critique of the postcolony on the basis of class, race, and gender oppression and her overarching concern for the nation and its place in the world signal her postcolonial feminism.

I focus on Nyawĩra's feminist nationalism and its connection to environmental activism, Ngũgĩ's most significant contribution to representations of gender in African literature. I also interrogate the discourses of economic globalization as these clash with environmental and minority rights, which are articulated in a national framework. Once students get over their fascination with the five theories to explain the Ruler's illness, with the magic realism, with the grotesquerie of the ruling elite and their spectacles of power (Bakhtin's *Rabelais and His World* and Foucault's *Discipline and Punish* would come in handy here), and with the suspenseful development of the affair between Nyawĩra and Kamĩtĩ, the question of her agency is bound to attract attention. That the women in *Wizard* work together and the men work against one another will likely attract the typical response from male students that this is a novel attacking men, though some might remark how progressive Ngũgĩ's view of women is. Such responses can be channeled to a discussion of gender performativity, oriented specifically to the motivations for Nyawĩra's agency.[2]

Ngũgĩ remaps the national space in *Wizard* as the site of women's agency. Nyawirã helps heal the environment (nature), which has been violated by the greed of men, and she taps into the ecofeminist notion that women are better able to manage the environment because they are more directly dependent on and associated with it. The national politics has become corrupted because it does not make space for women's voices. Where Ngũgĩ's mid-career novels (*Petals of Blood*, *Devil on the Cross,* and *Matigari*) imagined a utopian nation of workers to replace the official nation that had obviously failed, *Wizard* imagines a nation led by ecofeminist women. Aburĩria's men seek to compradorize the country for their own benefit, but Nyawĩra and her group nurture the country and guard it from becoming further indebted to global capital. National debt to multilateral donors impoverishes the average Aburĩrian, as the funds are channeled to white elephants that ensure kickbacks for the ruling elite. A debt-free nation is presented as a human right. Because the women feel the effects of poverty more immediately (the absence of food, water, firewood), they are at the forefront of the struggle to liberate the nation from global capital, to ensure that their children inherit a viable nation. The global financial institutions, part of the patriarchal order, accuse the Aburĩrian women of turning the country upside down with their agitation for equal rights, with their corruption of postcolonial modernity.

Lois West argues that there is a need to understand "the construction of nationalism as an inherently 'gendered' phenomenon," that men have presented the construction of nations and states as centered on power struggles between men, such as in wars (xiv). Similarly, Anthony D. Smith writes:

> [T]here are times . . . when the national struggle supersedes or subsumes all other struggles, including those of class and gender. This does not mean that "nationalism" as a discourse is not oriented primarily to the needs of men and for this reason possesses a "masculine" symbolic content. (208)

R. Radhakrishnan notes that "the advent of the politics of nationalism signals the subordination if not the demise of women's politics." He raises two important questions: "Why does the politics of the 'one' typically overwhelm the politics of the 'other'? Why could the two not be coordinated within an equal and dialogic relationship of mutual accountability?" (78). The simple answer is that, as West observes, nationalism is inherently gendered as male. By putting a woman at the head of the movement seeking to liberate the Aburĩrian nation from the comprador state elite, *Wizard* coordinates national politics and women's politics in an equal and dialogic relation of mutual accountability.

Writing on the experience of nationality, Jonathan Rée describes an ideal situation when he argues that in a democratic dispersal of monarchical hubris, each national subject can proclaim, "[T]he nation is mine" (89). In Aburĩria, the average citizen has little chance to claim the nation. A despot named His Holy Lord President II rules the country, stating categorically and often that there is no distinction between him and it (136). One of his praise songs iterates, "*His Mighty Ruler is the Mighty Country and the Mighty Country is the Ruler. . . . The Ruler and the Country are one and the same*" (161).

Feminist critics like West, Mary Russo, Ketu Katrak, Doris Sommer, Patricia Yaeger, Alison Blunt, and Gilian Rose note that historically women have been relegated to the private realm of the family, their claims to the nation articulated largely through patriarchal voices, but the people of Aburĩria are denied any claims, confined as they are to the large prison that passes for the Aburĩrian state. Women who violate the public male–private female binary are constructed by the state discourse as ungrateful criminals; as unnatural; as madwomen who have been "deluded into anarchy, no doubt, by a cunning [male] lover" (218). But the women of Aburĩria imagine the nation's territorial integrity, political independence, and sovereignty in ways that make the nation receptive to their assertion of equal rights. In other words, they articulate both their feminism and their nationalism. Robert Young notes that "women could be nationalist and feminist; they could also be nationalist without being feminist, and vice versa," depending on their positioning as post- and neocolonial or gendered subjects (370). The feminist nationalism in this novel is by far the best informed in African literature. The idea of a woman taking charge of a revolutionary nationalist movement with an environmentalist orientation is also a first in African literature.

Andrew Parker, Russo, Sommer, and Yaeger probe the "deeply ingrained . . . depiction of the homeland as a female body whose violation by foreigners requires its citizens and allies to rush to its defense." They argue that "this trope of the nation-as-woman . . . depends for its representational efficacy on a particular image of woman as chaste, dutiful, daughterly or maternal" (Introd. 5). Nyawĩra overturns the masculinist ascriptions of the apolitical, docile, chaste, dutiful, daughterly, and maternal qualities that the patriarchal order demands of its women. Recognizing the performativity of gender, she rebels against parental authority that would deny her the choice of a marriage partner, she walks out of an unfulfilling marriage, and she chooses not to have children. She unchains herself from the stereotype of the nurturing mother, the subservient and passive female, and the fertility of the Mother Africa trope that characterized African literature of the 1960s and 1970s. She is beautiful, but that beauty is used in a nonsexual way, for political ends, and she is able to perform ugliness to escape detection. She is the first heroine in Ngũgĩ's writing since *A Grain of Wheat* not to have had a moral fall (from having a child out of wedlock, from prostitution) that requires her to redeem herself through social activism.

Nyawĩra stages her resistance through self-modernization, through the denial of cultural practices in a state that advocates anachronistic traditions as escape from "stressful modernity" (621). She appropriates elements of modernity at the same time that she unmasks the crass materialism in Aburĩria. She deploys the trope of the nation as woman, arguing, "The condition of women in a nation is the real measure of its progress. *You imprison a woman and you have imprisoned a nation*" (253). She is not talking about mere maternity here, a big change from earlier African literature where woman was equated with Mother Africa, with fertility, and with eternal abstract beauty.

Nyawĩra brings an internationalist dimension to the Movement for the Voice of the People, the national underground movement that she comes to head. A feminist internationalism is evident in her reading of emerging women's voices from Africa and India. Summarizing the writings of Buchi Emecheta (Nigeria), Tsitsi Dangarembga (Zimbabwe), and Mariama Bâ (Senegal), she observes, "Women bear the brunt of poverty. What choices does a woman have in life, especially in times of misery? She can marry or live with a man. She can bear children and bring them up, and be abused by her man." These African women writers give "words to similar thoughts about the condition of women in Africa." She recommends to Kamĩtĩ, her mate, Arundhati Roy's *The God of Small Things*, Meena Alexander's *Fault Lines*, Susie Tharu's *Women Writing in India* and *We Were Making History*, "about women in the struggle!" When Kamĩtĩ confesses to having read only "the epics of Indian literature"—the Mahabharata, Ramayana, Bhagavad Gita, Purana, Rigveda, and Upanishads—Nyawĩra has a ready answer: "I am sure that those epics and Puranas, even the Gita, were all written by men. . . . The same men who invented the caste system. When will you learn to listen to the voices of women?" (83).

Wizard of the Crow is an attempt to make readers listen to the voices of women. It is the story of three women (Nyawĩra, Racheal, and Vinjinia to an extent) who refuse to break when subjected to male abuse and who create institutional structures to stop that abuse. These three inspire other women (and men) at the grass roots who bear the brunt of poverty, deconstruct the patriarchal discourses through which the Aburĩrian state perpetuates itself and in so doing articulate the voices of women in a dialogic process with nationalist politics, and redefine the private realm and the public space as not mutually exclusive.

A discussion of Nyawĩra's character should show how her nationalist credentials mark her as a subversive. She opposes the building of Marching to Heaven, the tower meant to immortalize the Ruler of Aburĩria. Her opposition is patriotic, because the tower would put the nation into permanent debt, but she and her group are considered traitors (86). The ruling elite are ecstatic about the project:

> The Aburĩrian masses . . . [will] forgo clothes, houses, education, medicine, and even food in order to meet any and every condition the [global] Bank may impose on the funds it releases for Marching to Heaven. . . . We swear by the children of the children of the children of the children of our children to the end of the world . . . that we shall pay back every cent of the principle along with interest on interests ad infinitum. (248)[3]

Obviously this Third World state (whose currency has the name *Burĩ*, meaning "free," "useless") cannot afford this fetish of modernity.

The bank's willingness to fund the tower can prompt an interesting discussion of the strings attached to Third World aid. Opposition to the tower as a rallying point for women's rights and civil rights and the connection of this resistance to the protest of Racheal, the Ruler's wife, whom the Ruler thought he had silenced, shows the futility of dictatorial power in the face of civil disobedience. The women point to the link between the nation's poverty and the greed of the state elite working with transnational capital as the unfinished business of decolonization. The complicity of the Global Bank in perpetuating traditional patriarchal practices becomes evident in its refusal to fund the construction of Marching to Heaven on the grounds that the women of Aburĩria have taken "women's liberation too literally and too far" by countering male violence with female violence. The representatives of the bank berate Aburĩria's ruler: "Everything is upside down in your country. Your women are challenging the natural order of things, even setting up what they call people's courts" (499). Both in the private realm and in public space, women challenge the patriarchal order. They envision the nation as debt-free and sovereign, including economic liberation in the struggle for political liberation.

Unlike the men, Nyawĩra presides over an egalitarian order. It is an inclusive comradeship of men and women fighting to liberate what is left of their country and nation from the grips of transnational capital. The novel's interrogation of the supranational formations advocated in globalization studies shows that at the heart of the new global order are national interests, which the novel labels "corpolonial." According to Tajirika, a confidant of the president, the Global Bank and the Global Ministry of Finance "are clearly looking to privatize countries, nations, and states." Tajirika explains their argument:

> [T]he modern world was created by private capital. The subcontinent of India, for instance, was owned by the British East India Company, Indonesia by the Dutch East India Company, our neighbors by the British East African Company. . . . What private capital did then it can do again: own and reshape the Third World in the image of the West without the slightest blot, blemish, or blotch. . . . The world will no longer be composed of the outmoded twentieth century divisions of East, West, and a directionless Third. The world will become one corporate globe divided into the incorporating and the incorporated. We should volunteer Aburĩria to be the first to be wholly managed by private capital, to become the first voluntary corporate colony, a corpolony, the first in the new global order. With the privatization of Aburĩria, and with the NGOs relieving us of social services, the country becomes your real estate. You will be collecting land rent in addition to the commission fee for managing the corpolonial army and police force. (746)

Evident is the rulers' adoration of the West, imagined here as being "free from spot or blemish," the Webster's dictionary definition for *white*. The elite's amenability to global capital in whatever form is also evident, and as long as the corpolonial state retains the instruments of violence—the army and the police—the Ruler is comfortable. His objection to the logic of corpolonialism has to do with his personal loss of status, not with notions of sovereignty

The new global order is also touted by the United States envoy in Aburĩria, who envisions

> a free and stable world where our money can move across borders without barriers erected by the misguided nationalism of the outmoded nation-state. The goal is to free up the resources and energies of the globe. All your countries and people will benefit. (580)

The envoy's vision invites class discussion on the place of the nation-state in the new global order and the notion of freedom that the envoy celebrates. The novel is clear that the West values only the freedom that gives global capital unlimited mobility; the West does not care about the ecological devastation that capital leaves in its wake or about the obvious inequality of the borderless countries.

The women are aware that the forces of globalization are impoverishing the people of Aburĩria. They must restage a popular nationalism to defeat global capital. Their new nationalism makes possible the liberation of the nation from the patriarchal state elite.

The women lead the way in recovering what Pheng Cheah describes elsewhere as "a postcolonial national identity formation [that] is in part a response to neocolonial economic globalization." Cheah argues, "[T]he uneven accumulation of capital and distribution of wealth and resources on a global scale [exacerbate] the unequal distribution of political power and economic resources within decolonized countries" ("Given Culture" 310). As Nyawĩra and her group make clear, the ruling elite in Aburĩria owe their power and wealth to patriarchal networks both local and global. To overcome the elite and their foreign allies, the subalterns of Aburĩria must think globally but also act locally. In the national context, they must resist the elite's attempt to mobilize the citizenry in the name of tradition that favors the rights of men and disempowers women.

In the postcolonial era, then, the women wage a new struggle to dethrone the official nation. Their struggle exemplifies Cheah's idea of "national consciousness formed through negative identification, induced by political-economic factors such as interstate relations within a neocolonial capitalist world economy" (300). Cheah observes that "although contemporary globalization has complicated the nation-state form, it has not rendered it obsolete as a form of political organization" (291).

Class discussion of Aburĩria as a failed state should recognize that the citizenry still mobilize around the inherited postcolonial state that they seek to legitimate as a nation. That mobilization is part of Nyawĩra's catechism. The novel deconstructs the logic of globalization, showing that even as the West touts a borderless world, it is essentially advancing a Euro-American agenda that enhances the growth of Western capital. Thus if the Aburĩrian state had the interests of its citizens at heart, it would transform itself into a popular nation-state rather than a satellite for Euro-American interests. Cheah argues:

> [P]opular rearticulations of postcolonial national identity are ethically imperative and cannot be dismissed per se as statist ideologies that hinder the rise of the more equitable cosmopolitan consciousness. . . . (312–13)

The phrase "equitable cosmopolitan consciousness" is utopian. All the nations depicted in the novel act instead out of patriotic cosmopolitanism, advancing statist ideologies while preaching the advantages of globalization.

In *Wizard*, the women leaders of the mass movement see what the male rulers cannot, that global order is not equitable; it does not safeguard the interests of Aburĩria. Therefore they must say, "The nation is mine," even at the risk of state violence. They must challenge the men to join in rescuing the nation from the global political and economic order that makes them exiles in their own country.

In Aburĩria, loyalty to country is loyalty to the Ruler. It is enforced through an elaborate disciplinary apparatus of state power that in effect erases the people's selfhood. The state deterritorializes its citizens by robbing them of country in the appropriative gesture that makes the Ruler and country coextensive, that identifies the Ruler's life as the nation's history. This identification makes the claim to a state-based nationalism problematic. As the women lead the effort to delink the state from the nation or the nation from the body of the president, they stage a popular nationalism that foregrounds women's questions, dethrones male violence and male conceptions of the natural place of women, and heals an environment that has been destroyed by male greed.

As the head of the Movement for the Voice of the People, Nyawĩra rewrites the image of the strong woman in Ngũgĩ's earlier writing. She organizes the women of Aburĩria as a collective whose rallying cry is that when you hurt one woman, you hurt all women; when you empower a woman, you empower the nation. Her movement has a strong basis in ecofeminism, whose central mission is to heal the natural and social environment that has been violated by global capital placed in the hands of a rapacious patriarchal order. This reclamation is a return to nature as life's sustaining force and as the realm that unites both man and woman in a nonhierarchical order. The movement's farms evoke Wangari Maathai's Green Belt Movement and model a utopian nation in which human beings live in harmony with one another and with nature. For an informed discussion of the synergy between Nyawĩra's ecofeminism and the nationalist struggle in *Wizard*, students could be asked to do research on Wangari Maathai, the first African woman to win the Nobel Peace Prize (2004), predominantly for her environmental activism. Graduate students should be encouraged to read Wangari's memoir, *Unbowed*. They will find references to her divorce; to her growing consciousness of the interplay between changing feeding habits, changing crop cultivation patterns, and environmental degradation; to her reforestation projects around Africa; to her opposition to the building of a tower, like the fictional Marching to Heaven, to immortalize the Kenyan dictator Moi in 1990; to her participation in a political protest in 1992 that ended in the mooning of police, which seems to inform the mooning ritual in *Wizard*; and to her leadership of the resistance to the grabbing of Karura Forest in 1998 by developers.

Writing about ecofeminism in the Green Belt Movement, Rosemary Ruether notes that besides its reforestation efforts, the movement teaches its predominantly female members "sustainable agriculture with an emphasis on restoration of traditional food crops" and "rediscovery of traditional knowledge of care for the land and solidarity with one another," not only emphasizing "what caused impoverishment of the land and how to restore it" but also embracing "a vision of love for the land as an extension of themselves" (103). The movement "seeks to restore the land and human community based on the presence of the divine in and through one another, not one that directs one's life to an otherworldly heaven" (104). Ruether connects the ecofeminism in the movement to ecofeminism generally, noting the members' "banding together in communities of accountability" as a means "to overcome the centralized systems of control over humans and non-human nature forged by colonialism and neocolonialism." Emphasizing ecofeminists' "rejection of a splitting of the divine from the earth and its communities of life to project 'God' as a personified entity located in some supercelestial realm outside the universe and ruling over it," Ruether notes that "the concept of god is deconstructed. The divine is understood as a matrix of life-giving energy that is in, through, and under all things" (124–25).

In *Wizard*, the deconstruction of divinity is linked to the defetishization of the Ruler of Aburĩria, who considers himself God's peer, and to the people's self-empowerment to tap the life-giving energy in them. In deconstructing the Ruler's divinity, its masculinist trappings, and the patriarchal roots of Aburĩria's much vaunted development, Nyawĩra enacts an ecofeminist nationalism. There are clear parallels between the Green Belt Movement and Movement for the Voice of the People, especially in their environmental restoration projects, in their social and political activism, and in the character Nyawĩra and the person Wangari Maathai.

The search for the inner divinity in all people informs Nyawĩra's theology and activism. She heads a movement that approximates Ruether's "communities of accountability," which undermine centralized and patriarchal systems of domination (124). The women, recognizing that they have been dominated by the men in the same way that men seek dominance over nature in the race for profit, demand social justice, especially centered on women's rights, national sovereignty, and the ecological health of their nation. They harness the power in themselves as individuals and as a community that evokes the Taoist balance, mind-body wholeness, and a simplicity in lifestyle that ensures that they take from nature only what they need and also give back to nature. That imagined nation is modeled on the equal rights of the subalterns who rise to restore their country's territorial integrity, sovereignty, and political independence. The women are feminists, nationalists, and environmental activists whose agency is an intrinsic part of the new national struggle. They forge a new revolutionary army whose mission is to correct the shortcomings of the anticolonial resistance. Its operative principle of taking from and giving to fellow human beings and the natural environment promises renewal. Kamĩtĩ observes of their model farms:

> Elsewhere Aburĩrian soil was dying from being doused with pollutants, imported fertilizer. Here they were working with nature, not against it. The forest was a school to which they often came to hear what it had to tell them: You take, you give. . . . (738)

The Seven Principles of Grace fashioned by Kamĩtĩ and Nyawĩra lead to mind-body wholeness, balance between the social and natural, and a holistic life. Before contemplating formal marriage or children, they have work to do to clear the rot and pollution over the land and clean the atmosphere (725). That cleaning is simultaneously environmental, social, and political. It can be achieved only by a community that recognizes the divinity in each of its members.

Wizard of the Crow is a fascinating novel on many levels. Its romance, political intrigue, multiple narrative perspectives, spectacle, fantasy, and magic realism easily engage the undergraduate student who loves a good story. Graduate students find engaging the novel's metacommentary on gender, nationalism, the discourses of globalization, and the politics of representation. The novel is also a significant contribution to environmental writing in African literature. It reopens the discussion of how the local concerns of much environmental writing can be harmonized with the broader concerns of postcolonial criticism. Its structuring of an allegorical national framework to address the crises of environmental preservation in an era of multinational corporations gobbling up natural and human resources without responsibility; its recognition of the need to recover marginalized voices and their histories as a way of challenging the developmentalist narrative of postcolonial or neocolonial modernity; and its enactment of a rooted cosmopolitanism all lead to the rapprochement that Rob Nixon advocates between environmentalism and postcolonial literary studies. Adding feminism to this mix should prompt discussion about some major, urgent questions of our age.

NOTES

I wish to acknowledge the help of Jean Kidula, La Vinia Jennings, and Peter Kareithi in my writing of this essay.

[1] The most pertinent characters are Muthoni in *The River Between*, Mumbi in *A Grain of Wheat*, Wanja in *Petals of Blood*, the Woman in *The Trial of Dedan Kimathi*, Warĩĩnga in *Devil on the Cross*, Gũthera in *Matigari*, and Nyathira in *Mother, Sing for Me*.

[2] I got these responses when I taught the novel in an undergraduate class in which most of the students had not encountered Ngũgĩ's earlier writing. But three students had taken a lower-division course in which we read *A Grain of Wheat*, and they were impressed by the difference between Mumbi and Nyawĩra. Some may choose not to use *Wizard* in an undergraduate class because of its length, but its wide sweep of African events and of the malaise of postcoloniality more generally makes it valuable whether one is teaching a course on African or postcolonial literatures. Its division into books that were published separately in the Gĩkũyũ edition allows one to read and discuss them as self-contained units. A brief discussion of the pitfalls of decolonization in Africa in the 1960s and 1970s and the emergence of the big man as a fixture on the political scene and as a type character in the African novel of disillusionment should provide context for *Wizard*. I encouraged my students to read Achille Mbembe's "Provisional Notes on the Postcolony."

[3] "Principle," for *principal*, may have ironic intent.

Transformation through Make-Believe in *Wizard of the Crow*

Steve Gronert Ellerhoff

Wizard of the Crow, Ngũgĩ wa Thiong'o's longest novel, may also be his most accessible. Not only does Ngũgĩ construct the pan-African experience in the postcolonial twenty-first century, he also draws from the continent's rich literary tradition and places its people in a global context. The work's length, 766 pages in its first hardcover American edition, may daunt students, but the instructor should point out to them that the chapters in each of the novel's six books are quite short, some of them just a page. Furthermore, one could teach one book at a time, giving students intellectual nourishment in digestible portions. Luckily for the instructor, the novel has what undergraduate students hunger for: pathos, intrigue, and flights of comedy high and low. Its satire is tempered with sadness and wisdom and ultimately gives us a hopeful take on transforming not just Africa but the whole world. *Wizard* is also perfect for introducing students to African literature, because it references and even points the way to other important novels by African writers, such as Amos Tutuola's *The Palm-Wine Drinkard*, Ayi Kwei Armah's *The Beautyful Ones Are Not Yet Born*, Peter Nazareth's *In a Brown Mantle* and *The General Is Up*, not to mention Ngũgĩ's own *Devil on the Cross*. *Wizard* makes vivid many challenges African nations face in the contemporary world: AIDS, military dictatorship, independence, and globalization.

This essay highlights some of the threads in what is a complicated novel, showing that, despite its length, *Wizard* is absolutely teachable and of great value. The first section explores Ngũgĩ's creation of Aburĩria, a fictitious African nation, as the setting of his work. The second section draws out the role of pretending as it affects the lives of the main characters and shapes our understanding of Ngũgĩ's hopes for Africa and the world. The third and final section reiterates the argument for *Wizard*'s use in the classroom.

A Fictitious African Nation

Becoming through pretending, adopting a role or identity one has not inhabited before, is the central tension for the protagonists in *Wizard of the Crow*. Kamĩtĩ wa Karĩmĩri and Grace Nyawĩra—an unemployed postgraduate and a secretary-cum–underground freedom fighter, respectively—don the mantle of Wizard of the Crow, a role they create on a whim and embody at the expectation of others. In that role, they see their nation's unnamed dictator, the Ruler, deposed and their countrymen more proactive in the country's place in the world. But the novel is not a simple morality play. The powers that shape its characters and landscape stretch from the personal to the political, from the local to the global, and from comic reverie to mythic transcendence. A knowing absurdity is at work in the novel, as is satire, and any interpretation must take into account Ngũgĩ's at times ironic and often hilarious tone.

The Wizard arises to fill a need in Ngũgĩ's fictional African nation, the Free Republic of Aburĩria. Aburĩria is placed in a global context on the first page, which cites the Ruler's failure to appear on *Meet the Global Mighty* on the Global News Network. Later we are shown the country as the government self-consciously feels tourists see it:

> In Aburĩria . . . tourist pictures of beggars or children with kwashiorkor and flies massing around their runny noses and sore eyes were prized for their authenticity. If there were no beggars in the streets, tourists might start doubting whether Aburĩria was an authentic African country. (35)

Ngũgĩ invents a nation instead of using an existing one. Allegory calls for such invention: by creating an imagined nation, he is free to talk about the big picture without historical facts and connotations of a specific nation interfering with the story.

Nazareth, a literary critic, African novelist, and Ngũgĩ's friend and former classmate, used allegory in his two novels, *In a Brown Mantle* and *The General Is Up*, inventing Damibia, a small landlocked African nation. A Ugandan of Goan descent, he writes his Damibian novels from a South Asian perspective, dealing particularly with the expulsion of Ugandan Goans, including him, on account of race at the order of Idi Amin, a very real dictator who "made the announcement on the basis of a dream from God" ("International Players" 6). *In a Brown Mantle*, published weeks before Amin expelled all Asians from Uganda on 5 August 1972, seemed to prophesy that tumultuous event, its Goan narrator forced to leave "sickened beyond cure of the political scene" (149). Damibia, like Aburĩria, is under the control of an insane and unnamed dictator, also referred to as the Ruler. Nazareth's sequel, *The General Is Up*, explores an expulsion in great detail, containing in the author's note the following sleight of hand: "Any resemblance to real events, persons or countries is an unfortunate coincidence"(n. pag.) Possibly taking a hint from Nazareth, Ngũgĩ widened his novel's scope to encompass the pan-African postcolonial experience in the new era of globalization.[1]

We see Aburĩria for the first time through Kamĩtĩ during an out-of-body experience (38). Tired and weary, he leaves his body lying on a trash heap, changes into a spirit bird, and views the nation from on high, seeing its entirety in all four cardinal directions and noting each region's physical features, much as one might when viewing a map. Kamĩtĩ sees Aburĩria as a nation of the world. He observes hungry people, homes ranging from shacks to mansions, industries both rich and spent, animals both fed and starving, and he is awakened to his place in the whole: "So I am not alone, he heard himself say to his bird self" (39). In Ngũgĩ's novel, the center of the world, the point where all lines of human experience intersect, is Aburĩria.[2] Kamĩtĩ, a twenty-first-century rationalist, educated with a BA and MBA in India, must broaden his understanding of life and its interconnectedness before he is ready to assume the transformative role of healer.

Off to See the Wizard

The Wizard of the Crow first appears as a deus ex machina. Kamĩtĩ and Nyawĩra, pursued by a foolish policeman named Constable A. G. Arigaigai Gathere, are cornered in Nyawĩra's house—and quite unaware of each other because it is dark—when salvation arrives in the form of a Bugs Bunny tactic. Nyawĩra providing the supplies he requests, Kamĩtĩ hangs a mass of rags tied to a bone and a dead lizard and frog over the door and props outside a cardboard sign he has fashioned on the spur of the moment: "WARNING! THIS PROPERTY BELONGS TO A WIZARD WHOSE POWER BRINGS DOWN HAWKS AND CROWS FROM THE SKY. TOUCH THIS HOUSE AT YOUR PERIL. SGD. WIZARD OF THE CROW" (77). A. G., superstitious, retreats in fear that demons are after him. Relieved that their strategy worked, Kamĩtĩ and Nyawĩra celebrate with laughter, then realize that they know each other. A last-ditch trick to evade a cop saves two people who will go on to save the spirit of their people.

Kamĩtĩ and Nyawĩra forget the Wizard of the Crow, but A. G. does not. His superstition and gift for embellishment breathe life into the yet-to-be embodied witch doctor. His story that the wizard sent jinn to lure him to the shrine goes through the Ruler's advisers to the top. As a result, A. G. is promoted. Crediting the wizard with his promotion, A. G. is the first person to take Nyawĩra for the wizard when he returns to the house. Assuming that she is a protean being, he thanks her, then tells anybody who will listen that the Wizard of the Crow takes many forms. He thus opens the door for her as well as Kamĩtĩ to don the mantle.

Because the people now know where the wizard lives, Kamĩtĩ and Nyawĩra have the transformation thrust upon them. It is decided that Kamĩtĩ, with his knowledge of herbs and the use of a mirror, should assume the role full-time. Soon the Aburĩrians, in need of healing, start showing up at the house in droves. He tends to all, scratching out the enemy of each in a mirror and relieving the people of the stench-stained money that has infected them. When ten policemen appear, seeking the same good fortune he bestowed on their colleague A. G., he accepts:

> The ten men spoke, each stressing the importance of the magic of the mirror and sprinkling every sentence with what they assumed to be his name, till he himself began to see it, a sign in neon lights flashing before him: THIS IS THE SHRINE OF THE WIZARD OF THE CROW. (133)

Before long, corrupt businessmen and leaders in the Ruler's office are coming to be healed, for they are sicker than anyone else in the nation. Titus Tajirika, a businessman and Nyawĩra's crooked boss, who makes a fool of Kamĩtĩ when Kamĩtĩ applies for a job at the beginning of the book, falls ill with a disease that comes to be known as white-ache, a condition paralyzing black men from the desire to be white. As Kamĩtĩ has risen to his office to serve his people, Tajirika has been transformed by greed and warped desires into a white man. He runs to the wizard for healing. The Wizard of the Crow, playing both mesmerist and psychoanalyst, walks Tajirika and his wife, Vinjinia, through a psychological transmogrification. Tajirika becomes a slave forced to take his white master's name. He chooses the name Clement Clarence Whitehead, and his wife becomes Virgin Beatrice Whitehead. They must speak only English, hold themselves as English colonial types, and embrace their destiny "as a homeless ex-colonial couple living solely on the memories of what used to be" (188). Kamĩtĩ's walkthrough cures them of their white-ache, leaving them begging to keep their blackness.

Nyawĩra too administers healing through the mirror and good counsel, when Kamĩtĩ goes off to live in the woods and seek his shamanic roots. She first hangs a sign on the wall outside her house, announcing the wizard's absence but A. G. notices her in the street, and she plays along when he addresses her as the wizard. She has learned that the government is hunting her down for her involvement in disrupting its plans for Marching to Heaven, a crackpot modern-day Tower of Babel. A. G., being a fool, does not know she is the woman he is supposed to detain. Realizing the wizard's power, "[s]he was very grateful for being mistaken as the Wizard of the Crow and would assume the role no matter what happened" (222). She goes on to help people, including Vinjinia.

Together, Kamĩtĩ and Nyawĩra bring to the Wizard of the Crow the powers of the male and the female, making the figure more powerful by infusing into it their own talents and perspectives. It is no surprise that they fall in love. Through their healing work, they draw up a list of seven suggestions for healthy living, which they title the Seven Herbs of Grace and hand out to the people they call their patients. They help the needy and destitute start changing their lives for the better. The wizard's legend grows stronger, which increases the dangers of their work.

Demons are not in short supply in the novel; each of its six books is named for a different kind of demon. Kamĩtĩ and Nyawĩra face great hardship at the hands of the parliament ministers—especially Kamĩtĩ, who most associate with the wizard. Arrested, he is forced to heal cabinet members, most of them transformed already by apocryphal cosmetic surgeries: Machokali with his eyes enlarged to the size of lightbulbs, Sikiokuu with enormous ears, Big Ben Mambo whose botched enhancement has left him with a long tongue like a dog's. The cabinet members underwent surgery to embody the eyes, ears, and command of the Ruler. The wizard is called on to tend to the Ruler himself, who falls ill on a trip to the United States with a disease that causes his body to balloon to

Pantagruelian dimensions and float as though filled with hot air. The corruption is so complete that there is little Kamĩtĩ can do for these people. He defends himself by faking white-ache and ultimately shattering the mirrors they have provided. When ordered at a public assembly to divine Nyawĩra's whereabouts, he gives himself away.

The greatest trial of the wizard comes not from the captors who fear him but from his address to the nation at a ceremony designed to assuage public fear over the Ruler's condition, which many believe to be a mysterious pregnancy. Kamĩtĩ, hesitating at the lectern before the media and the men and women of Aburĩria, is humbled:

> He had taken on the identity of the Wizard of the Crow as a cover, a joke, and now he was expected to be true to that identity. He was hardly here of his own volition, and now he had to speak as if he had come willingly! He hated lies and lying, even for private gain, and now he was expected to lie publicly for another's gain. He had wanted to root his life in truth—even as a diviner he had tried his best to avoid falsehood—and here he was, his life hanging on a false confession! (679)

This scruple echoes his feelings shortly after he first assumed the wizard's identity:

> At first I thought I was merely playing a role, briefly. I was proud that I never once dispensed magic that could harm anyone; and I never really lied to my clients. I never employed conjuring tricks to mesmerize. I worked with thoughts and images already in their own minds. But still I pretended to be what I was not. Did I not heal under falsehood? Imagine going to a doctor only to learn afterward that he has no training in his craft, no license to practice? I was a quack of a wizard. (207)

The truth, however, is that the Wizard of the Crow is not an imaginary figure. Because the people believed in him, he became in fact a great healer. Rising to the occasion, Kamĩtĩ delivers a speech about transformation for the country and its people. Explaining the rumor of the Ruler's pregnancy in terms of the nation's condition, he says, "Just as today is born of the womb of yesterday, today is pregnant with tomorrow" (681). He is joined onstage by Nyawĩra, wanted by the government for acts of treason. The nation's great healer declares that the nation's great leader of the underground resistance has healed him, and this declaration inspires a joyous, singing, dancing rebellion on the spot. Kamĩtĩ and Nyawĩra have come together, sacrificing themselves as the Wizard of the Crow for the sake of their people's well-being.

Ngũgĩ does not show Aburĩria healed of all ills. His message is one of hope for the world, not perfection, and as the celebratory rebellion starts, Tajirika, crooked businessman turned defense minister, the person underestimated by everyone, including the Ruler, launches a coup and seizes control. The Ruler is shot, deflated, and fed to crocodiles. Kamĩtĩ too is shot, in public at the assembly. He does not die, though it is assumed by the people that he does. The wizard's ghost is thought to haunt those who would misrule Aburĩria, and Kamĩtĩ and Nyawĩra are freed from their role as the wizard. A new insane ruler is in office; the white-ache of Tajirika returns to such a degree that he has his arm surgically replaced with a white man's. But the Movement for the Voice of the People and the Aburĩrian People's Resistance are stronger and more organized than ever. There is still hope for the nation's transformation for the better, just as there should be for all African nations and for all nations of the world.

The Protean Novel and Popular Criticism

The novel itself is a transformed work. Originally written in Gĩkũyũ and titled *Mũrogo wa Kagogo*, it was translated by Ngũgĩ into English, the translation taking it from a localized cultural community into an international one. He explains the tensions in the task of self-translation:

> The biggest challenge was in trying to figure a way of rendering in English the playfulness of the Gikuyu language. Gikuyu is very tonal, and the same word could mean and suggest different things depending on the tone. Trying to translate the musicality of one language into that of another is always difficult. But still, translation is the common language of all languages. (qtd. in Byrd)

So Ngũgĩ, in donning the responsibilities of translator to bring Aburĩria to a world audience's attention, becomes a wizard in his own right. Elizabeth Owuor agrees: "Thiong'o's work isn't simply about Africa. It's also about similar autocratic leaders from around the world, as well as the local and global frameworks that allow for their existence." In writing a novel that pretends to be about Africa, he has produced one that is really about the world, a myth for all of us. "And the only myth that is going to be worth thinking about in the immediate future," Joseph Campbell says, "is one talking about the planet, not the city, not these people, but the planet, and everybody on it" (32).

The thrust of *Wizard* is its appeal to the reader to transform the world. David Hellman makes a strong point that contextualizes *Wizard* apart from the canonical American tradition:

> The author couldn't care less about the conventions of Western literature; instead [he relies] on the open narrative of African folktales and also a sort of New Testament randomness. Ngũgĩ is not playing literary games here; he's telling his story his way. . . . From an ingrained Western perspective this could be annoying, which could lead to this novel not receiving

> the recognition it deserves. But to enjoy this book readers should first abandon any expectations they may have of literature and just surrender themselves to the story.

Hellman also notes that the novel is one "most would pray [does] not end up on their book group or college reading lists" because of its length but concludes that "it is essential reading for a world that only seems now to finally be waking up to its own reality, bathed in a vision of ever potential hope."

No epic should be trimmed for the sake of clarity, and students' capabilities should not be underestimated when a novel has so much to offer them. Teachers of undergraduates will find that many of their students have already consumed eight-hundred-page novels about wizards, thanks to the global popularity of J. K. Rowling's Harry Potter series. Ngũgĩ's novel about African wizards and the perils of globalization from an African perspective will do much to enlighten and broaden the awareness of a readership already familiar with best-selling epics of sorcery.

NOTES

[1] Nazareth informs me that when he saw Ngũgĩ at Northwestern University, Evanston, in 1985 at the annual meeting of the African Literature Association, he gave him a copy of *The General Is Up*, published by the Writers Workshop, Calcutta, the year before.

[2] This kind of shamanic vision, in which every place is the center of the world, appears in many cultures. Joseph Campbell, analyzing the great vision of Black Elk, shaman of the Oglala Sioux, contextualizes the vision in a way that resonates with Kamĩtĩ's experience: "That is a real mythological realization. It distinguishes between [Black Elk's] local cult image, Harney Peak, and its connotation as the center of the world. The center of the world is the *axis mundi*, the central point, the pole around which all revolves. . . . So is the central mountain of the world Jerusalem? Rome? Benares? Lhasa? Mexico City?" (89). Ngũgĩ sets the *axis mundi* in the Free Republic of Aburĩria, and his burgeoning shaman, Kamĩtĩ, realizes the small country is his own center of a greater whole, the world. The novel's action, played out in this localized setting, therefore has global implications.

NOTES ON CONTRIBUTORS

Pius Adesanmi is a recipient of the Penguin Prize for African Writing for his book *You're Not a Country, Africa*. He teaches African literature at Carleton University, Ottawa.

Michael Andindilile is lecturer at the Literature in English Department, University of Dar es Salaam, and a postdoctoral teaching fellow at the English Department of Fordham University. His current project is "The Anglophone African Literary-Linguistic Continuum."

F. Odun Balogun is professor in the English Department of Delaware State University and author of *Ngũgĩ and African Postcolonial Narrative* and *Tradition and Modernity in the African Short Story*.

Steve Gronert Ellerhoff is completing a PhD in English at Trinity College Dublin. He writes fiction, is a scholar involved with the Kurt Vonnegut Society, and is helping the Smithsonian National Museum of the American Indian in its tribute to the Kiowa rock guitarist Jesse "Ed" Davis.

Ali Erritouni is associate professor in the English Department of Kent State University at East Liverpool. He has studied in Morocco and the United States. His articles focus on the utopian imagination in African literature.

Uzoma Esonwanne is associate professor in the Department of English and the Centre for Comparative Literature at the University of Toronto.

Simon Gikandi is Robert Schirmer Professor of English at Princeton University and author of *Ngũgĩ wa Thiong'o* and coeditor, with Abiola Irele, of *The Cambridge History of African and Caribbean Literature*. He has written many books on postcolonial and African literatures.

Michael Harris is professor in the English Department at Central College, Iowa, and author of *Outsiders and Insiders: Perspectives of Third World Culture in British and Post-colonial Fiction*. He has written many articles on postcolonial literature. In 1998–99, he taught in the Department of Literature at the University of Dar es Salaam as a Fulbright senior lecturer.

Emilia Ilieva is associate professor in the Department of Literature, Egerton University, Kenya, and translator of *Petals of Blood* into Bulgarian. She has written articles, translations, and reviews in Bulgarian, Russian, and English journals.

Oliver Lovesey is associate professor of English in the Department of Critical Studies, University of British Columbia, Okanagan; author of *Ngũgĩ wa Thiong'o*; and editor of *Victorian Social Activists' Novels*.

W. O. Maloba is professor of history, black American studies, and women's studies and assistant vice president for Affirmative Action and Multicultural Programs at the University of Delaware. He is author of *Mau Mau and Kenya: An Analysis of a Peasant Revolt* and *African Women in Revolution*.

Kate McInturff, an expert on women's human rights norms and Canadian human rights policy, works with local, national, and multilateral organizations to implement international agreements that will make women's human rights an everyday reality. She currently campaigns for those rights for Amnesty International, Canada.

Evan Mwangi is associate professor in the English Department of Northwestern University. A journalist and university professor in both Kenya and America, he has written articles and chapters on African narrative, poetry, and drama as well as several study guides on aspects of African literature.

Peter Nazareth is professor of English and African American world studies at the University of Iowa. A novelist and critic, he has written many books and articles and edited *Critical Essays on Ngũgĩ wa Thiong'o*.

Gĩchingiri Ndĩgĩrĩgĩ is assistant professor of English and Africana studies at the University of Tennessee, Knoxville. He has been a member of the editorial board of the Gĩkũyũ-language journal *Mũtiiri*. He is author of *Ngũgĩ wa Thiong'o's Drama and the Kamĩrĩĩthũ Popular Theater Experiment*.

Ngũgĩ wa Thiong'o is distinguished professor of English literature and comparative literature at the University of California, Irvine.

Brendon Nicholls is lecturer in African and postcolonial literatures at the University of Leeds. He is the author of *Ngugi wa Thiong'o, Gender, and the Ethics of Postcolonial Reading* and *Nadine Gordimer's July's People*.

James Ogude is professor of African literature in the School of Literature and Language Studies at the University of the Witwatersrand, South Africa. He is the author of *Ngugi's Novels and African History: Narrating the Nation*. He also coedited *Urban Legends, Colonial Myths: Popular Culture and Literature in East Africa* and *Rethinking Eastern African Intellectual Landscapes*.

Bonnie Roos is associate professor of English in the Department of English, Philosophy, and Modern Languages at West Texas A&M University. Her articles have appeared in *Modernism/Modernity*, *Research in African Literatures*, and *Yale Journal of Criticism*. She is also coeditor of *Postcolonial Green: Environmental Politics and World Narratives*.

Peter Simatei is associate professor of comparative literature in the Department of Literature, Theatre, and Film at Moi University, Kenya. He is the author of *The Novel and the Politics of Nation-Building in East Africa*. He has written essays on African-Asian diaspora literatures.

Gayatri Chakravorty Spivak is University Professor at Columbia University and founding director of the Institute of Comparative Literature and Society. She is author of *A Critique of Postcolonial Reason*, *Death of a Discipline*, *Outside in the Teaching Machine*, and *An Aesthetic Education in the Era of Globalization*.

Patrick Williams is professor of literary and cultural studies and director of the Centre for Diaspora and Migration Studies at Nottingham Trent University, England. He is author of *Post-colonial African Cinema*, *Ngũgĩ wa Thiong'o*, and *Colonial Discourse and Post-colonial Theory*.

CONTRIBUTORS AND SURVEY PARTICIPANTS

Pius Adesanmi, *Carleton University*
Edna Aizenberg, *Marymount Manhattan College*
Steven M. Almquist, *University of Iowa*
Apollo O. Amoko, *University of Florida*
Michael Andindilile, *Fordam University, University of Dar es Salaam*
F. Odun Balogun, *Deleware State University*
Charles Cantalupo, *Pennsylvania State University*
Steve Gronert Ellerhoff, *Trinity College Dublin*
Ali Erritouni, *Kent State University*
Uzoma Esonwanne, *University of Toronto*
Bennett Yu-Hsiang Fu, *National Taiwan University*
Simon Gikandi, *Princeton University*
Shane Graham, *Utah State University*
Andrew Gurr, *University of Reading*
Michael Harris, *Central College*
Emilia Ilieva, *Egerton University*
Lyn Innes, *University of Kent*
Fredric Jameson, *Duke University*
W. O. Maloba, *University of Delaware*
Kate McInturff, *Gender and Peacebuilding Working Group, Peacebuild; Amnesty International*
Evan Mwangi, *Northwestern University*
Peter Nazareth, *University of Iowa*
Gĩchingiri Ndĩgĩrĩgĩ, *University of Tennessee, Knoxville*
Ngũgĩ wa Thiong'o, *University of California, Irvine*
Brendon Nicholls, *University of Leeds*
Susie O'Brien, *McMaster University*
Bernard Joseph O'Donnell, Jr., *University of Florida*
James Ogude, *University of the Witwatersrand*
Garnette Oluoch-Olunya, *Kenyatta University*
Bonnie Roos, *West Texas A&M University*
Peter Simatei, *Moi University*
William Slaymaker, *Wayne State College*
Gayatri Chakravorty Spivak, *Columbia University*
Helen Tiffin, *University of Tasmania*
Senorina Musanga Wendoh, *University of Nairobi*
Patrick Williams, *Nottingham Trent University*

WORKS CITED

Achebe, Chinua. *Anthills of the Savannah*. New York: Anchor, 1987. Print.

———. "The Novelist as Teacher." *Hopes and Impediments: Selected Essays*. New York: Doubleday, 1988. 40–46. Print.

———. *Things Fall Apart*. London: Heinemann, 1958. Print.

Adesanmi, Pius. "Africa, India, and the Postcolonial: Notes towards a Praxis of Infliction." *Arena Journal* 21 (2004): 173–96. Print.

Ahmad, Aijaz. "Jameson's Rhetoric of Otherness and the 'National Allegory.' " *Social Text* 17 (1987): 3–25. Rpt. in *In Theory: Classes, Nations, Literatures*. London: Verso, 1992. 95–122. Print.

Aidoo, Ama Ata. *Our Sister Killjoy; or, Reflections from a Black-Eyed Squint*. London: Longman, 1977. Print. African Creative Writing Ser.

Ajayi, Ade. "The Continuity of African Institutions under Colonialism." *Emerging Themes of African History*. Ed. T. O. Ranger. Nairobi: East African, 1968. 189–200. Print.

Amoko, Apollo Obonyo. *Postcolonialism in the Wake of the Nairobi Revolution: Ngugi wa Thiong'o and the Idea of African Literature*. New York: Palgrave-Macmillan, 2010. Print.

———. "The Resemblance of Colonial Mimicry: A Revisionary Reading of Ngũgĩ wa Thiong'o's *The River Between*." *Research in African Literatures* 36.1 (2005): 34–50. Print.

Amuta, Chidi. *The Theory of African Literature: Implications for Practical Criticism*. London: Zed, 1989. Print.

Anderson, David. *Histories of the Hanged: The Dirty War in Kenya and the End of Empire*. New York: Norton, 2005. Print.

Anonby, John A. *The Kenyan Epic Novelist Ngũgĩ: His Secular Reconfiguration of Biblical Themes*. Lewiston: Mellen, 2007. Print.

Appiah, Kwame Anthony. *In My Father's House: Africa in the Philosophy of Culture*. Oxford: Oxford UP, 1993. Print.

Appiah, Kwame Anthony, and Henry Louis Gates, Jr., eds. *Africana: The Encyclopedia of the African and African American Experience*. 2nd ed. New York: Oxford UP, 2005. Print.

Arendt, Hannah. *On Violence*. San Diego: Harcourt, 1970. Print.

Aristotle. *Poetics*. Ed. D. A. Russell and M. Winterbottom. *Classical Literary Criticism*. Oxford: Oxford UP, 1972. 51–90. Print.

Arnold, Guy. *Kenyatta and the Politics of Kenya*. London: Dent, 1974. Print.

Ashcroft, Bill, Gareth Griffiths, and Helen Tiffin, eds. *The Post-colonial Studies Reader*. London: Routledge, 1995. Print.

Bâ, Mariama. *So Long a Letter*. Portsmouth: Heinemann, 1981. Print.

Bakhtin, Mikhail. *The Dialogic Imagination*. Trans. Caryl Emerson and Michael Holquist. Austin: U of Texas P, 1981. Print.

———. *Rabelais and His World*. Trans. Helene Iswolsky. Bloomington: Indiana UP, 1984. Print.

Balogun, F. Odun. "Naturalist Proletarian Prose Epics: *Petals of Blood* and *Grapes of Wrath*." *Journal of English* [Sana'a U] Sept. 1983: 88–106. Print.

———. *Ngũgĩ and African Postcolonial Narrative: The Novel as Oral Narrative in Multigenre Performance*. Quebec: World Heritage, 1997. Print.

———. "Ngũgĩ's *Matigari* and the Refiguration of the Novel as Genre." Cantalupo, *World* 185–96.

Bardolph, Jacqueline. "Ngugi wa Thiong'o's *A Grain of Wheat* and *Petals of Blood* as Readings of Conrad's *Under Western Eyes* and *Victory*." *Conradian* 12 (1987): 32–49. Print.

Barnett, Donald L., and Karari Njama. *Mau Mau from Within: Autobiography and Analysis of Kenya's Peasant Revolt*. New York: Monthly Rev., 1966. Print.

Benjamin, Walter. "Theses on the Philosophy of History." *Illuminations*. Ed. Hannah Arendt. Trans. Harry Zohn. New York: Harcourt, 1955. 255–66. Print.

Benson, T. G. *English-Kikuyu Dictionary*. Oxford: Oxford UP, 1975. Print.

———. *Kikuyu-English Dictionary*. Oxford: Oxford UP, 1964. Print.

Berman, Bruce, and John Lonsdale. *Unhappy Valley: Conflict in Kenya and Africa*. London: Currey, 1992. Print.

Biersteker, Ann. "Gĩkũyũ Literature: Development from Early Christian Writing to Ngũgĩ's Later Novels." *The Cambridge History of African and Caribbean Literature*. Ed. F. Abiola Irele and Simon Gikandi. Cambridge: Cambridge UP, 2004. 306–28. Print.

———. "*Matigari ma Njirũũngi:* What Grows from Leftover Seeds of 'Chat' Trees?" Cantalupo, *World* 141–58.

Boahen, Adu. *African Perspectives on Colonialism*. Baltimore: Johns Hopkins UP, 1987. Print.

Boehmer, Elleke. "The Master's Dance to the Master's Voice: Revolutionary Nationalism and the Representation of Women in the Writing of Ngũgĩ wa Thiong'o." *Journal of Commonwealth Literature* 26.1 (1991): 188–97. Rpt. in *Postcolonial Literatures: Achebe, Ngũgĩ, Desai, Walcott*. Ed. Michael Parker and Roger Starkey. Houndmills: Macmillan, 1995. 143–54. Print.

Boland, Eavan. "Daughters of the Colony: A Personal Interpretation of the Place of Gender Issues in the Postcolonial Interpretation of Irish Literature." *Eire-Ireland* 32.2–3 (1997): 9–20. Print.

Booth, Wayne C. *The Rhetoric of Fiction*. 2nd ed. Chicago: U of Chicago P, 1983. Print.

Boyarin, Jonathan. "Space, Time, and the Politics of Memory." *Remapping Memory: The Politics of TimeSpace*. Ed. Boyarin. Minneapolis: U of Minnesota P, 1994. 1–38. Print.

Breidlid, Anders. *Resistance and Consciousness in Kenya and South Africa: Subalternity and Representation in the Novels of Ngũgĩ wa Thiong'o and Alex La Guma*. New York: Lang, 2002. Print.

Breytenbach, Breyten. "An Afrikaner Trapped in No Man's Land." Interview by James Wood. *Guardian Weekly* 9 Jan. 1994: 28. Print.

———. *The True Confessions of an Albino Terrorist*. London: Faber, 1984. Print.

Brown, Nicholas. *Utopian Generations: The Political Horizon of Twentieth-Century Literature*. Princeton: Princeton UP, 2005. Print.

Brutus, Dennis. *"Letters to Martha" and Other Poems from a South African Prison*. London: Heinemann, 1968. Print.

Bullock, Jim. *Bowers Row: Recollections of a Mining Village*. Wakefield: EP, 1976. Print.

Bunche, Ralph Johnson. "The Irua Ceremony among the Kikuyu of Kiambu District, Kenya." *Journal of Negro History* 26.1 (1941): 46–65. Print.

Bunyan, John. *Grace Abounding to the Chief of Sinners*. London: Oxford UP, 1966. Print.

———. *The Pilgrim's Progress*. Oxford: Oxford UP, 1966. Print

Byrd, Christine. "UCI Professor Ngugi wa Thiong'o Publishes Long-Awaited Novel." *UC Newsroom*. U of California, 7 Aug. 2006. Web. 16 Sept. 2011.

Campbell, Joseph. *The Power of Myth*. New York: Doubleday, 1988. Print.

Camus, Albert. *The Plague*. Trans. Stuart Gilbert. New York: Vintage, 1991. Print.

"Can Ngũgĩ's Writings 'Sow' a Grain of Peace in Learning Institutions?" *Sunday Nation* 15 Aug. 2004, Lifestyle: 12. Print.

Cantalupo, Charles, ed. *Ngũgĩ wa Thiong'o: Texts and Contexts*. Trenton: Africa World, 1995. Print.

———, ed. *The World of Ngũgĩ wa Thiong'o*. Trenton: Africa World, 1995. Print.

Carlson, Marvin. *Theater Semiotics: Signs of Life*. Bloomington: Indiana UP, 1990. Print.

Carothers, J. C. *The Psychology of the Mau Mau*. Nairobi: Government Printer, 1954. Print.

Chakava, Henry. "Publishing Ngũgĩ: The Challenge, the Risk, and the Reward." Cantalupo, *Ngũgĩ* 13–28.

Chakrabarty, Dipesh. "Postcoloniality and the Artifice of History: Who Speaks for Indian Pasts?" *Representations* 37 (1992): 1–26. Print.

Chaliand, Gérard. *Revolution in the Third World*. New York: Viking, 1989. Print.

Cheah, Pheng. "Given Culture: Rethinking Cosmopolitical Freedom in Transnationalism." *Cosmopolitics: Thinking and Feeling beyond the Nation*. Ed. Cheah and Bruce Robbins. Minneapolis: U of Minnesota P, 1998. 290–328. Print.

———. *Spectral Nationality: Passages of Freedom from Kant to Postcolonial Literatures of Liberation*. New York: Columbia UP, 2003. Print.

Chinweizu. *The West and the Rest of Us*. New York: Random, 1975. Print.

Clark, John Pepper. "The Legacy of Caliban." *Black Orpheus* 2.1 (1968): 16–39. Print.

Cochrane, Judith. "Women as Guardians of the Tribe in Ngũgĩ's Novels." Killam, *Critical Perspectives* 90–100.

Conrad, Joseph. *"Heart of Darkness" and Other Tales*. Ed. Cedric Thomas Watts. Oxford: Oxford UP, 1998. Print.

———. *Lord Jim*. London: Blackwood, 1900. Print.

———. *Nostromo*. London: Dent, 1960. Print.

———. *Under Western Eyes*. London: Penguin, 1999. Print.

Cook, Michael, and Michael Okenimkpe. *Ngũgĩ wa Thiong'o: An Exploration of His Writings*. 2nd ed. Oxford: Currey, 1983. Print.

Dangarembga, Tsitsi. *Nervous Conditions.* Seattle: Seal, 1988. Print.

Davidson, Basil. *Africa.* Chicago: Home Vision, 1984. Videocassette.

———. *The People's Cause: A History of Guerrillas in Africa*. Harlow: Longman, 1981. Print.

Davies, Carole Boyce, and Anne Adams Graves, eds. *Ngambika: Studies of Women in African Literature*. Trenton: Africa World, 1986. Print.

Davies, Ioan. *Writers in Prison*. Toronto: Between the Lines, 1990. Print.

De Marinis, Marco. "Dramaturgy of the Spectator." *TDR: The Drama Review* 31.2 (1987): 100–14. Print.

Derrida, Jacques. "Signature: Event: Context." *Limited Inc*. Evanston: Northwestern UP, 1988. 1–23. Print.

De Soto, Hernando. *The Mystery of Capital: Why Capitalism Triumphs in the West and Fails Everywhere Else*. New York: Basic, 2000. Print.

Dimov, Dimitar. Тютюн [Tobacco]. Sofia: Balgarski Pisatel, 1974. Print. Vols. 2 and 3 of Събрани съчинения в пет тома [Collected Works in Five Volumes].

Dirks, Nicholas. "Introduction: Colonialism and Culture." *Colonialism and Culture*. Ed. Dirks. Ann Arbor: U of Michigan P, 1992. 1–25. Print.

Dirlik, Arif. "The Postcolonial Aura: Third World Criticism in the Age of Global Capitalism." *Critical Inquiry* 20.2 (1994): 328–56. Print.

Downing, John, ed. *Film and Politics in the Third World*. New York: Autonomedia, 1987. Print.

Dramé, Kandioura. *The Novel as Transformation Myth: A Study of the Novels of Mongo Beti and Ngũgĩ wa Thiong'o*. Syracuse: Maxwell School of Citizenship and Public Affairs, Syracuse U, 1990. Print.

Eco, Umberto. *The Role of the Reader: Explorations in the Semiotics of Texts.* Bloomington: Indiana UP, 1979. Print.

"Editors' Introduction." *Rethinking Marxism* 19.3 (2007): 291–97. Print.

Egan, Susanna. "Breytenbach's *Mouroir*: The Novel as Autobiography." *Journal of Narrative Technique* 18.2 (1988): 89–104. Print.

Ekeh, Peter. "Colonialism and the Two Publics in Africa: A Theoretical Statement." *Comparative Studies in Society and History* 17.1 (1975): 91–112. Print.

Elkins, Caroline. *Imperial Reckoning: The Untold Story of Britain's Gulag in Kenya* New York: Henry Holt, 2005. Print.

Evans, Jennifer. "Mother Africa and the Heroic Whore: Female Images in *Petals of Blood*." *Contemporary African Literature*. Ed. Hal Wylie, Eileen Julien, and Russell J. Linnemann. Washington: Three Continents, 1983. 57–65. Print.

———. "Women and Resistance in Ngũgĩ's *Devil on the Cross*." *African Literature Today* 15 (1987): 131–39. Print.

Fanon, Frantz. *Black Skin, White Masks*. Trans. Charles Lam Markmann. New York: Grove, 1967. Print.

———. "The Pitfalls of National Consciousness." Fanon, *Wretched* 148–205.

———. *The Wretched of the Earth*. Trans. Constance Farrington. New York: Grove, 1963. Print.

Felman, Shoshana, and Dori Laub. *Testimony: Crisis of Witnessing in Literature, Psychoanalysis, and History*. New York: Routledge, 1992. Print.

Foucault, Michel. *Discipline and Punish*. Trans. Alan Sheridan. New York: Vintage, 1979. Print.

———. "What Is an Author?" *Language, Counter-memory, Practice: Selected Essays and Interviews*. Ed. Donald F. Bouchard. Trans. Bouchard and Sherry Simon. Ithaca: Cornell UP, 1977. 113–38. Print.

Fox, Claire. "Writing Africa with Another Alphabet: Conrad and Abish." *Conradiana* 22.2 (1990): 111–25. Print.

Fox, Robert Elliot. Rev. of *Poems of Black Africa*, by Wole Soyinka. *African Literature Today: 11 Myth and History*. Ed. Eldred Durosimi Jones. London: Heinemann, 1980. 209–12. Print.

Freire, Paolo. *Pedagogy of the Oppressed*. New York: Continuum. 1993. Print.

Furedi, Frank. *The Mau Mau War in Perspective*. London: Currey, 1989. Print.

Ghai, Yash Pal. "It's Not Enough to Ethnicise Reforms." *Standard* 24 Aug. 2008: 16. Print.

Gikandi, Simon. "Moments of Melancholy: Ngũgĩ and the Discourse of Emotions." Cantalupo, *World* 59–72.

———. *Ngũgĩ wa Thiong'o*. Cambridge: Cambridge UP, 2000. Print.

———. "The Postcolonial Wizard." *Transition: An International Review* 98 (2008): 156–69. Print.

———. "Round Table: The Epistemology of Translation: Ngũgĩ, *Matigari*, and the Politics of Language." *Research in African Literatures* 22.4 (1991): 161–67. Print.

Gilroy, Paul. *The Black Atlantic: Modernity and Double Consciousness*. Cambridge: Harvard UP, 1993. Print.

Gĩtĩtĩ, Gĩtahi. "Recuperating a Disappearing Art-Form: Resonances of Gĩcandĩ in Ngũgĩ wa Thiong'o's *Devil on the Cross*." Cantalupo, *World* 109–28.

Glenn, Ian. "Ngũgĩ wa Thiong'o and the Dilemmas of the Intellectual Elite in Africa: A Sociological Perspective." *English in Africa* 8.2 (1981): 53–66. Print.

Gordon, David. "Mau Mau and Decolonization: Kenya and the Defeat of Multi-racialism in East and Central Africa." *Kenya Historical Review* 5 1 (1977): 329–48. Print.

Greenfield, Kathleen. "Murdering the Sleep of Dictators: Corruption, Betrayal, and the Call to Revolution in the Works of Ngũgĩ wa Thiong'o." Cantalupo, *World* 27–43.

Gugler, Josef. "How Ngũgĩ wa Thiong'o Shifted from Class Analysis to a Neo-colonist Perspective." *Journal of African Studies* 32.2 (1994): 329–39. Print.

Habila, Helon. *Waiting for an Angel*. New York: Norton, 2002. Print.

Hall, Stuart. "When Was the Post-colonial? Thinking at the Limit." *The Post-colonial Question: Common Skies, Divided Horizons*. Ed. Iain Chambers and Lidia Curti. London: Routledge, 1996. 242–60. Print.

Harris, Wendell V. *Literary Meaning: Reclaiming the Study of Literature.* New York: New York UP, 1996. Print.

Hegel, Wilhelm Friedrich. *The Philosophy of History*. 1899. Trans. J. Sibree. New York: Dover, 1956. Print.

Hellman, David. "Allegory of Post-colonial Africa Takes Flight." Rev. of *Wizard of the Crow,* by Ngũgĩ wa Thiong'o. *San Francisco Chronicle*. SFGate.com, 13 Aug. 2006. Web. 17 Sept. 2011.

Henderson, Ian, and Philip Goodhart. *The Hunt for Dedan Kimathi.* London: Hamilton, 1958. Print.

Hobsbawm, Eric. "Inventing Traditions." Hobsbawm and Ranger 1–14.

Hobsbawm, Eric, and Terence Ranger, eds. *The Invention of Tradition*. Cambridge: Cambridge UP, 1983. Print.

Howe, Irving. *Politics and the Novel*. Morningside ed. New York: Columbia UP, 1987. Print.

Innes, C. L. *The Cambridge Introduction to Postcolonial Literatures*. Cambridge: Cambridge UP, 2007. Print.

Irele, Abiola. *The African Experience in Literature and Ideology*. London: Heinemann, 1981. Print.

———. *The African Imagination: Literature in Africa and the Black Diaspora*. Oxford: Oxford UP, 2001. Print.

Irigaray, Luce. "Women-amongst-Themselves: Creating a Woman to Woman Sociality." *The Irigaray Reader*. Ed. Margaret Whitford. Malden: Blackwell, 1991. 190–97. Print.

Isegawa, Moses. *Abyssinian Chronicles*. New York: Vintage, 2000. Print.

Iser, Wolfgang. "Do I Write for an Audience?" *PMLA* 115.3 (2000): 310–14. Print.

Jacobs, J. U. "Breyten Breytenbach and the South African Prison Book." *Theoria* 68 (1986): 95–105. Print.

———. "Confession, Interrogation and Self-Interrogation in the New South African Prison Writing." *Kunapipi* 13.1–2 (1991): 115–27. Print.

Jameson, Fredric. *Postmodernism; or, The Cultural Logic of Late Capitalism*. London: Verso, 1991. Print.

———. *Situations of Theory.* London: Routledge, 1998. Print. Vol. 1 of *The Ideologies of Theory: Essays, 1971–1986.*

———. "Third-World Literature in the Era of Multinational Capitalism." *Social Text* 15 (1986): 65–88. Print.

JanMohamed, Abdul. "Ngugi wa Thiong'o: The Problems of Communal Regeneration." *Manichean Aesthetics: The Politics of Literature in Colonial Africa*. Amherst: U of Massachusetts P, 1983. 185–223. Print.

Jean Juarès. Wikiquote, 6 Mar. 2011. Web. 3 Apr. 2012.

Jeyifo, Biodun. "The Nature of Things: Arrested Decolonization and Critical Theory." *Research in African Literature* 21.1 (1990): 33–46. Print.

Jones, Eldred Durosimi. *The Writing of Wole Soyinka*. 3rd ed. London: Currey, 1988. Print.

Kabira, Mũkabi Wanjikũ, and Karega Mutahi. *Gĩkũyũ Oral Literature*. Nairobi: Heinemann, 1988. Print.

Kacandes, Irene. *Talk Fiction: Literature and the Talk Explosion*. Lincoln: U of Nebraska P, 2001. Print.

Kagumba-Sibanda, Phoebe. "Kenyan Professor Wins Hearts in Canada." *Standard* 27 July 2008, Sunday Magazine: 12–13. Print.

Kagwanja, Peter Mwangi. "Facing Mount Kenya or Facing Mecca? The Mungiki, Ethnic Violence, and the Politics of the Moi Succession in Kenya, 1987–2002." *African Affairs* 102 (2003): 25–49. Print.

———. "'Power to Uhuru': Youth Identity and Generational Politics in Kenya's 2002 Elections." *African Affairs* 105.4 (2006): 51–75. Print.

Kalu, Antonia. "African Literature and the Traditional Arts: Speaking Art, Molding Theory." *Research in African Literatures* 31.4 (2000): 48–62. Print.

Kamau, Kiarie. "A Mellowed Ngũgĩ? Writer Is Still As Critical As Ever." *Sunday Nation* 16 Sept. 2007, Lifestyle: 12. Print.

Kanogo, Tabitha. *Squatters and the Roots of Mau Mau, 1905–63*. London: Currey, 1987. Print.

Kariuki, Josiah Mwangi. *"Mau Mau" Detainee: The Account by a Kenya African of His Experiences in Detention Camps, 1953–60*. Harmondsworth: Penguin, 1964. Print.

Kasanga, Luanga A., and Mambo Kalume. "The Use of Indigenized Forms of English in Ngũgĩ's *Devil on the Cross*: A Linguistic and Sociolinguistic Analysis." *African Languages and Cultures* 9.1 (1996): 43–69. Print.

"Kenyans Still Afraid of Ngũgĩ Books." *Saturday Nation* 21 Aug. 2004: 3. Print.

Kenyatta, Jomo. *Facing Mount Kenya: The Tribal Life of the Gikuyu*. New York: Vintage, 1962. Print.

Kershaw, Greet. *Mau Mau from Below*. Oxford: Currey, 1997. Print.

Kibicho, Charles, and Peter Karanja. "Conference Covenant." *Sunday Nation* 24 Aug. 2008: 43. Print. Address at National Pastors' Conf., 20–23 Aug. 2008.

Killam, G. D., ed. *Critical Perspectives on Ngugi wa Thiong'o*. Washington: Three Continents, 1984. Print.

———. *An Introduction to the Writings of Ngũgĩ*. London: Heinemann, 1980. Print.

Ki-Zerbo, Joseph. "African Intellectuals, Nationalism, and Pan-Africanism: A Testimony." Mkandawire 78–93.

Koff, David. *Mau Mau*. Dir. Anthony Howarth and Koff. Anthony David Productions, 1979. Videocassette. Part 2 of *The Black Man's Land Trilogy*.

Kujumdzhiev, Krastjo. "Димитър Димов и неговият роман" [Dimitar Dimov and His Novel]. Поручик Бенц [and] Осъдени души [Lieutenant Benz (and) Doomed Souls]. Sofia: Balgarski Pisatel, 1974. 5–31. Print. Vol. 1 of Димитър Димов: Съчинения в пет тома [Dimitar Dimov: Collected Works in Five Volumes].

Kumar, Amitava. Introduction. Kumar, *World Bank Literature* xvii–xxxiii.

———, ed. *World Bank Literature*. Minneapolis: U of Minnesota P, 2003. Print.

Kunene, Daniel P. "African Language Literature: Tragedy and Hope." *Research in African Literatures* 23.1 (1992): 7–15. Print.

Kurtz, J. Roger. "Ngũgĩ wa Thiong'o." *British Writers: Supplement 8*. Ed. Jay Parini. New York: Scribner's, 2003. *Literature Resource Center*. Gale Cengage Learning, n.d. Web. 17 Sept. 2011.

Kurtz, Stanley. Testimony before the Subcommittee on Select Educ., Comm. on Educ. and the Workforce, US House of Representatives. 19 June 2003. Web. 17 Sept. 2011.

La Guma, Alex. *The Stone Country*. London: Heinemann, 1974. Print.

Laitin, David D. "Can Language Be Planned?" *Transition* 54 (1991): 131–41. Print.

Lamming, George. *In the Castle of My Skin*. New York: Longman, 1979. Print.

LaPin, Deirdre. "Women in African Literature." *African Women South of the Sahara*. Ed. Margaret Jean Hay and Sharon Stichter. Harlow: Longman, 1984. 102–18. Print.

Larson, Charles R. *The Emergence of African Fiction*. Bloomington: Indiana UP, 1971. Print.

Lazarus, Neil. *Resistance in Postcolonial African Fiction*. New Haven: Yale UP, 1990. Print.

———. "(Re)turn to the People: Ngũgĩ wa Thiong'o and the Crisis of Postcolonial African Intellectualism." Cantalupo, *World* 11–26.

Leigh, Ione. *In the Shadow of the Mau Mau*. London: Allen, 1954. Print.

Levi, Primo. *Survival in Auschwitz*. Trans. Stuart Woolf. New York: Collier, 1961. Print

Levin, Tobe. "Women as Scapegoats of Culture and Cult: An Activist's View of Female Circumcision in Ngũgĩ's *The River Between*." Davies and Graves 205–22.

Leys, Colin. *Underdevelopment in Kenya: The Political Economy of Neo-colonialism, 1964–1971*. Berkeley: U of California P, 1974. Print.

Lindfors, Bernth. "Ngũgĩ wa Thiong'o's Early Journalism." *World Literature Written in English* 20 (1981): 23–41. Print.

Lindfors, Bernth, and Bala Kothandaraman, eds. *The Writer as Activist: South Asian Perspectives on Ngũgĩ wa Thiong'o*. Trenton: Africa World, 2001. Print.

Little, Kenneth. *African Women in Towns: An Aspect of Africa's Social Revolution*. London: Cambridge UP, 1973. Print.

Loflin, Christine. "Ngũgĩ wa Thiong'o's Visions of Africa." Nazareth, *Critical Essays* 261–80.

Lonsdale, John. "The Moral Economy of Mau Mau: Wealth, Poverty, and Civic Virtue in Kikuyu Political Thought." *Violence and Ethnicity*. Ed. Bruce Berman and Lonsdale. Athens: Ohio UP, 1992. 315–504. Print. Bk. 2 of *Unhappy Valley: Conflict in Kenya and Africa*.

Lovesey, Oliver. "Initiation for the Nation: Ngũgĩ wa Thiong'o's Njamba Nene Series." *Voices of the Other: Children's Literature and the Postcolonial Context*. Ed. Rod McGillis. New York: Garland, 1999. 193–210. Print.

———. "I Will Marry When I Want." *Modern African Drama*. Ed. Biodun Jeyifo. New York: Norton, 2002. 611–14. Print. Norton Critical Ed.

———. *Ngũgĩ wa Thiong'o*. New York: Twayne, 2000. Print.

———. "Ngũgĩ wa Thiong'o's Postnation: The Cultural Geographies of Colonial, Neocolonial, and Postnational Space." *Modern Fiction Studies* 48.1 (2002): 139–68.

Rpt. in *Postcolonial Literary Studies: The First Thirty Years*. Ed. Robert P. Marzec. Baltimore: Johns Hopkins UP, 2011. 199–224. Print.

Luttwak, Edward. *Coup d'État: A Practical Handbook*. London: Penguin, 1968. Print.

Lyons, Harriet D. "Genital Cutting: The Past and Present of a Polythetic Category." *Africa Today* 53.5 (2007): 3–17. Print.

Maathai, Wangari. *Unbowed*. New York: Knopf, 2006. Print.

Maduakor, Obi. *Wole Soyinka: An Introduction to His Writing*. New York: Garland, 1986. Print.

Magubane, Zine, ed. *Postmodernism, Postcoloniality, and African Studies*. Trenton: Africa World, 2003. Print.

Maina wa Kinyatti, ed. *Kenya's Freedom Struggle: The Dedan Kimathi Papers*. London: Zed, 1987. Print

Maloba, W. O. *African Women in Revolution*. Trenton: Africa World, 2007. Print.

———. *Mau Mau and Kenya: An Analysis of a Peasant Revolt*. Bloomington: Indiana UP, 1998. Print.

Mapanje, Jack. "Where Dissent Is Meat for Crocodiles." *The Chattering Wagtails of Mikuyu Prison*. Oxford: Heinemann, 1993. 80–81. Print.

Marsh, Zoe, and G. W. Kingsnorth. *A History of East Africa: An Introductory Survey*. Cambridge: Cambridge UP, 1972. Print.

Marx, Karl. *The Eighteenth Brumaire of Louis Bonaparte*. New York: Intl., 1998. Print.

Marx, Karl, and Friedrich Engels. *The Holy Family; or, Critique of Critical Criticism*. 1845. Trans. Richard Dixon and Clement Dutts. *Marx and Engels Internet Archive*. Marxists Internet Archive, n.d. Web. 11 July 2012.

Maughan-Brown, David. *Land, Freedom, and Fiction: History and Ideology in Kenya*. London: Zed, 1985. Print.

Mazrui, Ali Al-Amin. *The Africans: A Triple Heritage*. WETA and BBC, 1986. Videocassette.

———. "Ideology, Theory, and Revolution: Lessons from the Mau Mau." *Race and Class* 28.4 (1987): 53–61. Print.

Mbembe, Achille. "Provisional Notes on the Postcolony." *Public Culture* 4.2 (1992): 1–30. Print.

Mbure, Sam. "Ngũgĩ wa Thiong'o and the Young Poet." Cantalupo, *Ngũgĩ* 29–32.

McClintock, Anne. "The Angel of Progress: Pitfalls of the Term 'Post-colonialism.'" *Colonial Discourse and Post-colonial Theory: A Reader*. Ed. Patrick Williams and Laura Chrisman. New York: Columbia UP, 1994. 291–99, 302–03. Print.

McLaren, Joseph. "Ideology and Form: The Critical Reception of *Petals of Blood*." Cantalupo, *World* 73–91.

Michaud, André-Paul. "Nature as Agency in Ngũgĩ's *The River Between*." Nazareth, *Critical Essays* 48–63.

Miller, J. Hillis. *The Ethics of Reading: Kant, de Man, Eliot, Trollope, James, and Benjamin*. New York: Columbia UP, 1987. Print.

Mitchell, Timothy. "The Object of Development: America's Egypt." *The Power of Development*. Ed. Jonathan Crush. New York: Routledge, 1995. 129–57. Print.

Mkandawire, Thandika, ed. *African Intellectuals: Rethinking Politics, Language, Gender, and Development*. Dakar: CODESERIA; London: Zed, 2005. Print.

Moolaadé. Dir. Sembène Ousmane. Perf. Fatoumata Coulibaly, Maimouna Hélène Diarra, and Salimata Traoré. Ciné-Sud Promotion and New Yorker Films, 2004. Film.

Morris, Richard B. "Confessions of a Scholar Seeking a Wider Audience." *Wisconsin Magazine of History* 63.4 (1980): 299–308. Print.

Mudimbe, V. Y. *The Invention of Africa: Gnosis, Philosophy, and the Order of Knowledge*. Bloomington: Indiana UP, 1988. Print.

Muriuki, Godfrey. *A History of the Kikuyu, 1500–1900*. Nairobi: Oxford UP, 1974. Print.

Murphy, David. *Sembene: Imagining Alternatives in Film and Fiction*. Oxford: Currey, 2000. Print.

Mutahi, Karega. "Language of Oral Literature." Kenya Oral Literature Seminar, Nairobi, 1991. MS.

Mwangi, Evan. *Africa Writes Back to Self: Metafiction, Gender, Sexuality*. Albany: State U of New York P, 2009. Print.

———. "Ngũgĩ at Seventy: Reminiscences of an African Literary Icon." *Sunday Nation* 31 Aug. 2008, Lifestyle: 2. Print.

Nama, Charles. "Daughters of Moombi: Ngũgĩ's Heroines and Traditional Gikuyu Aesthetics." Davies and Graves 139–50.

National Defense Education Act of 1958. Federal Education Policy History. Kevin R. Kosar, 3 June 2011. Web. 17 Sept. 2011.

National Security Education Program: Report to the United States Congress: September 2003. Natl. Security Educ. Program, 26 Aug. 2003. Web. 18 Sept. 2011.

Natsoulas, Theodore. "The Politicization of the Ban on Female Circumcision and the Rise of the Independent School Movement in Kenya: The KCA, the Missions, and Government, 1929–1932." *Journal of Asian and African Studies* 33.2 (1998): 137–58. Print.

Nazareth, Peter. "Conrad's Descendants." *Conradiana* 22.2 (1990): 101–09. Print.

———, ed. *Critical Essays on Ngũgĩ wa Thiong'o*. New York: Twayne, 2000. Print

———. "Dark Heart or Trickster?" *Korean Society of Nineteenth Century Literature in English* 9.3 (2005): 291–321. Print.

———. *The General Is Up*. Toronto: TSAR, 1991. Print.

———. *In a Brown Mantle*. Nairobi: Kenya Lit. Bureau, 1981. Print.

———. "International Players, Footballs, and Penalties." *Uganda South Asians Exodus Kololian Perspectives*. Ed. Narendra Wagle, Nazareth, Zulema de Souza, and Bina Mehta. Toronto: U of Toronto P, 2002. 1–11. Print.

———. "Introduction: Saint Ngũgĩ." Nazareth, *Critical Essays* 1–16.

———. *Literature and Society in Modern Africa*. Kampala: East African Lit. Bureau, 1972. Print. Also published as *An African View of Literature*. Evanston: Northwestern UP, 1974.

———. "Obituary Tova Raz." *Confluence* 5.5 (2006): 10. Print.

Ndĩgĩrĩgĩ, Gĩchingiri. "Character Names and Types in Ngũgĩ's *Devil on the Cross*." *Ufahamu* 9.3 (1991): 96–111. Print.

———. *Ngũgĩ wa Thiong'o's Drama and the Kamĩrĩĩthũ Popular Theater Experiment*. Trenton: Africa World, 2007. Print.

Neuman, Shirley. "Autobiography: From Different Poetics to a Poetics of Difference." *Essays on Life Writing: From Genre to Critical Practice*. Ed. Marlene Kadar. Toronto: U of Toronto P, 1992. 213–30. Print.

Newman, J. R. *The Ukamba Members Association*. Nairobi: Transafrica, 1974. Print. Transafrica Historical Papers 3.

Ngau, Peter M. "Tensions in Empowerment: The Experience of the 'Harambee' (Self-Help) Movement in Kenya." *Economic Development and Cultural Change* 35.3 (1987): 523–38. Print.

"Ngũgĩ: Let the Grain Sprout." *Saturday Nation* 31 July 2004: 8. Print.

Ngũgĩ wa Thiong'o. *Barrel of a Pen: Resistance to Repression in Neo-colonial Kenya*. London: New Beacon, 1983. Print.

———. *Baathitoora ya Njamba Nene* [*Njamba Nene's Pistol*]. Nairobi: Heinemann, 1984. Print.

———. "Beyond Nativism: An Interview with Ngũgĩ wa Thiong'o." By Ângela Lamas Rodrigues. *Research in African Literatures* 35.3 (2004): 161–67. Print.

———. *The Black Hermit*. Oxford: Heinemann, 1968. Print.

———. "Borders and Bridges: Seeking Connections between Things." *The Pre-occupation of Postcolonial Studies*. Ed. Fawzia Afzal-Khan and Kalpana Seshadri-Crooks. Durham: Duke UP, 2000. 119–25. Print.

———. *Caitaani Mũtharaba-inĩ* [*Devil on the Cross*]. Nairobi: East African Educ., 1980. Print.

———. "A Conversation with Ngũgĩ wa Thiong'o." Interview by D. Venkat Rao. Lindfors and Kothandaraman 157–67.

———. *Decolonising the Mind: The Politics of Language in African Literature*. Oxford: Currey, 1986. Print.

———. *Detained: A Writer's Prison Diary*. London: Heinemann, 1981. Print.

———. *Devil on the Cross*. Trans. Ngũgĩ. Oxford: Heinemann, 1982. Print.

———. *Dreams in a Time of War: A Childhood Memoir*. New York: Pantheon, 2010. Print.

———. "Enactments of Power: The Politics of Performance Space." Ngũgĩ, *Penpoints* 37–70.

———. "Europhone or African Memory: The Challenge of the Pan-Africanist Intellectual in the Era of Globalization." Mkandawire 155–64.

———. "Europhonism, Universities, and the Magic Fountain: The Future of African Literature and Scholarship." *Research in African Literatures* 31.1 (2000): 1–11. Print.

———. "For Peace, Justice, and Culture: The Intellectual in the Twenty-First Century." *Profession* (2006): 33–39. Print.

———. *Globalectics: Theory and the Politics of Knowing*. New York: Columbia UP, 2012. Print.

———. *A Grain of Wheat*. Rev. ed. London: Heinemann, 1986. Print.

———. *Homecoming: Essays on African and Caribbean Literature, Culture, and Politics*. London: Heinemann, 1972. Print.

———. Interview. *Weekly Review* (Nairobi) 9 Jan. 1978: 10. Print.

———. "An Interview with Ngugi wa Thiong'o." By Jacqueline Bardolph and Jean-Pierre Durix. Ngũgĩ, *Ngũgĩ wa Thiong'o Speaks* 157–65.

———. "Interview with Ngũgĩ wa Thiong'o." By Jurgen Martini et al. *Kunapipi* 3.2 (1981): 131–40. Print.

———. "Interview with Ngũgĩ wa Thiong'o." By Bettye J. Parker. Killam, *Critical Perspectives* 58–66.

———. "The Language of Struggle." *Transition* 54 (1991): 142–54. Print.

———. *Matigari*. Trans. Wangũi wa Goro. Oxford: Heinemann, 1987. Print.

———. "*Matigari* as Myth and History: An Interview." By Maya Jaggi. *Third World Quarterly* 11.4 (1984): 241–51. Print.

———. *Matigari ma Njirũũngi*. Nairobi: East African Educ., 1986. Print.

———. *Moving the Centre: The Struggle for Cultural Freedoms*. London: Currey, 1993. Print.

———. *Mũrogi wa Kagogo*. 3 vols. Nairobi: East African Educ., 2004–07. Print. Vol. 1 subtitle: *Mbuku ya Mbere na Kerĩ*; vol. 2 subtitle: *Mbuku ya Gatatũ*; vol. 3 subtitle: *Mbuku ya Kana, Gatano, Gatandatũ*.

———. "Ngũgĩ wa Thiong'o in Conversation." Interview by Harish Trivedi and Wangũi wa Goro. Ngũgĩ, *Ngũgĩ wa Thiong'o Speaks* 399–413.

———. "Ngugi wa Thiong'o Interviewed on His New Novel, *Wizard of the Crow*." *Socialist Worker Online*. Socialist Worker, 4 Nov. 2006. Web. 28 Sept. 2011.

———. "Ngũgĩ wa Thiong'o Speaks: 'I Am Not above the Contradictions Which Bedevil Our Society.'" Interview by Emman Omari. Ngũgĩ, *Ngũgĩ wa Thiong'o Speaks* 129–35.

———. *Ngũgĩ wa Thiong'o Speaks: Interviews with the Kenyan Writer*. Ed. Reinhard Sander and Bernth Lindfors. Trenton: Africa World, 2006. Print.

———. *Njamba Nene and the Flying Bus*. Trans. Wangũi wa Goro. Nairobi: Heinemann, 1986. Print.

———. *Njamba Nene na Cibũ Kĩng'ang'i*. Nairobi: Heinemann, 1986. Print.

———. *Njamba Nene na Mbaathi ĩ Mathagu* [*Njamba Nene and the Flying Bus*]. Nairobi: East African Educ., 1982. Print.

———. *Njamba Nene's Pistol*. Trans. Wangũi wa Goro. Nairobi: Heinemann, 1986. Print.

———. "A Note on the English Edition." Ngũgĩ, *Matigari* [1987] vii–viii.

———. "A Novel in Politics: The Launching of *Petals of Blood*." Ngũgĩ, *Writers* [1997] 83–94.

———. "On the Abolition of the English Department." Ashcroft, Griffiths, and Tiffin 438–42.

———. *Penpoints, Gunpoints, and Dreams: Towards a Critical Theory of the Arts and the State in Africa*. Oxford: Clarendon, 1998. Print.

———. *Petals of Blood*. Oxford: Heinemann, 1977. Print.

———. *Petals of Blood*. New York: Dutton, 1978. Print.

———. Preface. *"Secret Lives" and Other Stories*. London: Heinemann, 1975. xi–xiii. Print.

———. "Recovering the Original." *The Genius of Language: Fifteen Writers Reflect on Their Mother Tongues*. Ed. Wendy Lesser. New York: Pantheon, 2004. 102–10. Print.

———. *The River Between*. Oxford: Heinemann, 1965. Print.

———. *Something Torn and New: An African Renaissance*. New York: Basic Civitas, 2009. Print.

———. *This Time Tomorrow*. Nairobi: East African Lit. Bureau, 1970. Print.

———. "'Tolstoy in Africa': An Interview with Ngũgĩ wa Thiong'o." By Reinhard Sander and Ian Munro. Ngũgĩ, *Ngũgĩ wa Thiong'o Speaks* 43–56.

———. *Weep Not, Child*. London: Heinemann, 1964. Print.

———. "When the Margin Becomes the Center: African Identities in a Global Environment." Macalester International Roundtable: Complex Contradictions: African, American, and Middle Eastern Perspectives. Macalester Coll., Saint Paul. 10 Oct. 2003. Address.

———. "Why *Nostromo*?" 1964. TS.

———. *Wizard of the Crow*. Trans. Ngũgĩ. New York: Pantheon, 2006; Anchor, 2007. Print.

———. "Women in Cultural Work: The Fate of Kamiriithu People's Theater in Kenya." Ngũgĩ, *Barrel* 39–51.

———. "The Writer as Activist: An Interview with Ngũgĩ wa Thiong'o." By T. Vijay Kumar. Lindfors and Kothandaraman 169–76.

———. *Writers in Politics: Essays*. London: Heinemann, 1981. Print.

———. *Writers in Politics: A Re-engagement with Issues of Literature and Society*. Rev. ed. Oxford: Currey, 1997. Print.

Ngũgĩ wa Thiong'o, Taban Lo Liyong, and Henry Owuor-Anyumba. "On the Abolition of the English Department." Ngũgĩ, *Homecoming* 145–50.

Ngũgĩ wa Thiong'o and Micere Githae Mugo. Preface. Ngũgĩ and Mugo, *Trial* iii–vii.

———. *The Trial of Dedan Kimathi*. Oxford: Heinemann, 1976. Print.

Ngũgĩ wa Thiong'o and Ngũgĩ wa Mĩriĩ. *I Will Marry When I Want*. Oxford: Heinemann, 1982. Print.

———. *Ngaahika Ndeenda*. Nairobi: Heinemann, 1980. Print.

Nicholls, Brendon. "Clitoridectomy and Gikuyu Nationalism in Ngũgĩ wa Thiong'o's *The River Between*." *Kunapipi* 25.2 (2003): 40–55. Print.

———. "The Landscape of Insurgency: Mau Mau, Ngũgĩ wa Thiong'o, and Gender." *Landscape and Empire, 1770–2000*. Ed. Glenn Hooper. Aldershot: Ashgate, 2005. 177–94. Print.

———. *Ngũgĩ wa Thiong'o, Gender, and the Ethics of Postcolonial Reading*. Farnham: Ashgate, 2010. Print.

Nixon, Rob. "Environmentalism and Postcolonialism." *African Literature: An Anthology of Criticism and Theory*. Ed. Tejumola Olaniyan and Ato Quayson. Malden: Blackwell, 2007. 715–23. Print.

Njambi, Wairimu Ngaruiya. "Irua Ria Atumia and Anti-colonial Struggles among the Gikuyu of Kenya: A Counter-narrative on 'Female Genital Mutilation.'" *Critical Sociology* 33.4 (2007): 689–708. Print.

Njogu, Kĩmani. "Gĩcandi and the Reemergence of Suppressed Words." *TDR: The Drama Review* 43.2 (1999): 54–71. Print.

———. *Reading Poetry as Dialogue: An East African Literary Tradition.* Nairobi: Jomo Kenyatta Foundation, 2004. Print.

Nkosi, Lewis. "Reading *Matigari*: The New Novel of Post-independence." Cantalupo, *World* 197–206.

Nnaemeka, Obioma, ed. *Female Circumcision and the Politics of Knowledge: African Women in Imperialist Discourses*. Westport: Praeger, 2005. Print.

Noss, Philip A. "Translating the Ideophone: Perspectives and Strategies of Translators and Artists." *The Creative Circle: Artist, Critic, and Translator in African Literature.* Ed. Angelina E. Overvold et al. Trenton: Africa World, 2003. 40–58. Print.

Ntarangwi, Mwenda. "'I Have Changed My Mind Now': U.S. Students' Responses to Female Genital Cutting in Africa." *Africa Today* 53.5 (2007): 87–108. Print.

Obumselu, Ben. "The Background of Modern African Literature." *Ibadan* 22 (1966): 46–59. Print.

Ochieng, Philip. "The Afro-Saxon of Alliance High Who Decolonised His Mind." *East African* 6–12 Sept. 2004, Magazine: 2–3. Print.

———. "Revolutionary Ideas Dominate Ngũgĩ's Works." *East African* 2–8 Aug. 2004, Magazine: 1–3. Print.

———. "Some Critics Say There Are Two wa Thiong'os: The Artist and the Ideologue." *East African* 26 July–1 Aug. 2004, Magazine: 1+. Print.

Ochieng, William R. "Autobiography in Kenyan History." Kenyatta U, n.d. TS.

———. "Dignitaries Not Spared." *Weekly Review* 24 July 1981: 47–48. Print.

———. *A Pre-colonial History of the Gusii of Western Kenya, from c. A.D. 1500 to 1914*. Nairobi: East African Lit. Bureau, 1974. Print.

Odhiambo, E. S. Atieno. Rev. of *The Trial of Dedan Kimathi,* by Ngũgĩ wa Thiong'o and Micere Githae Mugo. *Kenya Historical Review* 5.2 (1977): 385–88. Print.

Odhiambo, E. S. Atieno, and John Lonsdale, eds. *Mau Mau and Nationhood: Arms, Authority, and Narration*. Oxford: Currey, 2003. Print.

Ogot, B. A., and W. R. Ochieng. *Decolonization and Independence in Kenya, 1940–93*. London: Currey, 1995. Print.

Ogot, Bethwell A. *History of the Southern Luo*. Nairobi: East African, 1967. Print.

———. *Kenya before 1900*. Ed. Ogot. Nairobi: East African, 1976. Print.

———. "Three Decades of Historical Studies in East Africa." *Kenya Historical Review* 6.1 (1978): 22–29. Print.

Ogude, James. *Ngũgĩ's Novels and African History: Narrating the Nation*. London: Pluto, 1999. Print.

Okolo, M. S. C. *African Literature as Political Philosophy*. Dakar: CODESRIA; London: Zed, 2007. Print.

Onwuemene, Michael. "Limits of Transliteration: Nigerian Writers' Endeavor toward a National Literary Language." *PMLA* 114.5 (1999): 1055–66. Print.

Osaaji, Mumia G. "Is the Old Firebrand Ngugi Finally Mellowing?" *Sunday Nation* 16 Sept. 2007, Lifestyle: 12. Print.

Osha, Sanya. "Discourses of Decolonization." 2007. TS.

Osundare, Niyi. *African Literature and the Crisis of Post-structualist Theorizing.* Ibadan: Options, 1992. Print. Dialogue in African Philosophy Monograph Ser.

———. "Caliban's Gamble: The Stylistic Repercussions of Writing African Literature in English." *Language in Nigeria: Essays in Honour of Ayo Bamgbose.* Ed. Kola Owolabi. Ibadan: Group, 1995. 340–63. Print.

Owuor, Elizabeth. "In Africa, a Tale of Two Parallel Worlds." *Christian Science Monitor.* Christian Science Monitor, 19 Sept. 2006. Web. 18 Sept. 2011.

Palmer, Eustace. *An Introduction to the African Novel.* London: Heinemann, 1979. Print.

———. "Ngũgĩ's *Petals of Blood.*" Killam, *Critical Perspectives* 271–84.

Parker, Andrew, Mary Russo, Doris Sommer, and Patricia Yaeger. Introduction. Parker, Russo, Sommer, and Yaeger, *Nationalisms* 5–18.

———, eds. *Nationalisms and Sexualities.* New York: Routledge, 1992. 5–18. Print.

Pavlov, Grigor. "Under Western Eyes." 1964. TS.

Pegushev, Andrei M. Повстанцы May May [Mau Mau Rebels]. Moscow: Nauka, 1978. Print.

Peters, Bradley T. "The Significance of Dream Consciousness in *Heart of Darkness* and *Palace of the Peacock.*" *Conradiana* 22.2 (1990): 127–41. Print.

Peterson, Derek R. *Creative Writing: Translation, Bookkeeping, and the Work of Imagination in Colonial Kenya.* Portsmouth: Heinemann, 2004. Print.

Prazak, Miroslava, and Jennifer Coffman. "Anthropological Perspectives on Female Genital Cutting: Embodying Tradition, Violence, and Social Resilience." *Africa Today* 53.4 (2007): v–xi. Print.

Presley, Cora Ann. *Kikuyu Women, the Mau Mau Rebellion, and Social Change in Kenya.* Boulder: Westview, 1992. Print.

Prince, Gerald. *Narrative as Theme: Studies in French Fiction.* Lincoln: U of Nebraska P, 1992. Print.

Quayson, Ato. *Calibrations: Reading for the Social.* Minneapolis: U of Minnesota P, 2003. Print.

Radhakrishnan, R. "Nationalism, Gender, and the Narrative of Identity." Parker, Russo, Sommer, and Yaeger, *Nationalisms* 77–95.

Radway, Janice A. *Reading the Romance: Women, Patriarchy, and Popular Literature.* Chapel Hill: U of North Carolina P, 2001. Print.

Ranger, Terence O. "The Invention of Tradition in Colonial Africa." Hobsbawm and Ranger 211–62.

Rée, Jonathan. "Cosmopolitanism and the Experience of Nationality." *Cosmopolitics: Thinking and Feeling beyond the Nation.* Ed. Pheng Cheah and Bruce Robbins. Minneapolis: U of Minnesota P, 1998. 77–90. Print.

Robbe-Grillet, Alain. "A Future of the Novel." *Twentieth-Century Literary Criticism: A Reader.* Ed. David Lodge. London: Longman, 1984. 467–72. Print.

Robson, Clifford B. *Ngũgĩ wa Thiong'o.* London: Macmillan, 1979. Print.

Rodney, Walter. *How Europe Underdeveloped Africa.* London: Bogle-L'Ouverture, 1972. Print.

Rosberg, Carl, and John Nottingham. *The Myth of "Mau Mau": Nationalism in Kenya*. New York: Meridian, 1966. Print.

Roseneau, Pauline Marie. *Postmodernism and the Social Sciences: Insights, Inroads, and Intrusions*. Princeton: Princeton UP, 1992. Print.

Roy, Modhumita. "Writers and Politics / Writers in Politics: Ngũgĩ and the Language Question." Cantalupo, *Ngũgĩ* 165–85.

Ruether, Rosemary Radford. *Integrating Ecofeminism, Globalization, and World Religions*. Lanham: Rowman, 2005. Print.

Rushdie, Salman. *Midnight's Children*. New York: Penguin, 1980. Print.

Said, Edward. *"Reflections on Exile" and Other Essays*. Cambridge: Harvard UP, 2000. Print.

Salih, Tayeb. *Season of Migration to the North*. Trans. Denys Johnson-Davies. London: Heinemann, 1969. Print.

Schipper, Mineke. *Beyond the Boundaries: Text and Context in African Literature*. London: Allison, 1989. Print.

Scott, James. *Domination and the Arts of Resistance: Hidden Transcripts*. New Haven: Yale UP, 1990. Print.

Sembène, Ousmane. *God's Bits of Wood.* Oxford: Heinemann, 1980. Print.

Shaffer, Brian W. "'Civilization' under Western Eyes: Lowry's *Under the Volcano* as a Reading of Conrad's *Heart of Darkness*." *Conradiana* 22.2 (1990): 143–56. Print.

Sharma, Govind Narain. "Ngũgĩ's Apocalypse: Marxism, Christianity, and African Utopianism in *Petals of Blood*." Killam, *Critical Perspectives* 292–306.

———. "Ngũgĩ's *Detained* as a Modern *Consolatio*." *Research in African Literatures* 19 (1988): 520–28. Print.

Shaw, Carolyn Martin. *Colonial Inscriptions: Race, Sex, and Class in Kenya.* Minneapolis: U of Minnesota P, 1995. Print.

Shklovsky, Victor. "Art as Technique." *Critical Theory since Plato.* Ed. Hazard Adams and Leroy Searle. Boston: Thomson, 2005. 796–805. Print.

Sicherman, Carol. "Ngũgĩ's British Education." Cantalupo, *Ngũgĩ* 35–46.

———. "Ngũgĩ's Colonial Education: 'The Subversion . . . of the African *Mind*.'" Nazareth, *Critical Essays* 17–47.

———. *Ngũgĩ wa Thiong'o: A Bibliography of Primary and Secondary Sources, 1957–1987*. London: Zell, 1989. Print.

———. "Ngũgĩ wa Thiong'o and the Writing of Kenyan History." Nazareth, *Critical Essays* 299–320.

———. *Ngũgĩ wa Thiong'o: The Making of a Rebel: A Source Book in Kenyan Literature and Resistance*. London: Zell, 1990. Print.

Silva, Tomaz Tadeu da. "The Poetics and Politics of Curriculum as Representation." *Pedagogy, Culture and Society* 7.1 (1999): 7–33. Print.

Smith, Anthony. *Nationalism and Modernism: A Critical Survey of Recent Theories of Nations and Nationalism.* London: Routledge, 1998. Print.

Sontag, Susan. *Regarding the Pain of Others*. New York: Farrar, 2002. Print.

Soyinka, Wole. *Death and the King's Horseman*. Ed. Simon Gikandi. New York: Norton, 2003. Print.

———. *The Man Died: Prison Notes of Wole Soyinka*. New York: Noonday, 1972. Print.

———. *Myth, Literature and the African World*. Cambridge: Cambridge UP, 1976. Print.

Spivak, Gayatri Chakravorty. "Can the Subaltern Speak?" *Marxism and the Interpretation of Culture*. Ed. Cary Nelson and Lawrence Grossberg. Urbana: U of Illinois P, 1988. 271–313. Print.

———. *Death of a Discipline*. New York: Columbia UP, 2003. Print.

———. "Echo." *The Spivak Reader: Selected Works of Gayatri Chakravorty Spivak*. Ed. Donna Landry and Gerald M. Maclean. New York: Routledge, 1996. 175–202. Print.

———. *In Other Worlds: Essays in Cultural Politics*. New York: Methuen, 1987. Print.

———. "Translating English." *Nation, Language, and the Ethics of Translation*. Ed. Sandra Bermann and Michael Wood. Princeton: Princeton UP, 2005. 93–110. Print.

Steinbeck, John. *The Grapes of Wrath*. New York: Viking, 1939. Print.

Stratton, Florence. *Contemporary African Literature and the Politics of Gender*. London: Routledge, 1994. Print.

———. "Gender on the Agenda: Novels of the 1980s by Ngũgĩ and Achebe." Stratton, *Contemporary African Literature* 158–70.

Thomas, Lynn M. *Politics of the Womb: Women, Reproduction, and the State in Kenya*. Berkeley: U of California P, 2003. Print.

Tignor, Robert L. *The Colonial Transformation of Kenya: The Kamba, Kikuyu, and Maasai, from 1900 to 1939*. Princeton: Princeton UP, 1976. Print.

Trevor-Roper, Hugh. *The Rise of Christian Europe*. London Harcourt, 1965. Print.

Tsabedze, Clara. *African Independence from Francophone and Anglophone Voices: A Comparative Study of the Post-independence Novels by Ngũgĩ and Sembène*. New York: Lang, 1994. Print.

Venuti, Lawrence. *The Translator's Invisibility: A History of Translation*. London: Routledge, 1995. Print.

Visser, N. W., ed. *Ngũgĩ wa Thiong'o*. Spec. issue of *English in Africa* 8.2 (1981): 3–120. Print.

Wali, Obiajunwa. "The Dead-End of African Literature?" *Transition* 10 (1963): 13–16. Print.

Wamue, Grace Nyatugah. "Revisiting Our Indigenous Shrines through Mungiki." *African Affairs* 100 (2001): 453–67. Print.

Warah, Rasna. "Ngũgĩ in Exile: Home Is Where the Art Is." *East African* 30 Aug.–5 Sept. 2004. 14. Print.

Warhol, Robyn R. "Neonarrative; or, How to Render the Unnarratable in Realist Fiction and Contemporary Film." *A Companion to Narrative Theory*. Ed. James Phelan and Peter J. Rabinowitz. Malden: Blackwell, 2005. 220–31. Print.

Warigi, Gitau. "Ngũgĩ a Genuine Icon to Many." *Sunday Nation* 1 Aug. 2004: 9. Print.

Watt, Ian. *The Rise of the Novel: Studies in Defoe, Richardson, and Fielding*. Berkeley: U of California P, 1967. Print.

Wellek, René. "The Concept of Realism in Literary Scholarship." *Concepts of Criticism.* New Haven: Yale UP, 1963. 222–55. Print.

Were, Gideon S. *A History of the Abaluyia of Western Kenya, c. 1500–1930.* Nairobi: East African, 1967. Print.

West, Lois. *Feminist Nationalism.* New York: Routledge, 1997. Print.

"White." Def. 3. *Merriam-Webster's Collegiate Dictionary.* 11th ed. 2003. Print.

White, Hayden. *The Content of the Form: Narrative Discourse and Historical Representation.* Baltimore: Johns Hopkins UP, 1987. Print.

———. *Tropics of Discourse: Essays in Cultural Criticism.* Baltimore: Johns Hopkins UP, 1978. Print.

White, Luise. *The Comforts of Home: Prostitution in Colonial Nairobi.* Chicago: U of Chicago P, 1990. Print.

———. "Domestic Labor in a Colonial City: Prostitution in Nairobi, 1900–1952." *Patriarchy and Class: African Women in the Home and the Workforce.* Ed. Sharon B. Stichter and Jane L. Parpart. Boulder: Westview, 1988. 139–60. Print.

Wilkinson, Jane. "African Diaries." *Autobiographical and Biographical Writing in the Commonwealth.* Ed. Doireann MacDermott. Sabadell: AUSA, 1984. 247–53. Print.

Williams, Patrick. "'Like Wounded Birds'?: Ngũgĩ and the Intellectuals." *Yearbook of English Studies* 27 (1997): 201–18. Print.

———. *Ngugi wa Thiong'o.* Manchester: Manchester UP, 1999. Print.

Wiltse, Edward. "The 'Mau Mau' in Hollywood: *Something of Value* and Counterinsurgency from Algiers to Alabama." Cantalupo, *Ngũgĩ* 71–86.

Yeats, W. B. "Easter, 1916." *The Collected Poems of W. B. Yeats.* Ed. Richard J. Finneran. New York: Macmillan, 1989. 180–82. Print.

Young, Robert J. C. *Postcolonialism: An Historical Introduction.* Oxford: Blackwell, 2001. Print.

Zabus, Chantal J. *Between Rites and Rights: Excision in Women's Experiential Texts and Human Contexts.* Stanford: Stanford UP, 2007. Print.

Zinn, Howard. *A People's History of the United States of America, 1492–Present.* New York: Harper, 1980. Print.

INDEX

Modern Language Association of America

Approaches to Teaching World Literature

Achebe's Things Fall Apart. Ed. Bernth Lindfors. 1991.
Arthurian Tradition. Ed. Maureen Fries and Jeanie Watson. 1992.
Atwood's The Handmaid's Tale *and Other Works*. Ed. Sharon R. Wilson, Thomas B. Friedman, and Shannon Hengen. 1996.
Austen's Emma. Ed. Marcia McClintock Folsom. 2004.
Austen's Pride and Prejudice. Ed. Marcia McClintock Folsom. 1993.
Balzac's Old Goriot. Ed. Michal Peled Ginsburg. 2000.
Baudelaire's Flowers of Evil. Ed. Laurence M. Porter. 2000.
Beckett's Waiting for Godot. Ed. June Schlueter and Enoch Brater. 1991.
Beowulf. Ed. Jess B. Bessinger, Jr., and Robert F. Yeager. 1984.
Blake's Songs of Innocence and of Experience. Ed. Robert F. Gleckner and Mark L. Greenberg. 1989.
Boccaccio's Decameron. Ed. James H. McGregor. 2000.
British Women Poets of the Romantic Period. Ed. Stephen C. Behrendt and Harriet Kramer Linkin. 1997.
Charlotte Brontë's Jane Eyre. Ed. Diane Long Hoeveler and Beth Lau. 1993.
Emily Brontë's Wuthering Heights. Ed. Sue Lonoff and Terri A. Hasseler. 2006.
Byron's Poetry. Ed. Frederick W. Shilstone. 1991.
Camus's The Plague. Ed. Steven G. Kellman. 1985.
Writings of Bartolomé de Las Casas. Ed. Santa Arias and Eyda M. Merediz. 2008.
Cather's My Ántonia. Ed. Susan J. Rosowski. 1989.
Cervantes' Don Quixote. Ed. Richard Bjornson. 1984.
Chaucer's Canterbury Tales. Ed. Joseph Gibaldi. 1980.
Chaucer's Troilus and Criseyde *and the Shorter Poems*. Ed. Tison Pugh and Angela Jane Weisl. 2006.
Chopin's The Awakening. Ed. Bernard Koloski. 1988.
Coleridge's Poetry and Prose. Ed. Richard E. Matlak. 1991.
Collodi's Pinocchio *and Its Adaptations*. Ed. Michael Sherberg. 2006.
Conrad's "Heart of Darkness" and "The Secret Sharer." Ed. Hunt Hawkins and Brian W. Shaffer. 2002.
Dante's Divine Comedy. Ed. Carole Slade. 1982.
Defoe's Robinson Crusoe. Ed. Maximillian E. Novak and Carl Fisher. 2005.
DeLillo's White Noise. Ed. Tim Engles and John N. Duvall. 2006.
Dickens's Bleak House. Ed. John O. Jordan and Gordon Bigelow. 2009.
Dickens's David Copperfield. Ed. Richard J. Dunn. 1984.
Dickinson's Poetry. Ed. Robin Riley Fast and Christine Mack Gordon. 1989.
Narrative of the Life of Frederick Douglass. Ed. James C. Hall. 1999.
Duras's Ourika. Ed. Mary Ellen Birkett and Christopher Rivers. 2009.
Early Modern Spanish Drama. Ed. Laura R. Bass and Margaret R. Greer. 2006.

Eliot's Middlemarch. Ed. Kathleen Blake. 1990.
Eliot's Poetry and Plays. Ed. Jewel Spears Brooker. 1988.
Shorter Elizabethan Poetry. Ed. Patrick Cheney and Anne Lake Prescott. 2000.
Ellison's Invisible Man. Ed. Susan Resneck Parr and Pancho Savery. 1989.
English Renaissance Drama. Ed. Karen Bamford and Alexander Leggatt. 2002.
Works of Louise Erdrich. Ed. Gregg Sarris, Connie A. Jacobs, and James R. Giles. 2004.
Dramas of Euripides. Ed. Robin Mitchell-Boyask. 2002.
Faulkner's As I Lay Dying. Ed. Patrick O'Donnell and Lynda Zwinger. 2011.
Faulkner's The Sound and the Fury. Ed. Stephen Hahn and Arthur F. Kinney. 1996.
Fitzgerald's The Great Gatsby. Ed. Jackson R. Bryer and Nancy P. VanArsdale. 2009.
Flaubert's Madame Bovary. Ed. Laurence M. Porter and Eugene F. Gray. 1995.
García Márquez's One Hundred Years of Solitude. Ed. María Elena de Valdés and Mario J. Valdés. 1990.
Gilman's "The Yellow Wall-Paper" and Herland. Ed. Denise D. Knight and Cynthia J. Davis. 2003.
Goethe's Faust. Ed. Douglas J. McMillan. 1987.
Gothic Fiction: The British and American Traditions. Ed. Diane Long Hoeveler and Tamar Heller. 2003.
Poetry of John Gower. Ed. R. F. Yeager and Brian W. Gastle. 2011.
Grass's The Tin Drum. Ed. Monika Shafi. 2008.
H.D.'s Poetry and Prose. Ed. Annette Debo and Lara Vetter. 2011.
Hebrew Bible as Literature in Translation. Ed. Barry N. Olshen and Yael S. Feldman. 1989.
Homer's Iliad *and* Odyssey. Ed. Kostas Myrsiades. 1987.
Hurston's Their Eyes Were Watching God *and Other Works*. Ed. John Lowe. 2009.
Ibsen's A Doll House. Ed. Yvonne Shafer. 1985.
Henry James's Daisy Miller *and* The Turn of the Screw. Ed. Kimberly C. Reed and Peter G. Beidler. 2005.
Works of Samuel Johnson. Ed. David R. Anderson and Gwin J. Kolb. 1993.
Joyce's Ulysses. Ed. Kathleen McCormick and Erwin R. Steinberg. 1993.
Works of Sor Juana Inés de la Cruz. Ed. Emilie L. Bergmann and Stacey Schlau. 2007.
Kafka's Short Fiction. Ed. Richard T. Gray. 1995.
Keats's Poetry. Ed. Walter H. Evert and Jack W. Rhodes. 1991.
Kingston's The Woman Warrior. Ed. Shirley Geok-lin Lim. 1991.
Lafayette's The Princess of Clèves. Ed. Faith E. Beasley and Katharine Ann Jensen. 1998.
Works of D. H. Lawrence. Ed. M. Elizabeth Sargent and Garry Watson. 2001.
Lazarillo de Tormes *and the Picaresque Tradition*. Ed. Anne J. Cruz. 2009.
Lessing's The Golden Notebook. Ed. Carey Kaplan and Ellen Cronan Rose. 1989.
Works of Naguib Mahfouz. Ed. Waïl S. Hassan and Susan Muaddi Darraj. 2011.
Mann's Death in Venice *and Other Short Fiction*. Ed. Jeffrey B. Berlin. 1992.

Marguerite de Navarre's Heptameron. Ed. Colette H. Winn. 2007.
Medieval English Drama. Ed. Richard K. Emmerson 1990.
Melville's Moby-Dick. Ed. Martin Bickman. 1985.
Metaphysical Poets. Ed. Sidney Gottlieb. 1990.
Miller's Death of a Salesman. Ed. Matthew C. Roudané. 1995.
Milton's Paradise Lost. First edition. Ed. Galbraith M. Crump. 1986.
Milton's Paradise Lost. Second edition. Ed. Peter C. Herman. 2012.
Milton's Shorter Poetry and Prose. Ed. Peter C. Herman. 2007.
Molière's Tartuffe *and Other Plays*. Ed. James F. Gaines and Michael S. Koppisch. 1995.
Momaday's The Way to Rainy Mountain. Ed. Kenneth M. Roemer. 1988.
Montaigne's Essays. Ed. Patrick Henry. 1994.
Novels of Toni Morrison. Ed. Nellie Y. McKay and Kathryn Earle. 1997.
Murasaki Shikibu's The Tale of Genji. Ed. Edward Kamens. 1993.
Nabokov's Lolita. Ed. Zoran Kuzmanovich and Galya Diment. 2008.
Works of Ngũgĩ wa Thiong'o. Ed. Oliver Lovesey. 2012.
Works of Tim O'Brien. Ed. Alex Vernon and Catherine Calloway. 2010.
Works of Ovid and the Ovidian Tradition. Ed. Barbara Weiden Boyd and Cora Fox. 2010.
Poe's Prose and Poetry. Ed. Jeffrey Andrew Weinstock and Tony Magistrale. 2008.
Pope's Poetry. Ed. Wallace Jackson and R. Paul Yoder. 1993.
Proust's Fiction and Criticism. Ed. Elyane Dezon-Jones and Inge Crosman Wimmers. 2003.
Puig's Kiss of the Spider Woman. Ed. Daniel Balderston and Francine Masiello. 2007.
Pynchon's The Crying of Lot 49 *and Other Works.* Ed. Thomas H. Schaub. 2008.
Works of François Rabelais. Ed. Todd W. Reeser and Floyd Gray. 2011.
Novels of Samuel Richardson. Ed. Lisa Zunshine and Jocelyn Harris. 2006.
Rousseau's Confessions *and* Reveries of the Solitary Walker. Ed. John C. O'Neal and Ourida Mostefai. 2003.
Scott's Waverley Novels. Ed. Evan Gottlieb and Ian Duncan. 2009.
Shakespeare's Hamlet. Ed. Bernice W. Kliman. 2001.
Shakespeare's King Lear. Ed. Robert H. Ray. 1986.
Shakespeare's Othello. Ed. Peter Erickson and Maurice Hunt. 2005.
Shakespeare's Romeo and Juliet. Ed. Maurice Hunt. 2000.
Shakespeare's The Tempest *and Other Late Romances.* Ed. Maurice Hunt. 1992.
Shelley's Frankenstein. Ed. Stephen C. Behrendt. 1990.
Shelley's Poetry. Ed. Spencer Hall. 1990.
Sir Gawain and the Green Knight. Ed. Miriam Youngerman Miller and Jane Chance. 1986.
Song of Roland. Ed. William W. Kibler and Leslie Zarker Morgan. 2006.
Spenser's Faerie Queene. Ed. David Lee Miller and Alexander Dunlop. 1994.
Stendhal's The Red and the Black. Ed. Dean de la Motte and Stirling Haig. 1999.

Sterne's Tristram Shandy. Ed. Melvyn New. 1989.
The Story of the Stone (Dream of the Red Chamber). Ed. Andrew Schonebaum and Tina Lu. 2012.
Stowe's Uncle Tom's Cabin. Ed. Elizabeth Ammons and Susan Belasco. 2000.
Swift's Gulliver's Travels. Ed. Edward J. Rielly. 1988.
Teresa of Ávila and the Spanish Mystics. Ed. Alison Weber. 2009.
Thoreau's Walden *and Other Works*. Ed. Richard J. Schneider. 1996.
Tolstoy's Anna Karenina. Ed. Liza Knapp and Amy Mandelker. 2003.
Vergil's Aeneid. Ed. William S. Anderson and Lorina N. Quartarone. 2002.
Voltaire's Candide. Ed. Renée Waldinger. 1987.
Whitman's Leaves of Grass. Ed. Donald D. Kummings. 1990.
Wiesel's Night. Ed. Alan Rosen. 2007.
Works of Oscar Wilde. Ed. Philip E. Smith II. 2008.
Woolf's Mrs. Dalloway. Ed. Eileen Barrett and Ruth O. Saxton. 2009.
Woolf's To the Lighthouse. Ed. Beth Rigel Daugherty and Mary Beth Pringle. 2001.
Wordsworth's Poetry. Ed. Spencer Hall, with Jonathan Ramsey. 1986.
Wright's Native Son. Ed. James A. Miller. 1997.